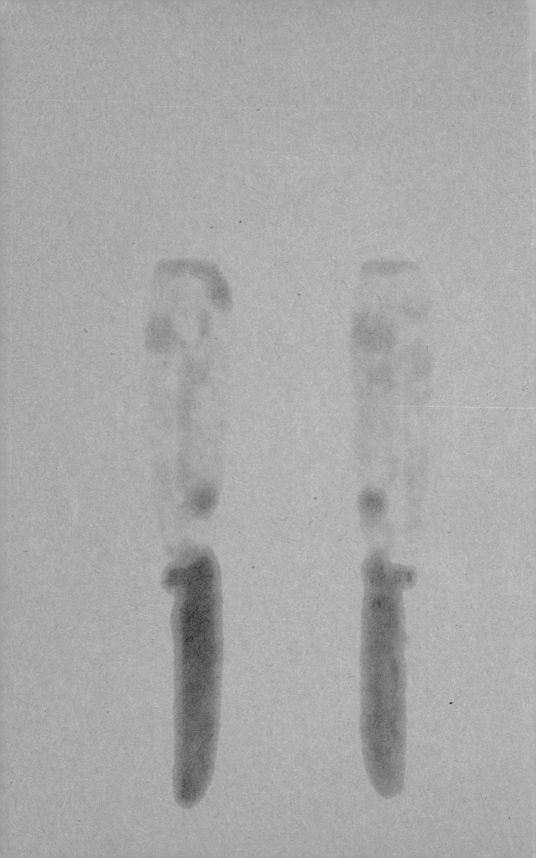

JEHOVAH'S WITNESSES IN CANADA

IN MEMORY OF
MY FATHER,
WHO TAUGHT ME TO HATE
INJUSTICE

Jehovah's Witnesses in Canada

CHAMPIONS OF FREEDOM OF SPEECH AND WORSHIP

M. JAMES PENTON

MACMILLAN OF CANADA
MACLEAN-HUNTER PRESS

*This book has been published with the aid of a grant
from the Humanities Research Council of Canada,
using funds provided by the Canada Council.*

Canadian Cataloguing in Publication Data

Penton, M. James, 1932–
Jehovah's Witnesses in Canada

"Select bibliography": p.
Includes index.

ISBN 0-7705-1340-9
1. Jehovah's Witnesses—Canada. 2. Religious
liberty—Canada—History. I. Title.

BX8525.8.C3P4   289.9   C76-017058-4

Printed in Canada for
The Macmillan Company of Canada, Limited
70 Bond Street
Toronto M5B 1X3

CONTENTS

COURT CASES

pREFACE

SEVERAL YEARS AGO when I began to research topics of religious conflict and discrimination in Canadian history, it quickly became evident that there were a number of satisfactory studies on many of Canada's minority faiths. But, surprisingly, in view of their importance as a rapidly growing and dynamic movement, there was no broad study, historical or otherwise, of Jehovah's Witnesses in Canadian society. This work is an attempt to alter that situation.

At first I was hopeful that my research would not take a great deal of time. As a member of a fifth-generation family of Jehovah's Witnesses, I had first-hand knowledge of many of the events that I describe. In addition, I was helped, most kindly, by many persons at the headquarters offices of Jehovah's Witnesses in Canada, Great Britain, and the United States. After a preliminary investigation, it became obvious that my task would be much harder than I had supposed. Many of the records of Jehovah's Witnesses in Canada had been lost as a result of the ban on their activities during the Second World War. Thus, much information had to be gleaned from newspapers, letters, typescripts, manuscripts, personal interviews, law reports, and public documents. And, in the case of the last-named source, I soon learned that some of the records I wanted to examine were not open to historians. Although some government departments in Ottawa were most helpful in opening files, others were not. After much work, I was able to assemble what I trust is a reasonably complete account of the history of what may well be Canada's most controversial religion.

One area of my research deserves special mention here—the matter of the treatment of conscientious objectors in the Canadian Army, in prisons, and in alternative-service camps in both the First World War and the Second World War. In the first instance, when I approached individuals who had been drafted for either military or alternative service during the wars, I was immediately given personal accounts of the cruel treatment which many, though certainly not all, claimed to have received. The historian cannot accept such information, however, without some strong supporting evidence from other sources. Thus, I spent many long hours sifting through the files of the Department of Militia and Defence, the Department of Defence, and the Department of Mines and Resources in the Public Archives of Canada in Ottawa. I also conducted a series of twenty-five additional interviews with other men involved in many of the events described later which happened in both Canada and Great Britain. And, as a result, I have come to feel that there is no reason to doubt the personal accounts of cruelty to conscientious objectors during the two periods of great patriotic fervour in our national history. Of course, this will come as no surprise to anyone who has read John Graham's *Conscription and Conscience*, David Boulton's *Objections Overruled*, John Rae's *Conscience and Politics*, or various statements in the British *Hansard*, all of which describe vividly the treatment to which conscientious objectors in England were subjected during the First World War.

Thanks are due to the many persons who assisted me with this work. Though it is impossible to mention them all, the following were especially helpful: Kenneth Little, Percy Chapman, Ralph Brodie, Edward Noseworthy, Jack Nathan, Arnold Macnamara, Jim Hogg, and Dale Colpitts, all presently or formerly of the Canadian Bethel Home of the Watch Tower Society in Toronto. Frank Platt and David Parry were of great assistance at Watch Tower House, London, England. I also owe appreciation to Mr. and Mrs. George Naish, Roberta Davies, Mr. and Mrs. Frank Wainwright, Mr. and Mrs.

Montague Mais, Mr. and Mrs. William Zarysky, Joseph Huppalo, Roy Hook, Clarence Leeson, Arnold Melin, and Walter Backous. My colleagues at the University of Lethbridge—especially Professors James Cousins and William Baker—made many useful suggestions, as did Dr. Joseph Boudreau of San Jose State College, California. Several members of my family also contributed much to the preparation of my manuscript. However, I am most indebted to three persons: W. Glen How, who was extremely generous in providing information, time, and suggestions; Eugene Rosam, who supplied much of the information used in Chapter 2; and Alex Trost, who not only contributed much of the medical information dealt with in Chapter 11, but was responsible for the discovery of the materials from the Lapointe Papers, which are discussed in Chapter 7.

I also want to express my gratitude to both the University of Lethbridge and the Canada Council for the financial support which made my research possible.

M.J.P.
Lethbridge, Alberta
May 10, 1974

INTRODUCTION

Religion is a matter between each man and his Maker, and the government has not the right to determine for the country what is truth, but ought to leave a matter so sacred to the conscience of each member of the community.

GEORGE BROWN *The Globe*, September 7, 1852

THE HISTORY OF religious discrimination and persecution in Canada since Confederation is not particularly well known. The popular view among most Canadians is that their country has had an even better record in its respect for religious freedom than has had the United States, a nation justly proud of its tradition of civil liberties. Scholars have also emphasized the supposedly high degree of religious freedom in Canada. Professor Searle M. Bates, writing in 1945, placed Canada in the category of those countries which enjoyed "essentially full and equal religious liberty".[1] Commenting on Bates's study, in which he listed seven freedoms as components of religious freedom, Professor D. A. Schmeiser of the University of Saskatchewan suggested that the first five—freedom of conscience, freedom of worship, freedom of association, freedom of propaganda, and freedom from civil disability —did not present much difficulty in Canada, although he admitted that the fourth had been strained by the controversy involving Jehovah's Witnesses in Quebec. Schmeiser also stated that the sixth freedom listed by Bates—freedom from discrimination against any or all religions by the state, and the manifesting of impartial sympathy toward their work—has been more commonly accepted in Canada than in the United States. He did recognize that Bates's seventh component freedom, freedom of the church or any part of it from connection with the state, was looked on differently in Canada than it was in the United States. But he argued that in practice the Canadian experience in this area has not varied greatly from the American one.[2]

The Canadian Bill of Rights, passed as an act of Parliament in 1960, declares firmly that Canada has respected and does respect the principle of religious liberty. It asserts that, along with other rights, freedom of religion has "existed and shall continue to exist without discrimination by reason of race, national origin, colour, religion or sex". Thus, the popular view of the matter, along with opinions of men like Bates and Schmeiser, is buttressed by an official pronouncement by Canada's highest law-making body. But the facts are somewhat different; there is quite another side to Canadian religious history, which many Canadians have been willing to ignore or overlook.

It is quite well known that during the period between the British Conquest of Quebec in 1759 and the establishment of responsible government in Canada, the British government and the colonial officials treated different religious organizations on different bases. The Quebec Act of 1774 restored to the Roman Catholic Church many of the rights and privileges that it had held under the French. The Constitutional Act of 1791 set aside the famous clergy reserve lands for the support of Protestant clergy,[3] and provided for the erection of endowed parsonages or rectories "according to the Establishment of the Church of England". This latter act, plus legislation in the new province of Upper Canada which long denied the ministers of many denominations the right to solemnize marriages,[4] caused much resentment among "non-conformist" Protestants. Thus, after a long struggle, there occurred in Canada what has come to be known as "the victory of voluntarism".

In 1851 the Parliament of Canada passed an act which stipulated that the government would initiate action and pay costs of testing the legality of patents under which over forty endowed rectories of the Church of England had been established in 1836.[5] The act also contained a section which was to have great significance in later years. It read:

Be it therefore declared and enacted, . . . that the free exercise and enjoyment of religious profession and worship, without discrimination or preference, so as the same do not be made an excuse for acts of licentiousness, or as a justification of practice inconsistent with the peace and safety of the province, is by the constitution and laws of this province, allowed to all her majesty's subjects within the same.

Thus, what was to become the Freedom of Worship Statute[6] of the Province of Canada came into being. A few years later, in 1854, when the issue of the use of funds from the clergy reserves was finally laid to rest, the voluntarists won their most important victory. Although the legislation by which this victory was accomplished stated that it was "desirable to remove all semblance of connexion between Church and State",[7] it did not do so.

Although most of the burning issues involving church-state relations were solved in the 1850s, the settlement arrived at was far from definitive. In Great Britain, the Church of England remained established; in the United States, the principle of separation of church and state, as clearly stated in the Virginia Statute of Religious Liberty and the First Amendment to the United States Constitution, became dominant. But in Canada, while the concept of religious establishment was abandoned and all religions were theoretically granted equality before the law, in fact government was left free to legislate both for and against specific religious denominations.

When four of the provinces of British North America came together in 1867 to form a Dominion called Canada, the British North America Act said very little about the subject of religion. Under Section 129 of that act, pre-Confederation legislation such as the Freedom of Worship Statute remained in force. It was deemed necessary, however, to give federal protection to publicly supported denominational schools in existence in any province at the time of Confederation.[8] Hence, in the very important area of education, the

Canadian experience was to deviate dramatically from the American one.

While in the United States any direct support for religious or "parochial" schools has been declared unconstitutional time and again, in Canada religious schools are specifically guaranteed financial support by federal legislation in some provinces, and other provinces are free to give or refuse such support as they see fit. It is evident that in the area of education at least, there is no separation of church and state. While many Canadians, particularly Roman Catholics, have argued that the Canadian approach provides greater religious freedom, this is a debatable point. In a number of instances in Quebec, to be detailed later, children of Jehovah's Witnesses were denied education because school boards held that they were not admissible to either the Protestant or the Catholic school systems,[9] the only publicly supported school systems in the province. In Saskatchewan, as late as the 1960s, a father was denied the right to send his child to a non-denominational public school because he was a Roman Catholic.[10] By now the courts have held that all children must be provided with education in tax-supported schools, but nothing has been done to overturn the Saskatchewan decision under which members of certain religious communities, notably Roman Catholics, whether or not they want to, may be forced to send their children to denominational schools.

Another section of the British North America Act which has permitted religious discrimination is the provision that the provinces have the sole right to determine who shall solemnize marriages.[11] When provinces have refused to recognize certain denominations, or the ministers or representatives thereof, members of the groups in question have had to have their marriages performed by the clergy of other faiths, civil functionaries such as justices of the peace, or they have had to go to other jurisdictions. In other words, some religions are "recognized" by the state while others are not.

Another form of discrimination, one of a most vicious sort, has involved the treatment of conscientious objectors. While it is true that Canadian governments have taken very humanitarian views by granting exemption from military service to several denominations when members of those faiths moved to Canada in large numbers,[12] other persons and religious groups have never been given the same consideration. During the First World War no provision was made for conscientious objectors who were not members of a "peace church",[13] and, even more important, several denominations opposed to military service were simply held not to be religious organizations within the terms of the Military Service Act.[14] In the Second World War the situation, although somewhat different, was no better. Perhaps as many as three hundred conscientious objectors were forcibly conscripted into the army,[15] and, as in the First World War, many were subjected to severe physical mistreatment.[16] At the same time, Mennonites, Doukhobors, and Quakers, as members of the traditional peace churches, generally had little difficulty in obtaining exemptions.

Canadian governments, both provincial and federal, have been guilty of violating the spirit and letter of the Freedom of Worship Statute and the high-sounding words of the Canadian Bill of Rights, by imposing specific disabilities on certain religions. For example, in 1920 British Columbia passed legislation which prohibited Doukhobors living in that province from voting in provincial elections,[17] in spite of the fact that many of them had committed no crime. In 1934 the federal government passed similar legislation, whereby all Doukhobors who were disfranchised by British Columbia were prohibited from voting in federal elections.[18] Thus British Columbia Doukhobors were denied the right to vote in any public election above municipal level simply because of their religion. Yet in the 1950s when the radical Sons of Freedom, a small sectarian group who had little in common with the more orthodox Doukhobors, refused to send their children to school because of religious objections, they were told their beliefs were not religious.[19] For years their children were seized by the police and placed in a detention camp at New Denver, British Columbia.[20]

Alberta, too, has passed legislation directed at specific religious groups. Because of a general fear of the possible rapid spread of Hutterite colonies, in 1947 the provincial legislature passed the Communal Property Act, which denied Hutterites and Doukhobors the right to establish agricultural colonies outside the terms of the act—a right not denied to any other citizens of the province. Interestingly, the act was upheld by the Supreme Court of Canada,[21] while a similar act in South Dakota was held unconstitutional by an American court.[22] It was only after the election of the present Conservative government of Alberta that the Communal Property Act was repealed.[23]

The best, or worst, instances of discrimination against, and outright persecution of, a religious community have not, however, involved groups such as the Doukhobors and Hutterites who are, for the most part, located in only certain areas of western Canada. Far better examples of how Canada has often failed to live up to its high professions of religious freedom concern another faith—Jehovah's Witnesses. For they, more than any other Canadian religion, not excepting the Doukhobors, have suffered at the hands of Canadian officialdom, the courts, mob violence, and social pressures. As the only religious denomination to be outlawed publicly by a Canadian government since the "victory of voluntarism",[24] their case is unique, and it provides an excellent study by which to determine how well or how badly Canada, since Confederation, has dealt with an unpopular religious minority. It also shows the important role a minority can play in fighting to defend its own rights within a democratic society, and thereby bolster the freedoms of others. Following is the story of Jehovah's Witnesses in Canada.

CHAPTER ONE

you are my witnesses, says Jehovah

Ye are my witnesses, saith Jehovah, and my servant whom I have chosen;
that ye may know and believe me, and understand that I am he: before me
there was no God formed, neither shall there be after me.

Isaiah 43:10, American Standard Version

JEHOVAH'S WITNESSES have played a unique role in Canadian
religious history. No other religious group has challenged the theological, social, national, and even scientific values of the larger society
to the same extent or with the same vehemence. In fact, the Witnesses
have been to Canadian and most modern societies what the early
Christians were to the Roman Empire of the first century, and what
the Anabaptists were to the European world of the sixteenth century.
Like both these groups, whom they regard as spiritual forefathers,
the Witnesses look for the present political systems of mankind to be
replaced by new heavens and a new earth under the kingdom of
Christ. They regard the world around them as satanically ruled, and
the religious, political, and economic institutions which support it as
deserving of destruction. Such beliefs have caused them to speak out
sharply and condemn many of the doctrines, institutions, and practices dear to others. As a result, Jehovah's Witnesses have undergone
more consistent opposition and both legal and popular persecutions

than members of any other religion, church, sect, or denomination in Canada since Confederation. Although a number of general studies of Jehovah's Witnesses have been made by both friends and foes, it is necessary to give once again a brief résumé of their background, beliefs, and nature, to make clear their position in Canadian history.

The Witnesses, known as International or Associated Bible Students and, less properly, as Russellites and Millennial Dawnites until 1931, first developed as an American movement in the 1870s under Charles Taze Russell[1] (1852–1916), better known as Pastor Russell, a Pittsburgh, Pennsylvania, businessman. Raised a Presbyterian, Russell was early to rebel against the doctrine of eternal torment for the wicked, and he lapsed into infidelity. His faith was restored in biblical Christianity a few years later by Jonas Wendall, an Adventist preacher, but Russell did not join the Adventists. In 1872 Russell and a few friends formed a small class primarily interested in studying the Scriptures to learn more about Christ's second coming. Through their studies, these Bible Students, as they soon became known, became convinced that the second advent or presence of the Lord would be invisible, seen only with the eye of understanding. To express this view, Russell wrote a pamphlet entitled *The Object and Manner of the Lord's Return*; fifty thousand copies were published at the author's expense.[2]

In 1875 Russell became acquainted with the *Herald of the Morning*, an Adventist paper edited by N. H. Barbour of Rochester, New York. Barbour and his fellows also believed in Christ's invisible presence. Russell was delighted and entered into a brief association with Barbour. The young Pennsylvanian also adopted Barbour's idea that the world had begun to undergo, since 1874, a "harvest period", during which the wheat of righteous mankind would be separated from the wicked tares. Russell then suggested that the "gentile times" would end in 1914, and the kingdoms of the world would become the Lord's. He was so fired by the new ideas that he called a meeting of Pittsburgh and Allegheny clergymen to encourage them to proclaim Christ's invisible presence and the oncoming end of the world. When all the ministers present refused to believe, he decided to devote his life to preaching the gospel. He sold five clothing stores which he owned and thereafter devoted his money, time, and energy to one of the greatest evangelistic campaigns in modern history.

In 1878 Russell broke with Barbour over the doctrine of Christ's atonement, which the latter had lately come to reject. As a result, on July 1, 1879, Russell began the publication of the magazine *Zion's Watch Tower and Herald of Christ's Presence.*[3] During the same year he married Maria Frances Ackley. Russell did not consider settling down to a quiet married life. During 1879 and 1880 he, and those associated with him, founded thirty congregations, from Ohio and Michigan in the west to Massachusetts in the east. By 1881 a new religious organization with specific practices and doctrines had arisen, and two missionaries were sent to Great Britain.[4] Already, Bible Students were placing vast quantities of books, booklets, tracts, and magazines with the public, and Russell felt that an organization was needed to co-ordinate their activities. Thus, he established the Watch Tower Bible and Tract Society, then known as Zion's Watch Tower Tract Society, which was incorporated under Pennsylvania law three years later, in 1884.[5]

Between 1882 and his death in 1916, Russell proved to be an amazingly active preacher, a prolific writer, and an able organizer. Over the years he travelled across the United States many times, visited Canada frequently, and made numerous overseas trips to Great Britain, Europe, and Asia. He wrote a number of books, the most famous of which were the six-volume *Millennial Dawn* series— later known as *Studies in the Scriptures*—plus numerous articles in the *Watch Tower*, in pamphlets, and in nearly four thousand newspapers in the United States, Canada, and Europe.[6] In all, his works totalled some fifty thousand printed pages, and by the time of his death nearly twenty million copies of his books had been printed and distributed throughout the world.[7] So much activity required organization. Russell therefore acted as director of hundreds of travelling colporteurs and, as president of the Watch Tower Society, dispatched a corps of travelling preachers, called pilgrims, to Bible Student congregations everywhere. When the headquarters of the Watch Tower Society was moved in 1909 from Pittsburgh to the brownstone parsonage of Henry Ward Beecher at 124 Columbia

Heights, Brooklyn, New York, it became necessary to establish a new legal corporation, the People's Pulpit Association, which in 1939 became the Watchtower Bible and Tract Society, Incorporated.[8] In 1914 a British corporation, the International Bible Students Association, was formed. Russell served as president of all these organizations and also as pastor of the many Bible Student congregations which elected him to that office. By the time of his death there were probably in excess of twenty thousand Bible Students throughout the world, and the *Watch Tower* had reached a circulation of fifty-five thousand copies per issue.[9]

The Watch Tower Society's second president, Joseph Franklin Rutherford,[10] was born in Morgan County, Missouri, in 1869. Raised on a farm by Baptist parents, Rutherford showed an early interest in law. He became a court stenographer, attended law academy, and spent two years under the tutorship of a Missouri judge. At the age of twenty-two he began to practise law at Booneville, Missouri. Several years later he served as public prosecutor and on a few occasions as special or substitute judge of the Fourteenth Judicial District of Missouri. The title "judge"[11] which he earned was to remain with him throughout his life.

Watch Tower representatives first contacted Rutherford with their message in 1894, and in 1906 he became a baptized Bible Student. In the following year he became legal counsel for the Watch Tower Society and its president, Pastor Russell. He also became a pilgrim and was sent out from Pittsburgh and New York to give public sermons. During the next decade he frequently represented Russell in litigation. When the pastor died in October 1916, Rutherford was chosen as one of a committee of three to head the Watch Tower Society until the annual general meeting of that organization's shareholders in January 1917.[12] At that meeting, he was elected president by a unanimous vote.[13] He displayed great energy and immediately began a thorough revitalization of Bible Student activity which had been lagging since 1914.

The first years of his administration were fraught with difficulties. Most Bible Students, if not all, had expected the world to come to an end in 1914.[14] When it did not, some became disgruntled. More serious was a schism which developed at the Watch Tower headquarters, the Brooklyn Bethel, during the summer of 1917 and public animosity toward the Bible Students for their opposition to participation in the First World War. By 1918 the schism had widened to affect many Bible Student congregations; Watch Tower literature was banned in Canada; many American Bible Students were mobbed; and in the summer of that year, Judge Rutherford and six associates were convicted under terms of the United States Espionage Act and sentenced to serve twenty years in the Atlanta, Georgia, federal penitentiary. A seventh associate was sentenced to ten years. Although Rutherford and his companions were later found not guilty upon appeal to a superior court, they had spent nine months in prison before their release in the spring of 1919.[15]

From 1919 to the end of his presidency and life in 1942, Judge Rutherford proved to be as great a human dynamo as had Pastor Russell. He, too, travelled widely, spoke often, wrote much, and cared for the ever-increasing preaching campaign of the Bible Students. Again and again he was heard at Watch Tower conventions, over radio, and on thousands of phonograph records. He produced on the average one book per year, and his publications reached a total of thirty-six million copies.[16] The judge's major contributions, however, were primarily organizational. To emphasize the concept that every true follower of Christ should be a public preacher, he introduced Sunday house-to-house evangelizing in 1927, and the Bible Students' new name, Jehovah's Witnesses, was adopted on his recommendation in 1931. He also reshaped the entire nature of the movement from what it had been in Pastor Russell's day. Under Russell, Bible Student congregations, then known as *ecclesias* or more simply as "classes", were governed by locally elected elders. The only things that held them together were their recognition of Russell as their pastor, the Watch Tower Society as their spiritual guide, and a general feeling of fellowship as brothers in Christ. Judge Rutherford felt that this system was not in harmony with the Scriptures and over a period of years introduced "theocratic government". By 1938 all local congregational officers were appointed directly from Watch Tower Society offices; any form of local election had disappeared. While some of the old congregationally elected elder class objected to the changes, theocratic government welded Jehovah's Witnesses into a far more effective force for preaching and made them less liable to the danger of internal schisms. When Judge Rutherford died, he was succeeded in office by Vice-President Nathan Homer Knorr, without a ripple; nothing like the division of 1917 occurred again. Furthermore, the number of Witnesses had risen to 115,240 active house-to-house preachers,[17] whose general loyalty in the face of persecution proved quite amazing.

On January 13, 1942, the full membership of the Pennsylvania and New York societies met in the parlour of the Brooklyn Bethel and unanimously elected Knorr as Rutherford's successor.[18] Knorr,[19] born in Bethlehem, Pennsylvania, in 1905, was raised in the Reformed Church, but at the age of sixteen had become associated with the Bible Students. In 1923 he became a full-time colporteur and was invited to the Brooklyn Bethel, which has been his home ever since. By 1932 he had become general manager of the New York Watchtower Society's publishing office and plant. Two years later, he became a director of that corporation and in 1940 became a member and vice-president of the Watch Tower Bible and Tract Society of Pennsylvania. He gained almost all of his experience as a loyal Jehovah's Witness at the movement's central offices, and he carried on many of the programs initiated by Judge Rutherford.

Nathan H. Knorr, a much more mild-mannered man than his immediate predecessor, proved an even more able organizer. Just as hard-working as either Pastor Russell or Judge Rutherford, he has not personally extended his energies so much on speaking or writing— although he has done plenty of both. Under his administration the tendency to de-emphasize personality, which was begun under Judge Rutherford, has been carried to its conclusion. Since 1942 all Watch Tower Society literature has been published anonymously. Also, during the last four years, the general oversight of the world-wide activities of Jehovah's Witnesses has been taken over by a governing body of eleven men with a rotating chairmanship.[20] Although Knorr is one of that group and continues to hold the position of president of the major publication societies, he has willingly supported and promoted the creation of a collective leadership modelled on the body of apostles and elders at Jerusalem, which served as a governing body for the early church after Christ's death.[21] He has never attempted to direct attention to himself. Though a tall, strong-featured man, like both Russell and Rutherford, he has never manifested the charisma or striking personality traits of either. Yet under his administration, Jehovah's Witnesses have grown from a small band, mainly in the English-speaking world and Germany, to perhaps the fastest-growing religion bearing the name Christian in the world today.[22]

TABLE I

World-Wide Growth of Jehovah's Witnesses

Year	Active Publishers	Memorial Attendance Reported
1928	44,080	17,380
1938	59,047	69,345
1948	260,756	376,393
1958	798,326	1,171,789
1968	1,221,504	2,493,519
1974	2,021,432	4,550,457

During the Second World War the Watch Tower Society established, on a permanent basis, a system of circuit and district overseers to visit and co-ordinate the activities of congregations and circuits (about twenty congregations). It also provided for the holding of semi-annual circuit conventions and annual district conventions. While frequent local, national, and international conventions had been common under both Russell and Rutherford, the new program placed them on a more regular basis, more easily available to all Witnesses. The Society also established the missionary training school of Gilead at South Lansing, New York, and local Theocratic Ministry Schools in each congregation. Since 1943 Gilead has sent thousands of graduates throughout the world, and much of the Witnesses' growth must be attributed to their efforts. The local Ministry Schools have done much to turn the average Witness, who may be a carpenter, a farmer, or a public accountant, into a well-trained door-to-door preacher and public speaker.

This growth, plus a tremendous increase in the output of Witness literature, has taken place since the beginning of N. H. Knorr's presidency. In 1974, over 273,000,000 copies of the *Watchtower* and its companion magazine *Awake!* were distributed throughout the world as 471,111,385 copies of both publications rolled off the society's presses.[23] At the same time 2,021,434 Witnesses reported time preaching to their neighbours in 207 countries, territories, and islands in the sea.[24] Remarkable, too, have been some of the great Watch Tower Society conventions. In 1958 more than 252,000 met at an international assembly in New York City's two major baseball parks;[25] over 7,000 were immersed in Long Island Sound in what was the largest such baptism in history.[26] A district convention held at Vancouver in 1969 was undoubtedly the largest religious gathering ever held in Canada; more than 65,000 persons were present.[27]

It is not enough to look at the Witnesses of Jehovah from a purely organizational standpoint. In order to understand something of the dynamics of their faith, it is also necessary to examine their belief structure, a major task in itself. But in the same way that it is possible to outline some of the high points of their organizational history, it is also possible to sketch their basic beliefs.

Jehovah's Witnesses are, if anything, strict biblicists. To Pastor Russell, and all since his time, the Bible is the unerring, inspired word of God. Yet neither Russell nor Jehovah's Witnesses since his day have ever believed that they have had an infallible comprehension of the Scriptures. In fact, one of the keystones of their doctrine is the strongly held belief that they have gradually moved from spiritual darkness into spiritual light. Pastor Russell often emphasized Proverbs 4:18, which states: "But the path of the just is as the shining light, that shineth more and more unto the perfect day." From this he understood that God would gradually direct His faithful, chosen ones, who would seek Him, to a greater understanding of truth. Russell and his associates frequently used the term "Present Truth", by which they meant the amount of accurate understanding that the Almighty would allow them at any given time. For this reason many doctrines of the early Bible Students have undergone change; and the teachings of Jehovah's Witnesses today continue to evolve.[28] While this approach has often brought sharp criticism from outsiders, it has been a source of great internal strength. The Witnesses have therefore shown much interest since Russell's day in studying the Bible in its historical, archeological, and linguistic context,[29] to get a clearer understanding of its meaning. Constant re-examination has often caused them to reassess many of their teachings. As a result, the *Watchtower* has frequently indicated that many views expressed earlier in the Society's publications were erroneous.[30] Jehovah and His word are perfect; His Witnesses do not claim to be.

There is no doubt that they feel they are on the pathway of truth, however. They assert that, shortly after the apostolic age, Christians came under influences which were at variance with the teachings of Jesus and his earliest disciples. The development of a clergy class with monarchical bishops, the growth of the cult of saints and martyrs, the rise of monasticism, and the accommodation of Christians to popular pagan customs gradually brought about a great apostasy. So, too, did the general acceptance of certain Greek philosophical concepts which were grafted onto Christian doctrine somewhat prior to, and during, the great theological and Christological controversies of the fourth and fifth centuries. But perhaps most serious of all from the Witnesses' standpoint was the union of church and state under the Roman Emperor Constantine and his successors. And although Jehovah's Witnesses state that Protestantism did take some positive steps to return to the teachings of primitive Christianity, they feel its churches did not go far enough: not only did they continue to teach false doctrines, but in most instances they remained yoked to the secular governments of the world. Like Catholicism and Orthodoxy, the Protestant churches failed to act as faithful representatives of Jehovah and His Messiah. Thus, in the nineteenth century, God poured out His spirit on a small group of earnest Christians to cause them to restore pure worship and preach the good news of Christ's kingdom.[31] These saints of God, chosen for a special purpose, were, according to the belief of the Witnesses, members of a holy nation to whom the Lord would reveal His truths in His due time. As one sociologist has expressed it, Jehovah's Witnesses "have the feeling that they are God's instruments, agents of His work and will".[32]

Pastor Russell's *The Divine Plan of the Ages*, published in 1884, gives perhaps one of the clearest statements regarding the Witnesses' view of world history. According to it, human history since the Fall of mankind's original parents in Eden has been a struggle between

Jehovah and the chief adversary, Satan. Man lost paradise when he sinned; through God's grace he will ultimately regain it. During the long period between the Fall and man's ultimate restitution, however, Satan has struggled to turn him from the righteous worship of God. On the other hand, the Lord Jehovah has raised up a great cloud of witnesses—patriarchs, judges, prophets, apostles, and, above all, Jesus Christ—who have testified to the truth. As His plan unfolded He revealed His will to righteous men from Abel to Joseph, gave His law unto Moses and the nation of Israel, and prepared man for the coming of Christ. Jesus, the Messiah, born of the virgin girl Mary, came to atone for man's sins by giving Himself as a ransom sacrifice at Calvary. By so doing He opened Heaven itself to a small body of 144,000 saints—the spiritual Israel of God. Eventually, after His Church (the 144,000) has been chosen, Christ will come again to destroy Satan and all of his wicked system at the battle of Armageddon. Then the world will be restored to the paradisaic nature of Eden, and the great majority of mankind will be raised from the dead through the resurrection to life on a perfect earth. This restitution will take place during the thousand-year reign of Christ.

Such doctrines had a profound effect on the early Bible Students and have continued to mould the character of Jehovah's Witnesses ever since. If human history is part of a controversy between Jehovah and the Adversary, it is important for Christians to take a stand against all forms of wickedness. Again, if Jehovah intends to destroy the nations at Armageddon, then clearly those nations, and the political, religious, and socio-economic systems which support them, are evil. Pastor Russell held, therefore, that it was necessary for true Christians, the remnant of the elect of God, to separate themselves as far as possible from these evil-doers. As Christ indicated to His followers, they were in the world, but were not part of it. Consequently, Russell counselled that while Bible Students should honour all men and be obedient to earthly authorities in matters not contrary to divine law, they should refrain from participating in politics, voting, and killing their fellow men in the wars of the nations. He also condemned what he considered to be the false doctrines of Christendom, the corrupt practices of big business, the revolutionary tendencies of communism, the social gospel, and the theory of biological evolution.

From all such and from the improper desires of the eyes and the flesh, Bible Students were enjoined to keep themselves free.[33]

These concepts, plus the belief that the world's end was at hand, caused Russell and his associates to preach their message with great fervour. If the world was passing away, it was important to warn mankind. Ever since, although they have restated the time features described in *The Divine Plan*, Jehovah's Witnesses have continued to feel that the destruction of Satan's system is near. Russell long expected that the year 1914 might mark the end of that system; today the Witnesses believe that 1914 was the year in which Christ began ruling as king in fulfilment of Psalm 110:1, 2, and that it marked the beginning of a time of distress leading to the battle of Armageddon.[34] The Witnesses' great zeal, which both friend and foe have noted with admiration,[35] is therefore largely attributable to their sense of history and their eschatological faith. Probably not even Marxists believe that history is on their side to the extent that the Witnesses of Jehovah do.

Russell and his fellows' strong certainty that God had given them new light in response to their earnest seeking caused them to feel that the churches were in darkness on many issues. As the Bible Students examined the Scriptures, they quickly abandoned many of the teachings of both Roman Catholics and Protestants. Their rejection of hell-fire and purgatory came with a denial of the doctrine of the immortality of the soul. They became convinced that the soul lies dead in the grave until the resurrection. They also denied the Trinity, the hypostatic union (the doctrine that Christ is both wholly God and wholly man), and the Anselmian concept of the atonement.[36] Jehovah is a unity, not a trinity. Jesus (God's first spiritual creation) was a perfect man while on earth, but no more than that. When he died he ransomed man from sin, death, and the Devil. But it was neither necessary nor possible that he be a god-man.

When the Bible Students publicized such ideas far and wide, they convinced many. They also garnered a harvest of hostility, particularly from clergymen. Such animosity did not always arise out of purely doctrinal issues. Pastor Russell and the Bible Students became a living challenge to the very existence of the professionally trained and ordained clergy of all denominations. Only a handful of early Bible

Students had ever darkened the door of a theological seminary, and Russell's pastorate was by election, not by any form of denominational ordination. Even more significant was the fact that they pushed the concept of the priesthood of the believer to its logical conclusion. As far as the Bible Students were concerned, ordination as a minister came at baptism. All Christians who dedicated their lives to God and were baptized by water immersion could preach. Furthermore, within the Church of Christ, all are brothers; there must be no clergy-laity distinction. Almost from the beginning, then, Russell and his co-believers came to look upon the clergy as false shepherds. The clergy were making no real effort to preach the good news of Christ's kingdom; many of them were worldly; many were teaching God-dishonouring doctrines such as hell-fire and immortality; and, most despicable, they were making their living at it. Bible Students also came to look upon solicited church contributions and the collection plate as means whereby the false shepherds fleeced their flocks. What was most upsetting to many men of the cloth was that the Bible Students expressed their feelings everywhere they went, particularly in the great quantities of literature which they distributed. Russell himself focused unfavourable attention on the collection plate when he adopted, as a sort of trademark on all his meeting announcements, the words: "Seats Free, No Collection".[37]

The Bible Students stirred up a veritable hornets' nest; they attacked what Judge Rutherford referred to as the "unholy alliance" or "Preachers' Union".[38] In no time they became the object of a counter-offensive. Ministerial associations condemned "Russellite" doctrines and attacked the first Watch Tower president in the strongest terms. Certain newspapers also tried to picture him as an immoral charlatan of the worst sort. They focused attention particularly on what became known as the "jellyfish story" and the "Miracle Wheat episode".

The jellyfish story arose out of Russell's strained relations with, and separation from, his wife. For many years Mrs. Russell actively supported her husband, and even served as secretary-treasurer of the Watch Tower Society. She was a strong-willed, well-educated woman, however, and about 1894 she demanded freedom to publish what she wanted in the *Watch Tower*. Russell, guided by the Apostle Paul's admonition against women religious teachers, refused. The breach between the two widened, and in 1897 Mrs. Russell abandoned their home and her faith. Seven years later she filed a suit for legal separation against Russell, and in April 1906 the case came to trial; the separation was made legal.[39] But that was only the beginning of Russell's troubles. During the trial, Mrs. Russell claimed that the pastor had said to Rose Ball, a fifteen-year-old girl who had lived with them as a daughter: "I am like a jelly-fish, I float around here and there. I touch this one and that one, and if she responds I take her to me, and if not I float on to others."[40] The judge ordered the jury to disregard this statement;[41] Russell denied it completely;[42] and, under oath, Mrs. Russell admitted she did not believe her husband guilty of adultery.[43] Nevertheless, Pastor Russell was pictured by his adversaries as a divorced man and a proven adulterer, neither of which charge was true. The *Washington Post* wrote a particularly vicious editorial in which he was labelled the "Rev. Jellyfish Russell".[44] He then launched suit against that paper and was awarded one dollar damages. He appealed to a superior court, which granted a retrial so that a jury might assess heavier damages. But during the second trial, the *Post* agreed to a settlement out of court, to pay court costs, and to publish his sermons.[45] In a subsequent suit over the same issue, a Chicago paper, the *Mission Friend*, also sought a settlement and published a statement apologizing for having maligned him.[46] Still, the jellyfish story continued to be repeated by his adversaries with many of the subsequent facts of the case forgotten, or intentionally ignored.[47]

The Miracle Wheat episode occurred some years later. In 1904 a man by the name of Stoner, who knew nothing of Pastor Russell's religion, discovered in Fincastle, Virginia, an amazingly productive variety of wheat which he named Miracle Wheat. Seven years later, two Bible Students donated thirty bushels of it to the Watch Tower Society to be sold at a dollar per pound as seed grain. The proceeds—about eighteen hundred dollars—were to be used by the Society to carry on its activities. Russell obtained nothing personally from the proceeds, but his enemies claimed the sale was a religious fraud. A

New York newspaper, the *Brooklyn Daily Eagle*, attacked him and lampooned both Russell and Miracle Wheat in a cartoon. Again he sued, but in this instance he lost.[48]

Bible Students argued that attacks on their pastor were motivated by religious prejudice. In 1915 J. F. Rutherford penned a small pamphlet, *A Great Battle in the Ecclesiastical Heavens*, in which he took up the charges against Russell one by one, and blamed the latter's woes on the clergy. Whatever the facts behind such events as Pastor Russell's separation and the Miracle Wheat episode, there can be no doubt that he was unfairly maligned and, also, that clergymen were largely responsible.[49] To this day anti-Jehovah's Witness literature is filled with assaults on Russell. Bible Students' animosity toward the churches and the clergy grew, and, with it, criticism of men of the cloth.

Such censure of the clergy, both Catholic and Protestant, made the Bible Students the targets of ecclesiastical wrath, and developed in them the strong sense of burning anti-clericalism which has marked Jehovah's Witnesses ever since. To them the clergy are, with notable exceptions, the most despicable of men. Yet aside from Russell himself, the Bible Students did not suffer much for this attitude until the First World War. Then, because they opposed participation in the war and criticized the clergy for supporting it, they came into serious trouble with secular authorities. Their literature was banned in both Canada and the United States. Many suffered arrests, fines, imprisonment, and mobbings. As mentioned previously, Judge Rutherford and seven Watch Tower officers were imprisoned for a short time.

After the war, the Bible Student-Witnesses, like Hebrew prophets of old, pronounced doom on commerce, politics, and religion. They also took a strong stand against nationalism in any form. As a result, they once again experienced terrible persecution prior to, during, and after the Second World War. As one writer remarked, they have provided more modern martyrs than any single religious group in the twentieth century except the Jews.[50] Hitler said he would see "this brood exterminated in Germany".[51] Americans mobbed them by the thousands.[52] Canadian Minister of Justice Ernest Lapointe labelled them seditious,[53] and a host of British dominions and colonies outlawed them.[54] Since the Second World War Fidel Castro has called them "worms" and sent them to concentration camps.[55] Communist Russia has called them "capitalist agents" and dumped them in the wilds of Siberia or sent them to slave-labour camps.[56] Numerous Arab and African countries have declared them illegal and subjected them to veritable pogroms.[57] Greece has sentenced young men to death for refusing military service,[58] and for years Spain kept many in nearly perpetual imprisonment for the same reason.[59] In Argentina they are refused recognition,[60] in France the *Watchtower* was banned for many years,[61] and in Great Britain the highest court in the land has refused to recognize any Jehovah's Witnesses as ministers.[62] In the United States they have long represented the largest group of conscientious objectors imprisoned for their faith.[63] And as if these troubles were not enough, the Witnesses have gotten into a major squabble with modern medicine over their refusal to accept blood transfusions.

Jehovah's Witnesses have been far more than martyrs to their faith. They have had an impact on many of the societies in which they have lived far out of proportion to their small numbers. No other religious group has been so successful in its championship of unpopular causes. The Witnesses have been masters at appealing to Caesar. Although they regard the political process as fundamentally immoral, they have been quite willing to use certain democratic rights to gain their ends. They have often used the ancient rights of both individual and collective petition, and thereby have had their concerns dealt with by many of the great legislative bodies of the Western world. Issues which they have raised have been debated in the parliaments of Australia, Britain, Canada, and Sweden, and in the Congress of the United States. They have sometimes been indirectly responsible for the enactment of important legislation. But their most significant contribution has been through the courts, a fact commented on again and again by outside observers. In 1943 Charles Beard wrote:

Whatever may be said about the Witnesses, they have the courage of martyrs. And they have the money to hire lawyers and fight cases through the courts. As a result in recent days they have made more contributions to the development of the constitutional law of religious liberty than any other cult or group. Believe me, they are making it fast.[64]

A few years later Charles S. Braden said much the same:

Against every sort of opposition they press ahead. They fight by every legal means for their civil rights, the right of public assembly—sometimes denied them—the right to distribute their literature, the right to put God above every other loyalty. They have performed a signal service to democracy by their fight to preserve their civil rights, for in their struggle they have done much to secure those rights for every minority group in America. When the civil rights of any one group are invaded, the rights of no other group are safe. They have therefore made a definite contribution to the preservation of some of the most precious things in our democracy.[65]

Perhaps, however, the matter was best put by U.S. Supreme Court Justice Frank Murphy:

No chapter in human history has been so largely written in terms of persecution and intolerance as the one dealing with religious freedom. From ancient times to the present day, the ingenuity of man has known no limits in its ability to forge weapons of oppression for use against those who dare to express or practice unorthodox religious beliefs. And the Jehovah's Witnesses are living proof of the fact that even in this nation, conceived as it was in the ideals of freedom, the right to practice religion in unconventional ways is still far from secure. . . . To them, along with other present day religious minorities, befalls the burden of testing our devotion to the ideals and guarantees of religious freedom.[66]

Nowhere has this been more true than in Canada.

Who then are the Witnesses of Jehovah? Scholars writing about them have often assumed that their membership is drawn from among the lowest socio-economic classes of the societies in which they live, and that they represent essentially a protest movement. For example, W. E. Mann, writing about them in Alberta in the 1940s, stated that "Jehovah's Witnesses constituted an especially depressed and hard hit group", and argued that "in particular they appealed to the more depressed and backwoods farmers who had profound resentments against city ways and middle class values".[67] Mann also claimed that the Witnesses were "venomously opposed" to education.[68] Nearly two decades later, Douglas Wilson, making much the same evaluation, wrote: "Their appeal is, for the most part, to the heavily pressed and untutored; this is true in whatever country or region the sect appears."[69] Yet such appraisals are based on surprisingly little concrete data; in fact, a sophisticated statistical examination of Jehovah's Witnesses has never been made in Canada, or anywhere else in the Western world for that matter. Statements like those of Mann and Wilson therefore seem to be based on presuppositions which are rooted either in the prejudices of the Witnesses' adversaries or in the rather gross sociological over-simplification that, because they are a "sect", they must fit sociologists' definition of what a sect is.[70] Mann, for instance, apparently based many of his statements on information supplied to him by Anglican and United Church clergymen, hardly objective or knowledgeable sources with respect to the Witnesses. Wilson was evidently stating his own viewpoint, or repeating frequently made assertions; he gives no proof at all for his contention.

At least two scholars—one American and one British—who have examined the Witnesses have come to quite different conclusions. William Cumberland, writing in 1958 in a carefully researched doctoral dissertation, found that they were then, if anything, middle class.[71] Allan Rogerson, who briefly evaluated a statistical survey made by the American Department of Justice involving eight thousand young Witnesses who applied for exemption from military service during the Second World War and the works of two American sociologists (Stroup and Czatt) on the subject, concluded that in both the United States and Great Britain, Witnesses are "pretty average". While there are many poor people among them, there are "few layabouts".[72] Of course it is difficult to state from a social standpoint just what the Witnesses have been and are. Not only has careful research on them not been done, but they have been growing so fast for the past several decades that it would be strange if their status as a group had not changed somewhat. There are some data, however, which indicate that Rogerson's evaluation is correct. At least in Canada, it seems that Jehovah's Witnesses have been, and are, pretty average.

Most of the historical sources which deal with Canadian Bible Students in the nineteenth and early twentieth centuries tend to indicate that many were reasonably well educated persons of British or Northern European origin, many of whom were small businessmen, clerks, farmers, and professional persons. Thereafter, particularly in the 1920s and 1930s, many were drawn, it is true, from among farmers and labourers of British and new-Canadian origin. During that period Scandinavians, Germans, Poles, Hungarians, and, in particular, many Ukrainians became Witnesses of Jehovah. There is, however, no indication that they were any more down and out than were their neighbours. Their young men who were interned in the Second World War alternative-service camps represented the most prosperous and sophisticated group of conscientious objectors.[73] Finally, although the picture given is incomplete, the kind of data found in the national decennial censuses gives the best indication of the social status of Jehovah's Witnesses in Canada. According to these statistics, the majority of Bible Student-Witnesses have been concentrated primarily in areas which are not the least affluent parts of the country.[74] Their birth rate has been relatively low, too—a fact often, though not always, associated with higher incomes and educational levels. According to the last two censuses, their birth rate has been very close to that of the national average[75] and that of members of the United Church of Canada.[76] Although not absolutely definitive, these facts do suggest strongly that in ways not associated with their faith Jehovah's Witnesses are quite average Canadians.

That this is the case should not be surprising. To an extent greater than any religion in Canadian history, Jehovah's Witnesses have attempted to be "all things to all men" and, therefore, have been successful in making converts among almost all groups of Canadians. Even prior to the Second World War, they began to convert numerous French Canadians to their faith, and have been one of the most successful religious movements in attracting persons of French-speaking, Roman Catholic backgrounds to their fold.[77] Large numbers of post-war immigrants have also become Jehovah's Witnesses, among them British, Germans, Italians, Greeks, Portuguese, and Spanish.[78] In fact, so many Italians have been attracted that most large cities have Italian-speaking congregations.[79] There are also numerous Witnesses who have been members of such ethno-religious communities as the Mennonites and Doukhobors, plus members of such minority groups as Canadian Indians, Métis, Chinese, Japanese, East Indians, Negroes, and Jews. In fact, in places like Montreal, Toronto, Winnipeg, Vancouver, and a host of other cities, large and small, Witness congregations are a veritable ethnic *pot-pourri*. Nevertheless, as has been the case since the nineteenth century, the largest number are still of British-Canadian origin, especially in the urban areas. Although there are many older and middle-aged persons in practically every kingdom hall (the congregational meeting places), the number of young people is quite large.[80] As far as occupations are concerned, it is evident that many are farmers and blue-collar workers; and there are skilled artisans—carpenters, bricklayers, electricians—and numerous clerical workers, salesmen, accountants, and persons who hold managerial positions among them. It is true there are not a great many who are professionals, although nurses, druggists, medical doctors, chiropractors, school teachers, university professors, and lawyers are to be found among their ranks. Since they do not encourage their youth to acquire university educations, as some religions do, only a small number of professionals come from within their own community.

Yet during the last few years, it would be possible to meet such Witness professionals as a medical doctor in Vancouver, several young South American physicians studying post-graduate medicine in Montreal, a Vancouver pharmacist who was recently interviewed on national television for refusing to sell tobacco in his drugstore, and another West Coast druggist who became a Witness during the "dirty thirties" in the small dust-bowl village of Viceroy, Saskatchewan. In Langley, British Columbia, a doctor of homeopathy, a Witness, practises the ancient Chinese therapy of acupuncture. Witness chiropractors are found across Canada in such places as Toronto, Saskatoon, Lethbridge, and Penticton. In addition, there are nurse-midwives, registered nurses, and medical technicians, in places large and small, from the Atlantic provinces to the Pacific coast. Jehovah's Witnesses are also found on the faculties and staffs of universities, colleges, and public schools throughout the nation. Among them are professors of education, engineering, mathematics, and history, and an instructor of architecture at such places as Simon Fraser University, the University of Alberta, Lakehead University, the University of Lethbridge, and Alberta's Northern Institute of Technology. Witness lawyers live and practise law in a number of centres both in Ontario and in the Prairies. In Trail, British Columbia, the chief research geologist for the Consolidated Mining and Smelting Company of Canada serves as an elder in the local Witness congregation.

There are also many Witnesses in business, in sports, in the performing arts, and in the civil service. One, now retired, was the owner of a major van and moving company. Another was an important Manitoba developer and manufacturer. Two are independently engaged in the printing and publishing business in Toronto. The man who discovered a major gold deposit in the interior of British Columbia, and who is now a wealthy shareholder in the company which mines it, is a Witness. So, too, is an Alberta farmer and businessman who not long ago had more arable land under cultivation than any single individual in the Commonwealth of Nations. Then, among Jehovah's Witnesses in Canada, there are artists, architects, opera singers, art historians, engineers, professional hockey players, northern bush pilots, employees of the federal Department of Agriculture, social workers, along with Maritime fishermen, Quebec dairy farmers, Ontario factory workers, prairie ranchers, British Columbia loggers, and men and women in scores of other secular pursuits. Jehovah's Witnesses truly make up a varied cross-section of the population, from the highly trained and well educated to men and women of modest means and little sophistication.

It is not true that Jehovah's Witnesses are, or ever have been, "venomously" anti-intellectual. Their children have long been encouraged to get the most out of public schools, to finish their high-school education, and to learn a skill or trade.[81] Some do go to university as well, but it is true that they have often taken a dim view of higher education.[82] Not only are many aspects thereof seen as faith-destroying, but Witness parents tend to regard the social environment of many university communities as dangerous to good morals. But the principal reason that Witness youth are not encouraged to seek careers through education is that their time can be spent more profitably elsewhere—as heralds of a new and better system. It would certainly be wrong to infer that Jehovah's Witnesses as a group are well educated; it would be equally wrong to conclude that by national standards they are uneducated or under-educated.

What marks the Witnesses as distinct is their faith. To a degree perhaps unrivalled by any other religion in Canada they are drawn from practically all groups in the society at large. Unlike Mennonites, Hutterites, Doukhobors, and even Mormons,[83] they are not ethnically distinct from the general population. Yet Jehovah's Witnesses are *different*. Their unique lifestyle is therefore based on their religious beliefs.

As already stressed, Jehovah's Witnesses see themselves as distinct from their neighbours. They are a society within a society, or, as Marley Cole has put it, "a nation without a country".[84] They are what sociologists, following Ernest Troeltsch and his disciples, would call a sect-type religion,[85] without anything pejorative or unflattering intended. Because of the application of the term to them, however, many students of the Witnesses have been guilty of making unwarranted assumptions about them. In 1929 H. Richard Niebuhr published *The Social Sources of Denominationalism*. He posited that a sect faced with increasing success, the upward social mobility of its adherents, and greater accommodation with the world would almost automatically become a denomination, that is, a routinized and accommodated sect. As a result, many people have suggested that the Witnesses would necessarily move in status from a sect to a denomination.[86] While it is true that they show increasing signs of wealth and sophistication, there is, nevertheless, no proof that they are evolving as predicted. The more tactful approach that they have taken in winning converts since the Second World War does not indicate that their basic attitudes have changed. In fact, careful studies in late years have demonstrated that they are—along with the numerically insignificant Christadelphians, who hold many of the same beliefs—of a type which does not become routinized or accommodated. According to sociologist Brian Wilson, they have become an "established sect".[87]

In reality, since the organization of the early Bible Students in the 1870s, Jehovah's Witnesses have drawn away from the world, rather than toward it. Persecution, the rise of nationalism, and lately, the so-called new morality have caused them to take ever-firmer stands which separate them from society in general. In harmony with their concept of "new light" or "new truth", they have gradually but consistently taken stronger stands against such things as participation in non-combatant military service, political involvement, working in munitions factories, and employment by other religious organizations. They have also come to reject the celebration of all religious and national holidays (except the annual memorial of the Lord's Supper), the use of the cross, flag salutes, standing for national anthems, blood transfusions, and a few other medical practices.[88]

Their attitude toward personal morality has also become stricter. Among Jehovah's Witnesses, fornication,[89] as described in Matthew 5:32, has always been seen as the only legitimate basis for divorce. But, particularly since 1950, the Watch Tower Society has taken ever more clearly defined positions on sexual morality. It has held that for such sins as fornication, adultery, homosexuality, lesbianism, bestiality, polygamy, consensual marriage, and even heavy or intimate petting among the unmarried, one may be disfellowshipped from the congregation and shunned completely by all Witnesses outside the immediate family. Masturbation and unnatural sexual acts within marriage have also been sternly condemned.[90] But Witnesses do not have a fixation on sexual matters: a member of the congregation may also be excommunicated for drunkenness, the non-medical use of drugs, lying, stealing, physical violence, shady business practices, direct participation in political activities, the willing acceptance of blood transfusions, and apostasy.[91] But perhaps the most evident example of their growing moral strictness is their new attitude toward the use of tobacco. In the past, although smoking and tobacco-chewing were frowned upon, they were tolerated. With the rise of the drug culture in the 1960s, however, the Witnesses were forced to re-examine their stand on the matter. Many young people argued that the use of marijuana is less dangerous to health than tobacco; and the Watch Tower Society came to agree that tobacco was at least as harmful as marijuana, and therefore morally wrong. Thus the June 15, 1973, *Watchtower* magazine came out with an article which told tobacco users and all persons on non-medical drugs to "clean up" within six months or be disfellowshipped.

Naturally, no person practising any of the moral infractions considered above is regarded as a proper candidate for baptism and membership in a Witness congregation. Literally thousands have been expelled, too, since the institution of disfellowshipping.[92] Thus Witness moral standards are high or puritanical, depending on one's point of view—a fact which, in an increasingly permissive world, re-enforces their separateness.

Jehovah's Witnesses do not simply stress what they are against, although it may seem so to outsiders. Much emphasis has been placed on the family as the basic unit of Christian life, particularly since the publication of the book *Children* in 1941. Like their Catholic neighbours, they believe that the family that prays together stays together. To the Witnesses, however, family life is far more than praying unitedly. The husband-father is family head in a Pauline sense: not only is he charged with the basic responsibiilty of providing for his household and disciplining them in love, but he must study the Bible with his wife and children if possible, training them in proper moral values and the doctrines and precepts of the faith.[93] Wives and mothers are expected to be helpmates to their husbands and to show proper subjection.[94] Children, therefore, usually grow up in an atmosphere of respect for parental and congregational authority through which their lives are directed toward "Jehovah's service".

To each and every zealous Witness, outside of his own home the kingdom hall is the most important centre of his personal activities. On the average he and his family will attend four one-hour congregational meetings per week there and one somewhere else. Usually on Sundays—but in some congregations on other days of the week— there is a one-hour sermon directed at newly interested persons as well as at dedicated Witnesses. Then the congregation participates in an hour-long question-and-answer study of some biblical subject presented in the *Watchtower*. Usually on a Thursday or Friday, they gather for the "Service Meeting", a program of instruction relating to their preaching work, and the Theocratic Ministry School. One evening each week they attend small book-study group meetings composed of from ten to twenty persons and generally held in a private home, to study closely more complex and advanced doctrines. Everyone, young and old, male and female, is expected to prepare for these meetings and is permitted to comment, to take part in the Theocratic Ministry School, and to participate in demonstrations and skits. Only persons who have been rebuked or excommunicated for some extremely grave offence are denied some or all of these privileges. Great respect is shown the old; much attention is given to the young. Outside of meetings, visiting the sick or spiritually weak is a duty of all in the congregation. Hence there is an attempt to involve everyone, and to make him or her feel wanted. All zealous adult males have a special role, however. They seek positions of responsibility as elders (presbyters) or ministerial servants (deacons).[95]

Regular visits by travelling circuit and district overseers constantly make Witness congregations aware that they are members of a larger organization, which is felt to be universal in scope. So, too, do other events. Congregations frequently trade speakers and practically every Witness gets to know others beyond his own congregation by his attendance at circuit, district, and even international conventions. Many have travelled to other continents and even around the world to major assemblies, and have become rather international, if not cosmopolitan, in outlook. Besides acting as sources of religious training, such conventions serve a number of useful functions. Since Jehovah's Witnesses do not celebrate traditional holidays or birthdays, their assemblies act as gala occasions to travel, to enjoy spiritual instruction, and to have fellowship with their co-believers. Sometimes young people meet future marriage mates. But most important from their own standpoint, the Witnesses become well known to the communities where their conventions are held, obtain much friendly publicity—because of their cleanliness and order—and make new converts.[96]

Finally, one other major event makes them feel a world-wide inner cohesiveness and separateness from the world. Since the nineteenth century, it has been their custom to celebrate the Lord's Supper once a year on the eve of the traditional date (Nisan 14) of the Jewish Passover, according to the ancient lunar calendar. Although held to be a memorial in which the bread and wine are only representative of the body and blood of the Christ, this occasion has great significance. Those who partake of the "emblems" (unleavened bread and pure red wine) indicate that they have been called to heavenly life and are of the remnant of the 144,000 saints left on earth. As of now there are only about 10,000[97] of this group, which has declined in numbers over the years since 1935.[98] But all other Witnesses also try to be present to see this elect class testify to the fact that they have received a higher calling. The vast majority of Witnesses now hope to live on a paradise earth restored, but they make much of their association with old-time "anointed" Witnesses who have directed them since Judge Rutherford's time and, in a few cases, since the days of Pastor Russell. When memorial celebrations are held, there are often twice as many present as there are active Witnesses, a fact which shows how many well-wishers and sympathizers they have.[99]

Not all their activities are strictly religious, and while Witnesses may be puritanical in some ways, they are not pietistic. They enjoy television, movies, and the latest in stereophonic sound equipment, not unlike most of their neighbours. Many of them enjoy dancing. They have no prohibitions against any foods or drinks, except those containing blood. Most of them drink tea, coffee, and alcoholic beverages in moderation. They have no particular regulations regarding clothing styles, and the women generally use cosmetics. It is nevertheless true that their whole lives are affected by their religious outlook. They are admonished always to watch good programs, to listen to good music, and to read edifying books. While the Watch Tower Society refuses to establish specific styles of clothing or grooming, Witnesses are reminded that their appearance must be chaste, modest, and clean. Rock and roll music, mini-skirts, and long hair on men have not found favour among them. After all, ambassadors substituting for Christ need both to be morally upright and to give a good appearance to those without.

This latter aspect of their general attitude focuses attention on what is the central factor within the lives of Jehovah's Witnesses: their ministry, or preaching, to others. They are the single Christian religion in the world today which teaches that every member in good standing should be a preacher trying to win converts in a formal, regular manner. There are, in fact, no membership rolls among them, but every active Witness demonstrates that he is such by regularly

reporting how much time per month he has spent in public proselytizing. By so doing he becomes a regular congregational "publisher"
of the good news of Christ's kingdom.

Usually whole families of Witnesses are publishers. As soon as
children reach the age of understanding, they accompany their
parents in preaching activities. They go from door to door or on the
streets to place Watch Tower literature; they make return visits to
interested persons; and they join in home Bible studies at the homes
of prospective converts. Thus the children of Jehovah's Witnesses
constantly hear the Bible read and discussed, so much so that biblical
terminology becomes part of their everyday thinking and speech. As
Charles S. Braden remarked three decades ago: "No modern
Christians make a more constant use of scripture, or memorize it in
greater quantities than the Witnesses. To argue successfully with
them on scriptural grounds, one must know his scriptures better than
most members of even the fundamentalist churches do today."[100]

Seeking converts and constantly defending their faith at the doors
of others—sometimes in the face of householders who throw everything from arguments to buckets of water, and worse—strengthens
Witness zeal rather than dampens it. For this reason, particularly
since 1957, whole families have moved their places of residence "to
serve where the need is greater".[101] Many from western Canada and
Ontario have migrated to Quebec and the Maritimes. Others have
gone to South and Central America, Africa, Spain, and the islands in
the Pacific, often to learn a new language and always to announce
Jehovah's kingdom.

The greatest bulk of the preaching of Jehovah's Witnesses in new
areas has nevertheless been done by full-time evangelists who were
known as colporteurs until the late 1920s and who have been called
"pioneers" ever since. Naturally, relatively few can be pioneers because of personal responsibilities, but all are encouraged to keep their
ministry as a goal. As a result, many young men and women become
pioneers immediately after graduating from high school. So, too, do
couples without children, or those who have raised their families.
Even housewives become very effective full-time pioneer evangelists.

This ministry is not easy and requires faith. It may mean voluntarily
delaying or giving up marriage as suggested by Christ and the Apostle

Paul.[102] For young married couples it may mean giving up normal home life and children. But most significant is the fact that pioneers must be self-supporting and preach one hundred hours per month. "Special pioneers", who are assigned specific territories, do receive fifty dollars a month from the Watch Tower Society, but they must preach one hundred and fifty hours per month to outsiders. In spite of the difficulties Witnesses find in "pioneering", a substantial number have become, and have remained, such full-time preachers.[103]

Over the years zealous and able pioneers have been invited to serve as district and circuit overseers. Some have joined the headquarters staff of the Watch Tower Society's branch office at 150 Bridgeland Avenue, Toronto. A large number have been called to Gilead, the Society's missionary school, in preparation for missionary assignments, usually abroad. Canadian Gilead graduates have been very active in the Province of Quebec and in scores of other countries. Some have come to hold responsible offices such as that of branch supervisor in the countries to which they have gone.[104] Old-time pioneers, active before the establishment of Gilead, have also become prominent, even at the Society's central offices in Brooklyn. A. H. Macmillan, long a member of the Society's board of directors, was a Canadian. So, too, was Thomas Sullivan, until his recent death a member of the governing body of Jehovah's Witnesses. Leo Greenlees, another member of the governing body, though born in Scotland, spent most of his youth and adulthood in Canada, and may therefore be considered Canadian.

The importance of countrymen in such roles means little to Canadian Witnesses. They are in no sense nationalistic. Percy Chapman, one of their own greatly respected former branch supervisors, is English, and a second, Eugene Rosam, is American. Besides, they are opposed to the concept of glorifying individuals; although many pioneers may be loved and admired for their zeal, they are just brothers in Christ. After all, what every Witness—congregational publisher or pioneer—is primarily interested in is the preaching work. As many men as possible must be contacted before Jehovah sends His son to destroy the wicked at the great battle of God the Almighty. Perhaps their spirit is best captured in the words of one of their hymnal marches, "Forward, You Witnesses", a song composed in the concentration camps of Germany during the Second World War:

Firm and determined in this time of the end,
Prepared are God's servants the good news to defend.
Tho' Satan against them has vaunted,
In God's strength they keep on undaunted!

Justice and truth have been pushed aside by man.
Opposers the name of Jehovah seek to ban.
They must be restored to their places
By Christians with bold, beaming faces!

Soldiers of Jah do not seek a life of ease.
The world and its rulers they do not try to please;
Unspotted at all times remaining,
Integrity always maintaining!

Then forward, you witnesses, ever strong of heart!
Rejoice that in God's work you, too, may have a part!
Go tell far and wide God's new order is near,
That e'er long its rich blessings will be here!

CHAPTER TWO

The Early Years and the Beginning of a Time of Troubles

Render unto Caesar the things that are Caesar's, and unto God the things that are God's.

Mark 12:17, American Standard Version

BIBLE STUDENT DOCTRINES penetrated Canada soon after Charles T. Russell began his religious activities. As early as 1881 some of his associates in Pittsburgh began to send Watch Tower literature to friends and relatives in Ontario.[1] Letters were received by the Watch Tower Society from that province in 1882,[2] and in 1886 at least one Ontarian, William Brookman, probably an ex-clergyman, travelled to Pittsburgh to join Bible Students there in the annual celebration of the Lord's Supper.[3] Soon a number of small businessmen, artisans, and farmers, mostly of Anglo-Saxon, Protestant backgrounds, began to accept Bible Student teachings.[4] As a result, small congregations began to develop throughout Ontario.[5] In 1891, at the invitation of the Toronto congregation, Pastor Russell made his first visit to that city and addressed some seven hundred persons on the subjects "God's Kingdom" and "The Times of Restitution of All Things".[6] Thereafter, the number of congregations increased, and by 1901 there were at least eighteen in as many Ontario centres. They were to be found in most of the province's large cities and also in smaller places such as

Aylmer, Beamsville, Barrie, Lucknow, Preston, Smithville, and West Montrose. In addition, local conventions of several congregations took place frequently, and the *Watch Tower* regularly reported the visits of pilgrims to the various congregations.[7]

Ontario was not the only part of Canada where Bible Students began to appear. An equally fertile field for their teachings was western Canada. Manitoba had been made a province in 1870 and British Columbia joined Confederation in 1871; thereafter, particularly between 1890 and 1914, thousands of settlers poured into these provinces and the portions of the Northwest Territories that became Alberta and Saskatchewan in 1905. Thus Canada had a new frontier area which, in the tradition of the Anglo-American frontier, proved open to the spread of so-called sectarian movements, among them the Bible Students.

As thousands of settlers moved to the Canadian West to establish new homes, they were joined by a small number of Bible Students who brought with them the millennialist teachings of Charles T. Russell. Though some of them later became colporteurs, there was no attempt on the part of the Watch Tower Society to send missionaries to the West in those days. Since there were no Bible Student clergy either, they had no religious leaders to spread the movement. Yet western Canada soon became an important area for the growth and development of their faith. With the great diversity of religious groups which appeared in British Columbia and the prairie provinces during those years, there was a great deal of interest in religion. At the same time there were many settlers who belonged to no particular denomination and many more who, though formally church members, were less than devout. Persons who in their places of origin might have felt constrained to maintain family religious ties did not always do so in the new land. Consequently, since individual Bible Students continually preached to their neighbours, some of them adopted the new religion and aided in its dissemination.

In 1889 a man named William Peter Flewwelling of Carberry, Manitoba, came into possession of Volume 1 of Pastor Russell's *Studies in the Scriptures*. Flewwelling read it, and, convinced by its teachings, became the first Bible Student in western Canada. The following year he moved to Vancouver, where he was employed by

British Columbia Steel; he preached to fellow workers and helped to organize the first Bible Student meetings in Canada west of Ontario. In 1910 he moved to the farming community of Asquith, Saskatchewan, about twenty miles from Saskatoon. As a direct result of his efforts, numerous Saskatchewan congregations came into existence and, indirectly, several in the interior of British Columbia were started.[8]

Meanwhile other groups were forming throughout the West. Early in the 1890s, a small *ecclesia* was formed in Victoria at the home of a couple named Moore on Rudlin Street. Some time during the same decade this class rented a hall, and by 1913 there was a small congregation of from twenty-five to thirty persons.[9] By 1893 or 1894 a Bible Student woman, Mrs. McCallum, had settled twelve miles outside of Regina and had made at least one convert, a Regina school teacher named John Aitchison. The two therefore became the first Bible Students in what was to become Saskatchewan.[10] But no congregation was formed in that vast territory until another Bible Student, Lewis Levi Parney, moved to a homestead just north of the community of Rosetown at least six years later.[11] A few years earlier, in 1895, a Swede named Dalquist moved from the mid-western United States to a homestead at Calmar in that part of the Northwest Territories that was to become Alberta. Almost immediately he was followed by numerous Scandinavian families—the Hammers, Melins, Fredricksons, Andersons, Sundstroms, Fors, Franzens, Bloomquists, Bostroms, Engbergs, Sutherlands, Westlunds, Westlins, and Mobergs—who, like Dalquist, were Bible Students. As a result, a congregation was formed, and Pastor Russell's teachings were disseminated throughout the district.[12] In 1898 a man named Louis Zink moved from the United States to Brandon, Manitoba. From there he visited the nearby town of Rapid City and frequently discussed the Bible around the pot-bellied coal stove in the general store of A. W. Leflar. Within a short time Zink converted Leflar and a formerly staunch Anglican, Bowen Smith, who ran the Rapid City lumberyard. Leflar, Smith, and several others then formed a class—the first in Manitoba.[13] Thus as settlers moved into British Columbia and the Canadian Prairies from Ontario and, in particular, from the United States, small Bible Student congregations began to form. As they did, they sought converts. Within a few years many Bible Student classes dotted the West. In places like Winnipeg and Vancouver large congregations grew up. Although most of the Bible Students were of British or Northern European stock, they also began to make converts among persons of other ethnic backgrounds.

A colporteur named Arthur N. Marchant travelled through the Maritimes in 1895, and within a few years Bible Student congregations were established in all three Maritime provinces; by 1903 pilgrims were making visits to groups in about ten different centres.[14] Growth in Canada's Atlantic provinces was not as fast as it was in Ontario and the West, but Bible Students in the Maritimes did develop an active community some years before any of their co-believers were to be found in Quebec, even among that province's English-speaking minority.

The first public lecture given by a Watch Tower representative in Quebec was delivered in 1909 in Montreal.[15] Two years later the federal census recorded only one Bible Student in that city—the only one in the Province of Quebec It was not possible, therefore, to organize a congregation in Canada's largest city until 1916, and even then only under great difficulty. Early in that year Pastor Russell spoke to a full house at His Majesty's Theatre. The small company of local Bible Students so feared possible Catholic attempts to have the lecture stopped, however, that they advertised it only three days prior to the time Russell delivered it. Troubles retarded the growth of that first Quebec Bible Student congregation for some years. In addition, the congregation was almost entirely English-speaking; there was no real attempt to make French-Canadian converts until after the war.[16]

In the rest of Canada the situation was quite different. During the decade and a half immediately preceding the outbreak of the First World War, the Bible Students were rapidly becoming more numerous, more active, and generally well known. Pilgrims regularly visited greater numbers of congregations and delivered well-advertised public sermons. Pastor Russell also gave much attention to Canadian Bible Students. In 1903 he came to Toronto to address a convention at which eighteen hundred persons were present and fifty-eight were baptized.[17] Again, in 1912, he made a trip to Toronto when an eight-day gathering was held at the city's Exhibition Park. About one thousand persons attended and five hundred were turned away from his main talk, "Beyond the Grave", held at the Royal Alexandra Theatre.[18] Besides appearing at large conventions in Ontario's capital, he frequently spoke at small, one-day gatherings in the province's cities and towns. In 1904 he was present at Hamilton;[19] in 1906 he delivered his famous talk "To Hell and Back" at Chatham and in the Orange Hall in Brantford.[20] In succeeding years he preached in London,[21] in Woodstock,[22] and again in Hamilton.[23] During the fall of 1909 he toured the Maritimes,[24] and in January of the following year he addressed a convention in Winnipeg.[25] In 1911, and again in 1912, he travelled across western Canada, where he not only delivered public discourses but took time to ride over the Prairies by horse and buggy to visit scattered groups of Bible Students.[26]

Pilgrim visits, conventions, and Russell's well-advertised lectures were not the only ways through which the Bible Students spread their message. Colporteurs placed increasingly great amounts of literature as the years went by. Then in 1909 the Watch Tower Society released a new series of tracts which contained cartoons and sharp articles against what it considered to be the false teachings of Christendom, particularly Protestantism. Known at first as *The People's Pulpit*,[27] the tracts were published monthly and were distributed far and wide. Bible Students placed many thousands of them under doors, handed them out in front of churches on Sundays, and gave them to friends and associates.[28] About the same time, the Society established an international news syndicate to make Pastor Russell's sermons available to a much greater audience. Every week he produced a separate sermon of about two newspaper columns in length, which was telegraphed to newspapers throughout the United States, Canada, and Europe. The Society estimated that in this way Russell's teachings became available to between fifteen and twenty million persons.[29] Early in 1914 the Society also released the "Photo-Drama of Creation", a combined moving picture, hand-tinted picture-slide program synchronized with phonograph records which carried recorded talks and music. This production, which described biblical history and prophecy from Creation through the thousand-year reign of Christ, was shown throughout much of the United States and Canada and also did much to publicize Bible Student teachings.[30] Pastor Russell, the *Watch Tower*, and the Bible Students were therefore well known to most Canadians outside Quebec by the start of the First World War.

Even in those early days, although they experienced no overt persecution, they were less than popular with many of their fellow citizens. Russell's teachings, particularly the doctrine that hell is the grave and the dead are unconscious until the resurrection, caused as much irritation in Canada as in the United States. His frequent suggestions that the doctrines of hell-fire and purgatory were money-making rackets angered Canadian clergymen as much as it did their fellows south of the border. Bitter relations between Bible Students and their pious Protestant and Catholic neighbours often resulted. Occasionally, too, angered preachers would challenge Bible Student spokesmen to debate; on the Prairies, pioneer settlers occasionally drove many miles in horse-drawn conveyances to hear sharp disputations over the nature of hell or some other point of theological contention.[31] More often, though, clerical critics of the Bible Students thundered denunciations at the impious "no-hellers" from their pulpits or turned to the press to denounce Russell and the "Russellites".

The depth of clerical animosity toward the Watch Tower president was demonstrated by J. J. Ross, a Hamilton, Ontario, Baptist minister. In 1911 Ross penned a pamphlet which Russell regarded as so libellous that he pressed criminal charges against the Canadian preacher. After much delay the matter was eventually brought before a grand jury which ruled that the parties should resort to civil suit. According to J. F. Rutherford, Russell then dropped action since Ross was "irresponsible financially and could not be compelled by such a [civil] proceeding to publish a retraction".[32] Ross thereupon published a second pamphlet in which he accused Russell of having lied that he "knew Greek".[33] To this charge the pastor replied that all he had said was that he knew the Greek alphabet and, hence, could look up words in a concordance or Greek-English lexicon.[34] Ross's charge was nevertheless to be used over and over again—along with the "jellyfish" story and the Miracle Wheat episode related in Chapter 1—to blacken Russell's reputation and discredit Bible Student teachings.[35]

Most Bible Students remained loyal to their pastor. Bitter religious wrangling hurt them very little. With the advent of the First World War, however, the situation changed. Canada, as part of the British Empire, was brought into the struggle, and all Canadians were called upon to support the war effort. Patriotic fervour swept the nation, and many of the clergy preached what amounted to a crusade against Germany and her war-time partners. But the Bible Students looked upon the terrible international slaughter as the Devil's work and refused to have any part in it, thereby leaving themselves open to the charge of disloyalty, which, as the war dragged on, was to cause them serious trouble with the Government of Canada.

Long before the war, Pastor Russell had counselled that Christians should not volunteer for military service, and if they were conscripted they should refrain from killing their fellow men. A decade or more before Sarajevo, Russell had written:

Are not we subjects of the great King? And are not all the kingdoms of this world more or less identified with "the prince of this world", and his law of selfishness? Are not we therefore, strangers and pilgrims here, and to some extent aliens and foreigners? It is eminently proper that we should love and appreciate every good law and all the servants of earthly laws, and rejoice that quite the majority of the New Creation live under the highest forms of civil government [the United States and the British Empire] to be found in the world to-day, and appreciate this as a divine favor and blessing. Hence, we neither traduce our native country, its rulers, or its laws; but this does not mean that we must fight for these with carnal weapons, nor that we must increase our responsibilities by voting for them.

True, government may not always exempt those opposed to war from participating in it, although a very gracious provision of this kind has in the past been made for some who, like ourselves, believe war to be unrighteous; viz., the Friends or Quakers, exempted from military duty under specially generous laws. We may be required to do military service whether we vote or not, however; and if required we would be obliged to obey the powers that be, and should consider that the Lord's providence had permitted the conscription and that he was able to overrule it to the good of ourselves or others. In such event we would consider it not amiss to make a partial explanation to the proper officers, and to request a transference to the medical or hospital department, where our services could be used with the full consent of our consciences; —but even if compelled to serve in the ranks and to fire our guns we need not feel compelled to shoot a fellow-creature.[36]

Russell therefore opposed military service but did not rule out the possibility that true Christians could serve as non-combatants or "even in the ranks" when under duress. However, during the early years of the war, he apparently recognized the impracticability of conscientious objectors agreeing to serve in situations where they might have to kill or be killed. In addition, both he and Bible Students in general came to the immediate conclusion that the great European blood bath was both unjustified and unjustifiable. The *Watch Tower* of September 1, 1915, took a completely unbending stand against any form of combatant service in the military forces of the nations. It stated in no uncertain terms:

But some one replies, "if one were to refuse the uniform and the military service he would be shot."

We reply that if the presentation were properly made there might be some kind of exoneration; but if not, would it be any worse to be shot because of loyalty to the Prince of Peace and refusal to disobey His order than to be shot while under the banner of these earthly kings and apparently giving them support and, in appearance at least, compromising the teachings of our Heavenly King? Of the two deaths we would prefer the former—prefer to die because of faithfulness to our Heavenly King. Certainly one dying for his loyalty to the principles of the Lord's teachings would accomplish far more by his death than would the one dying in the trenches. We cannot tell how great the influence would be for peace, for righteousness, for God, if a few hundred of the Lord's faithful were to follow the course of Shadrack, Meshach and Abednego, and refuse to bow down to the god of war. Like these noble men they might say, "Our God is able to deliver us, if He chooses so to do; but if He does not choose to deliver us, that will not alter our course. We will serve Him and follow His direction, come what may."

Early in the war British Bible Students were faced with choosing to serve in the British armed forces or take their stand as conscientious objectors—something which might mean imprisonment, or even death. Canadian Bible Students realized that they also might soon be faced with similar decisions. The November 15, 1915, issue of the *Watch Tower* published excerpts from the Canadian Militia Act of 1906 showing that under it conscientious objectors were entitled to exemption from military service. A letter from a Canadian Bible Student, W. J. Hooper, published in the February 15, 1916, *Watch Tower* stressed, however, that no person would receive such exemption unless he filed an affidavit giving reasons for his desire to be excused from service with the local commanding officer of militia in the district in which he resided at least a month before he was to be drafted. The editor of the *Watch Tower*, in commenting on Hooper's letter in the same issue of the magazine, remarked that the matter was serious and advised every Canadian Bible Student between seventeen and a half and sixty years of age to submit a letter and affidavit, based on a statement prepared by J. F. Rutherford, to his local commanding officer of militia.

In consequence, in the spring of 1916 hundreds of Canadian Bible Students throughout much of Canada submitted affidavits to the effect that as members of the Bible Students Association they were required to " 'follow peace with all men' and do violence or injury to none". Furthermore, the affidavits stated that followers of Christ must practise non-resistance and that the provisions of the Militia Act R.S.C. (1906) Chapter 41 were "in conflict with the teachings of the Lord Jesus Christ".[37] Many public officials were enraged since, in the midst of war, such a stand seemed highly unpatriotic. W. H. Chittick, a London, Ontario, justice of the peace, wrote as follows to the Minister of Defence and Militia in Ottawa:

Honourable Sir,
I have the honour to call your attention in being called by telephone to a law office to administer the oath to a number of persons who are taking advantage of the Militia Act, which, I am sorry to say, allows such persons, especially in time of war. Had I the authority, I would

much prefer to sit on a Court Martial and to try them on a charge of disloyalty.

Enclosed herewith please find a certified copy of their pronounced religious views, and also the names of the persons who have affixed their signatures and sworn to such.

It is certainly an unpleasant duty for me to swear in such a class of men who should be offering their services on behalf of the Empire. Especially so, as I have sworn in a great number of recruits at The Armouries here and still engaged doing the good work, and I trust, Honourable Sir, that you will use your powerful influence to have such a section of the Militia Act expunged.[38]

Militia officers also wrote to Ottawa to complain that the matter was serious. As hundreds of affidavits were being submitted, they, too, suggested that the act be changed.[39] However, at the time, the office of the Adjutant General of Militia refused to become alarmed. In a letter dated April 3, 1916, Major General W. E. Hodgkins wrote to the district officer commanding at Winnipeg that since "no steps have been made towards the enrollment of men liable for service, the claims now made for exemption are premature". He noted: "As respects the suggestion that the claimants are disloyal and their action interferes with recruiting, it must be said that in doing what they have done they have not been transgressing any law."[40] But in spite of the fact that Hodgkins had indicated that no action could be taken in the matter, Pastor Russell and the Bible Students were now thoroughly unpopular with a large segment of Canadian officialdom. As a result, when the Watch Tower president attempted to attend an Associated Bible Students convention at Winnipeg in July 1916, he was taken from a train at Gretna, Manitoba, by Canadian immigration officers and forced to return to the United States.[41] No other action of any consequence was taken against the Bible Students in that year; yet Russell's death in October 1916, while he was on a trip to the south-western United States, began a time of troubles for them such as they had never experienced before.

During the months of November and December 1916 the Watch Tower Society was governed by an executive committee of three, composed of Vice-President A. I. Ritchie, Secretary-Treasurer W. E.

Van Amburgh, and J. F. Rutherford. When the annual general meeting of the Society was held on January 6, 1917, Rutherford was elected to replace Russell as the new Watch Tower president, and A. N. Pierson was elected as vice-president. Van Amburgh retained his post as secretary-treasurer.[42] Thus the Watch Tower Society inherited a strong leadership, particularly in the person of Rutherford, who immediately stepped up programs which Russell had begun before he died. The Brooklyn headquarters office was reorganized, the number of the Society's travelling representatives was increased, and Bible Students were encouraged to begin distributing tracts on Sundays outside churches and during regular house-to-house visits.[43] Rutherford also planned the establishment of a Canadian branch office of the Watch Tower Society, which subsequently was opened at Winnipeg on January 1, 1918.[44] But as the year 1917 moved on, serious problems arose for Rutherford and the Bible Students.

In the first place, personal animosity began to develop against Rutherford among certain Bible Students as they manifested a desire to weaken his control over the Society. Pastor Russell, a dynamic and charismatic person, had been noted for his kindness and warmth. He had come to be revered by many of his flock as the "faithful and wise servant" of Matthew 24:45–47 and the "seventh messenger of the church".[45] This belief, held apparently by almost all Bible Students, made it difficult for his successor. To make new decisions apart from those taken by Russell seemed almost heretical to some. Rutherford quickly became concerned with the continuing adulation of the pastor which, he felt, was tantamount to "creature worship". He also became suspicious of those who tried to curry favour with him and was often quite blunt in his dealings with them.[46] Besides, his personality was very different from that of his predecessor. Russell had been raised in the big-city atmosphere of Pittsburgh and was known for his gentle manner; Rutherford had grown up in the less sophisticated environment of rural Missouri and had developed many of the attributes of a stern, God-fearing man of law. Russell was, in fact, the mild pastor; Rutherford was more like a judge or prophet of ancient Israel. Internal trouble soon came to a head among the Bible Students and at the headquarters of the Watch Tower Society itself.

The source of the trouble was P. S. L. Johnson. Originally of

Jewish faith and then a Lutheran clergyman before becoming a Bible Student, he was sent by Rutherford—acting on Russell's expressed wish—to England to revitalize Bible Student activities there. Johnson, a brilliant speaker, apparently did not serve his British brethren well. When he arrived in London he attempted to assume powers never granted him by Rutherford, and claimed that "he, Johnson, was Pastor Russell's successor, indicating that the mantle of Pastor Russell had fallen upon him just as the prophet Elijah's cloak had fallen upon Elisha". The Society's British branch overseer complained to Rutherford, who appointed a special commission of prominent English Bible Students. Upon their recommendation, Rutherford recalled Johnson to the United States. He refused to return for some time, but after impounding Watch Tower funds in a London bank, he finally obeyed Rutherford's directive. When Rutherford refused to send him back to England, Johnson then sought support from the board of directors against the Society's president and administrative officers. In this he was largely successful; four of the seven directors, A. I. Ritchie, K. H. Hirsh, I. F. Hoskins, and J. D. Wright—Rutherford, Pierson, and Van Amburgh being the other three—determined to wrest control of the Society from Rutherford by turning him into a figurehead.[47] Yet no schism took place openly until July 17, 1917.

On that date Rutherford released the book *The Finished Mystery* at the breakfast table of the Brooklyn Bethel. Acting as Russell had in the past, Rutherford and the Society's officers authorized the publication of the new volume, which was advertised as the Seventh Volume of Russell's *Studies in the Scriptures*. In fact, it had been written by two members of the Bethel family, C. J. Woodworth and G. H. Fisher, and unmistakably reflected their styles of writing. Yet as was carefully pointed out in the volume itself, it was based on Pastor Russell's notes and was, in fact, largely, if not wholly, his posthumous work. Although the language in it was stronger than he customarily used, it certainly expressed his feelings.[48] The four directors, Johnson, and a minority of the headquarters staff nevertheless objected to its publication, and a five-hour debate followed.[49] Shortly thereafter the directors tried to seize open control of the Society but were unable to do so. Rutherford pointed out that the four had never been properly elected according to the Society's Pennsylvania charter and simply owed their positions—which had never been sanctioned by an annual general meeting—to personal appointments by Russell. The judge thereupon dismissed the four and replaced them with legally designated successors.[50] The directors then took their case to the Bible Student community at large, and by the fall of 1917 serious divisions began to appear within their ranks. In the spring of 1918, an opposition group, under a committee of seven, celebrated the Lord's Supper apart from Bible Students loyal to the Society.[51] Later, the ex-directors, Johnson, and others organized separate movements and began publishing their own journals;[52] most Bible Students, however, continued to support the Watch Tower Society's officers. In November and December 1917, in a referendum held upon the suggestion of the *Watch Tower* of November 1, the members of 813 congregations indicated their feelings toward the Society's president. Of 11,421 votes sent in to Brooklyn by mid-December, 10,869 favoured Rutherford.[53] In January he and those who supported him were again chosen as officers and directors of the Society; not a single schismatic was elected.[54]

The internal troubles which beset the Bible Students, serious as they were, were small in comparison to those they were soon to experience from the outside. During 1917 the slaughter of war continued in Europe, the Middle East, and on the high seas. That year also witnessed two revolutions in Russia and, in April, the entry of the United States into the great holocaust on the side of the Allies. War fever and a spirit of patriotism were sweeping much of the world. Just at that time the Bible Students determined to take an even firmer stand against war and those who supported it, particularly the majority of the clergy of Christendom. *The Finished Mystery* referred to patriotism as "a narrow minded hatred of other people", mocked the inconsistencies of statesmen who spoke of peace while arming their peoples for war, and remarked: "the most virulent and devastating disease of humanity now raging on earth is militarism." Britain, the United States, and other nations of the world, both great and small, were subjected to sharp criticism. But the most caustic barbs were reserved for those clergy who bolstered militarism. War was described as an "open violation of Christianity". Furthermore, read the seventh volume, "if war is right, then Christianity is wrong,

false, a lie. If Christianity is right, then war is wrong, false, a lie."
Hence war's "armed men are grown from the dragon's teeth of secret
diplomacy, imperialistic ambition, dynastic pride, greedy commer-
cialism, economic exploitation at home and abroad". The clergy who
supported such war stood condemned:

"In all the warring countries the professed ministers of Christ are acting
as recruiting agents. All kinds of arguments are used to persuade the
young men of the country, contrary to the teachings of the Master. The
same men who are accustomed to laugh at the declaration that the
Turkish soldiers in former wars were promised, in the event of death, a
sure passport to Heavenly Paradise—these same ministers are now
urging all the eligible with whom they have influence to prepare to go
to battle to lay down their lives. While the Germans have on every
battle flag and upon their soldiers' belts, 'God with us', the British
ministers are quoting Bible texts to encourage enlistment of their young
men and to throw a halo of glory upon their soldier dead." (z. '15–267.)
"The clergy are finding themselves in a tight place. They are expected
to be faithful to their country, right or wrong. They are expected to
preach the War as the will of God and the going to war as a meritorious
matter that will have Divine reward and blessing. They must encourage
recruiting, in obedience to the commands of their earthly king, and in
violation of the commands of the Heavenly King, who has directed
them to be peacemakers, and to follow peace with all men and do no
murder, either under legal sanction or otherwise." (z. '15–276.)
"Recently in Canada the Editor was astounded by the activity of the
preachers there—especially those of the Church of England. One
was out in Khaki uniform marching through the street with the
volunteers. Asked by a college friend, 'Did I see you in the ranks?' he
answered, 'Yes, I wanted to encourage the boys.' 'And did you think of
going to the front, to the trenches?' 'Not a bit of it!' He was merely
acting as a decoy to get others to the front, just as a bull which they
have at one of the Chicago stockyards meets the animals about to be
slaughtered and, tossing his head in the air, becomes their leader up the
gangway leading to the slaughter. There he knows his little niche, into
which he glides and is sheltered; while the others drive and press one
another forward to the slaughter." (z. '15–259.) [55]

Other comments of a similar nature appeared in other Watch Tower publications, particularly in a new series of tabloid tracts known as the *Bible Students Monthly*. Number 9, entitled "The Fall of Babylon—Why Christendom Must Now Suffer—The Final Outcome", was particularly vitriolic. Presented at a number of well-publicized lectures under the same title on December 30, 1917, this tract was circulated widely and caused a great furore. It quoted some of the sharpest anti-clerical statements found in *The Finished Mystery* and, regarding patriotic clerics, stated: "Ye have preached millions into a dreadful death in the trenches, have made them cannon-fodder by the thousands for blood guilty kaisers and czars, kings and generals of your evil order of things." In addition, this issue of the *Bible Students Monthly* showed on its back page a cartoon drawing of a crumbling wall, the stones of which were marked with inscriptions such as "Romanism, Popes, Cardinals", "Eternal Torment Theory", "Protestantism, Creeds, Clergy". Clergymen in black suits and cassocks were shown clinging to the tumbling stones.

The Bible Students later believed that it was that particular publication which caused the Canadian government to take action against them, and in part it was. But long before December 1917, pressure was being brought against them from many quarters within the country. For example, the *Victoria Week* of March 18, 1916, attacked Pastor Russell as "a liar, a humbug, a hypocrite and a fraud". After referring to the charges of adultery against him in the Ball case it noted: "Now that we know that his organization is simply a cover for a pro-German anti-recruiting propaganda, it is time for someone to act." A short time before, the *Ottawa Free Press* had published an article entitled "Pastor Russell's People Trying to Hurt Recruiting", in which it blamed the low number of volunteers in Montreal on the Bible Students.[56] Then in April 1917, when Judge Rutherford spoke at the Royal Alexandra Theatre in Toronto and stated that "a Christian should not take up arms", the Provincial Treasurer of Ontario, T. W. McGarry, cancelled the International Bible Students' moving-picture licence so that they could no longer show the "Photo-Drama of Creation".[57]

Not surprisingly, much of the pressure had been coming from the clergy. The Bible Students' jibe that clerics were using their churches as recruiting depots was quite literally true,[58] and the assertion that such actions were un-Christian stung. Hence, clerics issued passionate pulpit tirades against the Bible Students as enemies of both God and the state, and demanded that something be done to stop the "pernicious" circulation of Watch Tower publications. There were, of course, many army men, public figures, and government officials who heard and agreed, the most important of whom was Colonel Ernest Chambers, chief press censor for Canada.

Chambers, an old soldier and newspaperman, was, if anything, the type of man whom the Bible Students called a "super patriot". Although a hard-working and seemingly tireless man, he manifested little sense of humour and pressed anyone he considered disloyal with dogged determination. If he felt that his honour had been questioned, he could manifest a spirit of thoroughgoing vindictiveness. It was ominous then for the Bible Students, when they fell under his displeasure.

The chief press censor became aware of Bible Student literature in 1916. On August 12 he wrote to Colonel Sir Percy Sherwood, Chief Commissioner of Police in Ottawa, to ask if there was any reason why Pastor Russell's literature should be banned.[59] Sherwood replied by directing Chambers to W. D. Scott, Superintendent of Immigration. Scott thereupon wrote to Chambers about Russell in the most scathing terms. According to the Superintendent of Immigration, Russell was "a notorious faker" who had been exposed by the *Brooklyn Eagle*; both Scott and Sherwood had decided "that we had enough of Pastor Russell's kind already in the country without importing more trouble and opposition". Russell, in Scott's eyes, was also a man of low principles: "Neither his moral character nor his business character is unblemished."[60] A little over a year later Chambers received another missive, this time from J. Gwallia Evans of the Kingston, Ontario, Veterans' Association. Evans drew Chambers's attention to pages 250–53 of *The Finished Mystery*, the section which attacked militarism, and stated: "To me such teaching is conducive to treason if not inspiring treason itself."[61] In reply, Chambers stated that he had not seen the publication in question and asked Evans to send him a copy.[62] Evidently Evans complied, but at the time Chambers was extremely busy and showed no particular alarm over the "Russellites".

What did finally cause Colonel Chambers to focus his attention on them was a letter written by an Ottawa minister, the Reverend George Bousfield, to Colonel Sir Percy Sherwood on September 23, 1917. Local Bible Students had received another edition of the *Bible Students Monthly* and had distributed that anti-clerical tract to practically every home in the city, much to the chagrin of Bousfield. As a result, he protested to Sherwood and suggested that such publications should not be permitted.[63] Sherwood sent Bousfield's letter to Chambers, who then wrote the Ottawa clergyman that he agreed: action should be taken against the Watch Tower publication.[64] So, two days after he wrote to Bousfield, the chief censor corresponded with Secretary of State Martin Burrell to complain about the offending tract and to state that his attention had been

drawn to the objectionable character of this publication from a War Censorship standpoint by J. W. Dafoe, Esqu., Editor of the "Winnipeg Free Press", Malcolm R. J. Reid, Dominion Immigration Inspector for B.C. By the Editor of the Victoria, B.C. "Week"; by Colonel Sir Percy Sherwood, Chief Commissioner of Police; by W. D. Scott, Supt. of Immigration; by Rev. George Bousfield, 656 Rideau Street, Ottawa, and by others.[65]

In October, Chambers was moved to write Burrell again, this time to ask that *The Finished Mystery* be banned. The district intelligence officer at Winnipeg had taken up the matter of pages 250–53 with General Ruttan, the officer commanding Military District Number 10. In addition, the intelligence officer in question had interviewed W. T. Hooper, whom he described as "a strong peace propagandist". Hooper was quoted as having stated long before conscription was thought of that Bible Students would refuse to be conscripted.[66] Chambers, fully convinced that *The Finished Mystery* was thoroughly objectionable, asked the Secretary of State to have it suppressed under order in council P.C. 146 (January 17, 1917).[67]

The government seemed less than anxious to move on Chambers's request or to submit to pressure for action against the Bible Students. During November and December they continued to hold public meetings and to circulate both the *Bible Students Monthly* and *The Finished Mystery*. It is quite certain, therefore, that it was largely the *Bible Students Monthly* Number 9 which ultimately caused the government to go along with the press censor's recommendation. As a result of an earlier distribution of the fiery tract, the Vancouver Ministerial Association had taken umbrage. It had directed its secretary, Congregational minister the Reverend E. A. Cooke, to write to the Minister of Militia in Ottawa to complain about the literature being distributed by the followers of Pastor Russell. As instructed, Cooke wrote:

I have been instructed by the General Ministerial Association of Vancouver to bring to your attention a matter which seems to us to be of considerable public importance at this time. As you are aware the followers of the late "Pastor" Russell, who call themselves "International Bible Students", profess to be conscientiously opposed to war and military service, hence the Government of Canada has prohibited the entry of their agents and teachers into this country from the United States.

As a measure of National safety and of loyalty both to the Empire and to our gallant men at the Front we believe this to be wise and necessary. But would it not also be well to prohibit the propagandist literature of this body which is published in the United States and sent to Canada for distribution by these people? I am enclosing a sample copy of one of their publications which has been put into almost every home in this city. As you will see it is a "War Extra", and while ostensibly making an attack on the clergy, is really making a strong but subtle attack on the whole war policy of the nation and on our soldiers, who are, in effect, called murderers.

This is in perfect keeping with their teaching at their public gatherings in this and other cities of Canada, and, by means of wide circulation through the mails and by hand, reaches a much larger constituency. While we would earnestly deprecate anything in the nature of interference with religious principles, we do believe that in this time of National and Imperial crisis, the dissemination of such literature in

Canada is highly detrimental to the best interests of our people, and to the success of the great and righteous cause for which so many of our men have already laid down their lives.

We, therefore, request that you will be good enough to give this matter your careful attention, or bring it before the Government so that such steps as may be considered necessary may be taken at the earliest opportunity.[68]

This letter, forwarded by the militia department to Chambers, was in the hands of the Secretary of State when the storm over the *Bible Students Monthly* Number 9 broke. And a storm it was: the thunderous outcries against the Bible Students were loud and clear. In Winnipeg, the Reverend Charles G. Patterson, Presbyterian minister of St. Stephen's Church, read excerpts from that issue of the *Bible Students Monthly* and roundly denounced them from the pulpit. As a result, Manitoba Attorney General Johnson sent to him for a copy of the offending tract in order to examine its contents.[69] D. A. Campbell, district intelligence officer in Winnipeg, wrote the chief press censor to ask: "Cannot something be done to stop the publication or at least circulation in this country of this poisonous matter?"[70] His counterpart in Toronto also expressed concern based on a clergyman's complaint.[71] On January 24, 1918, the Deputy Attorney General of British Columbia telegraphed Chambers concerning a convention of Bible Students in the Pacific province, labelled their literature "peace propaganda", and remarked that the police believed that Germans were financing their publications.[72] But before the outcry against the Bible Students reached its peak, Chambers acted.

On January 14, 1918, the chief press censor wrote to Secretary of State Martin Burrell, in particular to draw his attention to the latest Bible Student broadside and to recommend that bans be placed on both the *Bible Students Monthly* and *The Finished Mystery*. He stated that on September 27, 1917, he had asked to have the former suppressed and on October 25 had requested that the latter be outlawed. On November 5 he had sent a copy of the *Bible Students Monthly* Number 5 to the Secretary of State and on November 27 had forwarded a copy of the Reverend Mr. Cooke's letter to him. After remarking that the publications of Pastor Russell's followers were objectionable because they caused disaffection and made recruiting difficult, he emphasized the complaints about them he had received from the chief of police at Hamilton and intelligence officers throughout Canada. He then stated:

The bitter attacks in these publications upon the churches of all denominations without distinction is noteworthy, even if the statements embodied in these attacks cannot be directly described as "objectionable" under the definitions of the term "objectionable" contained in the Consolidated Orders Respecting Censorship. The Canadian churches of all denominations, Christian and Jewish alike, rendered and are rendering invaluable service to the Country in sustaining a courageous and stout-hearted national spirit, a matter of the most vital importance. They have been incessantly active in the encouragement of every national patriotic and benevolent effort having any relation to the prosecution of the War, and they have freely and ungrudgingly contributed of their very best manhood and womanhood to the national cause.

I respectfully submit that the churches of this country have by their conspicuously patriotic conduct fairly established the right to claim to be organizations actively and usefully co-operating in the successful prosecution of the war, and as such are entitled to the protection against such outrageous attacks as those contained in the publications of the so-called Pastor Russell Movement—attacks due to the fact that the churches have patriotically done their duty.

I notice that the Central Appeal Judge has disallowed a claim to exemption from military service "on conscientious grounds" made by a member of the International Bible Students' Association.

I would once more strongly recommend the issue of Warrants prohibiting the possession within Canada of copies of this literature.[73]

Finally, in apparent response to direct pressures from Chambers as well as from other sources, the government yielded. On January 30, 1918, a warrant was issued outlawing both *The Finished Mystery* and the *Bible Students Monthly*. Possession of either could lay one open to a maximum fine of five thousand dollars and a prison sentence not exceeding five years. On February 9 and again on February 16 notice of the ban was placed in the *Canada Gazette*; yet Bible Students and the general public became aware of the government's action only on February 12 and 13 when printed notice of it appeared in the nation's newspapers.[74] Local police forces immediately began raiding Bible Students' meeting places, businesses, and homes to seize the now illegal publications and bring their owners before the courts.

CHAPTER THREE

ÇAKEN İNÇO bAbYLON

Patriotism is the last refuge of a scoundrel!

SAMUEL JOHNSON Boswell's *Life of Johnson*, April 7, 1775

As THE YEAR 1918 began, the International Bible Students faced a time of crises. In the first place they were suffering internal divisions caused by the schism at Brooklyn. Then with the coming of the partial ban on Watch Tower literature in Canada, they began to experience serious legal suppression. Yet one group of men—those of military age—were to suffer the full wrath of Canadian officialdom even before mid-February of that year. During the year 1917 conscription had come to Canada, and with it repeal of the 1906 legislation granting general exemption from military service to conscientious objectors. Although similar provisions continued to apply, the government felt that Bible Students could not claim benefit from them. The Military Service Act of 1917 stated specifically that a person would be granted a certificate of exemption if "he conscientiously objects to the undertaking of combatant service and is prohibited from so doing by the tenets and articles of faith, in effect on the sixth day of July, 1917, of any organized religious denomination existing and well recognized in Canada at such date, and to which he in good faith belongs."[1] According to the government's viewpoint, however, the Bible Students were not an "organized religious denomination". And when David Cooke, a young Winnipeg Bible Student, took the matter to court, Justice Lyman Duff, then central appeal judge, supported the government's contention.[2] Bible Students thus had no way out: they had to serve, or accept the consequences for failing to do so. The small number who could obtain no other form of exemption and would not serve when conscripted were to experience some of the worst treatment accorded conscientious objectors in Canadian history.

George Naish, later to be the presiding minister of Jehovah's Witnesses at Saskatoon, Saskatchewan, for many years, was, according to his own account, drafted against his will early in 1918. When he refused to don the uniform or to "soldier", he was subjected to long periods of detention with little food and inadequate sanitary facilities, was struck in the eye with an officer's swagger stick, was choked until unconscious, and, after being court-martialled three times, was sent to serve a ten-year prison sentence in Prince Albert Penitentiary in February 1919.[3] Naish received relatively mild treatment, however, in comparison to that meted out to several other Bible Students.

On Thursday, January 24, 1918, the *Winnipeg Tribune* headlined "Treatment of Drafted Men Under Probe" and went on to give a detailed account concerning the severe manhandling of two Bible Students, Robert Clegg and Ralph Naish—a brother of George Naish—and a Pentecostal, Charles V. Matheson, at Minto Barracks. On the following day the *Winnipeg Free Press* announced "Conscientious Objectors Said To Have Been Roughly Treated", and added further details to the *Tribune* story. According to a sworn affidavit published in both newspapers, Clegg asserted that he was denied blankets for refusing to obey military commands, was undressed, was held under an ice-cold shower for fifteen minutes, was violently lashed dry, was shortly thereafter subjected to a second cold-shower treatment, and was dragged across concrete floors to the detention room where he was left unconscious in a state of nervous collapse. Ralph Naish, who had undergone one cold shower, was left with him in detention. Later Clegg was found in such serious straits that he was taken to St. Boniface Hospital where a half-dozen attendants spent considerable time trying to revive him. According to the *Tribune,* his chart indicated that on admission to hospital on Tuesday, January 22, Clegg's temperature stood at 78 degrees Fahrenheit, and his condition sheet recorded that he was suffering from an acute chill.

The *Free Press* none the less reported that the attending physician denied that Clegg was ever unconscious, and military authorities claimed that the whole affair was greatly exaggerated.[4] But others felt otherwise. F. J. Dixon, MLA for Winnipeg Centre, raised the matter in the Manitoba legislature and stated: "If men are to be treated in this manner for adhering to the dictates of their conscience, and they cannot find any better way to handle them, it would be better to line them up against the wall and shoot them."[5] In a telegram to T. A. Crerar, federal Minister of Agriculture, he wired: "Conscientious objectors tortured in Minto Barracks[.] Given coldwater treatment till unconscious[.] Robert Clegg in hospital[.] Other cases[.] Please use your influence against this barbarism[.]"[6] Then in a subsequent letter, Dixon claimed there was no doubt about the facts of the case.[7] Crerar evidently felt likewise; when he forwarded Dixon's remarks to Major-General S. C. Mewburn, Minister of Militia and Defence, he indicated that he had "received other private information to the effect that the reports of severe treatment of conscientious objectors seemed well founded".[8] Two letters published in the *Free Press* and the *Tribune* also gave strong support to Clegg's allegations. A Bible Student, Mrs. E. C. Tingling, wrote that she had interviewed both Clegg and Naish and that some friends who had come to check on the two young men had met stretcher-bearers carrying Clegg to an ambulance while he was in an unconscious condition.[9] Private Paul E. Case of "E" Company, an American who had volunteered for service in the Canadian Army wrote also:

An International Bible Student, recently drafted under the Military Service Act, and a member of the first depot battalion stationed at the Minto street barracks, was admitted to the General hospital Tuesday evening suffering from exhaustion, caused by being forced to stand, by the military police of the barracks, under an ice-cold shower bath, one man for 15 minutes, until he fell exhausted. Another was given two ice-cold shower baths of 15 minutes' duration, each with an interval of 30 minutes between, when he fell exhausted. Both were then taken to the guard house and confined until night, when the condition of one became so alarming he was hustled off to the General hospital.

The soldiers of the barracks are highly incensed over such cruel treatment and have questioned if even Germany can beat it.

Truth is a very valuable asset and such a misrepresentation of plain facts as occurred in yesterday's issue of the Free Press regarding the matter has occasioned quite some ill-feeling among the soldiers who have many witnesses to the facts.

The article in the Free Press stated the two men were "manhandled roughly" by their "fellow soldiers", and that the military authorities at the barracks claim to know nothing of it. Let it be known, please, that such things do not "carry on" unless so ordered, neither are soldiers put in the guard house unless ordered to be confined there by a commissioned officer.

We, as men, regret there are those so debased who would tolerate such treatment on human beings when it would be unlawful to mete out such treatment even to a dog.[10]

The *Winnipeg Free Press* was so convinced by such information that it published a strong editorial in which it called on the Canadian government to "Stop it!" In its remarks, the *Free Press* referred to similar assaults on conscientious objectors in Britain, and then stated that the evidence that Clegg and Naish had been subjected to "hazing" and "physical coercion" was conclusive. Furthermore, said the editorial: "It is idle to pretend that in cases like this, the hazing is the result of spontaneous indignation by the companions of the recalcitrant; these things happen because some one in authority is desirous that they should happen."[11]

In the meantime, at least one Bible Student made direct representations to Prime Minister Sir Robert Borden,[12] and Winnipeg Bible Students hired lawyer E. J. McMurray to press criminal charges against the persons who had mistreated Clegg and Naish.[13] Yet little came of either the public outcry or the Bible Students' actions. Military officials had already held a court of inquiry, beginning on January 24, to investigate the "alleged ill-treatment of conscientious objectors".[14] It was little more than a judicial farce, however. At least one of the officers of the court had been directly involved with the disciplining of the objectors previously;[15] leading questions favourable to the men who had manhandled Clegg, Naish, and Matheson were asked;[16] and, most serious, there was no cross-examination of witnesses. Private Paul Case refused to testify unless the American Consul General were present.[17] After hearing twenty-four witnesses, the court did nothing. Even before the inquiry was over, Brigadier-General Ruttan, the general officer commanding Military District No. 10 in Winnipeg, had decided that the whole matter had been exaggerated and that Clegg had never been unconscious.[18] It is true that a few days later the provost sergeant at Minto Barracks was arrested under a warrant charging assault issued by the civil authorities, but a local magistrate turned him over to the military authorities.[19] Shortly afterward, he was completely exonerated and the whole matter was dropped.[20]

Of course the Department of Militia and Defence had become involved as a result of complaints funnelled through the Minister of Agriculture and the Prime Minister. But Major-General Mewburn did not seem any more anxious to take action in the matter than had officers at Winnipeg. When T. A. Crerar handed him Dixon's telegram, he turned it over to the Adjutant-General with the wry remark: "Probably a hot shower would be better than a cold one."[21] Later he reported and supported the findings of his subordinates in Winnipeg to Crerar[22] and Prime Minister Borden.[23] Finally the militia council decided that conscientious objectors who refused to obey military orders should be court-martialled and sent to civil prisons.[24]

Less than a month later public attention was again fixed on the subject of the treatment of conscientious objectors in Manitoba when the case of David Wells became known. Wells, a Pentecostal by persuasion, had been sentenced to Stony Mountain Penitentiary on January 26, 1918. Within three weeks he became violently insane, was removed to the Selkirk Asylum, and died of "exhaustion and collapse".[25] As a result, the Reverend William Ivens, later to become well known during the Winnipeg Strike of 1919, wrote to T. A. Crerar to protest bitterly over Wells's death and the plight of conscientious objectors outside recognized peace churches in general. Ivens charged that Wells had "been literally 'done' to death by . . . civil officials" and went on to remark: "It may be that his death was necessary to convince the Government that there are Conscientious Objectors in the Dominion outside of Pacifist Organizations who are prepared to die for their convictions rather than submit to perform military service."[26] Crerar evidently thought Ivens's assessment of the Wells case correct and brought the matter to the attention of the Prime Minister.[27] The Winnipeg Trades and Labour Council, also scandalized, petitioned the government as follows:

Whereas:– The public has been greatly shocked by the death of David Wells within three weeks after his incarceration at Stony Mountain penitentiary as a Conscientious Objector, And whereas on his entrance he was in superb physical condition, And whereas there appears to be a widespread opinion that his insanity and subsequent death reflect upon his treatment while in prison, we, the Winnipeg Trades and Labor Council request:

1) That an immediate and searching inquiry be instituted into the causes surrounding his death, and into the treatment accorded to Conscientious Objectors generally, and that the results of such inquiry be made public.

2) That in harmony with modern methods of penal reform a copy of the penitentiary rules and regulations as applied to all prisoners be made public.

3) That whereas it is evident that the present Military Service Act is discriminating in its application to Conscientious Objectors exempting those belonging to particular and specified sects but imprisoning others not belonging to such sects, we request that the Act be so amended as to apply equally to all bonafide Conscientious Objectors and that those Conscientious Objectors now suffering incarceration under the Act be immediately released by being placed in the same category as those belonging to the recognized sects.[28]

Such public concern seemed to have no effect on either the government or the military; for, in the spring of 1918, in accordance with a routine order of the military council, conscientious objectors who for passive resistance had been sentenced to civil prison were ordered to be sent overseas in the next succeeding draft.[29] In April 1918 five Bible Students—Robert Clegg, Ralph Naish, John Gillespie, Frank Wainwright, and Claude Brown—were shipped to England along with three other objectors on the troop ship *Melita*.[30] Later two other Bible Students, O. K. Pimlot of Belleville, Ontario, and Sydney Ralph Thomas of Haliburton, Ontario, were placed on the *Waimana* and also transported to England.[31]

At first military authorities on the troop ships, and again in England, did not know they were dealing with conscientious objectors and tried to make them obey military commands. When they would not, they were subjected to punishment which, according to their reports, was often brutal. Pimlot stated that at Seford Camp, Sussex, he was beaten till unconscious, was kicked repeatedly, and later was thrown into a trench and again knocked unconscious. Thomas asserted that he, too, was kicked repeatedly, was knocked unconscious by a policeman, was goaded in the ribs for an hour and a half with a stick, and "was dragged, shoved and kicked several miles into the country to the edge of a 150 foot precipice and threatened to be thrown over; was dragged by the feet and pounded over the head and face with gloves till the blood flowed freely."[32] Thomas also reported that "ten instructors took turns at beating him . . . shoved him against a target and fired at him from the other end of the range, tried to shoot him at close range and cursed because the gun would not go off, knocked him into a trench and pounded him with the butt of a gun until unconscious."[33] Robert Clegg and Ralph Naish claimed to have been subjected to similar treatment. Besides being repeatedly beaten with boxing gloves they were evidently forced at bayonet point "to attend religious services conducted by those whom they believed to be hypocrites".[34] After a short time, six Bible Students, Clegg, Naish, Wainwright, Gillespie, Brown, and N. S. Shuttleworth —formerly one of the three other objectors sent overseas from Manitoba, but by then a Bible Student convert—were sent to England's Wandsworth Prison. There, according to their accounts, they were again kicked, clubbed, and placed on a starvation diet.[35] Wainwright reported, however, that the treatment at Wandsworth was an improvement over that received by the Bible Students in military camp.[36] Finally, in the autumn of 1918, the young conscientious objectors were shipped back to Canada, where they arrived on November 11, Armistice Day. Shortly thereafter they were given dishonourable discharges and released from the army.[37]

While the handful of Bible Student draftees were experiencing difficulties for their refusal to perform military service, their brethren throughout Canada were also objects of official wrath. The ban on *The Finished Mystery* and the *Bible Students Monthly* caused police in many Canadian cities and towns to carry out raids on Bible Student meeting halls, homes, and places of business. Telegrams, letters, and news clippings poured into the chief censor's office from Victoria, Calgary, Edmonton, Montreal, and other places, notifying him of the seizure of the now illegal publications.[38] On February 18, 1918, the *Ottawa Evening Journal* announced that three wagonloads of literature had been seized in Ottawa, and five Bible Students, including W. C. Douglas of Douglas Brothers Printers, were arrested. Only in Winnipeg, where police and some officials were sympathetic to the Bible Students, were they given time to dispose of the outlawed book and tract before raids were carried out.[39]

Sentences imposed on arrested Bible Students were severe. In a letter to Ernest Chambers dated March 25, 1918, a Bible Student, W. G. Brown, asserted that seven of his brethren who were arrested on February 13 had been fined a total of twenty-five hundred dollars.[40] The *Ottawa Evening Journal* of March 9 related that two had been fined five hundred dollars each and sentenced to sixty days in jail; three others were fined five hundred dollars each. Later in March the home of another Bible Student, George Dinsdale of Peterborough, Ontario, was raided, and when a single copy of the *Bible Students Monthly* was found, he was tried and fined one hundred dollars.[41]

Bible Students were mixed in their reactions to the government's action; so much so that even today Jehovah's Witnesses look upon the period as one of captivity to Babylon and the clergy of Christendom.[42] Some destroyed their literature or willingly surrendered it to the police. Others either hid it for later distribution or, in a few cases, defied the government by keeping it openly in their homes.[43] W. C. Paynter of Tantallon, Saskatchewan, a Bible Student for twenty-five years, president of Co-operative Creameries, and a member of the Saskatchewan Food Control Board, at first stated the ban on *The Finished Mystery* was "Prussianism" and that he would willingly go to jail for five years in defiance of it. Later, he backed down, saying that he had not read the outlawed publication previously, but that, after having examined a copy of it, he would not have such a "disloyal edition" in his home.[44] Evidently, too, there were some Bible Students, disaffected by events at Brooklyn, who openly broke with their brethren and took a stand with the government. The *Vancouver Daily Province* of March 26, 1918, mentioned a letter from J. M. McCoy of Toronto to Secretary of State Burrell which attacked *The Finished Mystery* and claimed that about fifty persons in the Toronto area had withdrawn from association with the International Bible Students Association under its "present management". Nevertheless, most Bible Students remained loyal to their faith and the Watch Tower Society, although many of them were, for a time, unclear as to what their course of conduct should be.

Chambers and many of the Bible Students' adversaries were pleased with the bans, particularly when American authorities began raids on Bible Student centres in the United States. The Canadian press and the chief censor both believed, quite rightly, that these were sparked directly by the actions of the Canadian government.[45] By mid-March the Watch Tower Society determined to fight back, and many Bible Students in the United States and Canada were ready to support such a campaign. Already the International Bible Students Association had made legal representations to Chambers through a Toronto lawyer,[46] and numerous congregations had sent protests to Secretary of State Burrell or to Chambers himself.[47] But the campaign really did not get under way until Judge Rutherford wrote an open letter to Martin Burrell on February 20. Rutherford denied that *The Finished Mystery* and the *Bible Students Monthly* were pro-German, as he felt the Canadian government had been led to believe, and he blamed the clergy for the government's anti-Bible Student behaviour. Shortly thereafter, his letter, plus a "statement of facts", a protest by the Toronto congregation of Bible Students, and a petition to have the bans lifted, was printed and circulated throughout Canada.[48] In March, to support the efforts of Canadian Bible Students, the Watch Tower Society published a broadside known as *Kingdom News* No. 1 which headlined: "Religious Intolerance—Pastor Russell's Followers Persecuted Because They Tell the People the Truth—Treatment of Bible Students Smacks of 'Dark Ages'." Then followed an account of the banning of the two Watch Tower publications in Canada.

The Bible Students also attempted to have their story published by the press, with some success. Though the chief censor had his western Canadian subordinate notify newspapers in that part of Canada that they should refrain from printing such articles,[49] the newspapers were not entirely co-operative. The *Calgary Albertan* was regarded by at least one censorship official as "a happy hunting ground" for the Bible Students.[50] The editor of the *Calgary Herald* wrote that while he thought the International Bible Students themselves ought to be banned, as long as they were not, he wanted their business.[51] The *Victoria Daily Colonist* of March 24 published a full-page account of J. F. Rutherford's famous speech "Millions Now Living Will Never Die", taken from the *Los Angeles Tribune*. In the centre of the article was shown a large photo of the judge with outstretched arms pronouncing doom on the nations.

All of this brought only negative results. Ernest Chambers, an extremely proud man, would not admit that he was not acting independently. On March 15, he had written to J. F. B. Livesay, press censor for the West in Winnipeg:

If I had time I would get out a statement regarding the Bible Students Association affair, which would put a stop to their howling. As a matter of fact their present complaints are based upon lying of the worst kind. It is not a question of interfering with the expression of opinions on religious matters but one of preventing the circulation of matter calculated to interfere with the successful prosecution of the war.

The attempt of these poor fools to lay the blame for the action taken by the Censorship Authorities upon the Churches is too absurd for anything. Only two of their vile publications have been prohibited and those which retain the right of circulation contain probably the most objectionable matter of the lot, viewed from the ordinary Christian's point of view.[52]

When he saw a copy of the *Daily Colonist* article he was furious. Judge Rutherford, in an extremely accurate prophecy, had said that "Germany will not be conquered by British, American and other armies, because before that can be accomplished internal disruptions will destroy the German autocracy." He had also suggested the possible spread of bolshevism and had condemned the concept of divine-right monarchy as well as the clergy. Chambers, upon reading the article, wrote to the editor of the *Victoria Daily Colonist* informing him that "you have been unconsciously the victim of a deliberate scheme to get around the censorship imposed for good reasons on two objectionable books of the International Bible Students Association". Rutherford's speech, according to the press censor, contained the "most objectionable features of those books". The judge's remark about a revolution in Germany was seen as "calculated to dishearten the public and discourage them in the policy of persisting with the prosecution of the war". His statement against the divine right of kings was "a poisoned shaft . . . directed against the Ruler of this Empire", and since he had failed to note that "the Divine Right of Kings is a purely Prussian theory which has always been combatted and exposed by British authors and statesmen as ridiculous . . . Mr. Rutherford is either an ignoramus or a cultivator of treason." Those who had handed the article to the editor of the *Daily Colonist* "were motivated by treasonable motives".[53] Thus on March 29 and April 1 the chief press censor fired off two angry letters to Judge Rutherford —plus several others to Canadian Bible Students at about the same time—in which he charged him with "false and misleading statements". He stated over and over again that the Bible Students lied when they blamed the government's action in banning two of their publications on clerical influence and reiterated that the literature in question had been outlawed because of its general effect, not because it was German propaganda.[54]

Chambers was like the lady who protested too much; in fact, it was he who was blatantly lying. Early in February, just after the bans had been imposed on *The Finished Mystery* and the *Bible Students Monthly*, he had written to the Reverend E. A. Cooke at Vancouver as follows:

Reverend and dear Sir,—
On November the 12th last you wrote the Minister of Militia drawing his attention to the objectionable character of the literature issued in connection with what is known as the Pastor Russell Movement or the International Bible Students Association.

This literature had already been the subject of investigation and inquiry, but your communication conveying as it did the views of such an influential body as The General Ministerial Association of Vancouver, proved very useful in securing action in this very important matter. I have the honour to inform you that the Honourable the Secretary of State has issued a Warrant forbidding the possession within Canada of "The Bible Students Monthly", and also the Book entitled "Studies in the Scriptures—The Finished Mystery".

Your letter to the Minister of Militia sets forth a pretty clear case against these publications, and there is no doubt that the wily denunciations of constituted authority and the sinister reference to the divine right of kings etc., are calculated to cause disaffection to His Majesty. Moreover, the reference to the "War Spirit", to the making of "cannon fodder", to intoxication with the "war spirit", to sending into "dreadful death in the trenches" etc., etc., are certainly calculated and disloyally intended to interfere with the recruiting and administration of His Majesty's Forces.

The extent of the distribution of this literature, in my opinion is suspicious, for the very wide distribution which has been made must cost a great deal of money, and I would be surprised to learn that the people connected with this Pastor Russell Movement have much wealth of their own.

I consider that the bitter attacks in these publications upon the Churches of all denominations, without distinction, are noteworthy, even if the statements embodied in these attacks cannot be described as "militarily objectionable". The Canadian Churches of all denominations, Christian and Jewish alike, rendered and are rendering invaluable services to the Country in sustaining a courageous and stout-hearted national spirit, a matter of the most vital importance from a military point of view. In fact a loyal military spirit is one of the most important assets of a Country at a time like this. The Churches of Canada have been incessantly active in the encouragement of every national patriotic and benevolent effort having any relation to the prosecution of the War and they have freely and ungrudgingly contributed of their very best in manhood and womanhood to the national cause. I consider that the churches of the Country have by their systematically patriotic conduct established the right to claim to be public organizations actively and usefully co-operating in the successful prosecution of the War, and as such they are entitled to protection against such outrageous attacks as those contained in the publication of the so-called Pastor Russell Movement, attacks due to the fact that the Churches have patriotically done their duty.[55]

The Bible Students, and Judge Rutherford in particular, refused to believe that they were not the victims of religious pressures. When the judge answered Chambers's two letters of March 29 and April 1, he remarked that the clergy had opposed International Bible Student teachings for twenty-five years, and if they had stopped suddenly, it was surprising. With regard to Chambers's statement that the clergy had exercised no influence, he said:

There are other ways to bring about influence than by coming directly to an official. And when I use the word influence I do not mean to charge that you personally have had consultations with them. The statements in your letters are to the effect that you have received objections from municipal officers, police, army officials and others from one end of Canada to the other. I dare say you have not stopped to investigate why they brought this matter to your attention. If these various officers and others (which class is not designated) took it upon themselves to call your attention to a religious book, the presumption is that that class of men who have been long opposing are the ones who called it to their attention and influenced them to call it to your attention, or to the attention of the Secretary of State.[56]

Rutherford then cited the examples of clerical opposition, mentioned previously, to the Bible Students in Winnipeg and Guelph, denied that the two banned publications were in any way detrimental to the Canadian war effort, and stated again that the Watch Tower Society was in no way connected with "Hun propaganda". With regard to Chambers personally, he said:

I do not question your honesty of purpose in putting the ban on our publications. All men are subject to influence. In prohibiting the possession and circulation of "The Finished Mystery", I believe that you think you are doing right; but the day will come when you will see that you are really banning the message the Lord desired to be delivered to tell the people the truth.[57]

Chambers was hardly mollified, and in spite of his denials, he continued to suggest that the Bible Students were German-financed. In a conversation with Toronto Bible Student Ernest Whelpton, at the time the Bible Students had made direct representations to him, he had indicated as much, although at the end of the conversation he had evidently assured Whelpton that he was certain it was not so.[58] Still, in letters to others he was not above stating the belief that the Bible Students were either willing or unwilling dupes of enemy agents.[59] He found it impossible to believe that the Bible Students could obtain enough money through voluntary contributions to print the great quantities of literature they published. After all, the number of copies of *The Finished Mystery* and the *Bible Student Monthly* confiscated by Canadian police and sent to the chief press censor's office alone were enough to fill a small warehouse.

Motivated by deep feelings, Chambers was able to have three more publications of the Watch Tower Society banned before the end of May.[60] But the harshest actions taken against the Bible Students did not come in Canada. Sir Robert Borden's government seemed reluctant to move more firmly against them in spite of a constant clamour from Chambers, other officials, the military, and, above all, the clergy and some segments of the press. Almost no one came to the Bible Students' defence and nothing was said on their behalf in Parliament. Still, the government, evidently not anxious to suppress freedom of religion, moved slowly against a group which was openly opposed to supporting war and was thoroughly unpopular with much of the public.

The same was not true in the United States, however, for the American Attorney General had marked the officials of the Watch Tower Society for prosecution.[61] Numerous military and religious leaders were determined to see the Bible Students' movement crushed, if possible.[62] Therefore, when the Watch Tower Society published a tract entitled *Kingdom News* No. 3 which headlined "Two Great Battles Raging—Fall of Autocracy Certain—Satanic Strategy

Doomed to Failure—The Birth of Antichrist", American officials evidently decided to act. *Kingdom News* No. 3 was released on May 1; on May 6 warrants were issued for the arrest of eight officers of the Society—J. F. Rutherford, W. E. Van Amburgh, A. H. Macmillan, R. J. Martin, C. J. Woodworth, G. H. Fisher, F. H. Robinson, and Giovanni DeCecca.[63] Under the terms of the American Espionage Act it was charged that they

Unlawfully and feloniously did conspire, combine, confederate and agree together, and with divers other persons to the said Grand Jurors unknown, to commit a certain offence against the United States of America, to wit: the offense of unlawfully, feloniously and wilfully causing insubordination, disloyalty and refusal of duty in the military and naval forces of the United States of America when the United States was at war . . . by personal solicitations, letters, public speeches, distributing and publicly circulating throughout the United States of America a certain book called "Volume VII. Bible Studies. The Finished Mystery", and distributing and publicly circulating throughout the United States certain articles printed in pamphlets called "Bible Student's Monthly", "Watch Tower", "Kingdom News" and other pamphlets not named.[64]

After a trial of fifteen days, Rutherford and his fellows were convicted. On June 21, 1918, Judge Harlan B. Howe sentenced seven of them to twenty years each in the Atlanta, Georgia, federal penitentiary; DeCecca was given ten years. Thirteen days later, in spite of attempts to be released on bail pending appeal, the eight were taken south by train to Atlanta, where prison doors closed behind them.[65] While these events were taking place, other Bible Students were becoming victims of both prosecution and persecution throughout the country. Some were arrested and sentenced to prison for three years for having copies of *The Finished Mystery*, even after the offending pages 247–53 had been removed on orders from the Watch Tower Society. Others were mobbed, tarred and feathered, or forcibly ducked in cold streams. Some had their homes ransacked, and a few were even driven from their home communities.[66] At the Brooklyn

Bethel, an executive committee of five was established to keep the *Watch Tower* in print, but because of a shortage of coal and paper, the Society could not continue its New York operations. On August 26, 1918, the headquarters staff moved back to Pittsburgh in an attempt to keep the organization intact. Though they did manage to produce the *Watch Tower* without fail, in practically every other way the Society seemed dead.[67]

In Canada the publication of *Kingdom News* No. 3, distributed under the title the *Morning Messenger*, brought further troubles for the Bible Students. In Winnipeg, Charles Cutforth, the first branch overseer of the Watch Tower Society in Canada, submitted a copy of the tract to the press censor for Western Canada. Press censor Livesay thereupon read it and approved it for publication.[68] It was, in comparison with many Bible Student publications, rather mild, and Livesay saw nothing wrong with it.[69] It could, in no reasonable way, be considered pro-German. Not only did it forecast the "end of autocracy", a term commonly used to refer to the government of the German Reich, but spoke of "the autocratic Kaiser with his bloody hordes" and showed a large picture of Satan asking Kaiser Wilhelm, "Why do you call me god?" Nor did the *Morning Messenger* have much to say about war or politics. Most of its text was concerned with the struggle between Jehovah and Satan throughout the centuries from the Fall of man in Eden. It was, nevertheless, destined to cause a great outcry and it brought wrath down upon the heads of both the Bible Students and J. F. B. Livesay.

After Livesay notified the Bible Students' Winnipeg printer on May 10 that he could see nothing objectionable in the tract, Cutforth had it printed with a statement that it had been approved by the Canadian censor, and he shipped it to Bible Students throughout Canada for distribution. In mid-June repercussions came. Though the *Morning Messenger* had said nothing of an anti-war nature or anything that could be regarded as unpatriotic, it had quoted a statement from Lord's *Old Roman World* in its penultimate paragraph on the front page which identified the Church of Rome as "the antichrist" and "the devil's seed". On its back page it labelled the Kaiser as pro-Catholic. Roman Catholic leaders were violently incensed and P. B.

McCaffery, editor of the New Freeman Publishing Company Ltd., Saint John, New Brunswick, wrote to Ernest Chambers on June 10, as follows:

The enclosed pamphlet claims to have been passed by the Canadian censor. Will you kindly inform us if such is the case and, if so, just why such matter was deemed fit for circulation among the people of Canada?

Government regulations, as we understand it, make it an offence to circulate or print anything which may have the effect of causing dessention [sic] in the prosecution of Canadian war effort. Is not this calculated to cause dissention [sic].

As the official Catholic organ for the province of New Brunswick we feel that we are entitled to an answer.[70]

A few days later the Reverend Thomas O'Donnell, president of the Catholic Church Extension Society at Toronto, also wrote to the chief censor to complain: "It [the *Morning Messenger*] is a downright attack on the pope—a neutral power. It has the effect of causing disunion and strife at this period of stress when all minds should be set on Winning the War."[71] McCaffery then dispatched a second letter filled with wrath. Was there no penalty for forging the censor's imprimatur? Would not the law do anything? "When is it going to stop," he asked, "or will it finally bring about the regrettable violence on the part of those thus slandered and on the part of those circulating the matter. Personally we would not guarantee to keep our hands off anyone caught so doing."[72] Chambers also received many other complaints, including one from Senator George Lynch-Staunton,[73] the administrative commissioner of Montreal,[74] and the Minister of Justice himself.[75]

The chief censor was upset, to say the least. On June 13 he wired a frantic telegram to Livesay who was then visiting Toronto:

Please wire me immediately what form your authorization of Morning Messenger took [.] Did you pass the matter carried in the May issue [?] Did you sanction use of title passed by Canadian censor [?] Whole publication most objectionable and pernicious tending to weaken and detract from the united effort of the people of Canada in the prosecution of the war [.] That is the evident intention [.] Would like for the police names and addresses of all connected with the writing printing publishing and circulation of this matter [.] Did you know Bible Students were interested [?] An immediate reply most urgent [.][76]

The same day he prepared a report to the Secretary of State asking that the offending tract be banned[77] and replied in haste to O'Donnell, McCaffery, and Lynch-Staunton. In an effusive letter to the former, written on June 15, he was able to state that the government had already acted—the *Morning Messenger* was outlawed. Furthermore, he said:

I suppose you are aware that these people have attempted to obtain sympathy among the ignorant and biased by circulating the story that the action taken by the Censorship Authorities to restrict the circulation of their literature was due to clerical influence. This was done with a dual object of discouraging the Christian churches of this country and also with the deliberate intention of misrepresenting the action of Censorship Authorities.

I hope that you will never hesitate to bring to my attention any literary matter which comes to your notice which is objectionable within the definitions of the term "objectionable" contained in the Consolidated Orders respecting Censorship, copy of which I enclose herewith for your information.[78]

To Lynch-Staunton he remarked that there was a strong possibility that the Bible Students were German-financed. He was pleased, too, that his office had "started the ball rolling" leading to the arrest and trial of Watch Tower leaders on charges of conspiracy in the United States.[79] In his reply to McCaffery, he wrote: "The desirability of prosecuting all those concerned in the publication of the 'Morning Messenger' has been placed in the hands of the local police and military." He said also: "I might add that I have recommended that all of the literature of the International Bible Students' Association, past, present and future, be forbidden circulation in Canada but I do not know how far my report is likely to be acted upon at the moment."[80]

Livesay was so embarrassed over the matter that he offered to resign.[81] Such a drastic measure was unnecessary, however, because his chief was forgiving: after all, said Chambers, "we all make mistakes". Besides, Bible Student literature was such "insidious stuff" that one had to be fairly familiar with it to recognize its dangerous points.[82] In correspondence with Charles Cutforth, however, he adopted a different tone. Accordingly, Cutforth's use of the statement "passed by the Canadian Censor" on the *Morning Messenger* was "an insolent and dishonest attempt to prevent interference with the distribution of what was clearly and distinctly dangerous literature". In addition, the tract was "vicious, treasonable and insidious". Chambers demanded, too, that Cutforth give him the names and addresses of all official representatives of the Watch Tower Society in Canada.[83]

The episode had other repercussions. Several Bible Students in Ontario were given fines for possessing the *Morning Messenger*,[84] while in Victoria the city council "declared war on the Bible Students".[85] Mayor Todd prohibited them the use of city halls and theatres for meetings, following examples already set by Toronto and Vancouver, upon the request of veterans' organizations.[86] Still, no action was taken against Charles Cutforth or the Watch Tower Society's officers in Winnipeg. The Manitoba government would take no steps to prosecute, since Livesay had given permission to Cutforth to publish the *Morning Messenger*, and Winnipeg authorities were less than co-operative with Chambers. The local military district intelligence officer assured F. G. Aldham, Livesay's assistant, "quite good humoredly that his idea of the situation was that no Bible Student would ever be more than reprimanded in a Manitoba court of sedition". Lawyer E. J. McMurray had already had sixteen clients acquitted of charges of possessing *The Finished Mystery*, "and was equally confident in this case". Furthermore, L. Burgess, secretary of the local Bible Student congregation, was a member of the Winnipeg police force and the inspector of motor vehicles.[87] What the intelligence officer did not know was that the chief of police had personally notified Burgess of planned raids on the Bible Students' premises so that everything illegal could be hidden away.[88]

The conviction of the Watch Tower officials in New York a few days later—which Chambers called "a full and fair trial before a jury"[89]—gave the press censor much more ammunition to use against the Bible Students. He notified Aldham at Winnipeg that all newspapers were to refrain from even giving the time and place of Bible Students' meetings,[90] and he pressed the government to have all Watch Tower literature banned.[91] Finally, on July 18, 1918, the warrant was issued: "All publications, circulars, leaflets and other printed matter of the International Bible Students Association, Watch Tower Bible and Tract Society, Associated Bible Students" were prohibited. Possession of such, as in the case of the literature which had been declared illegal previously, could bring a fine of five thousand dollars and five years' imprisonment.[92]

Thus, during July and August, Chambers and police officials began a crackdown on Bible Students throughout the country. The secretary of the Victoria congregation, angered at Chambers's order prohibiting the advertisement of Bible Student meetings, accused him of the "intolerance of the Dark Ages" and indicated that it would have been better were he to have had a millstone placed around his neck and been cast into the sea.[93] But the prohibition of meeting notices was mild in comparison with other actions or proposed actions that the authorities were taking or hoped to take against the Bible Students. Police were continuing to carry out raids on Bible Students' homes, sometimes without warrants.[94] I. C. Edwards of Victoria was fined one thousand dollars and jailed for a Bible Student display on Yates Street in that city;[95] a German Bible Student in Vancouver was sentenced to two years' imprisonment for being in possession of banned literature;[96] and secret agents were dispatched throughout western Canada to obtain information to be used against Canadian Watch Tower Society officers and their brethren throughout the country.[97]

Ernest Chambers was anxious to see the Bible Students prosecuted and was willing to use almost any weapon against them. A novel idea came to him. Police Chief Langley of Victoria wrote to him in some consternation about lapel buttons Bible Students were wearing; he felt the buttons gave them a sense of *esprit de corps* and therefore should be banned,[98] although they bore nothing more insidious than a cross inside a crown. The chief press censor, upon reading Langley's letter, was struck by a different idea, however; perhaps, in fact, the buttons were "publications" already outlawed by the July 18 warrant. If so, then the Bible Students could be prosecuted for wearing illegal publications! Chambers wrote post-haste to Under-Secretary of State Thomas Mulvey to have the matter clarified,[99] but was disappointed when Mulvey replied that the offending buttons were not subject to press censorship.[100] The Under-Secretary, nevertheless, did suggest that the matter be referred to the police, and Chambers determined to pursue it.[101] Finally, Sir Percy Sherwood laid it to rest; he felt that Chambers had a good idea, but there simply was no law against the wearing of lapel buttons.[102]

Chambers was not daunted. Lieutenant D. A. Campbell, the military intelligence officer in Manitoba, felt that local courts were treating Bible Students too leniently. He contacted Chambers to tell him that he had carried out extensive investigations in the Grand View–Gilbert Plains area of the province and had had eleven Bible Students arrested for possessing illegal publications. So, in order to obtain rigorous sentences, he asked that the magistrates or the provincial authorities under whom they acted be instructed that more severe penalties should be meted out.[103] Yet his efforts were not particularly fruitful, since the trials were held before the chief press censor could act. The heaviest fine levied was fifty dollars.[104] Chambers did bring the intelligence officer's request to the attention of the Minister of Justice, however. Chambers complained that Manitoba magistrates were uniformly letting Bible Students off with warnings or extremely light sentences on various grounds—a serious state of affairs. He said: "Many of these individuals are peaceable people leading clean lives and with generally good reputations for honesty, etc. in the community in which they live. They are decided fanatics however and persist in circulating pronouncedly pacifist, socialist and anti-war literature."[105] Hence, as the intelligence officer requested, the magistrates should be instructed to be more severe. The Deputy Minister of Justice, in answering, refused to move directly on this request. The chief press censor was informed that jurisdiction over magistrates lay properly with the provincial authorities.[106] Nevertheless, the Deputy Minister stated that he would write to the Manitoba Attorney General,[107] and Chambers referred his friend in intelligence to that official.[108]

Fortunately for the Bible Students, no Canadian official higher than Ernest Chambers was seriously interested in carrying on a major campaign against them. They were not outlawed as a movement and could continue to meet together openly. But circumstances were still very difficult for them. Constant raids continued to be carried out on their homes in search of forbidden literature.[109] Their meetings were sometimes broken up by overzealous officials.[110] Fines and prison sentences continued to be imposed by the courts and social pressures from neighbours were often great. The end of the First World War in 1918 and the release of the Watch Tower Society's American officers in March 1919 did nothing toward ending the Canadian ban.

There was little that Canadian Bible Students could do in self-defence during this period, particularly while Judge Rutherford and the Watch Tower Society's officers were in Atlanta. Some of them, nevertheless, refused to bow before the constant harassment meted out by the Canadian chief censor's office, immigration officers, and police. In fact, throughout the fall of 1918 and all of 1919, they continued to correspond courteously with Chambers and others in positions of authority in attempts to have the war-time bans on their literature lifted.[111] In other ways, too, they did what they could to make the imposition of the bans difficult. For example, a British Columbia physician, Dr. Alexander McCarter, arrested on charges of having Watch Tower publications, determined to go to jail rather than pay a two-hundred-dollar fine. In order to keep the court from simply seizing his private assets, he had all of them transferred to his wife while his trial was pending.[112] In another instance, a semi-literate Bible Student, A. Sutherland of Victoria, caused the chief censor and several other officials much time and correspondence. During a raid for forbidden books and pamphlets the police had seized a copy of Leeser's translation of the Bible from Sutherland. Annoyed by the illegal seizure, he wrote to Chambers in appalling English and demanded the return of his Bible. Chambers, who could not understand why the book had been taken since it wasn't in an enemy language, found himself in a long and curious correspondence over "one Jewish Bible". Soon even the acting Under-Secretary of State became involved in the affair, although he wondered how Sutherland's Bible could, under the circumstances, be found.[113] Most curious of all, however, was the case of the "Pittsburgh Dailies". The Bible Students, well aware that their mail was being examined by the postal authorities, decided to play a bit of a trick on the chief censor. Early in 1919 Walter Salter, who by then had taken over as Canadian Watch Tower branch superintendent, wrote a letter to a Mr. Edwards in Pittsburgh, Pennsylvania, suggesting that he could assist his Canadian brethren by sending them copies of "Pittsburgh Dailies". The letter was seized and turned over to Chambers, who at once determined to hunt down what he believed were more seditious papers. A female Bible Student was interviewed in Winnipeg by a secret agent posing as a believer, but she simply replied that the "Dailies" were no longer much used. Chambers then wrote to an American vigilante in Chicago to have him check on Edwards and his address in Pittsburgh. However, when that was done, Edwards was nowhere to be found; his address was that of a vacant lot. Strangely, Chambers never seemed to realize that he had been hoodwinked.[114]

In April 1919 Salter took more positive steps by writing to Chambers again to request that the ban be removed from Watch Tower literature. He pointed out that he knew that Bible Student mails were being tampered with and stated that with the war's end there was no good reason for the government's restrictions. Watch Tower Society officers in the United States were out of prison; the *Watch Tower* had clearly spoken out against revolution and anarchy.[115] Chambers replied that the Bible Students were bad citizens, remarked that their acts wouldn't be forgotten, and refused to meet the Watch Tower branch supervisor.[116] Salter next wrote to Secretary of State Burrell to point out that with the exception of *The Finished Mystery*—still outlawed in the United States—Watch Tower literature was banned nowhere but in Canada. He asked: "Does it not, therefore, seem strange that the ban should continue in this country of freedom?"[117] Burrell's only response was to allow Chambers to reply on July 30 that the warrants were to remain indefinitely.[118]

In the meantime the chief censor continued to regard the Bible Students as a threat. Late in November 1918 he wrote that they were spreading "underhanded pacifist propaganda subsidized by German agents".[119] By March 1919 he claimed that their "literature [was] intended and distinctly calculated to create disaffection and encourage those who are advocating the overthrow of all constituted authority".[120] Others evidently agreed, for during 1919 arrests and prosecutions of Bible Students continued without let-up. The only beneficial action taken by the government toward them prior to December of that year was that, in April, the Postal Department decided to stop interfering with Watch Tower mails.[121]

Finally the ban did have to be removed; and unintentionally it was probably the Royal North West Mounted Police and Ernest Chambers himself who were responsible for its being lifted. By the fall of 1919 war hysteria had generally died down, and although it was replaced by labour troubles and fear of bolshevism, there was a general desire to end war-time restrictions. The Bible Students consequently became somewhat more bold and once again began to distribute literature, particularly the *Golden Age*, a new magazine released by the Watch Tower Society in the United States. However, a letter from the Society's Winnipeg office to P. H. Hardin at Claresholm, Alberta, regarding the circulation of the magazine fell into the hands of the RNWMP, as did Hardin's reply stating that the work of placing it was progressing. When informed of the situation, Ernest Chambers was once again furious: the Bible Students were guilty of a "slim and impertinent attempt to evade the law".[122] Thus the RNWMP arrested ten persons for being in possession of outlawed publications throughout southern Alberta in such widespread places as Claresholm, Lethbridge, Bow Island, and Medicine Hat.[123] But publicity at the time had the reverse effect from that expected by Chambers and the police. One of the Bible Students was arrested for having a hymn book; another, a booklet on "Our Lord's Return"; a third, a copy of Russell's book *The Divine Plan of the Ages*; a fourth, the *Scenario of the Photo-Drama of Creation*; and a fifth, a Watch Tower edition of the *Emphatic Diaglott*, an interlinear translation of the New Testament. In consequence, although the court was prepared to be harsh—one of the persons charged had to put up a one-thousand-dollar bond and arrange for friends to post an additional one thousand dollars—the Bible Students' threat to carry the matter to the "highest court in the land" caused the magistrate to back down. Eight of the defendants were fined three dollars each, while the other two, who proved they were not Bible Students, were dismissed without fines.[124] More important, the government decided, without further ado, to put an end to the prosecution of Bible Students. On January 1, 1920, the bans were ended.[125]

A few weeks later, Chambers, replying to a letter from Ernest Whelpton, stated that he was glad. After all, he had not liked censorship. "As an old newspaper man," he said, "the duties were of a hateful character in many respects but one had to undertake distasteful duties if his country so requires."[126] Of course the chief censor was only putting up a front and was guilty of the thoroughgoing dishonesty which he always seemed able to recognize in others but never in himself. On December 31, 1919, in a letter to the Deputy Minister of Justice, he had exhibited some irritation over the fact that the orders respecting censorship under the War Measures Act had been repealed and the bans ended. In a final paragraph in that letter he had stated with some heat: "The publications of the International Bible Students Association included most dangerous and pernicious pacifist and distinct pro-enemy propaganda all the more vicious because insidious and disguised under the form of religious cant."[127] But with the beginning of the new year, the Bible Students no longer concerned themselves with Ernest Chambers; they were already in the midst of a new preaching campaign.

CHAPTER FOUR

COMFORTING THE MEEK AND PREACHING GOD'S WRATH

We know that we are of God, and the whole world lieth in the evil one.

1 John 5:19, American Standard Version

THE IMPRISONMENT OF J. F. Rutherford and his seven companions in Atlanta gave critics of the International Bible Students every reason to believe that the movement was thoroughly discredited and would fade. But they had not counted on the depth of Bible Student commitment, or on the fact that mob violence and prosecutions before the courts of both Canada and the United States had awakened in them the conviction that they were being persecuted for righteousness' sake. Rutherford had stated on the day of his sentencing by Judge Howe that it was the happiest day of his life, since "to serve earthly punishment for the sake of one's religious belief is one of the greatest privileges a man could have". When he and his fellows were taken to the grand-jury room after hearing the trial judge's sentence, friends and family members greeted them with faces that were "almost radiant". "The whole company made the old building [the Brooklyn Federal Court House] ring with 'Blessed Be the Tie That Binds'. 'It is God's will' they told each other." Bible Students therefore determined to demonstrate open support for the imprisoned directors.[1] A general convention was held at Pittsburgh, Pennsylvania, on January 4, 1919, under the latest Watch Tower vice-president, C. H. Anderson. At the meeting, attended by some one thousand delegates from both the United States and Canada, Judge Rutherford was re-elected as president of the Watch Tower Society. W. E. Van Amburgh, another of the eight, was again chosen secretary-treasurer, and C. A. Wise, vice-president.[2] In addition, American Bible Students, convinced that the Society's directors had been convicted unjustly, started an all-out campaign to work for their release. Aided by libertarian newspapers, they deluged public officials with requests for support. In March 1919, they circulated a petition on behalf of Rutherford and his colleagues which obtained seven hundred thousand signatures. But before it could be submitted, the eight were released from prison.[3] On March 2, Judge Howe recommended to U.S. Attorney General Gregory that he have their sentences commuted. Howe was apparently interested in blocking their appeals. His move, however, failed, and Justice Louis Brandeis of the U.S. Supreme Court ordered that the Bible Student directors be released on bail.[4] On March 26, they were free men awaiting a new trial; on April 4, Judge Ward of the Federal Second Court of Appeal at New York declared: "The defendants in this case did not have the temperate and impartial trial to which they were entitled, and for this reason judgment is reversed."[5] A year later the United States government dropped all charges against them by a motion of *nolle prosequi*.[6]

Upon release from Atlanta Penitentiary, Judge Rutherford at once began a major reorganization of Bible Student activities. On May 4, 1919, he delivered a public lecture entitled "Hope for Distressed Humanity" at Los Angeles, California.[7] It was so well received that he determined to call a general convention at Cedar Point, Ohio, from September 1 to 7. There, after quoting Jeremiah the prophet, he declared that the Bible Students must become God's ambassadors to "bear the divine message of reconciliation to the world" and, to help them, he announced the publication of the new magazine, the *Golden Age*.[8]

Those were only the first steps which began to give new life to a movement which had seemed close to disintegration. On October 1, 1919, the Watch Tower Society's headquarters staff returned to Brooklyn and from there Judge Rutherford began to take steps which were to strengthen the Bible Students in their resolve to obey God rather than men. In compliance with orders from the war-time American government, the Society had cut pages 247–53 from *The Finished Mystery*, and Bible Students had joined in a national day of prayer in the United States in May 1918. Those actions the Society now repudiated, labelling them compromises with the world.[9] Judge Rutherford also began to make changes in Bible Student organization, which were ultimately to make the movement more efficient and better disciplined. Along with a new emphasis on preaching, an activity every Bible Student was now encouraged to engage in, Rutherford began to de-emphasize the roles of individuals and to bring democratically run congregations under Watch Tower Society supervision. In the fall of 1919 the Society appointed service directors in each congregation to care for the distribution of the *Golden Age*, and in the next year it reduced the positions of congregationally elected elders by insisting that they not act independently (as local boards of directors) without congregational consent.[10]

A few years later other doctrinal and organizational developments occurred under Rutherford's direction. Beginning in 1926 the Watch Tower Society placed a new emphasis on the name Jehovah and the relationship of Christians to Him.[11] In 1927 the Society abandoned the idea that Pastor Russell had been the "faithful and wise servant". Henceforth this "servant" was to be seen as the remnant of the elect of God on earth—those of the 144,000 saints who had not been joined with Christ in heavenly glory.[12] The stage was therefore set for the acceptance by the Bible Students of a new name. At a convention held in Columbus, Ohio, in July 1931, Judge Rutherford called on them to accept the new designation, "Jehovah's Witnesses", based on the text found in Isaiah 43: 10–12.

Most Bible Students did respond favourably to these changes, but a number were thoroughly disgruntled and left the movement. The war-time schism in Brooklyn had caused a number of divisions and more followed after the First World War. Some ultimately joined the Dawn Bible Students Association, an outgrowth of the group which had followed the former Watch Tower directors who had tried to oust Judge Rutherford from power in 1917.[13] Others followed P. S. L. Johnson,[14] and in Canada, particularly in the West, sizable numbers joined the so-called "Stand Fasters", or another movement, the Pastoral Bible Students.[15] Over a period of years, however, such groups tended to disappear, while those Bible Students who remained loyal to the Watch Tower Society began to experience a renewed vitality.

Peace, and a return to more normal conditions after the Red scare of 1919–20, gave them an opportunity to recuperate. After the secession of those opposed to the new leadership, loyal Bible Students set about winning new converts. They began to grow and flourish once more. Between 1922 and 1925 the number of persons throughout the world who attended their annual celebrations of the Lord's Supper rose from 32,661 to 90,434.[16] Thereafter, except in 1926, they continued to increase throughout the 1920s and the early 1930s. The Watch Tower Society's Brooklyn offices were enlarged, printing facilities were greatly increased, and Bible Students were becoming increasingly active and numerous overseas, particularly in Germany and in Central Europe.[17]

Bible Students did not stand still in Canada either. As a direct result of the Watch Tower Society's new policies, they began to experience a slow but steady growth. In January 1920, at the time the Canadian government ended its ban, the Society moved its branch offices from Winnipeg to Toronto in order to be closer to both the American Watch Tower headquarters and the national centre of population. Also, in accord with counsel from the *Watch Tower* and communications from Brooklyn, Canadian Bible Students began to participate in the new preaching campaign engaged in by their brethren in the United States and other countries. The *International Bible Students Association Year-book for 1922* reported that some nineteen hundred Canadian Bible Students had gathered to celebrate the Lord's Supper in the spring of that year.[18] Though incomplete, that report did give a rough indication of how many persons were still associated with the organization in the Dominion. The *Year-book* also claimed that the Bible Students were increasing and that their message was being spread far and wide.[19] That such was the case was demonstrated a few years later; the *1925 Yearbook* reported that in the previous year throughout Canada over three thousand had attended the Lord's Supper.[20]

At the same time, the Bible Students were forming a very different type of community from the one which existed prior to 1920. As indicated earlier, the first Canadian Bible Students were largely of either English-speaking or Northern European stock. Among them were many Anglo-Canadians, Americans, British, and Scandinavians. In spite of Ernest Chambers's suggestions that they were German-financed during the First World War, there were few Germans, Austrians, or Hungarians among them. But after the war, the older Bible Students, who were lost to schismatic movements, were more than replaced by converts from among Anglo-Canadians and other ethnic groups as well; for the first time, large numbers of immigrants of Slavic and Hungarian origin became Bible Students.

The *1925 Yearbook* showed that in Montreal in 1924, while eighty-six had gathered for the English-language memorial celebration of the Lord's Supper, eighty-five had come together for a similar Ukrainian service.[21] In Hamilton, fifty-one attended a Polish service.[22] Yet it was in western Canada that Bible Student teachings had the greatest appeal to Central and Eastern Europeans. In Winnipeg and in Edmonton, large Ukrainian Bible Student communities began to grow. But more outstanding was the growth of Bible Student support in northern Saskatchewan.

In and around the small town of Wakaw, Saskatchewan, great numbers of Ukrainians converted to the teachings of the Watch Tower Society almost *en masse*. In 1920, four men living in Wakaw —John Damchuk, Michael Adamowski, Emil Zarysky, and Joseph Katchowski—became aware of the International Bible Students as a result of the ban on *The Finished Mystery*. After they came in contact with a Ukrainian Bible Student colporteur from Winnipeg, they accepted the new teachings and began to form small Ukrainian-speaking *ecclesias*. Within a short time these small groups united, and by 1925 meetings were being held in Wakaw, often attended by three to four hundred Ukrainian-speaking Bible Students.[23] Evidently these converts, practically all ex-members of the Ukrainian Orthodox Church, had been deeply disgruntled with both their former religious institution and the clergy. They were, therefore, psychologically ready for the adoption of a new faith, and the Bible Students gained an important base among them. During succeeding decades, many dozens of Bible Student–Jehovah's Witness evangelists were to go out from Wakaw to comfort the meek and teach the destruction of Satan's world.[24]

In 1925, in response to Bible Student growth, the Watch Tower Society saw fit to establish a new corporation under Canadian law— the International Bible Students Association of Canada. The Society also determined to use a number of new means by which colporteurs and publishers could reach the Canadian public. For example, it organized special campaigns to contact French-, Ukrainian-, and German-speaking Canadians and to preach to other ethnic minorities.[25] It provided for what was known as the "school team" work conducted by special evangelists who held meetings at public schools,[26] and the "house car" work, which involved travelling colporteurs who moved from place to place distributing literature far and wide.[27] On the West Coast a sailboat was required to reach isolated persons in the scattered coastal communities of British Columbia and the Alaska panhandle.[28]

Of course the Bible Student–Jehovah's Witnesses were not always well received. Much war-time animosity lingered on. Some regarded them as unpatriotic, while others looked on them as religious fanatics, cranks, or nuisances. However, it was really the bitterness with which they denounced religious, political, and commercial organizations, plus the fact that they successfully sought converts everywhere they went, that caused religious and secular authorities to take action against them again.

Judge Rutherford had stressed the idea that the Bible Students should bear God's message of reconciliation to man in an attempt to win converts. But the judge and the Watch Tower Society felt equally strongly that they must publish Jehovah's wrath against the rulers of the nations. The Bible Students neither forgot nor forgave their adversaries for the persecution they had experienced in 1918 and 1919. Their literature, therefore, became increasingly harsh in its condemnation of the authorities of the world. In September 1920 the Watch Tower Society published a special issue of the *Golden Age*, which told in detail many of the war-time experiences of Bible Students who had suffered arrests, prosecutions, and mobbings. It also poured verbal vitriol upon the churches and political leaders. So harsh was this publication that some Bible Students were unwilling to distribute it.[29] In many ways, the *Golden Age* No. 27 was only the first in a long series of stern denunciations of the powers of the world. For during the period between the two world wars a flood-tide of books, booklets, magazines, and other publications which rolled off the presses of the Watch Tower Society inveighed against Christendom, politics, big business, and the League of Nations. The most condemnatory Scriptural terminology was used over and over again against the churches. The clergy were called "scribes", "pharisees", "hypocrites", "serpents", "offspring of vipers", and "whitewashed sepulchres", and the churches were described as "harlot-like organizations which committed whoredoms with the kings of the earth". Judge Rutherford, writing in the book *Deliverance*, which was published in 1926, stated:

The clergy of these various ecclesiastical systems [Catholicism, Protestantism, and Orthodoxy] bless the armies which are sent out by the commercial and political wings, and their blessing is extended regardless of which side these armies are fighting on. The clergy all pretend to pray to the same God for a blessing upon the warring armies on both sides. Their course during the World War proves this beyond a question, and is admitted by all. Of course they will all join in asking a blessing upon the Devil's armies as they assemble for Armageddon.[30]

A year later he wrote:

The pious hypocrites preach from their pulpits, telling the people what glory shall be theirs if they die upon the field of battle. These wicked instruments of Satan busy themselves amongst the contending nations, both sides claiming to represent the Lord and both representing the Devil.[31]

Then, in 1929, in the book *Life*, he repeated what was becoming a constant theme in Watch Tower publications:

Jesus was accused of every crime known to the calendar, yet guilty of none. The common people heard him gladly and believed on him. The clergy of his day, from whom better might have been expected, were the instruments used by Satan for his persecution. The clergy of the present time likewise misrepresent God. They advance their own wisdom to turn the minds of the people away from God and from his Word. The time has come when people must cast away the stumbling stones which the clergy have put in their pathway and must use their own mental faculties to understand the Scriptures.[32]

The Watch Tower president even censured the clergy because of their support for prohibition in the United States. In Pastor Russell's day the Bible Students had taken the position that the Bible clearly permitted Christians to drink alcoholic beverages so long as they did not become intoxicated. Furthermore, they were specifically enjoined to use wine, not unfermented grape juice, in the celebration of the Lord's Supper.[33] In 1930 Judge Rutherford gave several widely broadcast radio lectures in which he condemned prohibition as another example of the clergy's unrighteous imposition of their will on society contrary to God's word, the Bible. Later these lectures were published in a booklet entitled *Prohibition; the League of Nations: of God or the Devil, Which?*

Politicians and high financiers were also reviled and they, like the clergy, were panned in bitter cartoons which appeared, particularly in the *Golden Age*. Even national leaders and traditions were attacked. The Bible Students strongly disliked Woodrow Wilson who, they felt, had acquiesced in their persecution in 1918. Though they had little personal feeling against the three United States Republican presidents—Harding, Coolidge, and Hoover—who followed him, they associated them with political corruption, big business, and prohibition—three things which they profoundly detested. Hoover, a Quaker, was regarded as an insincere "milk-face", because as president he was also commander-in-chief of the American armed forces. Later, President Franklin Roosevelt was suspected as the leader of a political party with too much Catholic support, although Mrs. Roosevelt came to be respected by Jehovah's Witnesses for her favourable stand on civil liberties. In Canada, the situation was no different, and although Watch Tower publications seldom mentioned individual politicians, they indicated no love for certain Canadian institutions. In its February 25, 1925, issue, the *Golden Age* openly criticized the office of the governor general of Canada. It remarked: "Canada the land of the Free, loves its shackles, as is shown by the statement of the cost of the upkeep of one of its out-of-date British traditions." Then, to drive the point home it stated: "Over half a million per year to keep one amiable English gentleman fed and housed for a year is an expensive luxury when we consider that our citizens, because they cannot eat regularly, leave the country in droves to get jobs in the U.S.A." There was nothing pro-American in the magazine's observations either, for it concluded by saying: "In the meantime, the 'peaceful penetration' of American dollars goes on apace; and we witness the piecemeal buying of Canada by American dollars."

In addition, the Watch Tower Society held a series of conventions at which world rulers, both religious and secular, were declared to be objects of Jehovah's wrath. At Cedar Point, Ohio, in 1922, the League of Nations was labelled the "Devil's scheme", and the American Federal Council of Churches was charged with blasphemy for calling it "the political expression of the kingdom of God on earth". Bible Students were therefore admonished to "advertise the King [Christ Jesus] and the Kingdom" rather than an international peace organization which was bound to fail. In Los Angeles the following year, the clergy were denounced for their support of war and—in the case of modernists—for "their God dishonoring doctrines of higher criticism and evolution". To make the resolution known, forty-five million copies of it were printed and distributed. In 1924 the clergy were again indicted, this time in Columbus, Ohio. But in 1926 Judge Rutherford, at a convention in the Alexandra Palace, London, England, unleashed a verbal broadside at the British Empire and the League of Nations. The latter was described as the "abomination of desolation". In 1927 the Bible Students' annual convention was held in Toronto—in spite of opposition from the city's press—and Judge Rutherford gave a public address entitled "To the Peoples of 'Christendom' " which was broadcast over an international radio chain to listeners throughout Canada and the United States. At this time, another resolution was adopted which condemned the "unholy alliance" of politicians, big business, and the clergy of Christendom.

Finally, though a resolution passed at a Detroit, Michigan, convention in 1928 was directed at Satan himself, Judge Rutherford referred to "the men in office" and "the blind preachers who have misled the people". There was no doubt that the Bible Students regarded both as Satan's representatives.[34]

Such jeremiads were often received with hostility; clergymen, politicians, and businessmen did not like being labelled the Devil's tools. Still, during the 1920s, Bible Students were generally allowed to spread their message in English Canada with little interference from anyone. After all, they were not the only ones who used strong language, and many sympathized with what they had to say about the great ones of the earth. The labour movement and many farmers certainly agreed with what they said about the business community; Orangemen, and Protestants in general, appreciated their attacks on the Church of Rome; and as far as politicians were concerned, they were generally regarded as fair game by almost everyone. Nevertheless, Bible Students did meet some opposition. In August 1920, they were described as pro-Soviet by the Canadian Department of Labour.[35] The most frequent charges against them involved the issues of canvassing without a licence and violating the Lord's Day Act by preaching from house to house on Sundays. Even then, when brought before the courts, more often than not they were acquitted.

In February 1925 H. Bailes was brought before a Calgary, Alberta, magistrate for selling without a licence, but the magistrate's decision was in Bailes's favour.[36] A year later a French-Canadian Bible Student was arrested on the same charge in St. Boniface, Manitoba, as was Osmond Metcalfe, for preaching to the chief licence inspector at the Winnipeg City Hall annex offices in 1930. But in both cases the magistrates ruled that the accused had done nothing illegal.[37] In Ontario, after they began calling from door to door on Sundays in 1927, Bible Students were arrested on a number of occasions for violating the Lord's Day Act. Norman Dove was stopped while preaching on a Sunday in February 1929, as was A. G. Cameron on March 3. Both were brought to trial and acquitted,[38] but in the following year, Ontario policemen continued to arrest Bible Students on the same charge. Mrs. C. L. Nicoll, A. Hopkins, Fred Fruk, J. Whitehouse, and William Bold were arrested in Toronto,[39] and Mrs.

B. W. Holland and John and Robert Stephens in Port Elgin.[40] As in 1929, magistrates held them not guilty, and eventually Ontario police left the Bible Students alone.

In Quebec, the situation was much different. In 1924, for the first time, Bible Students began a concentrated drive to spread their teachings throughout the province. A small number of colporteurs began to distribute large quantities of literature—particularly the sharply anti-clerical publications *Immortality*, *Warning*, and *Indictment*—in both French and English.[41] Almost immediately they got into trouble. On August 11, 1924, both P. A. Robertson and Gerald Barry, the son of an Anglican priest, were arrested at Ste. Anne de Beaupré for selling a French edition of the book *The Harp of God*. According to Barry, they were first taken to the local priest's house where they had a long talk. They were then driven to Quebec City where they were lodged overnight in jail. The next day they were released on bail, and on August 28 they were acquitted of having violated a municipal licence ordinance.[42] In February 1925 nine colporteurs were arrested in English-speaking Westmount for canvassing without licences, but the city later decided to drop the charges.[43] The city of Rosemount reacted differently, and in April of the same year it took René Marcotte to court for selling books in its jurisdiction without a municipal licence. Recorder G. H. Semple handed Marcotte and the Bible Students an important victory when he held that under provincial law the representatives of religious organizations were exempt from licence requirements.[44]

This, however, did not stop the police from arresting Bible Students in other parts of Quebec. On May 11, 1925, a colporteur, Findley Lister, was arrested in Quebec City; on May 14 four of his fellows were charged in Lévis; on May 16 A. L. Deakman and P. A. Robertson were jailed for five days at St. Jerome along with two other Bible Students, G. H. Waterer and W. J. Waterer.[45] Though in every instance the charges were ultimately dropped or magistrates held them not guilty of violating any law, the Bible Students were faced with serious opposition from both the Quebec police and the municipal authorities.

The authorities cared nothing about licence laws, of course. In point of fact, they were disturbed by the nature of the Bible Students' activities. For the first time since the conquest of Canada by the British, a non-Catholic religious organization was making a serious effort to make converts among French Canadians, and also was distributing great quantities of openly anti-Catholic literature. In 1924 and 1925 the Bible Students had distributed some 115,000 copies of the leaflet *Indictment* alone.[46] Catholic clergymen and many laymen were furious. As a result they determined to put a stop to what the Bible Students were doing. Just how serious they were was demonstrated at the small town of Coaticook in the Eastern Townships on May 28, 1925. Two female Bible Student colporteurs were arrested and charged under the criminal code with blasphemous libel for distributing literature attacking the Roman Catholic clergy. Fortunately for them, the magistrate held that blasphemous libel must constitute an attack on the Deity, not just those who claimed to represent Him.[47] But if the police did not continue to press charges on the basis of blasphemous libel, they determined to continue to harass the Bible Students on licence-law charges.

Over the next few years Bible Students were arrested again and again at places large and small throughout the province. In September 1925 a colporteur was arrested at Lake Megantic.[48] In 1929 and 1930 others were brought to court at Lévis, Roberval, Causapscal, and Quebec City, always on licence-law charges.[49] Most of their troubles, however, occurred in Montreal, where they concentrated their efforts. So often were they arrested for canvassing without a licence that, despite repeated acquittals, they determined to take the City of Montreal to court. They launched a suit against the city in the name of colporteur A. Dufresne in November 1929. The case came before the superior court in January 1930, but was postponed. In February the city offered Dufresne seventy-five dollars damages and fifty dollars to cover court costs. It also agreed to permit the Bible Students to carry on their activities unhindered.[50]

Though indignation against the Bible Students was growing, the Quebec provincial government as yet had done nothing to support municipalities anxious to curb them. In the rest of Canada neither provincial nor municipal authorities seemed to care one whit what they did. True, there had been the few licence cases and, in Ontario, the "Lord's Day Act" cases; but, in general, the Bible Student-Witnesses were quite free to preach wherever they went and to proclaim Jehovah's coming destruction of the wicked. Yet in one important area, they were to run afoul of officialdom. They came into conflict with both the Liberal government of W. L. Mackenzie King and the Conservative administration of R. B. Bennett. The issue was over their use of radio.

CHAPTER FIVE

the battles of the air waves

Give me the liberty to know, to utter, and to argue freely according to conscience, above all liberties.

JOHN MILTON *Areopagitica*

QUICK TO USE any new medium of communication, the Bible Students took their message to radio very early. In 1922 the Watch Tower Society purchased land at Staten Island, New York, for its own radio station and in 1924 began broadcasting from station WBBR. About the same time, Canadian Bible Students began to obtain broadcasting licences. Between 1924 and 1928 they owned four Canadian stations: CKCX Toronto, CHUC Saskatoon, CHCY Edmonton, and CFYC Vancouver. They also operated station CJYC Toronto through a holding company, the Universal Broadcasting Company, and, in addition, they regularly obtained time on commercial radio stations to give sermons and Bible lectures.[1]

The five International Bible Students Association radio stations were apparently regarded with favour, or at least with tolerance, by the general public. Although much of their broadcasting time was devoted to sermons, they also played sacred and popular music, and produced programs of an educational nature and concerts for disabled veterans of the First World War.[2] Their broadcasts were considered by outside observers to be of very high quality.[3] By 1927, however, they were in serious trouble with the Department of Marine and Fisheries, the federal department responsible for the control of radio in Canada. When Judge Rutherford delivered the lecture "Freedom for the Peoples" over the air from the Toronto IBSA convention in 1927, he angered a large number of important persons, particularly in Ontario. Thus, pressure was brought to bear on the federal government to curtail Bible Student broadcasting.[4] But of equal importance in making the Bible Students unpopular with the Department of Marine and Fisheries were events which happened in Saskatchewan.

During the mid and late 1920s, a strong spirit of anti-Catholicism was sweeping much of English-speaking Canada. In Mexico, the revolutionary government of that country was locked in a bitter struggle with the Church of Rome over certain sections of the Mexican Constitution of 1917; in the United States there was also much anti-Catholic sentiment. Thus, traditional opponents of the Church of Rome in Canada, such as the Orange and Masonic Lodges, fanned anti-Catholicism to a white heat. The *Orange Sentinel* frequently carried articles on the Mexican situation which pictured Mexican Catholic leaders as arch-reactionaries and anti-democrats of the worst sort. In addition, many Protestants, particularly in Saskatchewan, were stirred up over the question of separate, French-language, Roman Catholic schools which, it was argued, discriminated against Anglo-Protestant children.[5] In consequence, a new and even more militant anti-Catholic movement came into being under the leadership of an ex-Catholic, Irish-Canadian extremist, J. J. Maloney:[6] this organization was the Ku Klux Klan. Unfortunately for the Bible Students, radio station CHUC rented two hours of broadcast time to Maloney while he was on a major organizing campaign for the Klan throughout Saskatchewan in the winter of 1927–28.

During the first two years of its existence, CHUC, the first Bible Student station in Canada, had been operated by representatives of the local congregation at Saskatoon, William P. Flewwelling and George Naish.[7] But by 1927 the situation had changed: Walter Salter had insisted that the station be placed directly under the control of the Watch Tower Society's Toronto branch. He appointed a new manager, Clifford Roberts, in charge of the Saskatoon studios of

CHUC. Salter, who was gradually becoming estranged from his breth-ren over what they considered to be his high-handed behaviour and personal arrogance, was quite interested in the money-making aspects of broadcasting. He ordered Roberts to put CHUC on a commercial basis, something which local Bible Students had carefully avoided as being contrary to the Lord's will. According to Salter's wishes, the new station manager began to sell radio time and made the serious mistake of permitting Ku Klux Klansman Maloney to broadcast over CHUC.[8]

On January 7, 1927, Commander C. P. Edwards, radio director for the Department of Marine and Fisheries, sent a memorandum to Alexander Johnston, Deputy Minister of the department, in which he claimed that CHUC was "in trouble again". He then went on to tell his superior about the Ku Klux Klan programs which, he stated, had been investigated by the Royal Canadian Mounted Police and re-ported to the department by them. Edwards remarked: "The station itself has not violated any of the regulations, but apparently they cater to this type of broadcast."[9] In fact, Edwards was being unfair. Except for Judge Rutherford's 1927 speech, Bible Student broadcasts had been relatively mild, and IBSA stations did not ordinarily rent time to extremists such as Maloney. CHUC had never really been in any serious trouble before, either. It is true that in January 1927 a sub-committee of the Saskatoon Board of Trade had requested that the Bible Student station be prohibited from preaching sermons over the airwaves ex-cept on Sundays. Yet this event was not important. A letter in the *Saskatoon Daily Star* showed that the Board of Trade did not support its sub-committee,[10] and numerous letters and petitions, many signed by non-Bible Students, indicated that the station's sermons were reasonably popular throughout Saskatchewan.[11]

In addition, when the Bible Students were made aware of the dis-pleasure of the Department of Marine and Fisheries over the Maloney broadcasts, Walter Salter, in effect, apologized. On January 18, 1928, he wrote to Deputy Minister Johnston and stated: "The criticism that I received, and possibly that you also received, revolved around the broadcasting of two lectures by one J. J. Maloney under the auspices of the KKK, who took advantage of the occasion to slander the Roman Catholic Church."[12] Salter then attempted to blame the whole affair on Roberts in Saskatoon. He asserted that the contract between CHUC and Maloney had never been authorized by "this office" and stressed that he would not tolerate "any of our stations slandering any other organization".[13]

But it is quite obvious that the Department of Marine and Fisheries was thoroughly annoyed with the Bible Students and was determined to put an end to their ownership of independent radio stations. Both the Minister of Marine and Fisheries, Arthur Cardin, and the Deputy Minister were staunch Roman Catholics; and Johnston was anxious to punish the Bible Students for the "indiscretion" of allowing criticism of his church to be broadcast over IBSA stations. When he received Commander Edwards' memorandum, he wrote on the bottom of it in red type: "The operations of CHUC should be carefully observed and considered when time for renewal of license arrives. A.J."[14]

A few months later in March 1928, Arthur Cardin not only refused to renew CHUC's licence but those of all Bible Student stations in Canada. The minister claimed that he received many complaints regarding the five stations and was simply acting in response to public wishes. Speaking in the House of Commons, he stated:

The matter being broadcast is generally described by complainants as having become intolerable; the propaganda carried on under the name of Bible talks is said to be unpatriotic and abusive of all our churches. Evidence would appear to show that the tone of the preaching seems to be that all organized churches are corrupt and in alliance with unrighteous forces, that the entire system of society is wrong and that all governments are to be condemned.[15]

The Bible Students did not accept Cardin's action quietly, but caused a nationwide storm. A petition addressed to Prime Minister Mackenzie King was circulated throughout Canada to solicit public support to have the radio licences renewed. It was signed by 458,026 citizens and in due course was presented to Parliament.[16] Public meetings were held from coast to coast at which influential citizens were asked to speak; a "statement of facts" was prepared and submitted to each Member of Parliament; thousands of letters and telegrams were sent to the government; and finally, personal interviews were arranged with Cardin.[17]

The Speaker of the House of Commons refused to receive the petitions on the grounds that they were improperly addressed.[18] Nevertheless, MPs had already presented many of them,[19] and the Bible Students were able to claim great public support. The public meetings were well attended, and civil libertarians and labour leaders chastised the Minister of Marine and Fisheries for his actions.[20] In Toronto, James Simpson, vice-president of the Trades and Labour Congress of Canada, denounced the government and personally defended Judge Rutherford:

In regard to the address delivered by Judge Rutherford at the great annual convention of the Association in the City of Toronto last year, it was a remarkable address, harmonizing the spiritual and moral claims of religion with the greater responsibilities of religious, denominational, fundamental and economic conditions. There are few ministers who seem to recognize that our existing industrial and financial conditions are but a reflex of the misapplications of the teaching of Christ to modern industrial life. I would like to see more of the pulpits used for such deliverance as that of Judge Rutherford. The result would be a greater appreciation of the Christian church on the part of the masses of the people. If Judge Rutherford did no more good during his visit here than expose the wrong done to the children and workers in Southern cotton fields by the bill passed by Congress, and the injustices suffered by coal miners, awakening in the minds of some such thoughts that would eventuate in a measure of relief to those unfortunate ones, his visit was well worth while. When the last trumpet is sounded he will, in my humble judgment, be much nearer the throne of heavenly grace than the ministers that criticize and condemn him.[21]

But the most dramatic support for the Bible Students came from western Canada, from Saskatchewan in particular. J. J. Maloney wired Prime Minister Mackenzie King:

CHUC broadcasting station informs me that the Deputy Minister of Marines has denied them renewal of their license because of Protestant lectures going over their station[.] Petitions with two hundred thousand names being circulated in this province which is 80 percent Protestant[.] I am calling your attention on the advice of the President of the Liberal Executive.[22]

A few weeks later, A. R. Pottle, radio inspector at Regina, sent a letter to C. P. Edwards in Ottawa, plus editorials over the radio-licence issue from Regina and Moose Jaw newspapers which were highly critical of the federal government. In his letter Pottle pointed out that the government's refusal to renew IBSA radio licences had become a *cause célèbre*. Eighty copies of a petition against the "cancellation" of CHUC's licence were circulating throughout the province; the Bible Students were carrying on a door-to-door canvass over the issue; and J. J. Maloney had obtained one thousand signatures at a KKK meeting in support of the relicensing of Bible Student stations.[23] Evidently, too, practically all Protestants in the province were convinced that the Bible Students were victims of Roman Catholic discrimination. For on April 17, 1928, J. Macklem, radio inspector at Saskatoon, reported to the Ottawa radio director: "There appears to be a tremendous amount of reaction in connection with this matter and a large number of societies, organizations of various kinds and churches are taking the matter up, not on behalf of the Bible Students, but in defence of the principle of religious societies being allowed to broadcast."[24] What was perhaps most outstanding was that Macklem reported that petitions in favour of relicensing CHUC were being signed in every Protestant church in the city, and two mass meetings of protest over the government's action had already been held—one under the auspices of the Saskatoon Ministerial Association.[25] Evidently the Bible Students had annoyed few, in western Canada at least, except members of the Church of Rome. For many, the issue surrounding their loss of the right to broadcast became one of a series of issues which was to lead to the defeat in 1929 of the Liberal government of Saskatchewan—which, like its federal counterpart, was viewed as too pro-Catholic—and to its replacement by a Conservative-led coalition under Dr. J. T. M. Anderson.[26]

In Parliament members of the Opposition debated the radio-licence question and accused Arthur Cardin and the Liberal government of outright religious discrimination.[27] J. S. Woodsworth, Labour Member of Parliament for Winnipeg North Centre, requested on behalf of A. A. Heaps, the Member for Winnipeg North, that all correspondence relating to IBSA broadcasting be tabled.[28] When Cardin complied with Woodsworth's request, the number and nature of anti-Bible Student complaints proved to be insignificant. Although there was much correspondence which referred to Bible Student activities prior to the time the Association had begun broadcasting in 1924, only seventy items from the files of the Department of Marine and Fisheries related to their radio activities. There were only three complaints from the Vancouver area, five from Edmonton, and six relating to Saskatoon; the remainder of the complaints were from Toronto. One was from a Baptist preacher, the Reverend W. A. Cameron, who claimed that the Bible Students had cut in on his radio service. A few related to interference with the Dempsey-Sharkey and Dempsey-Tunney boxing matches. Another correspondent complained that their programs were "too American", then stated in the same letter that they prevented him from getting American stations! There were, of course, other more general complaints and a petition signed by 199 individuals who were displeased with the nature of biblical interpretations presented by Bible Student speakers.[29] In contrast, the Bible Students were able to point to the mass public support they had obtained during the spring of 1928. But the Minister of Marine and Fisheries adamantly refused to yield to public demands or severe criticism from both opposition and government Members of Parliament.[30] After March 31, 1928, IBSA stations stayed off the air.

Bible Students and great numbers of Canadian Protestants believed that the major reason behind the government's refusal to renew their licences was religious, but the Opposition, discussing the matter in Parliament, pointed also to what seemed to be a flagrant act of political patronage at the expense of station CJYC Toronto. In attempting to have their stations relicensed, the Bible Students had gone to the press with their story. Many newspapers proved unwilling to support them, and some were openly hostile. The *Golden Age* stated that "the Press Associations have deliberately ignored everything given to them which would explain the charges made against the IBSA stations in Canada",[31] and charged the press with biased reporting. As an example, the *Golden Age* reprinted a *Toronto Daily Star* story, based on the complaints tabled in the House of Commons, which had thrown a very unfavourable light on Bible Student broadcasting.[32] If the Bible Students suspected that the *Star* had any direct interest in the question, they never voiced it, but, according to George Greary, Conservative Member of Parliament for Toronto South, the newspaper had benefited directly from the government's refusal to renew CJYC's licence.

Greary noted that CJYC and another Toronto station, CFRB, had been the only stations of the 580-kilocycle wave-length. Another wave-length, known as the 840-kilocycle wave-length, had been shared among United States broadcasters and three Toronto stations—CKCL, the Dominion Battery Company; CKNC, the Canadian National Carbon Company; and station CFCA, owned by the *Toronto Daily Star*. A third wave-length, the 960-kilocycle, had been given to the brewing company of Gooderham and Worts for the sole use of its station CKGW. When CJYC's licence was not renewed, CFRB, the other half-user of the 580-kilocycle wave-length, was given the 960-kilocycle wave-length to share with Gooderham and Worts. The two competitors of the *Toronto Daily Star* station were then moved to the 580-kilocycle wave-length and the *Star* station, CFCA, was given the entire Canadian share of the 840 wave-length. Said Greary: "The bald fact remains that they [the *Daily Star*] have been given the possession of an exclusive Canadian channel, and they can use this channel twenty-four hours a day and seven days a week." The Member from Toronto South then accused the *Star* of bringing influence to bear on the government and charged Cardin with entirely bad judgment.[33]

Besides pointing out what they believed to be the complicity of the *Toronto Star*, other Members of Parliament criticized Cardin and the government for violating freedom of speech and for prohibiting the Bible Students from owning radio stations when other religions continued to be allowed to do so.[34] T. W. Bird, Liberal Progressive from Nelson, Manitoba, claimed that the government's action in respect to the Bible Students had come as a result of pressures from three classes of Canadians: "those who were antipathetic to the religious views of the Bible Students"; people who were "very patriotic"; and "people who think the air should be monopolized by jazz music and prize fights".[35] MPS also gave the Bible Students favourable testimonials. Bird remarked that "they are amongst our best Canadian citizens; they can be classified as the very best of our Canadian citizens."[36] John Evans, Liberal Progressive from Rosetown, quoted R. G. Scott, M.D., Superintendent of the Anna Turnbull Hospital at Wakaw, Saskatchewan, and a Presbyterian minister, to the effect that "the Bible Student movement has done a lot of good and is still doing a lot of good".[37] The Minister of Marine and Fisheries remained unimpressed. He stoutly denied that he had acted out of either prejudice toward the Bible Students or favouritism toward the *Toronto Star.* The most he would do was promise to have the case of the Universal Radio Company placed before a commission which the government had agreed to establish to investigate the whole question of Canadian broadcasting.[38] This action led directly to the establishment of the Canadian Broadcasting Corporation,[39] but at the time it did nothing positive for the Bible Students. In effect, Cardin made it plain that no radio licences would again be granted to them under his ministry.

Nevertheless, the Bible Students did not go off the air. During the next few years they bought program time on about twenty-five Canadian radio stations and continued to give regular broadcasts.[40] In fact, Judge Rutherford's speeches, broadcast from recordings, began to be heard more often over Canadian radio. But his messages infuriated important segments of the Canadian public; when Conservative Prime Minister R. B. Bennett appointed Hector Charlesworth, the former editor of *Saturday Night,* chairman of the Canadian Radio Commission, it was not long before Rutherford's broadcasts over Canadian outlets were dropped. On January 18, 1933, the Canadian Radio Commission sent the following telegram to radio stations throughout the country: "Speeches of one Judge Rutherford, foreign anti-social agitator, must not be broadcast on Canadian stations until the continuity or records of same are submitted to Canadian radio broadcasting commission for approval. Hector Charlesworth, Chairman."[41]

When Judge Rutherford had delivered his famous July 1927 address in Toronto, he apparently had greatly angered Charlesworth, as well as other Canadians. As indicated, the Watch Tower president had issued a stinging denunciation of both Christendom and professional politicians. But what seemed to upset Charlesworth most was Rutherford's severe censure of the business community. Among other things, the judge had stated:

The masses of the people are entitled to self-government exercised by the people for the general welfare of all; but instead of enjoying such rights a small minority rules; that the money power of the world has been concentrated into the hands of a few men called high financiers, and these in turn have corrupted the men who make and execute the laws of the nations, and the faithless clergy have voluntarily joined forces with the high financiers and professional politicians, and that the said unholy alliance constitutes the governing powers that rule the peoples.[42]

Saturday Night responded to Rutherford's discourses with a bitter editorial; it appeared on the front page of the August 6, 1927, issue of the Toronto magazine and was probably penned by Charlesworth himself:[43]

Recently Toronto had the doubtful honor of entertaining once more a heavy-jowled flannel-mouth known as "Judge" J. F. Rutherford, Grand Vizier of the "Russellites" or the International Bible Students' Association, together with some thousands of his followers. What the said Rutherford is a "Judge" of we do not know,—perhaps of cigars, perhaps of fat swine,—perhaps he is called "Judge" by way of persiflage, just as an elevator man is called "Cap". What we wish to emphasize is that "Judges" and wandering orators of the Rutherford type are unwelcome guests. This is we hope the last occasion on which the Russellite Chieftain and his mob of "students" will be allowed to misuse important civic property like the Canadian National Exhibition Grounds. The average international convention is more than welcome in Toronto but its citizens want no more "Russellite" gatherings here. Such conventions bring small gain, since most of the delegates travel in "tin lizzies" and bring their dough-nuts with them.

Rutherford is no stranger in Toronto. He comes round every once in a while heralded by a slogan of which he is the author: "Millions Now Living Will Never Die". There is no harm in his cherishing that delusion; but when he violates the law of hospitality by abuse of the British Empire (which he regards as a section of one of the beasts of the Apocalypse); when he traduces every reputable clergyman and every well-to-do citizen in the community, he is going a little too far. It is true that he is equally abusive of fellow citizens in the United States but let him stay on his own soil and hurl his mud there. This same Rutherford spent a term in a detention camp after the United States entered the Great War, and prior to that time the "Russellites" had been in trouble with Canadian authorities because their extensive publishing department had sold out to Bernstorff and was caught in the act of distributing pro-German propaganda in Canadian towns and cities.

The war is over and peace-loving people are willing to let by-gones be by-gones, but they do object to wandering blatherskites and professional liars starting the war all over again on Canadian soil. That Rutherford is a lying demagogue is apparent from the text of his addresses, in which he exploits the old fallacy that there is one law for the rich and another for the poor, a condition which is certainly not true of Canada, or any part of the British Empire. Clerical dialecticians may be left to answer his attacks on Christianity and refute the charge that their master is Satan, if they wish. The day that the "common people" yield to his appeal and "forsake organized Christianity and its clergy as the instruments of the devil" will be a hey-day for Satan if that historic person still happens to be going about like a roaring lion. When the "Judge" indulges in tirades against capital and capitalists as oppressors of the common people, he not only prompts curiosity as to his own bank account, but utters a dangerous falsehood. It is true that there has been a great accumulation of capital in the hands of a comparatively small group, but it is also true, especially in America, that never have conditions been so good for the poor; never at any time in the history of mankind was labor so well rewarded, never was so much practical philanthropy practiced for the care of the weak and needy, never was so much capital freely available for the care and comfort of the under-privileged. Only a fool or a liar could deny these facts.

The reason this loquacious "Judge" has received so much attention of late is that he managed to bulldoze his way into control of the air during the progress of the Russellite convention of Toronto. He gave credit for this, not to himself, but to "Jehovah, the only true God", who, he said had "graciously used the National Broadcasting Company for his divine purposes". The tribal god of the Russellites certainly gained no popularity with users of radio thereby; their deliberations were a nightly nuisance on the air. On the night of July 21st reputable fathers of families anxious to listen in on the progress of the Dempsey-Sharkey prize fight were kept out by the high power oratory at the Toronto Coliseum. On Sunday, July 24th, the religiously inclined were prevented from hearing their favorite message because the leather-lunged Ruther-ford had the air. Millions now living would rather die than be compelled to listen very often to his discourses.

Charlesworth undoubtedly needed little urging to act against Rutherford; if the 1927 *Saturday Night* editorial was any indication, the radio commission chairman's animosity toward the Watch Tower president was little short of personal hatred. But Charlesworth may also have been motivated in January 1933 by complaints from others. A press dispatch appearing in the *Telegraph-Journal* of Saint John, New Brunswick, reported that three Anglican clergymen—the Rev-erend Canon R. P. McKim, Rector of St. Luke's; the Reverend W. C. V. Martin, Rector of St. Mary's; and the Reverend T. Hudson Steward, Rector of St. John's (Stone) Church—had sent a "dignified complaint" about Judge Rutherford's broadcasts to Charlesworth.[44]

Whatever the case may have been, Charlesworth's action created a storm. On January 19 Judge Rutherford released a tract entitled *Important Notice* which was a veritable broadside against the reli-gious and political authorities of Canada and the British Empire. Included in the leaflet, which was printed in 1,250,000 copies in English, French, and Ukrainian and distributed nationwide,[45] was the statement "that the clergymen of the Anglican church, contrary to their claim, do not in fact represent Jehovah God and Christ Jesus and his kingdom, but they do represent Satan the Devil and that thereby the people are deceived". Jehovah's Witnesses then proceeded to take up a petition for submission to Parliament which was circulated from coast to coast. Ultimately 406,270 signatures were obtained.[46] The Witnesses also flooded the radio commission with letters of protest, wrote letters to local newspapers, and held meetings in public halls throughout Canada.[47] Finally, after the petition was submitted to Parliament, two representatives of the Watch Tower Society interviewed Prime Minister Bennett who, according to them, "promised to have the radio commission appear before him and look thoroughly into the matter with a view to taking proper action".[48]

Some newspapers, particularly in western Canada, roundly criticized Charlesworth for attempting to muzzle free speech. The *Winnipeg Free Press* editorialized: "The best and safest plan for the Commission is to make up its mind that it is dealing with a free people and, therefore, despite any ideas in high places as to what is good for licence holders, will proceed to present as many facets as possible of world opinion."[49] The newspaper proceeded to ridicule Charlesworth personally in an Arch Dale cartoon which showed the radio commission chairman as King Canute trying to stem the radio waves carrying Rutherford's broadcasts from the United States. *Hush*, a Winnipeg periodical, suggested that Charlesworth, "that old Saturday Night Big Interest sweetheart", had banned Rutherford's broadcast at the order of the clergy and the same interests who had removed Winnipeg's Judge Stubbs from the bench.[50] *Justice*, a Halifax, Nova Scotia, publication, stated bluntly that it had been the "Tory War-Mongers" who had "ruled Judge Rutherford off the air" for his "stinging rebuke" of big business.[51] *Hush* and *Justice* reflected the attitudes of many labour spokesmen and radicals. Labour leaders, bitterly critical of the business community during the first years of the depression, were also sympathetic to Judge Rutherford, as James Simpson had been in 1928. The very statements that enraged Hector Charlesworth made Rutherford popular with large numbers of the working classes.

Much of the press and the public sided with Charlesworth, however, or viewed the matter lightly. The *Toronto Mail and Empire* compared the 1933 action taken by the chairman of the Canadian Radio Commission with Arthur Cardin's refusal to renew IBSA radio licences "in 1929 [*sic*]" and charged the Watch Tower Society with supplying "the unthinking with the most disturbing revolutionary thinking".[52] The *Moncton Daily Times* was particularly angered by the distribution of *Important Notices*, which it referred to as "blasphemous Rutherford leaflets".[53] On the other hand, the *Toronto Daily Star* treated the whole issue facetiously by suggesting that it would be great fun to listen to a debate between Rutherford and Charlesworth in Massey Hall, Toronto.[54]

The clergy apparently gave solid support to Charlesworth, as the radio commission later testified. At least one Anglican clergyman suggested that "Judge Rutherford's diatribe against the Anglican church as a whole would in itself warrant the Radio Commission of Canada in refusing the Russellites the existing facilities for broadcasting without first submitting the same to the broadcasting commission."[55]

In Montreal one young Witness, Edward Noseworthy, was convicted before Recorder G. H. Semple, a magistrate usually sympathetic to Jehovah's Witnesses, for distributing the *Important Notice*. According to Semple, the circular was "subversive of peace, order and good government".[56] Apparently what offended him was a question in it which asked: "Have the people of Canada reached such a state of low intellectuality that they need a 'wise' radio commission to approve what they shall hear from the Bible?"[57]

The issue involving the action of the radio commission and the circulation of the *Important Notice* first came before Parliament on March 2, 1933. Vincent Dupuis, Liberal Member for Laprairie-Napierville, raised a question on the orders of the day. Dupuis, angered at what he considered to be a "direct insult to the Anglican denomination" in the Watch Tower broadside, asked Postmaster General Arthur Sauvé what he was doing to prohibit the distribution of the offending leaflet by the postal department.[58] Several weeks later J. L. Brown, Liberal Progressive Member for Lisgar, Saskatchewan, remarked that he had received numerous letters "protesting against the action of the radio commission in banning Judge Rutherford's lectures" and asked the Minister of Marine, Alfred Duranleau, to make a brief statement to clarify the situation.[59] Duranleau later replied by reading a letter from the radio commission.

According to the letter, the radio commission had received many complaints about the "abusive and mischievous character of the speeches of Judge Rutherford being broadcast in Canada", but it had taken no action until it obtained copies of Rutherford's speeches from the Watch Tower offices at 40 Irwin Avenue, Toronto. Subsequently it had made Charlesworth issue his January 18 telegram. The commission also asserted that since Rutherford's lectures were transcribed they must be submitted to prior censorship before being broadcast in Canada: "As Rutherford lived in the United States and did not deliver his speeches in person in Canada, he could not be made amenable to Canadian laws." The commission claimed:

Anxious that it could be clear there was no intention of interfering with the legitimate exercise of free speech the commission requested the representative of the International Bible Students, the organization sponsoring Rutherford in Canada, to submit the records of the Rutherford speeches, together with the texts on which they were based. This request was not complied with, and the only response was the wide distribution of printed literature in Canada attacking the commission and religious institutions and clergy, in which the chairman of the commission was described as liar, thief, Judas and polecat, and therefore fit to associate only with the clergy.[60]

At the time, Brown and other members of the House of Commons seemed satisfied with the statement, but this was not the end of the matter. It was true, as the commission had asserted, that the Witnesses had unleashed a campaign of bitter invective against Charlesworth. In a series of articles in the issues of March 1, 15, and 29, the *Golden Age* had referred to the chairman of the radio commission by the terms mentioned in the commission's letter and many more in the same vein. This attitude, of course, incensed many Canadians who might ordinarily have sympathized with the Witnesses' arguments that Rutherford was being denied freedom of speech. But on April 21, Brown raised the matter in Parliament again. He had been visited by "one of Judge Rutherford's disciples" who had shown him a copy of the 1927 *Saturday Night* anti-Rutherford editorial and therefore felt constrained to demonstrate in the House of Commons that Charlesworth "was not unprejudiced". Thereupon he read some excerpts from the editorial into the record of *The Debates of the House of*

Commons and stated: "I repeat however that the action of the radio commission is not in harmony with my views in regard to the rights of a man to promulgate whatever doctrine he wishes."[61]

Thomas Reid, Liberal Member for New Westminster, revealed another interesting fact. He indicated that he had written to Charlesworth earlier concerning his January 18 telegram. Charlesworth, in reply to Reid's letter, stated that Judge Rutherford had called the radio commission chairman "a thief, a liar, a Judas and a polecat, and therefore fit only to associate with the clergy".[62] Charlesworth had also remarked: "You will see plainly that a man who interlards such attacks with his interpretations of prophecy is an objectionable person to have on the air in Canada."[63] When Reid quoted Charlesworth in letters to irate Jehovah's Witnesses, one of them wrote to Rutherford who, in turn, communicated with Reid as follows:

A letter just received by me quotes from a letter written by you on March 28th to Mr. A. Kennett of Vancouver, B.C., the following:

"Mr. Charlesworth makes the further statement that Judge Rutherford in his recent address called him a thief, a liar, a Judas and a polecat, and therefore, he stated, fit only to associate with the clergy."

Permit me to say, my dear sir, that never at any time in a public address have I even mentioned the name of Mr. Charlesworth and at no time have I ever indulged in such language as above quoted. Surely I should not be responsible for what others may say. I have never yet applied such epithets to any public man.[64]

Rutherford was stating the facts. Though he had roundly condemned clergymen, politicians, and entrepreneurs in general in the *Important Notice*, he had never stooped to personal invective and was as shocked as anyone at the harsh terminology used in the *Golden Age*. The editor, Clayton Woodworth, had apparently unleashed the bitter name-calling attack on Charlesworth without the judge's consent. The *Golden Age* made that clear,[65] and Woodworth later openly admitted that he had been reprimanded by the Watch Tower president.[66] The *Golden Age*'s lack of moderation had, nevertheless, already done the Witnesses' cause more harm than good, and while the matter was put straight in Parliament, the government, in the face of criticism from Brown, Reid, and J. S. Woodsworth, determined to support the radio commission.

The position taken by the commission and, therefore by the government, was that Rutherford was not being banned from radio in Canada; he must simply submit his lectures to prior radio commission censorship. The commission also asserted that other representatives of the Watch Tower Society or International Bible Students could continue to deliver sermons on Canadian stations.[67] The Witnesses were embittered by the government's decision, and many no doubt agreed with the characterization of Charlesworth in the *Golden Age*. Prior censorship of Rutherford's lectures, they felt sure, would take him off the air. As it was, the Watch Tower Society refused to submit records of Rutherford's speeches, and his voice was no longer heard over Canadian radio. Yet Charlesworth's action, taken at so much cost to his own reputation, probably hurt Judge Rutherford and Jehovah's Witnesses very little. Canadians could hear the Watch Tower president on American stations, and, while the Witnesses had obtained some bad publicity, they had also gained much sympathy. As was to be the case over and over again in future years, government actions to limit the activities of the Witnesses simply gave them more publicity and helped them to become more, rather than less, well known.

CHAPTER SIX

theocratic organization midst persecution

It must . . . be acknowledged that the conduct of the emperors who appeared the least favourable to the primitive church is by no means so criminal as that of modern sovereigns who have employed the arm of violence and terror against the religious opinions of any part of their subjects.

EDWARD GIBBON *The Decline and Fall of the Roman Empire*

THE YEAR 1933 was, in general, a difficult one for Jehovah's Witnesses. Not only did Hector Charlesworth put an end to Judge Rutherford's broadcasts over Canadian radio networks, but in the United States Roman Catholic action groups began to campaign to have him taken off the air as well.[1] In addition, large numbers of American Witnesses were arrested for distributing literature in contravention of municipal bylaws, particularly in New Jersey.[2] Overseas they were facing serious problems as well. They had already been under ban in Fascist Italy for a year; Japan restricted their activities; and, as one of its first oppressive acts, Hitler's new Nazi government outlawed them.[3]

The German situation was most grave. Early in April, less than two months after the Reichstag fire gave dictatorial power to the Nazis, the state of Bavaria declared Jehovah's Witnesses illegal. Roman Catholic clergy were given the responsibility for aiding the civil authorities by reporting members of the hated *Bibelforscher* or Bible Students (as the Witnesses were still known in Germany) for refusing to stop practising their faith.[4] During the same month the police also occupied the Watch Tower Society's offices at Magdeburg but, after finding nothing seditious, briefly restored them to their owners. In the month of June, however, the Bavarian ban was extended to Prussia and other parts of the Reich; and on June 28 the Society's Magdeburg properties were seized once again. The Witnesses were then already beginning to experience what one non-Witness later described as "sadism marked by an unending chain of physical and mental tortures, the likes of which no language in the world can express".[5]

The Witnesses reacted with increased militancy toward such events. In the United States they fought back by appealing to traditional American freedoms and damning their enemies as tools of the Devil. Pope Pius XI had decreed 1933 a holy year; Judge Rutherford delivered an April radio address over fifty-five stations entitled "Effect of the Holy Year on Peace and Prosperity" in which he forecast more troubles for the world.[6] In July, he released the booklet *Intolerance*, in relation to the New Jersey situation, after having delivered the text as a public talk—also widely broadcast—at Plainfield, New Jersey, while police machine-guns were pointed at his back.[7] In order to carry Rutherford's message as contained in *Intolerance* and in a similar booklet, *The Crisis*, throughout the United States, some 12,600 American Witnesses volunteered to invade unfriendly communities by the hundreds to contact people in every home.[8] Late in the year and early in 1934 these same door-to-door preachers, and many others, circulated a petition "vigorously protesting against Catholic intimidation and threats of freedom of speech over the radio". Nearly 2,500,000 signatures were obtained and submitted to Congress.[9]

In Germany the Witnesses first appealed to the authorities to check the persecution raging there, and when that did not work they openly defied the Nazi Führer and his regime. In June 1933 Judge Rutherford travelled to Berlin, where, with the aid of the American State Department, he sought to regain control of the Watch Tower properties at Magdeburg. While in Berlin he also read a "Declaration of

Facts" before an assembled audience of 7,000 who resolved to have the declaration made known to Nazi officials.[10] Later, when the persecution intensified, the Witnesses took stronger action. The November 1, 1933, issue of the *Watch Tower* carried an article entitled "Fear Them Not" in direct response to the German situation. In the following October, roughly 20,000 German Witnesses advised Hitler personally that they would obey God's commandments, as they understood them, at any cost: "If your government or officers do violence to us because we are obeying God, then our blood will be upon you and you will answer to Almighty God."[11] At the same time their brethren in other countries deluged Berlin with telegrams which read: "Hitler Government, Berlin, Germany. Your ill-treatment of Jehovah's Witnesses shocks all good people of earth and dishonors God's name. Refrain from further persecuting Jehovah's Witnesses; otherwise God will destroy you and your national party."[12]

Naturally, all these events, coupled with the action of the Canadian Radio Commission, had a profound effect on the Witnesses in Canada; like their co-believers in the United States and Germany, they went on the offensive. For instance, in the fall of 1933 they engaged in a blitz to place literature, this time in Quebec. They determined to swoop down on Quebec City like a plague of evangelistic locusts in the way that their brethren in the United States were doing with unfriendly towns. This necessitated bringing in Witnesses from great distances. There were none in Quebec City at the time and few in Montreal. But a convention was arranged for Montreal and a large contingent was brought in from Toronto. On the day following the convention forty carloads of 158 persons were dispatched to the Quebec provincial capital and at six-thirty in the morning they began to place Watch Tower booklets throughout the city.[13]

This event caused much local consternation. Forty-seven Roman Catholic bishops and archbishops were gathered from throughout the country for a plenary session of the Canadian episcopacy; and the Witnesses inadvertently met thousands of pious Catholics who, on their way to mass, were nonplussed by what they considered to be a general invasion of heretics. According to the Witnesses, "so great was the excitement in the town of Quebec that it well appeared that a foreign foe was trying to sack the city."[14] And they were not exaggerating. The Reverend Father Boulanger of Sacred Heart Church complained to the police,[15] and within half an hour they began to comb the city to make arrests.[16] But they succeeded in rounding up only twenty-nine of the Witnesses, who were finally charged with seditious conspiracy.[17] That was only part of what happened, though.

The police were determined to put an end to the circulation of Witness publications. They therefore seized about twenty-five "suitcases" of Watch Tower literature from eight cars[18] and made at least two highly questionable arrests which the Witnesses labelled "frameups". Lloyd Stewart, who claimed that he had never been involved in door-to-door pamphlet distribution, was arrested while on an errand about twelve hours after his brethren had called at Quebec City homes on the morning of October 3, 1933.[19] Frank Wainwright, by then secretary-treasurer of the International Bible Students Association of Canada, was charged with the possession of an obscene magazine which, he claimed, had been planted in his car by Quebec City policemen.[20] But, whether questionable or not, the actions of the police received hearty approval from most influential Quebec City citizens.

When the Witnesses were first brought to trial, a Roman Catholic canon testified that statements in their publications were a menace to government. A passage which particularly upset him was: "Although some of the clergy suppose they represent God, they in reality are servants of the devil and his empire."[21] Militia officer Henri DesRosiers, a crown witness who claimed to represent war veterans, also spoke against the accused.[22] Outside court, the Quebec City press censured the Witnesses severely. The English-language *Chronicle-Telegram* published an editorial entitled "Unwelcome Witnesses" in which it criticized religious proselytizing.[23] *Le Soleil* claimed that even Quebec Protestants were angered at Jehovah's Witnesses for the insult they had given to Catholic bishops.[24] Yet in the end most of the Witnesses who had been arrested for their part in the pamphlet blitz escaped punishment of any kind. Charges against most of them had to be dropped when the officers who had arrested them could identify only six of the thirty, including Lloyd Stewart, at their preliminary hearings. They had intentionally changed their appearance; the women, in particular, wore different hats.[25]

Others in other parts of the province of Quebec did not get off so lightly, for during the same year no fewer than fifty-nine Witnesses were charged with a variety of crimes including blasphemous libel, seditious conspiracy, violating the Lord's Day Act, disturbing the peace, and peddling without a licence.[26] When convicted, as they usually were in these cases, they were given severe sentences such as thirty days in jail for the rather minor offence of peddling without a licence.[27] In addition, the October 1933 pamphlet blitz caused the Quebec City council to pass Bylaw 184, which made it illegal for anyone to distribute printed materials in the city without police permission. Thereafter, anyone could be fined one hundred dollars for violating this ordinance.[28]

The Witnesses of Jehovah were in no way discouraged by Quebec's legal actions against them, neither were they very frightened by human government at any level. Thus they had determined to distribute the *Crisis* booklet with its story of persecution in New Jersey far and wide, particularly to men of public prominence, regardless of what anyone said. In Ottawa, where Parliament was in session in the spring of 1933, they decided to place it in the hands of practically every official, whether elected or appointed, from the Governor General down to anyone whose standing was above that of an ordinary clerk. Bank managers, businessmen, and clergymen were to receive their copies, too. So in order to deliver the booklet personally to individual government officials and Members of Parliament, they invaded the federal government buildings in droves.[29] The *1934 Yearbook of Jehovah's Witnesses* reported:

Early in the morning the workers, strong in the Lord and in the power of his might, visited the government buildings. When stopped by the government policemen they would tactfully leave, only to reappear later on another floor. As one worker was put out others continued the work, and the policemen had a merry time. By noon no serious difficulty had been encountered and 1,000 of the officials had been personally presented with a copy of the *Crisis* booklet.[30]

Naturally, spectacular events such as these made the Witnesses well known to almost everybody—exactly what they wanted. For whether their message was received favourably, rejected with anger, or simply ignored, at least it was heard. But far more important as far as their growth as a religious movement was concerned were several doctrinal developments and organizational changes within their own ranks.

The first of these was the exposition of a new doctrine. Pastor Russell had taught almost from the beginning of his ministry that the Bible Students were part of the elect class of 144,000 mentioned in Revelation 7 and 14, who would rule as king-priests with Christ during the millennium. In addition, he had stressed that the vast majority of mankind would inherit perfect life through the resurrection in a restored paradise-earth. But besides the "elect" and the majority of saved humans, the *Watch Tower* had taught that there was a third group, the "great multitude" of Revelation 7:9, who would receive heavenly life on a secondary plane. The *Watch Tower* also explained in 1923 that there would be a "sheep class", mentioned in Matthew 25:31–46, who would be divided from the "goats" in the time of the end. In 1932, Judge Rutherford had reasoned that these "sheep" were pictured by the ancient Rechabite Chieftain Jonadab who had joined King Jehu of Israel at the time of the destruction of the Baal priests of Queen Jezebel. Naturally these concepts were very complex, and, more significantly, they meant that the Witnesses saw their preaching work as directed only to the gathering of the 144,000 elect of God. Jehovah himself would deal with the other classes of mankind in His own due time. This all changed rather dramatically when, at a convention in Washington, D.C., in the spring of 1935, the Watch Tower president proclaimed that the "great multitude", the "sheep", of Matthew 25 and the "Jonadabs" were all one class who would receive everlasting life on earth as a reward for their obedience.[31] As a result, the Witnesses felt that they must gather great numbers of men to God's organization so that they could be saved from the impending battle of Armageddon for life on a new earth. Instead of simply preaching to gather the elect and announce the world's coming end, they began to make a far more concerted effort to make converts.

The second step taken by the Watch Tower Society also had great significance, particularly from the standpoint of the Witnesses' relation with secular authorities. When the Nazis first came to power they commanded Germans to salute the Swastika and called on the people to "Heil Hitler". Characteristically Jehovah's Witnesses regarded such acts as idolatrous state worship and refused to engage in them. Their "stubbornness" caused them much suffering, and it was over the issue of the flag and Hitler salutes that many of them were sent to concentration camps.[32] Their martyrdom was nevertheless regarded as highly laudable by their brethren in other countries, and when the custom of saluting the flag began to spread in the United States at about the same time, Judge Rutherford called on Witnesses throughout the world to refuse to participate in it, or in other patriotic exercises.

Though the custom of saluting the flag had occasionally been practised in the United States in the past, it had been uncommon outside the military.[33] In Canada, with its monarchial tradition, it was almost unknown. But with the spread of nationalism in the early 1930s, American schools began to insist that school children salute the national emblem. Thereupon, Judge Rutherford conducted a question-and-answer session on the subject at the Washington, D.C., convention on June 3, 1935, in which he told the conventioners that saluting the flag constituted unfaithfulness to God.[34]

Shortly thereafter, on September 20, a Lynn, Massachusetts, boy, Carleton Nicholls, enrolled in the third grade, refused to salute the American flag, and started a struggle which was to involve Jehovah's Witnesses in long and bitter litigation and to bring upon them severe persecution. The Associated Press publicized the incident; Judge Rutherford delivered a famous lecture "Saluting a Flag" on a coast-to-coast network; and the Witnesses' adversaries were given a prime issue to use against Witness children and parents alike.[35] Within a short time the flag salute began to spread to Canada,[36] although Canadian school authorities did not take strong action to enforce it until September 1940.

Very important, too, were changes in Witness organization. As indicated earlier, the Watch Tower Society had begun to appoint a service director for each congregation as early as 1919. Then in 1932 elective congregational elders were replaced by a democratically chosen service committee who were to aid the service director. The service director was given the new title "company servant" in 1936. But not until 1938 did the Watch Tower Society introduce "theocratic government" to Witness congregations, which in effect meant that henceforth all congregational officers—company servants and their assistants—were to be appointed by the Society.[37]

A few months later the Society provided also for the creation of "zones" of roughly twenty congregations each under travelling supervisors called "zone servants". During the period 1933–35 when the Witnesses had been organized for divisional campaigns—the mass invasions of unfriendly towns—the need for greater organization above congregational level had become obvious. Besides, if they were going to succeed in overcoming persecution and bans such as already existed in many countries, congregations needed to be more closely united. The zone servants were to visit each congregation for a week at a time to give aid and counsel as needed. The Society also provided for what were known as "zone conventions", at which the Witnesses were to receive admonition from zone servants and their administrative superiors (created at the same time) who ministered to a number of zones as "regional servants".[38]

These changes, doctrinal and organizational, had an amazing effect. The doctrine that great numbers of men should be converted for life on a new earth gave real impetus to the missionary activities of Jehovah's Witnesses. The flag-salute issue set them even more dramatically apart from the larger societies in which they lived and gave them more publicity. The organizational changes co-ordinated their activities and made it much easier for them to minister to interested persons and converts. They began to grow rapidly. In 1935 the Watch Tower Society reported an average of 2,218 Witness preachers in Canada;[39] by 1939 the number had risen to 4,269, or had nearly doubled;[40] and the major part of that increase occurred in 1938 and 1939.[41]

Such growth cannot be attributed entirely to new doctrines and organizational factors, important as they were. It occurred partly because each new convert was able, in turn, to contact more people. Pioneer evangelists were now preaching from British Columbia to the Maritimes, reaching persons of all social, ethnic, and religious backgrounds. During the summers, they proselytized mainly in the country; in the winters, they established camps in large cities such as Montreal, Toronto, and Vancouver, to carry on their activities. But wherever they went they made additional converts; and whenever one was baptized, he too would set off in car, home-made camper, horse-drawn Bennett buggy, boat, or whatever means of conveyance he could find, to preach to his fellow Canadians.

In addition, the fact that Judge Rutherford could no longer be heard throughout Canada on radio undoubtedly caused the Witnesses to become more active in their house-to-house preaching. Although the judge could sometimes be heard until 1937 over American stations, Witnesses both in the United States and in Canada recognized that he was being forced off the air altogether. The Watch Tower Society began to produce phonograph records of his speeches which could be played on portable phonographs, and since Canadian Witnesses felt strongly that they must bring the Watch Tower president's messages to the people, they increased the number of calls they made on their neighbours in order to do so. While this phonograph preaching was particularly resented by many, for a time it proved to be an effective means of proselytizing.[42]

Without doubt, world conditions also aided their growth. After the stock-market crash of 1929, many listened with increased attention to the message that they were living in the world's time of the end. In western Canada where the Depression was very severe, Witness teachings were received most favourably. British Columbia workers beset by labour troubles joined their ranks, as did farmers, businessmen, and a few professionals in Alberta and Manitoba. Saskatchewan, then regarded as Canada's "dust bowl", proved to be the most fertile territory for producing new Jehovah's Witnesses, if nothing else. The *1938 Yearbook* stated: "Saskatchewan has been labelled the 'Dust Bowl'. The farmers here have practically no money nor harvest, nor any feed even for cattle. They cry out for relief. In spite of these distressing conditions there has been more interest manifest by the people of Saskatchewan than in any other province."[43]

Jehovah's Witnesses were not experiencing easy times. For one thing, in 1936, Walter Salter, the branch overseer of the Watch Tower Society in Canada, was removed from his position and went into opposition to his former brethren. Evidently he did not agree with the *Watch Tower*'s new teaching regarding the "great multitude"[44] and fell out with other officers of the Watch Tower Society. In addition, there were serious questions concerning his moral behaviour.[45] Salter's defection apparently caused little stir. Although he wrote on Watch Tower stationery to Witnesses throughout Canada to spread his ideas, they remained almost one hundred per cent loyal to the Society.[46] Judge Rutherford then placed Percy Chapman from the Watch Tower's London, England, offices in charge of the Canadian branch.[47]

Much more serious were external problems. As they grew in both numbers and militancy, they faced greater opposition, particularly from Roman Catholic clergy and public officials. In 1935, Witnesses in western Canada encountered some persecution, especially among Ukrainians. On one occasion the Witnesses charged that one of their camps was destroyed; on another, they claimed that a priest-incited mob "threw decayed eggs at Jehovah's Witnesses"; and in a third instance they reported being mobbed at a railway station by a group of mockers with painted faces, dressed in old clothes and carrying tin pans and fiddles.[48] It was in Quebec, however, that they experienced their most trying difficulties. In the same year eleven were arrested on various counts, and the sedition cases of two who had engaged in the 1933 Quebec City blitz dragged on through the courts.[49]

True, in 1936 they did gain somewhat of a victory when the Supreme Court of Canada overturned the conviction of George Brodie and G. C. Barrett for seditious conspiracy, but it was, at most, a rather hollow win. Both had been held guilty at trial level and their conviction was affirmed by the Court of King's Bench. Fortunately for Brodie and Barrett, the original indictment against them had never specified the nature of their supposed conspiratorial actions. When the Quebec King's Bench denied a defence contention that the Crown had been obliged to do so, it had ruled contrary to a 1932 decision of the Ontario Appeals Court in a similar case. The Witnesses were therefore allowed to appeal for a final judgment to the Supreme Court of Canada, which reversed the decision, maintaining that the defence was right in insisting that the indictment must clearly specify the nature of seditious conspiracy.[50]

That decision in no way stopped Quebec authorities from charging the Witnesses with sedition; it simply caused them to be more careful. Hence, in the same year that Brodie and Barrett were acquitted by the Supreme Court, several Witnesses were convicted on an identical charge of seditious conspiracy for circulating pamphlets which criticized the clergy, big business, and the political elements. On appeal, the Court of King's Bench held: "If these pamphlets mean anything, they constitute an appeal to all to condemn and have a supreme contempt for all forms of organized authority, whether civil or ecclesiastical."[51]

That the Catholic clergy were behind most of the Witnesses' troubles was quite evident. Although Protestant clergymen, especially Anglicans, sometimes also caused them problems, information published in the press buttressed the Witnesses' contention that the majority of attacks of one sort or another made against them originated with members of the Roman hierarchy. For instance, on February 1, 1937, Archbishop Forbes of Ottawa issued a pastoral letter to all Catholic churches in his diocese which read:

We, by virtue of Canon 1398 of the Canon Law of the church, declare prohibited, and by these presents we prohibit in our diocese these writings, booklets, pamphlets, circulars. They are not to be allowed to be published, read, kept, bought or sold, nor to be translated into other languages nor to be passed out in any way. They are to be destroyed. To be perfectly clear, we wish, without excluding all the rest of the same type, to point to the writings of the so-called Witnesses of Jehovah.[52]

Of course the archbishop's letter expressed little more than a pious or impious hope, depending on one's point of view. In Protestant Ontario, neither provincial authorities nor the police had any notion of suppressing freedom of the press at the behest of a Roman Catholic clergyman. The Witnesses themselves were delighted with the archbishop's fulmination, for it gave proof to their contention that the Catholic Church was not favourably disposed to civil liberties when it was being critcized. Furthermore, it gave them another golden opportunity to distribute tracts far and wide. The Watch Tower Society printed a letter addressed "To All Sincere Catholics", mailed twenty-seven thousand copies to Ottawa citizens, and distributed another twenty-three thousand early one morning throughout the Ottawa area.[53]

On the other hand, Quebec authorities, in particular Quebec's new Union Nationale premier, were quite willing to take actions which would curb Witnesses' activities or those of any other unpopular minority. That was clearly demonstrated when the government of Premier Maurice Duplessis had passed in the provincial legislature the Quebec Communistic Propaganda Act, better known as the "Padlock Law". Under the terms of that act no person could use his house "to propagate communism or bolshevism by any means whatsoever". But more important, Article 12 of the act read: "It shall be unlawful to print, to publish in any manner whatsoever or to distribute in the Province any newspaper, periodical, pamphlet, circular, document or writing whatsoever propagating or tending to propagate communism or bolshevism."[54] While the new act was not specifically directed against Jehovah's Witnesses, almost any unpopular publication, including theirs, could be labelled as "tending to propagate communism". *Maclean's* magazine writer J. E. Keith noted:

Mr. Duplessis stated openly in the legislature that the idea of the Padlock Act was suggested by Cardinal Villeneuve. While ostensibly anti-communist, the law can also be used against anti-clericals, who are growing stronger every day in the province. It is significant that the only sedition charges laid in the Quebec courts in the past five years have not been against Communists, who attack the economic system but against Jehovah's Witnesses who attack the priesthood.[55]

Arrests of Quebec Witnesses continued. Percy Chapman reported that in 1938 once again "practically every charge was laid against us, including 'selling without a license', 'soliciting without a license', 'indecent assault', 'blasphemous libel', 'defamatory libel', 'distributing seditious literature', 'seditious conspiracy'."[56] If anything, things were more difficult for them in 1939: in that year forty-one cases involving 115 Witnesses were brought before Canadian courts, practically all of them in Quebec. In addition, Montreal police began raiding Witness homes and confiscated "much literature and many phonographs, records and even private papers".[57]

The Witnesses hired the services of an able Quebec criminal lawyer, R. L. Calder, to defend them, and they were often acquitted of the many charges against them, especially when they were able to have their cases heard by English-speaking, usually Protestant, judges and juries.[58] For example, when two Witnesses were charged with "blasphemy" and brought to court at Sherbrooke, Judge White, in addressing the jury, said: "These people believe these statements to be true; they have faith in these teachings, hence they have a right to promulgate them, and even if it does hurt some of us, that does not constitute blasphemy." The jury rendered a verdict of not guilty.[59]

For three months in 1939, the Witnesses dispatched a boat, equipped with powerful sound equipment, phonographs, records, and literature, up and down the St. Lawrence River. Though met with hostility everywhere—the crew were stoned and shot at, their moorings were cut, and much of their equipment was seized by Quebec City police—the newspapers gave much publicity to the work of the boat, and the opposition to it. Jehovah's Witnesses also wrote all members of the Quebec legislature, asking them to raise the question of the conviction of two Witnesses on charges of sedition for distributing the tract *The People's Greatest Need*. When they obtained no results, they sent some fourteen thousand copies of the same letter to businessmen, professionals, and newspaper editors; and, although the legislature continued to ignore their pleas, they gained some public sympathy.[60] Even in Quebec they were making converts, often among French Canadians. "In spite of this opposition," wrote Percy Chapman, "the work in the province of Quebec makes increase. More publishers are taking part in the service of door-to-door preaching, the majority of these coming from the Catholic church."[61]

Jehovah's Witnesses nevertheless believed that, given a chance, their enemies would try to suppress them completely. They were convinced that they were targets of an international conspiracy led by the Roman Catholic hierarchy and its allies. Although outside commentators have accused them of being guilty of hysterical know-nothingism in their bitter attacks on the Church of Rome, they certainly did have good reason for being somewhat hysterical.

In the United States, particularly in Catholic areas, they were facing ever-increasing opposition. Gimbel Brothers Department Stores had sponsored Judge Rutherford's broadcasts in the early 1930s. But in 1936, a Roman Catholic priest, James J. Clarke, started a boycott campaign which received the support of Dennis Cardinal Dougherty, the archbishop of Philadelphia, to force the managers of that department-store chain to stop giving financial support for the Watch Tower president's radio addresses. In spite of legal action and Witness petitions, the boycott proved successful. On September 26, 1937, Judge Rutherford announced that he would no longer use commercial radio for broadcasting the "Kingdom message".[62] However, what was more serious to American Witnesses was that they, like their brethren in Quebec, were being arrested in droves on every conceivable charge related to their ministry. They were beginning to suffer serious mob violence; their children were being expelled from school over the flag salute; and their conventions were often interfered with or broken up by thugs or by police. During 1938 the Watch Tower Society reported that 471 Witnesses had been arrested in the United States;[63] in 1939, over 600 were charged on a variety of counts.[64] At New Orleans in 1938, the local police cut telephone lines to a Witness convention in that city so that the conventioners could not receive a talk delivered at New York by Judge Rutherford.[65] In 1939, some 500 followers of Canadian-born Father Charles E. Coughlin's Christian Front tried to break up an assembly of Witnesses at Madison Square Garden, New York, but were driven off by cane-carrying ushers without any aid from the police.[66]

Overseas persecution was getting worse, too. In Germany hundreds of Witnesses had already been rounded up and sent to concentration camps. Many were forced to undergo "German baptism" or immersion in a barrel filled with liquid manure. Others had been beaten severely and some killed, while many more were being gathered up for transportation to the new camps of Buchenwald and Dachau. Most terrible of all was that, under an August 1938 law, the Third Reich declared that anyone who refused military service or incited others to refuse would be executed or, in less extreme instances, placed in prison or protective custody. "Since such refusal was an article of belief for Jehovah's Witnesses, they were thus all practically brought under sentence of death."[67] Hungary, Italy, and other countries also were carrying on persecution against them.[68] Even in democratic Britain, they faced violent opposition. Not only were many of them mobbed, but the Irish Republican Army tried to stop a Watch Tower convention at London's Kingsway Hall by phoning a bombing threat and later setting off five bombs which caused a great deal of damage and injury near the convention centre.[69]

Understandably, Jehovah's Witnesses were developing a rather strong persecution complex. Neither is it surprising that they blamed the Roman Catholic clergy for a majority of their problems. There could be no doubt that in Quebec, in the United States, and in other places, many of the attacks on them, whether by legal authorities or by mobs, were inspired by Catholic action. And when the Watch Tower Society published an article written by a German priest, in the pamphlet *Face the Facts*, the Witnesses could hardly be blamed for holding the hierarchy partly responsible for the persecution of their German brethren. The article in question, taken from *Deutschen Weg* of Berlin, May 29, 1937, stated in translation:

There is now one country on earth where the so-called "Earnest Bible Students" [Jehovah's Witnesses] are forbidden. That is Germany! The dissolution of the sect which, at that time, had found a strong foothold in Germany, did not come to pass under Brüning [chancellor of the German Reich before Hitler], although the Catholic Church in Brüning's time urged to have this done. However, the "most Catholic chancellor" Brüning answered that he had no law which authorized him to dissolve the sect of the "Earnest Bible Students".

When Adolph Hitler had come to power and the German Episcopate repeated their request, Hitler said: "These so-called 'Earnest Bible Students' are trouble-makers; they disturb the harmonious life among the Germans; I consider them quacks; I do not tolerate that the German Catholics be besmirched in such a manner by this American 'Judge' Rutherford; I dissolve the 'Earnest Bible Students' in Germany; their property I dedicate to the people's welfare; I will have all their literature confiscated." Bravo!

However, the American Episcopate, even Cardinal Mundelein, is not able to have Rutherford's books, in which the Catholic Church is slandered, to be taken away from the bookmarket in the United States![70]

Persecution only made Jehovah's Witnesses more militant toward what they regarded as the devil's world, in particular the clergy. In

1937 the Watch Tower Society published the book *Enemies* which pictured the political and economic powers of the nations as ridden by religion, specifically the Church of Rome. To make this clear the book contained a colour picture showing a politician and an entrepreneur together, under a wooden yoke on which there rested a giant serpent with a man's head crowned with a papal tiara. In extremely strong language, political and commercial organizations were likened to the ancient heathen nations which surrounded Israel; the churches of Christendom were compared to the harlot sisters, Oholah and Oholibah, of Ezekiel 23. Nor was *Enemies* atypical; most of the Society's literature produced in the late 1930s was vitriolic in its condemnation of the Witnesses' adversaries. *Fascism or Freedom*, which contained a detailed statement concerning Roman Catholic persecution of the Witnesses in the United States as well as in Germany, stated: "Today Hitler and Mussolini, the arbitrary dictators, threaten the peace of the whole world, and they are fully supported in their destruction of freedom by the Roman Catholic Hierarchy, which fact is shown by the Catholic press today."[71] *Consolation*, the successor to the *Golden Age*, constantly lampooned the hierarchy and contained cartoons which pictured priests as fat pigs. Even the Society's yearly calendars, displayed openly in Witness homes, frequently bore harshly anti-clerical messages. One of them carried a vivid picture of a drunken, semi-nude harlot (as described in Revelation 17–18) riding on a seven-headed, ten-horned beast which was about to turn on her. Like the serpent in the book *Enemies*, she wore a tiara.

The Witnesses also hurled the charge over and over again that the Church of Rome was sympathetic to fascism and had openly co-operated with Franco, Mussolini, and the Nazis. They often spoke of a Nazi-Fascist-Catholic conspiracy to persecute them. Wherever they went, they made their views known. They continually increased the distribution of their literature, and they carried Judge Rutherford's ever-more-stinging speeches from door to door on portable phonographs and often used sound trucks to play them to whole villages throughout the United States and Canada. Most spectacularly, they often paraded through cities and towns by the hundreds and sometimes by the thousands bearing placards which bore slogans such as

"Religion is a Snare and a Racket".[72] Seldom before in history had a small religious minority turned on its persecutors with such vehemence and with such widely broadcast denunciations.

In Canada the Catholic response to the Witnesses' campaign was to try to put an end to it in any way possible. Of course Quebec authorities were doing what they could to put them out of commission, but provincial officials in the rest of Canada would do nothing. For example, on July 14, 1938, a group of Witnesses appeared at the small northern Saskatchewan community of Makawa armed with literature, phonographs, and a sound truck. Their activities immediately aroused the extreme ire of Abbé J. B. Cabana, the local parish priest. The abbé thereupon sought to have "these people" forcibly ejected from his parish[73] and contacted the Attorney General of Saskatchewan's Liberal government to have their activities stopped.[74] When that official replied that it was a religious matter only, Cabana then wrote to federal Minister of Justice Ernest Lapointe to seek help. He sent Lapointe four Watch Tower publications and remarked: "All of their publications are seditious, revolutionary." *Consolation* he described as "a demon", and, he stated, if something were not done to end their widespread criticism of both religion and French Canadians, the Witnesses might become dangerous.[75]

Cabana's correspondence, written between January and March 1939, was followed by other Catholic complaints to the Minister of Justice. During March, Lapointe received anti-Witness letters from the Société Saint-Jean-Baptiste de Beauport,[76] L'Union des Jeunesses Catholiques Canadiennes de Sherbrooke,[77] Le Conseil Central des Syndicats Catholiques et Nationaux de Sherbrooke, Inc.,[78] and from Abbé Arthur Pigeon, parish priest of Huntingdon, Quebec.[79] Among other things, some of these missives demanded that the government bar the Witnesses the use of the mails.[80] Lapointe, though guarded in his answers, was obviously sympathetic to such requests from the Catholic community and forwarded several letters to the Postmaster General for possible action.[81]

A few months later, after the outbreak of the Second World War, the *Canadian Messenger of the Sacred Heart*, a Jesuit publication based in Toronto, published an article entitled "Doctrine and Practice of the Witnesses of Jehovah". Following a detailed report of old attacks on Pastor Russell and Judge Rutherford and a denial that the Catholic Church was persecuting the Witnesses, it stated:

"Whatever may be the profession of Jehovah's Witnesses," says Father Thurston, "there is no room for doubt that the practical effect of the Watch Tower activities is to stimulate Communism, not to say anarchy, and to undermine all feeling of reverence for authority. It is not only the churches that are brought into disrepute but every existing form of civil government is decried and caricatured."[82]

Although Canadian Jehovah's Witnesses were only partly aware of what was going on, there was a strong feeling among them that it was their turn next. In 1938 Percy Chapman stated: "The fight is on, and well we know it in the Quebec district."[83] When in the following year the Watch Tower Society determined to hold an international convention in New York—the one at which the Madison Square Garden riot occurred—Witnesses in Canada attempted to have Judge Rutherford's lecture brought in to a number of convention centres by long-distance telephone. On June 14, just two days before the lecture was to be given, Bell Telephone cancelled an agreement to make facilities available within Ontario and Quebec.[84] In western Canada, pressure was also brought to bear to keep the lecture from being heard by telephone at Saskatoon and Lethbridge. But at the last moment, "in spite of opposition raised by government officials", it was brought to those centres.[85] Shortly thereafter the Watch Tower Society's Canadian branch overseer wrote:

The enemy has made a desperate attempt to break up the work in certain parts of the land, particularly in the province of Quebec. It would appear that, were he able to break into and stop the work in that province, he would quickly attempt to make inroads in the ranks of the [Witness] army in other parts of the Dominion.[86]

Chapman was not wrong. Less than a year from the time he penned those words, Jehovah's Witnesses in Canada were declared seditious and were outlawed.

CHAPTER SEVEN

banned as seditious

Then innocent parties should not be discriminated against, or as Burke says, you cannot indict a nation; no more can you indict an entire race or all members of any religious sect.

WILLIAM LYON MACKENZIE KING
Debates of the House of Commons of Canada, June 30, 1934

OPPOSITION TO Jehovah's Witnesses became far more intense in the first half of 1940. Ralph Brodie, a worker at the Watch Tower Society's Toronto offices, was seized by the Royal Canadian Mounted Police and placed in detention without trial under the Defence of Canada Regulations on the specific charge of having fascist sympathies.[1] In Quebec, a Montreal jury recommended to the Chief Justice of the Superior Court that the executive of the Watch Tower Society be arrested "so that this work stop".[2] That jurist, Chief Justice Greenshields, agreed and stated further that Judge Rutherford, as author of the book *Enemies*, was fortunate "he had not met a good Anglican or a good Catholic with a horse whip".[3] The Witnesses replied by circulating a tract, from one end of the country to the other, sarcastically entitled *It Must Be Stopped!*[4] However, their position had become decidedly vulnerable, particularly during the months of May and June. France was in a state of collapse before victorious German armies; Britain and the Commonwealth stood momentarily alone before the Third Reich. Then, on June 3, the United States Supreme Court handed down a decision in the case of *Minersville School District* v. *Gobitis* in which it ruled that public school boards could require Witness children to salute the American flag or, upon refusal, expel them from school.[5] It was that decision which sparked many of the American assaults on Jehovah's Witnesses from the summer of 1940 through all of 1943.[6] As a result of such events, Canadian Witnesses were becoming definitely more unpopular. They were viewed by many as an unpatriotic minority who refused to serve in time of need and who despised the national symbols. Dr. H. A. Bruce, Conservative Member of Parliament for Parkdale, Toronto, said that the government had not gone far enough in listing seditious organizations for suppression under the Defence of Canada Regulations and should outlaw many more, among them Jehovah's Witnesses.[7]

The Witnesses became somewhat alarmed, and those in Winnipeg adopted the following hurriedly prepared and badly written but explicit resolution:

We Christians, who are witnesses of Jehovah and are commanded by the Scriptures to preach the Gospel of the Kingdom, state that we are loyal Canadians, and are for the freedom Canada stands for. We are emphatically opposed to the Nazis, Communists, Fascists, and the 5th Column. Also, we are opposed to the betrayers of the people who are in favor of the Totalitarian form of Government. Our work is not done in secret, but rather out in the open, and members of the Government, the police, and many of the people in Canada, are cordially invited to attend our meetings, and see for themselves the falsity of the statement, that we are a subversive movement. Further, like our brethren in Germany (many who have been shot for refusing to shoot British and French soldiers, and who are sitting in concentration camps for fighting Hitlerism) are noble Christians, and are being brutally treated because they will not bow down to the Totalitarian form of Government. That we Christians, in this land, will fight Hitlerism, Fascism, Nazism, Communism, the Fifth Column, and all the dictators (even if it means our lives), with the word of God, the Bible, just as our Master Christ Jesus did, and that shortly at Armageddon Jehovah God will destroy the dictators and their regimented forces.[8]

Their representatives also approached E. J. McMurray to request that he prepare a statement on their behalf and submit it to the federal government. In consequence, on June 19 the Winnipeg lawyer wrote to Minister of Mines and Resources T. A. Crerar and stated that on the basis of his personal knowledge the Witnesses "were a group of good-living, God-fearing people; of sound, middle-class Canadianism", who were neither communists nor socialists. He stressed that their activities were purely religious and should have no more political significance than those of Anglicans, the Salvation Army, or the Quakers. He drew attention to the persecution of the Witnesses in Germany as outlined in British White Paper Number 2 and the book *Crusade Against Christianity* and quoted from the *Montreal Daily Star* of January 6, 1940, which had reviewed those two publications. In closing, McMurray remarked:

Jehovah's Witnesses are opposed to Communism, Nazism and Fascism, as set forth in their resolution [which he enclosed], and it would seem to be an extraordinary thing that these people who are opposed to Communism, Nazism and Fascism should be the object of any suspicion in this country at this time, particularly in view of the fact that they are not in the Motherland which is now in close grips with the common enemy![9]

Crerar dutifully forwarded McMurray's letter to Minister of Justice Ernest Lapointe who replied: "Mr. McMurray's letter will, you may be assured, receive every consideration."[10] Yet on the very day that Lapointe answered Crerar, July 4, 1940, notice appeared in the *Canada Gazette* that the Minister of Justice had caused an order in council to be passed declaring Jehovah's Witnesses illegal as a subversive movement.[11] Apparently, some time before the Witnesses had made representations to the government, Lapointe had made up his mind to take some sort of action against them. In a letter dated May 27, 1940, Lieutenant-Colonel Henri DesRosiers, by then Deputy Minister of National Defence, had written to the Minister of Justice about Jehovah's Witnesses and the Toronto journal *Flash*, both of which he labelled "sowers of discord". The Deputy Minister indicated that he would mention the Witnesses only in passing, since he was then aware that steps were about to be taken to curb their "nefarious work".[12] Still, Lapointe had evidently not decided exactly what he would do with respect to them at that time; nor did he do so until near the end of the following month.

On June 6 James H. Gallagher, a Catholic layman from Kingston, Ontario, sent Lapointe a copy of the *Canadian Messenger of the Sacred Heart* anti-Witness article of the previous autumn and called his attention to the paragraph quoted earlier.[13] But the most that the Minister then did was to send copies of the article—and an accompanying letter from Gallagher calling for the Witnesses' suppression—to the Royal Canadian Mounted Police and Fulgence Charpentier, chief press censor for Canada, for consideration.[14] The Minister of Justice still evidently wanted advice as to what steps he should take against the Witnesses. As a result, Charpentier and his colleague, Wilfrid Eggleston, commissioned their assistant in Toronto, Charles S. Grafton, to examine the *Canadian Messenger of the Sacred Heart* article and comment on the Witnesses. Grafton replied to his superiors on June 25:

Unless there are more flagrantly subversive types of periodicals issued and distributed in Canada by the Watch Tower organization than Consolation, upon which I made a memorandum in Ottawa, I would urge that the approach through censorship to the serious problem presented by the sect, Witnesses of Jehovah, is the wrong one. As inferred in that memorandum, the trend toward an almost militant stand against Nazism taken in a late June issue, weakens considerably any case censorship might build up against this particular publication.

He then went on to state that he considered the "Watch Tower organization one of the most efficiently organized rackets of all time". But censorship, he felt, "would be the weakest point from which to attack". He had other ideas:

The Department might not wish to press the issue of saluting the flag, since it might invite a widespread martyrdom, but its operatives might more closely follow parades of the sect which are often staged, and in which inflammatory, yet indiscreet, slogans are often displayed on banners. It would seem that the Department's operatives might obtain evidence of subversive doctrines as uttered in assemblies. Their actions, their utterances seem more logical points to attack than what they read and attempt to distribute. Ban on the latter would obviously follow success achieved in the former directions.[15]

Charpentier and Eggleston concurred:

We agree that the Witnesses of Jehovah are circulating literature and carrying on activities which are probably quite undesirable at the present time, but we have never been able to satisfy ourselves that we had any right under the Defence of Canada Regulations to recommend that action be taken against them.[16]

As late as June 28, therefore, the date on which they wrote to Lapointe, the press censors were unitedly opposed to any overt move against the Witnesses. But by that time the Minister of Justice was receiving advice from other quarters which proved much more influential.

The Anglican Synod of the Diocese of Kootenay, meeting at Kelowna, British Columbia, on June 9, adopted the following:

Be it resolved that this Synod of the Diocese of Kootenay petitions both the Federal and Provincial Governments to have the organization known as "The Jehovah Witness" thoroughly examined by the police and that action be taken if found necessary.[17]

Thirteen days later Grote Stirling, Conservative Member of Parliament for Yale, sent Lapointe a copy of the resolution and asked that he accede to the request of the Kootenay Synod.[18] Meanwhile, *L'Action Catholique* of Quebec had taken up the cudgels. On June 22 it published a blistering editorial entitled "Les pires saboteurs", in which it claimed that the "sabotage" carried on by Jehovah's Witnesses was worse than that of enemy agents. Furthermore, said editor Louis-Philippe Roy: "We will not hesitate to say that the authorities should do much more in this regard for the protection of the public."[19]

Evidently *L'Action Catholique* was speaking for the Canadian Catholic Hierarchy; for on June 27 Monseigneur Paul Bernier, the chancellor of the archdiocese of Quebec, wrote to Lapointe's private secretary, Maurice Bernier, as follows:

His Eminence the Cardinal [Villeneuve] would be pleased if you would draw the attention of the Right Honourable Mr. Ernest Lapointe, Minister of Justice, to the enclosed leading editorial concerning the publications of *The Watchtower* or *Jehovah's Witnesses.*

Certain books and booklets still being sent by post, especially the magazine Consolation, are the most demoralizing and destructive of the spiritual forces of the nation.

I thank you in advance, dear sir, for the attention that you will give to this communication.[20]

Lapointe evidently felt that the recommendations of his church were of primary importance. On July 4 his private secretary replied to Monseigneur Paul Bernier:

I have made it my duty, on receipt of your letter of June 27, to comply with the wishes of His Eminence the Cardinal, and to draw the attention of the Minister to your request and also to the editorial published by L'Action Catholique on the subject of the Watchtower, Jehovah's Witnesses and Consolation.

Mr. Lapointe has authorized me to communicate to you by phone the confidential message that the organization called Jehovah's Witnesses will be declared illegal this very day, with the express wish that you communicate it to His Eminence the Cardinal.

This communication is to confirm what I have said to you by phone.

I understand that His Eminence the Cardinal will, in due course, be informed of the ministerial decree concerning Jehovah's Witnesses.[21]

Shortly thereafter, Cardinal Villeneuve wrote personally to express his pleasure at what Paul Bernier described as the "prompt and happy solution" of outlawing "the so-called 'Witnesses of Jehovah', the plague of Christianity in America".[22]

When a question was raised on July 16 in the House of Commons as to why Jehovah's Witnesses had been banned, Ernest Lapointe was not present. But Prime Minister Mackenzie King, acting on behalf of the Minister of Justice, read a statement prepared by him in explanation. It stated:

The literature of Jehovah's Witnesses discloses, in effect, that man-made authority or law should not be recognized if it conflicts with the Jehovah's Witnesses' interpretation of the Bible; that they refuse to salute the flag of any nation or to hail any man; and, that they oppose war.

The general effect of this literature is, amongst other things, to undermine the ordinary responsibility of citizens, particularly in time of war.[23]

The Defence of Canada Regulations clearly spelled out what being declared illegal meant for the Witnesses or anyone else similarly proscribed. Section 39C read in part:

2) Every person who is an officer or member of an illegal organization, or professes to be such, or who advocates or defends the acts, principles or policies of such illegal organization shall be guilty of an offence against this Regulation.

3) In any prosecution under the Regulation for the offence of being a member of an illegal organization, if it be proved that the person charged has—

a) attended meetings of an illegal organization;
b) spoken publicly in advocacy of an illegal organization; or
c) distributed literature of an illegal organization by circulation through the Post Office mails of Canada, or otherwise

it shall be presumed, in the absence of proof to the contrary, that he is a member of such illegal organization.

4) a) All property, rights and interests in Canada belonging to any illegal organization shall be vested in and be subject to the control and management of the Custodian, as defined in the Regulations respecting Trading with the Enemy, 1939;
b) Subject as hereinafter provided, and for the purposes of the control and management of such property, rights and interests by the Custodian, the Regulations respecting Trading with the

Enemy, 1939, shall apply *mutatis mutandis* to the same extent as if such property, rights and interests belonged to an enemy within the meaning of the said Regulations;

c) The property, rights and interests so vested in and subject to the control and management of the Custodian, or the proceeds thereof, shall on the termination of the present war be dealt with in such manner as the Governor in Council may direct.[24]

The Witnesses were taken by surprise. Much of their correspondence and literature in transit was seized by the postal authorities,[25] and their meetings were temporarily curtailed. In addition, property worth approximately one hundred thousand dollars[26] and nearly seventy-five thousand dollars in cash[27] were confiscated from the Watch Tower Society and local congregations of Jehovah's Witnesses by government officials. If, however, the Minister of Justice believed that the ban would end or even drastically inhibit their activities, he was wrong; they immediately went underground. Title pages showing the Watch Tower Society as printer and publisher were torn from King James Version Bibles so that Witnesses could continue to use them in their preaching work. Watch Tower literature disappeared into false closets, hidden places in the woods, haystacks, and abandoned rooms in lignite coal mines on the Prairies. Secret meetings were organized under the guise of picnics, birthday parties, dances, and family gatherings. Return visits on sympathetic persons continued to be made, and in November, only five months after the announcement of the ban, over seven thousand Witnesses conducted a night-time "blitz" by distributing a small booklet entitled *End of Nazism* on the doorsteps of thousands of sleeping Canadians from British Columbia to Nova Scotia. Less than ten were apprehended.[28]

A major source of continuing aid to the outlawed Witnesses was their brethren in the United States; for while American Witnesses were suffering unparalleled mob violence and public censure, they were protected from legal proscription by the American courts, acting under the American Bill of Rights. They could continue to preach publicly, hold conventions, and publish literature for distribution both in the United States and in Canada. Also, although the border between the two countries had been closed on July 1, 1940—just four days before announcement of the ban—to any Canadian not holding a valid passport, it was impossible to keep Canadian Witnesses from entering the United States both legally and clandestinely to attend conventions and to obtain outlawed literature. In consequence, tons of books and booklets were illegally brought into Canada. Canadian Witnesses themselves were soon back in the business of printing and publishing their own literature however. Printing shops which were underground presses in the most literal sense possible were established in southern Ontario and northern Saskatchewan. In spite of a nationwide shortage, newsprint was obtained from Witness sympathizers and, within a short time after the beginning of the ban, Canadian editions of the *Watchtower* began to be circulated regularly throughout the country.[29]

But if Jehovah's Witnesses continued to meet, proselytize, print, and distribute literature, they now experienced legal repression of a kind never before imposed on any religious group in Canadian history. As early as July 9, police at Windsor, Ontario, seized large quantities of Watch Tower publications and arrested a Witness, Gordon Cripps, under the terms of the Defence of Canada Regulations.[30] Throughout the remainder of the summer and during the autumn, raids were conducted on Witness homes. Several tons of printed matter were confiscated in Toronto;[31] and, in Sault Ste. Marie, Ontario, eighteen were charged as members of an illegal organization.[32] Sentences at first were often severe. Charles Morrell, private secretary to Supreme Court of Canada Chief Justice Sir Lyman Duff, and himself a Jehovah's Witness, later reported that in 1940 twenty-nine Witnesses were initially sentenced to 300 months in prison, although on appeal those sentences were reduced to a total of 209 months or more than six months apiece, often simply for possessing banned literature.[33] Many others were given shorter jail terms, fines, and, where there were relatively lenient judicial officials, suspended sentences. Only rarely were Witnesses acquitted.

More serious to some Witnesses than raids and arrests for possession of banned publications or for holding illegal meetings was the flag-salute and patriotic-exercises issue. When school terms began throughout the country about the first of September, patriotic teachers and public school authorities demanded that all children salute the flag and join in standing for or singing the national anthem. As taught by their parents, Witness children generally refused and were often expelled from classes—in some cases for as long as four years. For example, a particularly nasty situation developed in Hamilton, Ontario. Two days after school started two pupils were suspended from school and sent home. By October 9, the number of suspended children had risen to twenty-seven.[34] The matter was then brought to the attention of the provincial government in Toronto, and investigators were sent to Hamilton. The investigators indicated shortly that the children's objections to the exercises were "purely religious", and government officials stated that "there is neither law nor regulation which compels a student to salute the flag".[35] They also remarked that Jehovah's Witness children might properly be excused from taking part in the exercises.[36] Nevertheless, the Hamilton Board of Education determined to stand firm on the issue, and the provincial government decided not to interfere. Witness parents then formed a private "kingdom school" under an experienced teacher to keep their children from being charged with truancy and to provide a means of education for them.[37]

Pupils similarly suspended or expelled in other parts of the country could not always be sent to "kingdom schools" or other private educational institutions. Expulsion from public schools often meant that they were denied any form of education except what they could obtain from parents or friends on an informal basis.[38] But that was not the most serious aspect of the whole affair. When Witness parents appealed to certain public authorities concerning the problems that their children faced, they received little sympathy. In addition, both parents and children could face legal action plus attempts on the part of public officials to remove the children from their homes and place them under state control. When a Red Deer woman, Mrs. Hilda McGregor, applied to William Aberhart, the Bible-quoting Social Credit Premier of Alberta, for aid in the matter, he replied in no uncertain terms:

Dear Madam:
Your letter of the 25th at hand and I note the difficulty you are having in connection with request of saluting the flag in the schools.

The British flag has always stood for liberty, justice and fair play and the standing to one's feet when the National Anthem is sung or the saluting of the flag when it flies is merely the British way of once more acknowledging our belief in these great Christian principles of democracy.

I feel the children ought to be taught constantly to recognize great principles. The refusal therefore to salute the flag would be recognized as disloyalty to the British principles just as the refusal to stand when the National Anthem is sung or if a gentleman refuses to remove his hat would be looked upon as disloyalty to the British Empire. Surely that would be outside the realm of freedom.

It is not the right of any British subject to rebel against his country. If I were you therefore I would instruct the children in the meaning of the saluting of the flag. I would even go so far as to show them the three Christian crosses that constitute the flag and the symbolism that is contained therein. Red standing for sacrifice; white standing for righteousness and fair play and blue for loyalty to God and man.

If the children with your consent refuse to salute the flag it becomes a very serious offence especially in a time like this when there are unfortunately in our midst those who are disloyal to the British Empire. I am quite satisfied that if the children are suspended from school that the military authorities will immediately take up the case with the parents and they might be charged by the Federal authorities under the War Measures Act as being rebels. I do not know what punishment would be meted out to you.

I would therefore certainly recommend that you do not make a mountain out of a mere trifle. Teach the children the meaning of the flag and tell them that when they salute the flag it is just the same as raising their hands when they have the right answer to a question. I am sure that as British born people you must have British idealism at heart and you will be glad to have your children brought up under the British flag.

I assure you that there is no real argument that could be offered for us not to declare our loyalty to the British ideals at a time such as this. Of course you will be held responsible no doubt for the action of the children. The local School Board has the right to demand obedience on the part of the children in such exercises and would of course suspend a child whose parents refuse him an opportunity of carrying out his duties in school.

If the military authorities decide to intern the parents the children would of necessity be taken care of and be sent to school under the authority of those who would look after them. The whole situation is too unhappy to be worth any objection being taken in such a simple matter.[39]

Though no actions of the kind envisioned by Aberhart occurred in Alberta, his remarks indicated, in fact, what could happen. For in other provinces attempts were actually made, in both 1940 and the following year, to intern Witness parents when convicted under Defence of Canada Regulations for making statements to their children—such as that it was wrong to salute the flag or sing "God Save the King"—which were regarded as seditious by the authorities.

The most extreme instance occurred in the London, Ontario, suburban community of Merwin Heights. Two Witness children, Marion and Denis Leeson, aged nine and eight, respectively, were in attendance at the Merwin Heights Public School; like children throughout much of the nation, they were called on to salute the flag and sing the national anthem. On September 23, 1940, they were sent home from class by their teacher, Miss Leila Bilyea, and after being readmitted briefly, some time later, they were again expelled from school.[40] In the meantime, their teacher had contacted the school inspector, the school board, and the Ontario Provincial Police, all of whom were determined to take action against Clarence and Agnes Leeson, the children's parents.[41] On September 20 two Ontario Provincial Police, Constables Milligan and Macmillan, had raided and searched the Leeson home for Watch Tower literature with a warrant issued under the terms of Section 39c of the Defence of Canada Regulations. They found only one old copy of the *Consolation* magazine with its cover torn off, but, according to Leeson, they seized both his and his wife's personal Bibles, one of which he believes is still being used to swear in witnesses in a London court.[42] Then, on October 11, Milligan and Macmillan again appeared at the Leeson home. Mrs. Leeson was placed in custody and taken to jail while the Leesons' four children—one a sickly child under twelve months of age—were placed in the hands of the local Children's Aid Society. The police next went to Leeson's place of employment, arrested him, and escorted him to jail. A terrible experience for Clarence and Agnes Leeson followed. They were held in jail for eleven days with no charge laid against them and without being allowed to communicate with anyone. They had virtually no information concerning their children. In the meantime the police sought authority from the Attorney General of Ontario to prosecute them under the Defence of Canada Regulations. Finally the Leesons were released from jail, but only after they had both been charged with advocating the principles of Jehovah's Witnesses contrary to Section 39C of the Defence of Canada Regulations and of having made statements intended or likely to cause disaffection to the King in violation of Section 39A of the same regulations.[43]

The Leesons came to trial before Magistrate C. W. Hawkshaw in Middlesex County Police Court on November 6, 1940. On November 29, Magistrate Hawkshaw held them guilty on both charges and sentenced them each to four months in jail and fined them $100 each plus court costs. According to the *London Daily Free Press*, the fines and costs totalled $500.40. If they refused to pay their fines, the magistrate stated that the Leesons would have to serve an extra three months in jail. Following sentencing they were escorted to their cells.[44] On December 5, the Leesons were freed on $2,000 bail each while their lawyer, J. L. Cohen of Toronto, appealed their cases to the Supreme Court of Ontario. That body eventually postponed hearing the charges against them indefinitely, and the Leesons were not made to serve their jail sentences or to pay their fines. Yet they had suffered terribly and were to continue to do so. Clarence and Agnes Leeson had been forced to spend eighteen days in jail and to appear in court some five or six times at a cost of about $3,000 to themselves. But more serious was the effect on their children. Marion and Denis were not allowed to return to school for two years, and both they and the two younger Leeson children suffered serious psychological damage.[45]

At Saskatoon, Saskatchewan, O. M. Woodward was sent to jail for a month, also under Section 39C of the Defence of Canada Regulations. The judge who sentenced him held that it was a crime to teach or defend the principles of Jehovah's Witnesses, even to his own children.[46] Shortly thereafter, a police magistrate in Manitoba took the same position. A Witness named Clark had written to the local school board to request that his children be excused from saluting the flag. As a result, he too was arrested under the Defence of Canada Regulations. In court Police Magistrate Lauman declared: "If the accused is not for his children taking part in the flag salute exercise or singing the National Anthem then he must be against it. To be against the salute of the flag he is opposed to everything for which it stands—law, order, our civilization." The conviction was later quashed by the Manitoba Court of Appeal.[47] But the Woodward and Clark cases, along with that of the Leesons, showed how far some Jehovah's Witnesses' enemies were willing to go against Witness parents.

In another instance, school authorities actually tried to have Witness children taken from their parents. In Hamilton the Board of Education was not satisfied with seeing the children of Jehovah's Witnesses expelled from school, and had six of them—Arthur Ellison, Thomas Young, Peter Sharbanow, Donna Hanco, and Walter and Frank Valchuck—taken before Hamilton Magistrate H. A. Burbidge, family and juvenile court judge, on charges of juvenile delinquency. On January 6, 1941, Burbidge ordered that Arthur Ellison, Thomas Young, and the two Valchuck boys be handed over to the Hamilton Children's Aid Society and placed in foster homes. Appeal was made to Chief Justice Rose of the Supreme Court of Ontario, who quashed the order with the remark that "the children should not have been brought into court on an issue of this kind". He then advised the two parties to settle the matter out of court. In the meantime, the Valchuck boys had already been held at the Juvenile Observation Home in Hamilton for two weeks.[48]

It is true that these instances were among the most extreme involving the flag-salute and patriotic-exercises affair. Also, in some provinces, provincial officials attempted to blunt the persecution of Jehovah's Witnesses in connection with the whole issue. Alberta Premier Aberhart, in spite of his annoyance with the Witnesses, openly tried to keep local officials from expelling their children from provincial schools. Acting as Attorney General, he asserted that there was no law against refusing to salute the flag.[49] Saskatchewan provincial authorities went even further. Minister of Education Estey—later to serve as justice of the Supreme Court of Canada—ordered local school boards to leave Witness children alone and threatened principals and school teachers with severe discipline if they refused to educate them.[50]

Yet in 1940 and 1941 the tide of public opinion was running strongly against Jehovah's Witnesses. Some newspapers insisted that their children be forced to conform.[51] The Reverend J. Gordon Boner, president of the Edmonton Ministerial Association proclaimed: "Freedom of conscience must be guarded, but . . . it is a Christian duty and apostolic injunction to obey the state."[52] Numerous school boards, often prompted by veterans' groups or British settlers,[53] decided, therefore, to press the Witnesses as hard as possible. Throughout English Canada, many Witness children were expelled from schools; and, as a result of the cases described, their parents experienced real fear that they might be imprisoned and their children taken away from them. What Premier Aberhart had written to Mrs. McGregor was somewhat more than bluster and hyperbole.

The year 1941 brought increased actions against the Witnesses. On January 13, as a legal afterthought, the Watch Tower Bible and Tract Society and the International Bible Students Association were declared illegal.[54] Shortly thereafter, the Watch Tower Bible and Tract Society Incorporated was also outlawed.[55] Thus, by the spring of the year, every organization in association with the Witnesses of Jehovah was proscribed under Canadian law. Individual Witnesses were still arrested, many were forced out of employment,[56] and threats of internment continued to be made.

Witnesses reacted to legal repression with both fortitude and outspoken denunciations of their adversaries. Trials gave them a chance to express themselves, and in reviewing the trials, newspapers often publicized Witness statements throughout the country. For example, when an elderly woman, at first too ill to appear in court, was offered a suspended sentence if she would stop attending the meetings of Jehovah's Witnesses and distributing subversive literature, she replied, "I will not deny Jehovah nor will I agree not to do his will. So you may as well impose the sentence."[57] As a result, she was given a month in jail, but her comments were publicized widely.[58] A similar event occurred in Edmonton, Alberta. A police spy accepted baptism as a Witness "convert" in order to obtain information against members of the local congregation. In court, he later gave evidence which resulted in the imprisonment of many who had accepted him as a spiritual brother. The facts of the case gave the Witnesses much sympathetic publicity, however, and after the trial local newspapers reported: "A brown paper parcel, containing a rope, was found Wednesday morning in the door of the court room, with the words, 'For Judas Iscariot'."[59]

Public martyrdom began to gain the Witnesses sympathy. They were not slow in pointing out to both the public and the officials that, while they were held to be seditious in Canada, in Great Britain they were allowed complete freedom to carry on their activities. They reiterated time and again in written appeals to elected representatives and others that the ban had been imposed on them because of undue Roman Catholic influence on the Liberal government in Ottawa. For example, in May 1941 copies of a letter addressed to Attorney General Gordon Wismer of British Columbia and signed simply "Christian" were sent to crown prosecutors, magistrates, and judges throughout the Pacific province, to Prime Minister Mackenzie King, and to Members of Parliament. It read in part: "England, Scotland and Wales, freely permit Jehovah's Witnesses to carry on their work with the full knowledge of the Right Honourable Winston Churchill and every member of the Government. Why, then, is this good work of announcing God's Kingdom in harmony with the prayer of Jesus— 'Thy Kingdom Come'—banned in Canada?" After detailing a number of cases of alleged police and prison-guard brutality against the Witnesses, and a night raid on a home in West Vancouver, it went on to state: "The persecution of Jehovah's Witnesses in Canada smacks of what is going on in Hitler Germany, since Hitler got control." It labelled the Roman Catholic Church as the chief cause of the woes of the Witnesses: "It is very manifest that the Roman Catholic Hierarchy is the fifth column. . . . One by one they have suppressed Jehovah's Witnesses, not because they are subversive, but because they are exposing Catholic action." In reference to the Minister of Justice, it stated: "Evidently the whole of Canada has yielded to a pompous son of the church of Rome."[60]

Such arguments did not fall on deaf ears. To many Canadians of varied persuasions, the government ban on Jehovah's Witnesses seemed just one among many misuses of war-time power. Along with the Witnesses, the Minister of Justice had declared illegal a number of organizations—the Ukrainian Labour Farmer Temple Association, the League of Peace and Democracy, Technocracy Incorporated— which had not been demonstrably linked with seditious movements in any way.[61] Lapointe also refused for a time to free nine out of twenty-four internees who had been recommended for release by a committee established to review such cases by the Minister himself.[62] Then, too, the government was charged with interfering with legitimate freedom of the press. Not only had the literature of illegal organizations been outlawed and the circulation of other journals prohibited,[63] but a pamphlet written by Mrs. Dorise Nielsen, United Progressive Member of Parliament for North Battleford, Saskatchewan, and an outspoken critic of the ban on Jehovah's Witnesses, had been seized by the Royal Canadian Mounted Police.[64] Civil libertarians were shocked; the press began to question the government's use of the Defence of Canada Regulations, and the Minister of Justice received particularly severe public criticism.

Lapointe and a number of Liberal MPs attempted to defend the government's actions but came under sharp attack in the House of Commons even after Prime Minister Mackenzie King moved, on February 27, 1941, to establish a special select committee, representative of all parties, to suggest revisions for the Defence of Canada Regulations.[65] T. C. Douglas, Co-operative Commonwealth Federation Member for Weyburn, raised issue after issue regarding the violation of civil liberties and, in the cases of Jehovah's Witnesses and Technocracy Incorporated, censured the government for having declared them illegal without having given adequate reasons for having done so. He argued that "the regulations ought to be altered so as to give those people an opportunity of appearing before some judicial or quasi-judicial body, so that they may state their case and have a hearing. That is the very least we can give to any organization or individual."[66]

Replies of government members tended, if anything, to strengthen Douglas's charges of government unfairness and capriciousness. When he mentioned Technocracy Incorporated, Paul Martin, Liberal Member for Essex East, called out "incipient fascists".[67] Somewhat later, G. A. Cruickshank, the Member for Fraser Valley, stated for the government that Technocracy had, in effect, been outlawed because Mr. Howard Scott (Technocrat leader) had "attempted to tell the Prime Minister [Mr. Mackenzie King] how to run Canada, what we should do in connection with the war". Furthermore he said: "I remember hearing the Minister for National Defence For Air [Mr. Power] refer to a member last year and saying if he were the Minister of Justice, the member would be interned. That is just what I would like to do with Howard Scott and with anyone who is a supporter of Howard Scott."[68] With regard to Jehovah's Witnesses, government members expressed either sarcasm or bitterness. Douglas's reference to an individual who could not collect money loaned to the Witnesses before the ban because of the seizure of Watch Tower funds brought a reply from Lapointe to the effect that "he made a poor investment".[69] Cruickshank stated simply: "I am not speaking disrespectfully, and I do not wish it to be so understood when I refer to the organization known as Jehovah's Witnesses. We can say to them, however, that we can thank God we have the Minister of Justice [Mr. Lapointe]."[70]

In spite of criticism, the Minister of Justice was in no mood to revise, immediately, a government policy which had much popular public support. War hysteria remained high; German armies poured over additional areas of Europe. On June 22, 1941, the *Wehrmacht* attacked the Soviet Union and by November was knocking at the gates of Moscow. War erupted in the Pacific on December 7, and Japanese forces swept quickly throughout the Western Pacific and Southeast Asia. In Europe, Asia, and Africa, the Allies were in retreat, and Canada was constantly called on to contribute more to stem the Axis tide. By a majority of Canadians, Jehovah's Witnesses continued to be regarded as unpatriotic slackers, and they continued to be prosecuted. Yet in some ways, during 1942 their position improved in spite of the continuation of the ban.

Individual Witnesses were, in general, becoming more adept at avoiding arrest, especially by carrying on their preaching activities with the Bible alone rather than with Watch Tower literature. The courts, particularly in Ontario, were beginning to show increased sympathy to them. In one outstanding instance, a Toronto magistrate dismissed a case against Lloyd Stewart for trying to have twenty-five thousand copies of the book *Children* printed by the T. H. Best Printing Company. In fact, Magistrate R. J. Browne, who must have known what the book was, maintained: "There is no evidence before the court that the books entitled *Children* are authoritative issues of an illegal organization known as Jehovah's Witnesses."[71] Prosecutions became more scattered; Witnesses in some parts of the country were able to hold meetings with up to five hundred persons present without molestation by the police.[72] But of greater importance was the fact that spokesmen for the Watch Tower Society were able to appear before the select committee of the House of Commons to give reasons why they believed the bans against both Jehovah's Witnesses and their legal corporations should be lifted.

The select committee agreed to hear representations from Jehovah's Witnesses on June 25 from ten-thirty in the morning to one o'clock in the afternoon, in part at least upon the urgings of CCF Members of Parliament. Two Witnesses, Charles Morrell and Robert McNaul, appeared and presented a brief which served as the basis for a discussion which lasted ultimately until six o'clock in the evening. Members of the committee were favourably impressed, and, although the Witnesses expected opposition from several government members, in the end the committee unanimously recommended the removal of the ban on Jehovah's Witnesses.[73] Charles Morrell was not wrong in noting, however: "As between the Committee's recommendation, if favorable, and the rescinding of Orders in Council there is a great gulf. . . . The government doesn't need to act on the Committee's recommendation."[74] Jehovah's Witnesses were to remain a proscribed religion for sixteen additional months.

The report of the select committee was tabled on July 23, 1942,[75] with a full statement of its findings published almost immediately by the *Montreal Standard*;[76] but Parliament took no action in the fall of 1942 or during the following winter, spring, and summer. Indeed, numerous Witnesses' homes continued to be raided, and many Witnesses were arrested under both the War Measures Act and other legislation. A man named Sherwin was convicted under Sections 217 and 262 of the Customs Act for having illegally imported literature which had been in his home for ten years.[77] RCMP also raided the home of Charles Morrell and even went so far as to confiscate a copy of the brief which had been placed before the select committee of the House of Commons, and later refused to release it.[78]

The government was faced with a rising tide of criticism, and Louis St. Laurent, Minister of Justice following the death of Ernest Lapointe in November 1941, was hard pressed to defend the continued legal suppression of Jehovah's Witnesses. The report of the select committee of the Commons had emphatically recommended the removal of the ban and the Department of Justice made no objections, but the Minister steadfastly refused to rescind the order in council sponsored by his predecessor without a specific resolution on the matter from the Commons.[79] The fact that the select committee had not placed its report before the House for adoption permitted him to do this, in spite of the fact that the government needed no such parliamentary support to act. St. Laurent and the government must have been made extremely uncomfortable, though, when Ralph Maybank, Liberal Member from Winnipeg South and a member of the select committee, stated earlier in the Commons why he personally had refrained from moving the adoption of the report when he had been charged with the sole responsibility of doing so:

A certain number of people did not want to discuss this question. I have no hesitation in saying that many of my good friends from the province of Quebec urged in conversation with me that the adoption of the report should not at that particular time be moved; that the report probably would have just as much effect if it were not formally adopted. They said, and I recognized the justice of their contention, "It is going to make a division in the country at the present time; everybody is very hot about this, and we think, Maybank, if you will let it go, in the long run that will turn out to be the wiser course."[80]

Even more damaging to the government's position must have been the Winnipeg Liberal's remarks, made at the same time respecting the ban on Jehovah's Witnesses in particular. "I have the case of the government—and the mounted police—against Jehovah's Witnesses," said Maybank, "and, Mr. Speaker, I would hesitate to read that case here in this house. As a matter of fact, the case against Jehovah's Witnesses, as presented to us at any rate, is just laughable. That is all there is to it."[81]

St. Laurent had somewhat relaxed restrictions on the Witnesses and other illegal groups. Under the terms of an order in council of February 15, 1943, the Defence of Canada Regulations were amended so that membership in an illegal organization was no longer held to be a crime so long as one did not *act* as an officer or member of such organization.[82] Also, on the same date, a statement was added to Section 39c of the Regulations to the effect that "No person shall be guilty of an offence against this regulation by reason of attending a meeting the sole purpose of which is religious worship or instruction."[83] Thus, in theory at least, Jehovah's Witnesses could now admit their faith and attend religious meetings, but in fact the police generally seemed unaware of the subtleties of the new measures.

That this was so was made evident by two instances in the Province of Quebec. In the first, a number of Witnesses were gathered on April 19, 1943, in a hall in Montreal to observe the Lord's Supper. During the service ten or eleven members of the RCMP entered and, though asked to wait until the meeting was ended, insisted on breaking it up by demanding that all persons present show their war-time registration cards. When three women were unable to produce them, they were taken to the police station.[84] The second instance occurred in St. Georges de Beauce, where Mrs. H. H. Mullins and a companion, Mrs. Boucher, were arrested and charged with distributing banned publications and as members of Jehovah's Witnesses under Sections 15A and 39c of the Defence of Canada Regulations. Mrs. Mullins and Mrs. Boucher had distributed pamphlets which did not carry the name of the printer. As a result the Royal Canadian Mounted Police raided Mrs. Mullins's home, seized a large quantity of the pamphlets, and, under instructions from the provincial Attorney General, arrested the two women. Mrs. Mullins, who refused to accept bail, remained in jail from July 8 to July 19, 1943, when she was finally released on her own recognizance.[85]

It was events such as these which brought great pressure on the government to end the ban. In reference to the April 19 Lord's

Supper raid, Angus MacInnis, CCF member for Vancouver East, stated sharply:

Suppose the police were to go into any gathering or any church in the evening and ask the congregation to show their registration cards; how many would be found in any congregation of, say, one hundred who would have their cards? Suppose such a thing had happened when the Roman Catholic church was holding a celebration on the streets of Ottawa not so long ago. How we would make the welkin ring with protests! . . . I do not know; I cannot understand, why there should be this continual persecution of Jehovah's Witnesses, because that is what I call it.[86]

Furthermore, when speaking of a Department of Justice brief submitted in defence of the ban on the Witnesses to the select committee, he said: "There was not enough material in it to shut up a dog, let alone a human being."[87] The police and Quebec and federal authorities were most embarrassed, however, when John Diefenbaker, then Progressive Conservative Member of Parliament for Lake Centre, raised the Mullins case in the House of Commons on July 15, by demonstrating that the pamphlets distributed by Mrs. Mullins and Mrs. Boucher were no more than excerpts from the French Catholic Crampon Version of the Bible; the very version on which St. Laurent himself admitted he had taken his oath of office.[88]

In replies to the queries and criticisms of MacInnis and Diefenbaker, the Minister of Justice felt constrained to make statements concerning the Witnesses and government policy toward them. Though he indicated that he had only hearsay evidence as to why the ban had been originally imposed on them—he had then been in Quebec City practising law—he remarked that the Watch Tower published "tens of millions of tracts", produced thousands of phonographs with speeches by the "so-called Judge Rutherford", and outfitted sound trucks. He also noted that the Witnesses regarded all religions but their own as those of the Devil. He claimed that the real reason for declaring them seditious, however, was their opposition to war. "There is no war according to their theory that is anything but the machinations of the devil himself, and . . . their view is that human-made laws have no binding force upon the individual if they happen to contravene what these gentlemen regard as being proper human behaviour."[89] Commenting later, he remarked: "They will not salute the flag; that, according to them, is an act of idolatry. At the present time—and the same situation is continuing—they are detrimental to the war morale of this nation."[90] In conclusion, he affirmed that the responsibility for the administration of justice and the prosecution of Jehovah's Witnesses lay with the provincial Attorneys General.[91]

The opposition was satisfied neither with the Minister of Justice's attack on the Witnesses nor with his defence of government policy. Speaking a week after St. Laurent's first statement, John MacNicol, Progressive Conservative Member for Toronto-Davenport, invoked the traditions of his Scottish Covenanter ancestors and bluntly said, with regard to the treatment of Mrs. Mullins, that he would not "stand for any persecution".[92] T. C. Douglas twitted the government for the April 19 Montreal Lord's Supper raid, criticized the continued legal repression of Jehovah's Witnesses in Canada when nothing of the kind existed in the United States, Great Britain, or Australia, and stated that if individuals were obstructing recruitment they could be charged with such without outlawing a whole religion.[93] Ernest Hansell, Social Credit Member for Macleod and a minister of the Church of Christ, attacked St. Laurent's statement, sentence by sentence, and argued that neither the quantity of their literature nor the fact that the Witnesses regarded theirs as the only true faith made them subversive. In fact, on the last point he challenged "the Minister of Justice to rise in his place and say that that is not the attitude of his own church".[94] When reference to the Witnesses' refusal to fight was made by a government member, Hansell stated: "There are other people who do not believe in fighting. There are the Doukhobors, and how many people in this house believed in not fighting only a few years ago?"[95]

Perhaps the most pointed opposition comments made at the time were those of Clarence Gillis, ccf Member for Cape Breton South, and Victor Quelch, Social Credit Member for Acadia. Gillis testified: "I have some [Jehovah's Witnesses] as friends and neighbours, and I know they are the best citizens in the community. They practise the

brotherhood of man; their creed is 'Love thy neighbour as thyself'."
He went on to state: "According to the Ottawa *Citizen* of recent
date, if General Eisenhower's mother were living in this country she
would be under the ban; she is a member of this group."[96] Quelch
said: "But it does make one wonder whether the action against
Jehovah's Witnesses is largely on account of their attitude toward the
Roman Catholics, instead of their attitude of a subversive nature."
When a French-Canadian Member cried, "It is a shame!" Quelch
replied: "You may say that it is a shame, but that question is being
asked all over the country."[97]

The government strenuously denied Quelch's suggestion. G. C.
Crerar, the Minister of Defence stated: "I can say this and I have
knowledge of whereof I speak. There is not a single particle of
evidence to support the allegation which the hon. member made in
his . . . remarks."[98] While Quelch stated that he had not made an
allegation but only asked a question which was being asked all over
the country,[99] Crerar responded:

It was close to an allegation, if it was not an allegation. I think all
members will agree on reflection that it is a most unwise statement to
make. He raised the question whether the policy of the government so
far as Jehovah's Witnesses was concerned was inspired by their attack
on the Roman Catholic church. That is the only inference that could
be drawn from his statement. I wish to say that the inference has no
foundation whatsoever, and I want that to go across this country. The
raising of issues of this kind, the planting of seeds of doubt and suspicion
is the greatest disservice that can be rendered to Canada at the present
time.[100]

In spite of the Opposition's efforts, the Minister of Justice adamantly refused to legalize Jehovah's Witnesses without a resolution
supporting such action from the House of Commons. He made that
clear on more than one occasion.[101] Nevertheless, the government was
now under intense pressure from outside Parliament, as well as from
inside, to remove the ban. The tide of war had turned completely;
Axis armies were in retreat in all theatres, and with a decrease in
public hysteria, Canadians began to be more concerned about civil

liberties. Also, there was the serious question of government policy toward the Communist Party of Canada. The 1942 select committee of the House of Commons had recommended that the party—banned since the spring of 1940—be made legal along with Jehovah's Witnesses and Technocracy Incorporated, although in the case of the Communists, the committee had not been unanimous.[102] As a result, the government, embarrassed no doubt by the existence of an official anti-Communist policy while war-time propaganda hailed the heroism of Canada's Soviet allies, gradually abandoned the prosecution of party members and began to release Red internees.[103] At the same time many police and public officials continued, without let-up, to press Jehovah's Witnesses. The suspicion therefore grew that the government, and the Minister of Justice in particular, refused to act in accord with the wishes of the Opposition on the advice of the now defunct select committee because it wanted, above all, to continue the suppression of Jehovah's Witnesses. Whatever the case may have been, pressures to lift the ban from the Communist Party helped both the Witnesses and the Technocrats. It would be difficult for St. Laurent to remove it from an organization which had long preached revolution without doing the same for the apolitical Jehovah's Witnesses or the politically unimportant Technocrats.

Independently, however, in the summer of 1943 Jehovah's Witnesses were also benefiting from a more favourable press in Canada and the English-speaking world in general. The report of the select committee and Opposition statements in Parliament had had their effect. The fact, too, that Ida Eisenhower, the mother of the Allied Supreme Commander in Europe and North Africa, was a Witness made the charge of sedition against her Canadian brethren seem somewhat hollow. Yet perhaps of even greater importance, as far as public opinion was concerned, were several important decisions by the Supreme Courts of the United States and Australia, which threw a more favourable light on the activities of the Witnesses of Jehovah.

On May 3, 1943, Jehovah's Witnesses won an amazing series of cases before the United States Supreme Court. Out of thirteen cases involving them, the court decided twelve in their favour.[104] Most important was the court's verdict in *Murdock* v. *Pennsylvania*,[105] which reversed a previous position taken by the Supreme Court itself in *Jones* v. *City of Opelika*,[106] and practically put an end to the arrests of American Witnesses for failing to obey licence-tax ordinances while conducting door-to-door preaching. Then, on June 14, 1943—Flag Day in the United States—the Supreme Court once again gave the Witnesses important legal victories. In *Taylor* v. *Mississippi*,[107] the court held that the beliefs and teachings of Jehovah's Witnesses could not be regarded as seditious. But of equal, if not greater, importance, the court also reversed its earlier ruling in the *Gobitis* case and, in *West Virginia Board of Education* v. *Barnette*,[108] determined that Witness children could no longer be forced to salute the American flag. The court stated. "If there is any fixed star in our constitutional constellation, it is that no official, high or petty, can prescribe what shall be orthodox in politics, nationalism, religion or any other matters of opinion or force citizens to confess by word or act their faith therein."

On the very same day that the United States Supreme Court rendered its verdicts in the *Taylor* and *Barnette* cases, the Supreme Court of Australia handed down its decision in *Adelaide Company of Jehovah's Witnesses, Inc.* v. *The Commonwealth*.[109] It held that a ban placed on the Witnesses in that country in January 1941, on the personal initiative of Prime Minister Menzies, was clearly unconstitutional. As a result of greater recourse to the courts and broader constitutional guarantees in Australia than existed in Canada, the Adelaide Company (congregation) had been able to have the matter heard judicially. Justice Williams, speaking for the Supreme Court, referred to the "perfectly innocent principles and doctrines" of Jehovah's Witnesses and ruled: "As the religion of Jehovah's Witnesses is a Christian religion, the declaration that the association is an unlawful body has the effect of making the advocacy of the principles and doctrines of the Christian religion unlawful and every church service held by believers in the birth of Christ an unlawful assembly."

These rulings by the most august judicial bodies in the United States and Australia became well known in Canada and, to a large degree, they served the Canadian Witnesses. Even before the American and Australian court decisions, the press in Canada had begun to demand that the government implement the recommendations of the select committee of the House of Commons. In an editorial of

February 24, 1943, entitled "Three Banned Organizations", the Toronto *Globe and Mail* castigated the Minister of Justice in very strong terms. Said the *Globe and Mail*: "Mr. St. Laurent, the Minister of Justice, seems determined to convince the Canadian people that he is a very stubborn politician, whose liberalism is only skin deep and whose contempt for Parliament is as profound as any dictator's." After discussing the creation of yet another committee to review the Defence of Canada Regulations and the former select committee's report, the *Globe and Mail* remarked in reference to the latter: "Its report urged that the ban now imposed upon the organized existence of three groups, the Communists, the Jehovah's Witnesses and the Technocrats, be removed as soon as possible, but nothing has been done about implementing this recommendation and Mr. St. Laurent evidently intends to continue disregarding it."[110] Several months later even some newspapers which had supported the government's original action in outlawing Jehovah's Witnesses began to suggest that the ban against them be removed. For example, the *Calgary Herald*, a rather consistent adversary of the Witnesses over the years, which had referred to them in the harshest of terms in July 1940 and had suggested that the ban be continued after the Second World War,[111] asked, on August 14, 1943: "Was Canada Wise to Ban This Religious Cult?" After mentioning the Montreal Lord's Supper raid and the *Barnette* decision, it suggested: "By banning the cult we have placed its members in the position of martyrs, which we imagine is something to their liking. As such it may be expected their zeal will be intensified and their determination to disregard the law firmer than ever. To them it means religious persecution—something they will regard as a sweet morsel under the tongue."

In the end, the many pressures were too great, even for "a very stubborn politician" like Louis St. Laurent. On October 14, 1943, upon the request of the Minister of Justice, the Governor General signed an order in council deleting the name Jehovah's Witnesses from the Defence of Canada Regulations subversive list.[112] Jehovah's Witnesses throughout Canada rejoiced; the ban was over, at least in part.

CHAPTER EIGHT

RECONSTRUCTION AND ALTERNATIVE SERVICE

It is neither safe nor prudent to do aught against conscience.

MARTIN LUTHER *Before the Diet of Worms*

DURING THE MORE THAN THREE YEARS of the ban, Jehovah's Witnesses had suffered greatly. It is estimated that well over five hundred were arrested on varying charges throughout the Dominion during that period,[1] a great number indeed in view of the fact that when they were outlawed in 1940 there were fewer than seven thousand active in all of Canada.[2] Many, illegally attending Watch Tower conventions south of the border in those years, were apprehended by American authorities,[3] imprisoned, and later deported to Canada, where they came under increased surveillance. But what was most disturbing to them was the constant fear, by day and by night, of police raids; the constant spying by neighbours;[4] and social pressures, both at work and at school. Often, too, even when individual Witnesses stopped to speak to one another on public streets, they were warned by police to move along.[5] Such official and unofficial suppression, however, had just the opposite effect from that intended by the government. The *Calgary Herald* was not wrong in assuming that it was a "sweet morsel under the tongue": they prospered. They looked upon the ban as a sure proof that they were being persecuted for righteousness' sake. Legal opposition to their activities strengthened their resolve to carry on with them; like the apostles, they rejoiced "that they were worthy to suffer shame for his [Christ's] name". Attending meetings, dropping prohibited booklets on doorsteps at night, and smuggling banned publications across the United States border or the Great Lakes became a serious but somewhat exciting game. Even arrest and conviction did not deter them, for to suffer such was a mark of pride among Witnesses, although they were far more interested in eluding the police to spread their beliefs.

In spite of the difficulties and obstacles the Witnesses faced, many Canadians received and accepted their message. Literature left in the night was sometimes read, and even members of police forces occasionally developed a sympathy for Jehovah's Witnesses based on their reading of the illegal publications. In a few cases policemen even became converts.[6] As the *1945 Yearbook of Jehovah's Witnesses* stated: "For more than three years the ban had been enforced against every activity of Jehovah's witnesses. . . . However, the progress of the truth and the 'hunting' and 'fishing' for the Lord's 'other sheep' went on." According to that same publication, "whereas in 1940 there was an average of 6,081 publishers engaging in the field each month, in the month of June 1944 there were 10,345 participating."[7] When Canadian Witnesses celebrated the memorial of the Lord's Supper in the spring of 1944, nearly sixteen thousand persons attended.[8]

Legal suppression, severe but spotty, had, if anything, increased the zeal of the Witnesses, created among them a unified élan, and greatly increased their numbers. Yet when news was flashed across the country that the ban was ended, it "was immediately hailed with joy as the prelude to greater activity".[9] A letter was dispatched to all congregations from Watch Tower Society overseers in Toronto which highlighted above all the militant determination of the now legalized faith:

JEHOVAH, the God of the free, through his great Emancipator, has burst another Devil-inspired band of restraint upon the Lord's servants. . . . The publishers of The Theocracy had determined that no matter what persecution came; regardless of whether any raised their voice on their behalf, the name of Jehovah *would* be praised; the New World *would* be proclaimed; the King's enthronement *would* be announced, as long as life and breath remained with them. Their faithful keeping of integrity has been recognized and blessed of Jehovah. . . . For all his loving-kindness and tender mercies manifested towards us, what shall we say? what shall we do? There is only one answer—FORWARD JEHOVAH'S WITNESSES.[10]

Congregations immediately began engaging kingdom halls and advertising them as in pre-ban times. A national headquarters, again under the superintendence of Percy Chapman, was established and began to publish a new magazine in English, entitled *Thy Word Is Truth*, with articles from the *Watchtower*. Within a year, nearly thirty thousand subscriptions were obtained for it, and editions in French and Ukrainian began to be published.[11] But the Witnesses were still under many legal restraints. Although they could publish all Watch Tower literature in Canada through commercial printers and could reproduce articles from the *Watchtower* magazine in *Thy Word Is Truth*, the government still prohibited the importation of all literature from the United States on the grounds that the Watch Tower Society was still illegal. Even King James Version Bibles printed without comments by the Society were denied entry into Canada by the Customs Department.[12] The International Bible Students Association also remained banned. The government therefore refused to return its confiscated properties, and since some kingdom halls had been owned through the Association, local Witness congregations had difficulty regaining their usage. Speaking in Parliament, A. H. Bence, Progressive Conservative Member for Saskatoon, remarked: "They are forced into the position where they must go and rent, from the custodian of enemy property, the very hall which they themselves bought with their own money through the medium of this organization which is still banned."[13]

If, however, Jehovah's Witnesses had been able to bring pressure to bear on the government while under the ban, they now increased their efforts by resorting to further stratagems to have their position legally accepted in every way possible. Not only did they continue to write letters to Members of Parliament with the result that their cases were discussed repeatedly on the floor of the House of Commons, but they turned once again to the ancient right of petition and to the courts. Legal counsel approached the government to have the ban removed, at least from the International Bible Students Association, so that Witness property might be returned, but to no avail.[14] The Witnesses, therefore, undertook to present a petition to the House of Commons, and the month of June 1944 was set aside as a time to get signatures for it. By the middle of the month, 223,448 were obtained,[15] but the government, undoubtedly impressed, decided to act before the petition could be presented to Parliament. By an order in council dated June 13, 1944, and made public three days later, the government abruptly legalized the International Bible Students Association of Canada.[16]

Other Witness victories came in 1944, in connection with the flag-salute issue. For some time the Witnesses had wanted to challenge the decisions of the many local school boards who had expelled their children from school. Heartened by the *Barnette* case they sought recourse to the courts in both Alberta and Ontario. But in the 1943 case of *Ruman* v. *Lethbridge District Trustees*, the Supreme Court of Alberta held that the Lethbridge School Board had acted within its power under the Alberta School Act.[17] Yet the *Ruman* decision was no more than a temporary victory for those Albertans who insisted on attempting to force Witness children to perform the required patriotic exercise. In its 1944 session, the provincial legislature, under the government of Premier Ernest Manning, amended the School Act to read that children need not salute the flag as long as they respectfully remained at attention during the exercise.[18]

More important, as far as most Canadian Witnesses were concerned, was the 1945 decision of the Supreme Court of Ontario in *Donald* v. *Hamilton Board of Education*.[19] According to the facts of the case, Robert Donald's two sons, Robert Jr. and Graham, had been suspended from school in September 1940 for refusing "on religious principles to sing 'God Save the King', and to repeat the Pledge of Allegiance, and to salute the flag". Two years later, after having taken private instruction and having passed high-school entrance exams, Robert Jr. was expelled from a Hamilton high school, again at the behest of the board. Donald then took the matter to court but lost at trial level. Upon appeal, however, the trial judge's decision was reversed, and the Witnesses were thereby given a sound legal basis for refusing to participate in patriotic exercises under Canadian law. The Supreme Court unanimously held that Section 7, Subsection 1, of the Ontario Public School Act was of "some importance" when it stated: "No pupil in a public school shall be required to read or study in or from any religious book, or join in any exercise of devotion or religion objected to by his parent or guardian." Furthermore, the court referred to Regulation 12 of the act which stated much the same thing and thereupon agreed with the appellants that if they regarded patriotic exercises as religiously objectionable, they could claim exemption from them on those grounds. Justice Gillanders remarked, in speaking for the court, that he found it "difficult to understand how any well disposed person could offer objection to joining in such a salute on religious or other grounds", but went on to state that "it would be misleading to proceed on any personal views on what such exercises might include or exclude". In that connection he adopted a portion of Justice Jackson's opinion in *West Virginia State Board of Education* v. *Barnette* which read in part:

Symbols of the State often convey political ideas just as religious symbols come to convey theological ones. Associated with many of these symbols are appropriated gestures of acceptance or respect; a salute, a bowed or bared head, a bended knee. A person gets from a symbol the meaning he puts into it, and what is one man's comfort and inspiration is another man's jest and scorn.

After quoting from another American case, *New York* v. *Sandstrom*, in which a New York court had held in favour of Jehovah's Witnesses on the flag-salute issue, Justice Gillanders went on to say:

The regulations relating to both public and high schools specifically contemplate that a pupil who objects to joining in religious exercise may be permitted to retire or remain, provided he maintains decorous conduct during the exercises. To do just that could not, I think, be viewed as conduct injurious to the moral tone of the school or class.

Donald received $378 damages for the expenses that he had incurred in paying private tuition for his children. But of much greater general significance was the fact that the Supreme Court of Ontario had established a judicial precedent which gave Jehovah's Witnesses some constitutional protection against school authorities who might attempt in future to force their children to participate in patriotic exercises.[20] The court declared that Jehovah's Witnesses might consider such exercises religious if they so chose; the Supreme Court of Canada did not disagree: the Hamilton Board of Education attempted to appeal to that court, but it refused to hear the case and allowed the judgment of the Ontario Supreme Court to stand. As a consequence, Witness children were permitted to return to school throughout the Dominion, and, except for a few isolated instances since the Second World War, the issue of the flag salute and attendant exercises was laid to rest.

During 1945 the government finally legalized the Watch Tower Bible and Tract Society and the Watchtower Bible and Tract Society, Incorporated. Percy Chapman and Hayden C. Covington, the American legal counsel for the two societies, visited Minister of Justice St. Laurent to request that the bans on those organizations be lifted. The Minister adamantly refused, whereupon the two Witnesses threatened to have another petition circulated beginning May 1, which they confidently expected would obtain over one million signatures.[21] To drive the point home, they contacted Prime Minister Mackenzie King personally to have "the facts laid before him".[22] They were as good as their word: the petition campaign began on the designated date.[23] But again the government gave way. The war was ending and the Liberals faced an upcoming June election with uncertainty. The Prime Minister caused the bans to be removed.[24] By a memorandum sent from the Deputy Minister of National Revenue, Customs and Excise to customs officers, all Watch Tower literature was allowed free entry into Canada as of May 15, 1945.[25] One week later the bans on the publishers of the literature were lifted by order in council.[26] Thus, after nearly five years, Jehovah's Witnesses and all organizations associated with them were once again recognized as legal throughout Canada.

Witness reorganization and growth were continuing also. A "Reconstructors Theocratic Assembly" was held in Toronto's Maple Leaf

Gardens in November 1944, and on the final day approximately eleven thousand persons attended.[27] In the following month the custodian of enemy property restored the ownership of the former headquarters and Bethel home of Jehovah's Witnesses in Canada to the International Bible Students Association.[28] Printing operations were begun at once, and in 1945 alone nearly 16,500,000 pieces of literature were produced.[29] In that same year over twenty-five hundred public meetings were held in Canada and 67 new congregations were formed, bringing the total to 470.[30] But perhaps most surprising of all was that the *1946 Yearbook of Jehovah's Witnesses* could boast that "Canada probably has more publishers in proportion to its population than any other country".[31]

Yet for one group of Jehovah's Witnesses—men of military age—restrictions were to increase from 1943 onward to the end of the war and for a year afterward. The direct involvement of Canadian forces in Italy, France, and the Low Countries brought increased demands for more troops. The government was therefore able to bring pressure to bear on any group not willing to be drafted for overseas service and, in consequence, to place hundreds of Jehovah's Witnesses either in the army or in alternative-service work camps, at the very time that it was permitting most other conscientious objectors to return to their homes.

The National Resources Mobilization Act of June 1940 had given the government almost complete control over national manpower and had permitted the establishment of national registration in August of the same year. The act also allowed for the call-up of men for military training and for the establishment of a home-defence "zombie army". At the same time the government was not anxious to go any further. Opposition to total mobilization was strong in Quebec, and to placate feeling there the National Resources Mobilization Act contained a provision against conscription for overseas service. Conscientious objectors nevertheless found themselves in difficult circumstances, because most of them were personally opposed to any sort of military service whatsoever. Consequently, groups such as the Mennonites and the Doukhobors appealed to agreements made by their forefathers with former Canadian governments which exempted them from such service. Public demands were made, however, that the "conchies" be drafted along with everyone else, and some politicians and newspapers argued that agreements made with former generations were no longer binding.[32] To blunt attacks made on them, the Mennonites quickly came forward with the suggestion that their young men be allowed to perform alternative service of a civilian nature.[33] The government agreed. It was not interested in stirring up issues which would focus attention on an already nationally divisive problem, and Prime Minister Mackenzie King was known to be personally sympathetic to the Mennonite community.[34]

Under National War Service regulations, provision was made for those "Mennonites, Doukhobors and conscientious objectors" who were to be exempted from military service to perform alternative-service work. The regulations also provided that the Minister of National War Services could enter into agreements with any other federal or provincial minister of the Crown whereby he would be responsible for the supervision of alternative-service workers.[35] As a result, work camps were established under the authority of the Minister of Mines and Resources in several national parks in western Canada beginning in June 1941. During the summer, camps were organized in Alberta at Banff, Jasper, and the Kananaskis Forest Experiment Area; at Prince Albert National Park in Saskatchewan; and at Riding Mountain National Park, Manitoba. Another camp was established at Kootenay National Park, British Columbia, in the fall, and later, others were erected at Petawawa and Montreal River in Ontario.[36] In addition, many alternative-service workers were placed under the supervision of the Dominion forester acting for the British Columbia government.[37]

From 1941 to 1944 the overwhelming majority of workers in the camps were Mennonites, though there were also sizable numbers of Hutterites and Seventh-Day Adventists. For instance, as of March 31, 1942, a total of 1,277 men had been called up for alternative service. Among them, 890 were Mennonites, 71 were Seventh-Day Adventists, and 24 were Hutterites, while the remainder were of various religions or no stated religion whatsoever.[38] Later many more Hutterites were called up, for they proved to be excellent workers. Surprisingly, the government or government officials saw fit to exempt most Doukhobors from such service. Out of the 1,277 mentioned, only one was a Doukhobor,[39] and while many others were ultimately called to the camps, they were few indeed in comparison to the total Doukhobor population.

What then was the relation of Jehovah's Witnesses to alternative service? Certainly a strange and involved one. In the first place, although every Witness regarded himself as a minister, and ministers of religion were exempted from military service, it was useless to claim to be a minister of a banned organization between July 4, 1940, and October 14, 1943. Many young pioneer evangelists, trying to continue their activities during that time, were arrested and often given severe prison sentences, sometimes with hard labour.[40] Even to claim status as conscientious objectors was dangerous, for on occasions when Witnesses did so and admitted that they were members of a banned organization, they were charged, convicted, and sent to jail.[41] Some in alternative-service camps from 1941 to 1943 were openly listed as Jehovah's Witnesses and some, in order to escape possible prosecution, as International Bible Students.[42] It is quite likely, too, that some of the persons described as of "no religion" were actually Witnesses. But during the period in question, the majority of Jehovah's Witnesses of military age escaped both imprisonment and alternative service. Many of them, especially farmers, received postponements of one sort or another.

As the War progressed, greater pressure was brought to bear on conscientious objectors in general, and Jehovah's Witnesses in particular. By the spring of 1942 the question of military conscription for overseas service had become a heated national issue. To satisfy French-Canadian feelings, Prime Minister Mackenzie King had stated in 1939: "So long as this government may be in power, no such measure will be enacted." In April 1942 he asked Canadians to release him from that guarantee by voting "yes" to a plebiscite held to give the government a free hand. Although sixty-four per cent did, French Canada reacted bitterly, and in order to maintain national unity, the government decided to continue its policy of conscription for home defence only. Yet the very nature of the conscription debate tended to focus unfavourable attention on conscientious objectors in English Canada, where most of them lived, and as of June 1942 the government decreed that "they cannot claim exemption on the plea that they are both c.o.'s and farmers".[43]

Still, it was only after the removal of the ban in October 1943 that the government began to take major steps against Jehovah's Witnesses of military age. In the first place, mobilization boards continued to refuse to recognize any Witness as an ordained minister exempt from mobilization regulations under the law. Since there was no clergy-laity distinction among them, and since all believed that they were ordained to preach at baptism, the government steadfastly refused to accept the claims for ministerial status of any of them. Minister of Justice St. Laurent, speaking in the Commons on May 15, 1944, stated:

The second point [for which they had been banned] was the propaganda to the effect that one could be an ordained minister of Jehovah's Witnesses by making an individual compact with the Almighty, that by doing so one became an ordained minister not subject to mobilization regulations. That is something which I look upon as contrary to the policy which this state has to maintain in war time.[44]

The Witnesses regarded the government's policy in this matter simply as another example of persecution. It was true that the position they took on mobilization was regarded as extreme even by some who felt that earlier measures against them had been wrong. Not only did they insist that all baptized Witnesses were ministers and ought to be exempted from military service, but they had come to feel that voluntary alternative civilian service was wrong and could not be accepted either. They were well aware that they would not be given blanket exemption, however, and ordinarily most of their young men would have quietly accepted some form of incarceration, as did their brethren in the United States. But what they specifically resented was that the government refused to recognize circuit and congregational overseers, pioneer evangelists, and even those working at the headquarters of Jehovah's Witnesses of Canada in Toronto as ordained ministers. Percy Chapman expressed that feeling when he wrote:

A strenuous effort was put forth during the year [1944] to have the government recognize the Christian ministers as "ordained of God", but not even those who preside over large congregations have been acknowledged as ministers. This is truly surprising! The country lifts the ban on Jehovah's witnesses, recognizes their right to worship, finds in its midst upward of 15,000 persons attending meetings, and yet will acknowledge none as ministers.[45]

When Jehovah's Witnesses refused to be drafted and were not recognized as conscientious objectors, they were turned over to military authorities in apparent attempts to force them to accept military service. According to friends and relatives who visited them, they were sometimes subjected to extremely brutal treatment amounting to physical torture. Opposition Members of Parliament received reports of such alleged occurrences from Windsor, Ontario, and Winnipeg,[46] and the matter was quickly aired in Parliament. Ernest Hansell read an affidavit from a Mrs. Elva Patzer which asserted that she had visited her brother, Gordon Mark Morrow, at Fort Osborne barracks at Winnipeg on April 23, 1944. "At the time his face was swollen, and one hand was bruised across the back of the wrist." Morrow had informed her that "three members of the army had previously struck him with their sticks behind the ears, on his hands and wrists, and then they had in addition struck him with their fists". He had also claimed that "some soldiers tied a loaded pack on his back, which was secured by a rope fastened around his throat, that he was violently pushed around, and the rope cut off his breath". Finally, he had asserted that the soldiers "threw him violently to the floor and then jumped on him with their knees" which caused him internal pain and led him to believe "that he had a broken rib or ribs".[47] A similar instance was reported in a statement by Stephie Klymuik of Whytewold, Manitoba, concerning another Witness at Fort Osborne, Adam Remando. She had visited him on April 16, a week before Mrs. Patzer had seen Morrow. At that time, according to her declaration: "Remando then informed me he had been put on a bread and water diet for refusing to put on the uniform, that his clothes had been violently torn from him and destroyed, and he was forcibly dressed in a uniform and ordered to pick up a gun, which he refused to do." In addition, he had asserted that "he was beaten and badly injured and put under an ice cold shower for twenty minutes, and that later on a gun was tied to his arm for several days".[48]

J. L. Ralston, the Minister of National Defence, remarked that the affidavits were hearsay evidence,[49] and submitted a report from Brigadier MacFarlane, district officer commanding Military District Number 10 at Winnipeg, which denied the allegations of mistreatment. MacFarlane did admit that four Witnesses—Martens, McGuire, Morrow, and Remando—"refused to take off their civilian clothes and their clothes have [sic] to be removed", but he said that the military board which had investigated the matter was "of the opinion that practically no force was necessary in order to remove the clothing and certainly no man was struck in any manner". He also stated that Morrow had been x-rayed twice with negative results and he denied that cold-water treatment had ever been used.[50] No mention was made of Morrow's swollen face or bruised wrist as described by his sister, but nearly three weeks had passed between her visit and the investigation.

Although the Minister of National Defence insisted on regarding the charges of brutality as unfounded, the matter was an embarrassment. Speaking in Parliament, M. J. Coldwell, leader of the ccf, questioned the validity of the military investigating itself in secret. Said he: "I suggest to the minister that, in view of the nature of these charges, if these courts are held in secret, he would be well advised to have an open inquiry into these cases in order that all parties can be satisfied."[51] The military had, of course, no intention of doing so— and with good reason. For the Witness conscripts at Fort Osborne told the same accounts in secret before the investigative military board that had been mentioned in Parliament,[52] and their statements could in no way be labelled "hearsay evidence". Yet, as long as such matters were kept in camera, military authorities could claim that Jehovah's Witnesses were just trying to embarrass them.

Thus, throughout 1944 and well into 1945, whenever Witness conscripts refused to obey orders and received rough treatment, the military attempted, very successfully, to keep their complaints from becoming public. Officers, in statements to their superiors, stated that, after all, since the Witnesses were recalcitrants, how could they expect not to be manhandled. Yet, when the Witnesses complained of brutality or beatings in army camps, officers investigating such charges almost always denied that the "alleged" events had occurred. They argued that they must accept the word of officers or noncommissioned officers above that of "self-styled conscientious objectors". Broken noses or badly bruised bodies were evidently wounds which the Witnesses had inflicted on themselves or which had occurred as accidents.[53]

Still, it is probably quite true that most Jehovah's Witnesses who were drafted into the Canadian Army were not mistreated physically. Generally, when they refused to obey commands, the worst that happened to them—and some other conscientious objectors—was that they were court-martialled and sent to prison. But such measures were extreme. All Witnesses claimed to be conscientious objectors and argued that they should never have been placed under military jurisdiction in the first place; and even the government was forced to concede that there was more than a little reason to their contention. Late in March 1944, T. C. Douglas asked in the House of Commons just how many men were in prison for refusing to obey military orders as conscientious objectors.[54] Less than a month later, perhaps as a direct result of this question, twenty-eight men—mostly Jehovah's Witnesses—in jail at Regina, Saskatchewan, were granted rehearings and sent to alternative-service work camps as bona fide conscientious objectors.[55] Still many others were imprisoned, particularly in Headingly Jail in Winnipeg, and were not released until near the end of 1945.[56] But this was the fate of only a few dozen.

In most cases, beginning early in the winter of 1944, the police rounded up Witness men of military age to take them to jail for refusing alternative service and, after short terms, to alternative-service camps. Although some pioneer evangelists moved so frequently that police could not apprehend them, most were arrested and eventually sent to the camps. Their claims for ministerial exemption were denied, and in many cases they were the last to be released. But pioneers were a minority of Jehovah's Witnesses in the camps; most were farmers or farm labourers.

Technically, farmers and farm workers should have been able to escape being sent to the camps. As the Deputy Minister of Labour stated in a letter of December 27, 1943, to Dr. Charles Camsell, Deputy Minister of Mines and Resources, there was an increased emphasis on agricultural production. He noted too: "The great majority of men postponed as conscientious objectors come from farms, and if they did not claim to be conscientious objectors when requesting postponement, I think the majority would be postponed as essential agricultural workers."[57] As a result of this analysis, Deputy Minister of Labour Arnold MacNamara indicated that most conscientious objectors should "be returned to agricultural employment under Alternative Service work contracts, and that some other labor be found to do the necessary work . . . in the National Parks or the British Columbia forests."[58] Great numbers of Mennonites, Hutterites, and other conscientious objectors were, in consequence, sent home, and the total number of camp workers was reduced considerably. It would therefore have seemed reasonable to have left many Jehovah's Witnesses home on farms, but such was not to be the case.

In the first place, the government argued that they were completely uncooperative and unwilling to abide by the law. Under the terms of an order in council dated Wednesday, April 7, 1943, alternative-service workers employed in agriculture could receive a maximum of twenty-five dollars per month plus board and lodging; and all other wages that they would ordinarily receive above that amount—usually about fifteen dollars—would be paid by their employers to the Canadian Red Cross Society.[59] In addition, if a conscientious objector were a self-employed farm owner, he too might have to turn over a portion of his income to the Red Cross.[60] Thus, Jehovah's Witnesses of military age who were working on farms were, in effect, required to pay a special assessment which was levied on them and other conscientious objectors because of their opposition to war, although they were not supposed to be liable to military service. If they refused to pay they would be arrested and, if convicted, sent to jail and then to alternative-service camps. Most other conscientious objectors agreed to pay the forced contribution, but not the Witnesses. In the first place, they regarded Red Cross donations as indirect support of the war. But more significantly, they felt that the April 1943 order in council was totally discriminatory and simply a handy tool with which the government could bedevil them. Why, they asked, should a man who was a bona fide farmer or farm labourer be required to pay a forced contribution to the Red Cross because he belonged to a faith which regarded war as wrong, when no such regulation applied to other men who were exempted for agricultural purposes? Why, also, should a man be subject to alternative-service regulations simply because of his belief, if he was in no way liable to military service? Evidently there was nothing "alternative" about alternative service.[61] In such cases conscientious objectors were being penalized simply because of their beliefs, not because they had broken any law or because the government was granting them any special exemption. In reply to the government's contention that they were uncooperative and unwilling to abide by the law, they asserted that the law was nothing but another subterfuge to harass them; and there was much evidence to support their allegation.

Not only did their neighbours, who were not opposed to war on religious grounds, receive agricultural postponements without paying forced contributions, but many other conscientious objectors were permitted to escape that requirement as well. The Witnesses were aware that few Doukhobors had ever been called for alternative service, and they agreed with John Diefenbaker that the government had simply given its "approval to the flouting of these regulations by these people".[62] While many others were left alone by Selective Service officials, however, the same officers carried on a concerted campaign against Jehovah's Witnesses. For example, in several cases involving Witnesses engaged in agriculture at Quill Lake, Saskatchewan, Judge J. N. Hanbidge of the District Court of Humboldt noted:

I would just add one thing and that is this, that in the course of evidence it was mentioned that these men were just picked out to make an example. That may be necessary but it seems strange to me where all Conscientious Objectors are not put on the same footing that the Alternative Service Officer should happen to pick out two farmers who were farming in a very large way and apparently very essential on the land, engaged in an occupation which the authorities at Ottawa deemed so essential that they worded Section 9, "The Board shall, upon application of a person employed in agriculture grant him a postponement order until further notice."[63]

But in most instances the courts were completely unsympathetic to the Witnesses. Selective Service officers were usually allowed to use their own discretion in interpreting regulations involving conscientious objectors.[64] Thus, when they would not pay Red Cross donations, hundreds of young Witnesses were taken from farms throughout Canada and shipped to alternative-service camps at the very time that the nation was crying desperately for more farm workers.

Arrests of Witness men of military age were generally carried out quietly by the police, although in one instance they created a stir by attempting to arrest several at a funeral. The enforcement officer of National Selective Service at North Bay, Ontario, notified the Royal Canadian Mounted Police when he saw an obituary notice in the *North Bay Nugget* which indicated that Donald Morrison, for whom a warrant as a delinquent had been issued, would officiate at interment services at the nearby community of Balsam Creek on July 9, 1944. The RCMP in turn contacted the Ontario Provincial Police and the military provost police with the result that members of each force attended the funeral. As the funeral party was leaving the cemetery, the police arrested Morrison and chased several other men across nearby fields in vain attempts to apprehend them. The episode was reported to John Diefenbaker, who in turn brought it to the attention of the Minister of Justice. Even Louis St. Laurent's sensibilities were shocked, and the RCMP officers involved were reprimanded.[65]

The methods used in interning Witnesses were harsher than those employed for other conscientious objectors. In practically every case from early 1944 on, they were escorted to the camps by policemen and were sentenced to alternative service for as long as the government might choose to hold them. They were, in effect, prisoners rather than voluntary workers, and therefore relations between them and the officials and men who governed them were not particularly good. Time and again, park superintendents, medical officers, and civil servants accused them of being poor workers and malingerers, and orders were sent from Ottawa to force them to work or have them sent to prison. As the result of a complaint by Dr. A. J. Tripp of Invermere, British Columbia, that many of the men at Kootenay Park were malingering and had attempted to induce him to recommend their discharge, the controller of the lands, parks, and forest branch of the Department of Mines and Resources wrote to park superintendents at Banff, Jasper, and Riding Mountain:

There is abundant evidence of a tendency to malinger on the part of conscientious objectors performing alternative service, particularly Jehovah's Witnesses and it is important, if we are going to get any work out of these people, to put teeth in the regulations. An example should be made of men who appear to be the ringleaders in this form of misdemeanor.[66]

For their part, Witness internees complained that they were often treated harshly, and that sometimes, when they were sick, prejudiced medical officers insisted on ignoring their real needs. Ross Bletsoe of Mimico, Ontario, who had reported to the Montreal River camp in 1942, prior to the time that Jehovah's Witnesses had taken a unified stand against alternative service, claimed that he had been struck on the shoulder with a twenty-five-pound stone, had contracted a chill, and was confined to camp for a month with a fever of up to 104 degrees with no medical attention. After being contacted by a fellow worker, his parents paid to have a physician travel two hundred miles to see him. When the camp doctor finally arrived he diagnosed Bletsoe's case as pleuropneumonia and said if it did not clear up in a month, he would have to go to Sault Ste. Marie and be x-rayed for tuberculosis. Further, a wisdom tooth had caused him "temporary lock jaw". The camp foreman, on being told that he had not eaten for days, replied: "He is not dead yet. Let him drink water." Bletsoe ultimately recovered without medical assistance.[67] Walter Backous, who had served ten months at hard labour in the Lethbridge, Alberta, jail for refusing alternative service,[68] reported an experience similar to Bletsoe's when he was in the alternative-service camp at Banff. Feeling ill, he reported to the camp physician, who, according to Backous's report, accused him of malingering and said he should be fighting on the Russian front. He was apparently so obviously ill and running a high fever that the camp superintendent allowed him to return to his home at Bassano, Alberta. There his family physician diagnosed his case as scarlet fever.[69]

Men at the Petawawa camp in the cold months of 1944 complained that they were so inadequately clothed that they had to use all the small amount of money they received to buy extra clothing to keep from freezing. Consequently, the families of married men were left practically destitute. Thus, both the men and their wives made the matter known to government officials at every level and caused members of the Opposition to discuss it in Parliament. A Timmins, Ontario, woman, a Mrs. McKnight, wrote: "Because of our Christian beliefs, in this democratic country are my child and I to starve? My friends are tired of keeping me in groceries and rent, and I am unable to work."[70] Mrs. Alfonse Vaillancourt of the same city complained that her husband had only enough money for himself at camp while she and their children were poorly clothed.[71] Mrs. Ernest Jutras of Kirkland Lake, Ontario, stated: "I have a young baby five months old. Due to the lack of necessities he has been sick for more than two months, and is now seriously ill. I tried (but in vain) to get support from the authorities, causing me to descend to mendicancy."[72] Mrs. Gordon Lane of London, Ontario, protested that she had had two serious operations in the past two years and could not work to support her family. What little cash she had had on hand had gone to buy warm clothing for her husband at Petawawa, "as none was supplied to him". She was left in a rather critical position.[73]

Humphrey Mitchell, the Minister of Labour, whose department had by that time taken over responsibility for alternative-service workers, brushed the complaints aside. He said: "It must be remembered we are dealing with one brand of religious people, namely, Jehovah's Witnesses. It is very difficult to deal with them." Although he indicated that he meant this in a "kindly way", he remarked: "Many of the letters that are received in my department are of an emotional character like the people themselves." With reference to the dependants of conscientious objectors, he claimed that "they were treated just as fairly as the men in the fighting forces", and if they were in serious need, they should appeal to provincial not federal officials, since "the province in which that family resides will take care of those people and we bear the expense".[74]

The Minister of Labour was not being entirely candid. On October 30, 1943, the Minister of Mines and Resources had written to him about the serious conditions under which alternative-service workers laboured and indicated that from the beginning it had been recognized that "the men would receive less remuneration than soldiers". He had also made it quite clear that "our officers remarked . . . that alternative service workers might find themselves in a difficult position because they were receiving no clothing allowance, nor separation allowance where the worker had dependants." In closing he had stated: "All I wish to do is bring to your attention the undoubted fact that there is a difficult situation which will not become any better by delay."[75] More specifically, nearly three months before Mitchell suggested that the wives of Jehovah's Witness alternative-service workers were exaggerating their plight, his own parliamentary assistant, Paul Martin, had answered a question from T. C. Douglas by saying with regard to the families of men committed to the camps: "Unfortunately their dependants have to rely on their own resources, these cases being parallel to the cases of men committed to prison."[76]

Months later, in January 1945, supplementary clothing supplies were sent to the men at Petawawa and some of the other camps as well.[77] No funds were forthcoming for their dependants, however, and government officials began to express bitterness at Witness complaints. "In the case of Jehovah's Witnesses, we realize that they complain about everything," wrote L. E. Westman, Chief Alternative Service Officer of the Department of Labour. He indicated, however, that their protests were generally ignored: "Relatively we pay little attention to their complaints and I assure you that there are a great many that are never forwarded to the superintendents [of the camps]."[78]

The Witnesses did far more than complain. Although they had developed their manner of protest into a fine art which often brought results, they also fought in the courts attempts to conscript them for military and alternative service. As already indicated, they were particularly interested in having various organizational overseers and pioneer evangelists recognized as ministers in order to have them exempted from mobilization requirements. So, when authorities would not agree, they engaged them in a series of legal contests.

Under the terms of the National War Services regulations, it was provided that certain persons should "be exempted from being called out". Among such were "Regular Clergymen or Ministers of religious denominations".[79] Of course Jehovah's Witnesses did not want to be regarded as clergymen, but they did want to be classified as ministers of a religious denomination; and they had judicial precedents to buttress their claim to that status.

At the time, the terms specifying the exemption of ministers of religion from conscription were almost identical in the United States, Australia, Great Britain, and Canada. Furthermore, Jehovah's Witnesses faced the same problem in each of those countries: not one was willing without litigation to recognize even full-time overseers or pioneer evangelists as ministers. It is true, however, that United States Selective Service authorities in Washington, D.C., did admit that they could be designated as ministers under the terms of the American Selective Service Act,[80] but local draft boards often refused to grant the necessary IV-D classification, and many young Witnesses were sent to prison. Only in 1945 did the United States Court of Appeals Seventh Circuit discharge a Jehovah's Witness from Selective Service custody on the grounds that he had not been properly classified, since he was a minister of religion.[81] As early as March 5, 1943, however, an Australian court had reversed the conviction of a Witness, Frank Grundy, for refusing to be conscripted, on the basis of the plea that, in fact, he was an ordained minister.

In the *Grundy* case the Crown argued that Frank Grundy could not be a minister of religion under the terms of the Australian Defence Act 1903–41, since Jehovah's Witnesses were not a religion. The Crown Counsel contended that: " 'Religion' as used in the Defence Act means an organized religion within a ministry but Jehovah's Witnesses are only an organized society for putting out publications and, as they claim to be opposed to religion, their beliefs and actions cannot be a religion." In addition, he contended that "the faith of Jehovah's Witnesses is not a bona fide religion". On the other hand, Grundy's counsel argued that the Australian Parliament had intended the word religion to be understood in its popular sense, and within that meaning, Jehovah's Witnesses were a bona fide religious organization of which Grundy was a minister. The court found for Grundy; his appeal was allowed and his conviction quashed.[82]

Of importance to the positions taken by both the American and the Australian courts were constitutional provisions which provided for the separation of church and state. The First Amendment to the

United States Constitution was quoted almost verbatim in Section
116 of the Australian Constitution Act. Thus the governments of
both countries were enjoined from making "any law establishing any
religion or prohibiting the free exercise thereof".

The situation was different in Canada, of course, where, as in
Great Britain, no such provision existed. Nevertheless, there were
both British and Canadian precedents which, it seemed, might serve
to support Jehovah's Witnesses' contention that at least some of them
should be classified as regular ministers. During the First World War
the Court of Appeals in England had held that a part-time minister
of the Strict Baptist Church who served six days a week as a solicitor's
clerk could be exempted from military service because he preached
regularly on Sundays.[83] Similarly, the Saskatchewan Court of King's
Bench granted a writ of *habeas corpus* to a man named Bien on
August 30, 1943, because he had been inducted into the army in
spite of the fact that he claimed to be a minister of the Church of
Christ. The court made no particular issue over the facts that the
Church of Christ was far less "organized" in a formal sense than
Jehovah's Witnesses, and that Bien spent six days a week as a
farmer.[84] Yet the judiciary was to prove as adamant toward the
Witnesses in this matter as was the government itself.

In practically every case where the question of the ministerial status
of Jehovah's Witnesses was adjudicated, the courts decided against
them. Though they usually agreed that the Witnesses constituted a
religion, they denied that even their circuit overseers could be regarded as "Regular Ministers of a denomination". A judge of a
Saskatchewan court held that the term "regular" did not apply to
them.[85] The British Columbia Court of Appeal followed the ruling of
the Scottish High Court of Justiciary in *Saltmarsh* v. *Adair*, a 1942
case, and declared that they could not be regarded as ministers.[86] In
Greenlees v. *Attorney General for Canada*, an Ontario judge took
the same view,[87] but when appeal was made to the Ontario Court of
Appeal, that body refused to address itself to the question of Greenlees' ministerial status; it found that Jehovah's Witnesses were not a
denomination.[88]

All of these cases were originally tried during the time that the
Watch Tower Bible and Tract Society of Pennsylvania and its

associate New York corporation remained under the ban. Therefore, since all Witness overseers and pioneers had originally been appointed by those organizations, the courts claimed that they could not be ministers of Jehovah's Witnesses.[89] Also, since Jehovah's Witnesses were not incorporated or governed independently of the banned societies, they were held not to be a denomination.[90] Since no province had granted any Witness the legal right to solemnize marriages, that, too, was used as an argument to deny that they were in any way ministers under the terms of the National War Services regulations.[91]

W. Glen How, a young Witness attorney soon to become known as one of Canada's most brilliant constitutional lawyers, attempted to appeal the *Greenlees* case to the Supreme Court of Canada. But it refused to hear the case, since that court could not accept cases in which no monetary interest was involved.[92] When How pressed to have the matter heard before the Privy Council in London, the government ended the matter by withdrawing the National War Services regulations. By that time the war had long since ended, and the issue was settled, at least as far as the government was concerned.

From the point of view of Jehovah's Witnesses, the *Greenlees* case was a disappointment. Nevertheless, they did gain some favourable publicity through it,[93] and by fighting every attempt to conscript them, they caused the government some discomfiture. Occasionally they even made the authorities look foolish. In one rather amusing instance in Saskatchewan in 1944, the District Court of the Judicial District of Yorkton acquitted a pioneer evangelist, John Jazewsky, for failing to respond to a separate call from the National Selective Service to accept civilian alternative service at the same time that he had been ordered to report for military induction. The judge commented that, to his mind, the maintenance of two sets of proceedings against Jazewsky smacked "somewhat of persecution".[94]

In the meantime, Witness internees in the alternative-service camps used every legal device to obtain as much freedom as possible. For example, they demanded the right to call on the homes of nearby townspeople on Sundays to spread their beliefs, and when this was refused, they complained that their freedom of worship was being restricted. Though the Minister of Labour denied their contention, he took time to write personally to Minister of Justice St. Laurent to obtain a statement on the matter from the Department of Justice. Mitchell remarked: "Since it is likely that a number of letters will be received by Members of Parliament and Members of the Cabinet from Jehovah's Witnesses now in camp, it will be helpful . . . if I would have a statement from you specifically indicating what you consider to be a fair interpretation of freedom of worship."[95] Also, when the RCMP took proceedings against two men at Camp Petawawa for malingering, they fought the actions so tenaciously in the courts that the Chief Alternative Service Officer notified the director of lands, parks, and forests that great care had to be taken in bringing such proceedings. For, said Westman, "We anticipate that on Jehovah Witness [*sic*] prosecutions there will be found opposing legal talent."[96] In some ways the Witnesses almost intimidated those who kept them in detention. In his book *The Theory and Practice of Hell*, Eugen Kogon comments that in the concentration camps of Nazi Germany "one cannot escape the impression that psychologically speaking, the SS was never quite equal to the challenge offered them by Jehovah's Witnesses".[97] The same may be said for the men who ran the alternative-service camps; eventually they took great care in dealing with their charges. As internees later reported, their guards sometimes grumbled that "these Jehovah's Witnesses are all a bunch of lawyers".

Yet the government would not relent of its policy; as Mennonites and others left the camps, Jehovah's Witnesses continued to be brought in. The records of the five alternative-service camps in the national parks of western Canada indicate that during the period from April 1, 1944, through March 31, 1945, out of a total of 595 camp workers, 226 were Jehovah's Witnesses, 206 Mennonites, and 101 Hutterites.[98] But during the following year, out of a total of 456, there were then 283 Witnesses, 100 Mennonites, and only 44 Hutterites.[99]

National Selective Service officers continued, too, to circumscribe the freedom of Witness men outside the camps, although after the war they stopped sending them to the camps. Under National Selective Service civilian regulations, as established by Privy Council Order 246 of January 19, 1943, all persons "not gainfully employed" could be required to accept work as designated by Selective Service officers. Many officers interpreted the regulations as broadly as possible and ordered certain pioneer evangelists, who were not subject to military conscription, to accept regular work in industry. Even in the spring of 1946, when thousands of returned veterans created a serious labour surplus, Selective Service continued this practice. Thus, nearly a year after the war, becoming a full-time missionary of Jehovah's Witnesses could, and sometimes did, bring threats of prosecution,[100] although no such action was contemplated against the missionaries of any other religion.

Of course the government defended its policy in these matters. Deputy Minister of Labour MacNamara claimed that his department had tried to release as many conscientious objectors as possible from the alternative-service camps, to have them "employed in those essential occupations in which their individual skills can best serve the national interests".[101] At the same time he argued that the ninety-one who remained in the camps after March 31, 1946, could not be released because: "We cannot be in a position to allow a man who would not take up arms for his country to be employed in a job that a man who has fought and risked his life in the Armed Services was seeking."[102]

But it was becoming obvious that, once again, the government would soon have to yield. On May 30, 1946, the Ontario Court of Appeal handed down a decision in the case of *Rex* v. *Evans* which brought an end to the powers of Selective Service officers over pioneer evangelists. According to the evidence presented in the court, William Lloyd Evans, a pioneer, had been ordered to accept work at the First Co-operative Packers of Ontario at Barrie on March 15, 1945, as a person "not gainfully employed". When he refused, he was arrested, tried, and sentenced to three months in jail and fined one hundred dollars. The defence argued that Evans was gainfully employed since he received up to forty dollars a month as a missionary. The magistrate ignored that argument, however, and when Evans appealed to the County Court, the "Judge was of the opinion that the matter of whether the appellant was 'gainfully employed' was one in the discretion of the Selective Service Officer, and that it was not his duty to pass upon the right or wrong of the decision". But the Appeal Court did not agree: Evans's conviction was quashed.[103] *Saturday Night* editorialized:

Whatever other objections may be laid against them, the Witnesses of Jehovah perform a useful function in about any society as defenders of the rights and liberties of the common citizen. They have just achieved a notable victory, after two appeals, in securing a judgment from the Ontario Court of Appeal that a Selective Service Officer has no right to place his own interpretation on the expression "person not gainfully employed". One of the "missionaries" of the society was ordered to work for a packing company on the ground that he was not gainfully employed when he was actually earning up to $40 a month in his missionary capacity. His remuneration was not large, and many people feel that his occupation was not very essential, but the regulations are silent on both these points. It would have been a national disaster had it been held to be the law that a man cannot be employed as a missionary at $40 a month by the Witnesses of Jehovah, when plenty of people are employed at similar work and similar remuneration by other religious bodies of higher social standing.[104]

It was not a court decision, however, which finally brought about the release of the men still in the camps. Glen How, acting under the direction of the Watch Tower Society, carried on a well-organized campaign to bring pressure on the government both through direct appeals and through members of the Opposition. In reply to the Deputy Minister of Labour's policy statement on conscientious objectors, How circulated a brief entitled "Representations with Respect to Alternative Service" in which he argued that MacNamara's remarks regarding the reasons for keeping the men in the camps were contradictory and misleading. MacNamara claimed the men must accept "essential occupations" or remain in the camps; yet there was no labour shortage requiring their services for such occupations. The Deputy Minister also claimed that they must be held in the camps to keep them from taking jobs from veterans, an argument which seemed in direct contradiction to his statement that they must accept "essential occupations" or stay in the camps. Finally, How pointed out that since the Department of Labour was aware that all of the internees in question were missionaries, it knew very well that, if they were released, they most certainly would not take work from job-hungry veterans.[105] In How's sight, the government was maintaining a system which treated Jehovah's Witnesses like "English serfs of the middle ages, and American slaves in the southern states".[106] In a letter to Minister of Labour Mitchell, dated June 1, 1946, he wrote:

The continued failure of the Department to give any relief or even adequately explain this situation, leaves me no alternative but to advise those adversely affected by this continued enforced labour, that their sole recourse is to the courts. I am reluctantly forced to this position by the attitude of the Department. An extensive test case to probe the authority of the Crown under the Emergency Powers Act, seems most inadvisable at the present time.[107]

No such test case needed to be launched. Ever since early in 1944, members of the Opposition had asked question after question about conscientious objectors, particularly about Jehovah's Witnesses in the alternative-service camps.[108] Now, with less than one hundred men—all Jehovah's Witness missionaries—still in internment, Opposition questions again began to make the government look guilty of persecuting one particular religious group. The government was also anxious to grant an amnesty to the great number of unapprehended army deserters still at large in the country, particularly in Quebec, and it was obvious that to do so without releasing Jehovah's Witnesses would look highly discriminatory indeed. Thus, the government apparently decided to yield on the matter when, on July 10, 1946, John Diefenbaker rose in Parliament to ask: "How many Jehovah's Witnesses are still being held in concentration camps?"[109] On July 23 Minister of Labour Mitchell tabled a copy of order in council p.c. 3030 which provided that, effective August 15, 1946, control over conscientious objectors for alternative service would end. A six-year struggle between Jehovah's Witnesses and the Liberal government of William Lyon Mackenzie King was over; the Witnesses' civil liberties were restored entirely, except in Quebec.

CHAPTER NINE

QUEBEC'S BURNING HATE

Catholic patriots, entrusted with the government of a Catholic State, will not shrink from repressive measures in order to perpetuate the secure domination of Catholic principles among their fellow-countrymen.

MONSIGNOR RONALD KNOX *The Beliefs of Catholics*

AT THE END OF THE WAR Jehovah's Witnesses turned their attention to the Province of Quebec. In English Canada peace brought them relief from most official opposition, and after the fall of 1946 few restraints of any kind were placed on their preaching activities. It is true in a few cases that they were charged with distributing literature without a licence, but, without exception, the courts upheld their right to do so. For instance, in 1949 in the case of *Rex* v. *Kite*,[1] Judge P. O. Harrison of the County Court of Nanaimo held that Eustace Kite should not have been arrested for handing out handbills on the streets of Nanaimo, British Columbia, under a municipal street and traffic bylaw. Saskatoon Magistrate B. M. Wakeling took a similar position in *Rex* v. *Naish*[2] in the following year. In addition, the courts began to protect individual Witnesses from assaults while engaged in door-to-door evangelism.[3] Then, too, beginning with the CCF government of T. C. Douglas in Saskatchewan, one by one the provinces of English Canada gradually granted them the right to solemnize marriages.[4] Thus, with little opposition they were able to spread their message throughout western Canada, Ontario, and most of the Maritimes. During the 1950s they were to gain the distinction of being Canada's "fastest growing religion".[5] But in Quebec circumstances were different.

On Saturday, September 15, 1945, a number of Witnesses were advertising a public lecture in Lachine, Quebec, for the following day. Before the day was out local youths attacked them, tore up their placards, handbills, and literature, and drove them into the combined home and clockmaker's repair shop of Witness Joseph Letellier. There they were besieged by a crowd of hundreds who hurled stones and tomatoes at the building and broke the store's plate-glass window. When Letellier rushed to the phone to call the police, "someone smashed his fist into the elderly man's face, inflicting a long cut and knocking his glasses to the floor". Later, police did set up barricades around the Letellier building, but mobsters climbed over rooftops and continued to shower it with stones. As a result, the entire front of the building was wrecked, and valuable clocks inside were destroyed. One young Witness woman was struck "full in the chest" by a stone, and only after five hours were the five occupants able to make their escape through a narrow alley to an automobile which their friends had provided.[6]

On the following day, when they attempted to hold the advertised public lecture at the Banque Canadienne Nationale hall, a crowd threatened to riot again. Because of the circumstances, the local bank manager stated he could not risk having the building damaged and promised to refund the rent that the Witnesses had paid for the use of it. They then determined to hold the lecture at the home of a Mrs. Blickstead but could only do so surrounded by a score of Lachine and Provincial Police.[7]

Six days earlier, a similar event had occurred at Chateauguay. The Montreal *Gazette* reported that on September 9 "a crowd estimated at more than 1,000 men, women and children, many armed with canes and sticks, broke up an outdoor Bible lecture of the Witnesses of Jehovah here today by showering them with tomatoes, potatoes and rocks and overpowering the speaker's voice with two powerful sirens." The *Gazette* further reported that at least one Witness was "jumped upon by about 10 men who allegedly kicked and beat him" and "that the home of R. W. Weaner, in whose yard the lecture was held, was considerably damaged, with windows broken, and walls spattered with tomatoes and potatoes". In this instance, the police did nothing to stop them, but, earlier in the day, "acting under instructions of René Lussier, town secretary, and police Chief Mc-Clintock", they had arrested fifteen Witnesses for distributing circulars without a licence.[8]

The Witnesses, as tenacious as ever, tried on the following Sunday to hold another public lecture, with the same results. Seventeen, most of them women and youths, were arrested, again on the charge of distributing circulars without a licence. Again they met at the Weaner home, and again they were attacked, this time by a crowd of about fifteen hundred who began to shower them "with potatoes, cucumbers, rotten eggs and a few rocks". The eight policemen present told the Witnesses that they could not control the situation and ordered them to shut down their loudspeakers unless they wanted Mrs. Weaner charged with disturbing the peace. Montreal restaurateur Frank Roncarelli, attending the lecture with his two sons, was seized by a group of youths and beaten until rescued by the police. The tires of a bus which had brought many Witnesses from Montreal were deflated, and some forty passengers were forced to flee on foot under police escort two miles to Woodland, Quebec, to take trains and buses back to the city. On the way they were overtaken by youths who set upon them. "The hoodlums seized all the literature carried by the Witnesses and burned it in a field."[9] The *Montreal Daily Star* reported: "Pamphlets and Bibles were torn to shreds and littered the lawns of the summer homes facing St. Louis."[10] In the mêlée several Witnesses were injured, but no arrests were made.[11]

Lachine and Chateauguay showed the depth of French-Canadian, Roman Catholic feeling against Jehovah's Witnesses, and if they had any doubts about the attitudes of Quebec officials as apart from the populace, they were soon dispelled. Although the federal government in Ottawa was no longer able to do much to inhibit the activities of Jehovah's Witnesses—much as certain members of it might have liked to do so—in Quebec neither the Roman Catholic Church nor civil authorities had any intention of ending their anti-Witness campaign.

Catholic clergymen, including Cardinal Villeneuve,[12] continued to inveigh against them. Priests preached bitter sermons about "these apostles of heresy" and sometimes suggested the use of a broom, stove poker, or kettle of hot water on them when they called at Catholic homes.[13] Catholic writers argued that they were the tools of communism,[14] and now, once again, policemen, public officials, and, above all, Premier Maurice Duplessis decided to suppress them through the most sweeping series of arrests ever carried out against any religious movement in Canadian history. Although the adverse publicity from the Lachine and Chateauguay riots did temporarily curb legal actions against them—the Quebec Superior Court granted some seven writs of prohibition to restrain recorder's courts from hearing Witness cases in Montreal and Verdun[15]—arrests continued. By September 1946, some eight hundred charges were pending against Jehovah's Witnesses in those communities. Percy Chapman reported that "so serious has the fight become in these cities that over $100,000 in property bond is lodged on behalf of the brethren in Montreal alone".[16] At the time, there were only about three hundred Witnesses in the entire province.[17]

Catholic Quebec seriously underestimated its adversaries, however. The Witnesses of Jehovah, as they were so often called in *la belle province*, had already been hardened by six years of total or partial attempted suppression by federal authorities; they were not particularly daunted by the actions of one province. Furthermore, they were willing to accept almost any type of martyrdom, especially if it would discredit the Roman Catholic Church. They were fully aware that when their German brethren had been suppressed in 1933, the German Catholic clergy had openly supported the Nazi authorities in attempting to crush them. They were also convinced on the basis of strong evidence that federal government action against them had originated mainly in Quebec and from Roman Catholic influences within the government. Thus, they were filled with a deep desire to "preach Christ's Kingdom to the people of Quebec and to expose the hierarchy". In consequence, the Witnesses responded to mob violence and to the sweeping arrests of late 1945 and the year 1946 by sending more missionaries to Quebec from Ontario and western Canada. By the fall of 1946, particularly after the release of the young missionaries from the alternative-service camps in August, there was already a hard-core contingent of completely devoted Witness evangelists in Canada's largest province, prepared, under all circumstances, to accept any form of violence or legal action that might come their way. And, as Witness missionaries poured into the province, the Watch Tower Society launched a nation-wide publicity campaign against Quebec officialdom and the Catholic hierarchy in order to arouse public sympathy, particularly in English Canada.

On November 7, 1945, the magazine *Consolation* published an article entitled "Sodom, Gomorrah, and Catholic Quebec", which began with the statement: "Apologies might be due because of the title. But if so, they are not due Catholic Quebec, but Sodom and Gomorrah." Then, by quoting long excerpts from Montreal newspaper reports, letters to editors, and a protest of United Church clergymen to Premier Duplessis, it gave the story of the events at Lachine and Chateauguay and denounced those events in the strongest terms. Yet not until a year later did the Witnesses really go on the offensive by releasing the tract *Quebec's Burning Hate.*

On November 2 and 3, 1946, between fourteen and eighteen hundred Jehovah's Witnesses from Ontario, Quebec, and the United States gathered for an assembly in Montreal. Present among other Watch Tower officers were Hayden C. Covington and the Society's president, Nathan Knorr. It was those two who were to launch a propaganda war to make Jehovah's Witnesses' struggle with Quebec officialdom known from one end of Canada to the other, with little credit to Quebec. Beginning on November 3, Covington addressed the crowd on the topic "Freedom" and argued that "Quebec province has a Freedom of Worship Act just as strong in its guarantee of freedom as does the United States in its Constitution".[18] But it was Knorr, speaking at a quarter past three in the afternoon that same Sunday, who personally released the publication which was to create such a nation-wide storm.[19]

The leaflet, the full title of which was *Quebec's Burning Hate for God and Christ and Freedom Is the Shame of All Canada*, was itself a scorcher. It gave detailed accounts of the Lachine and Chateauguay mobbings and of a similar event at Quebec City and an attack on Iroquois Indian Witnesses by other Indians at Caughnawaga, just outside of Montreal, in September 1946. It also described the arrest and long legal fight of septuagenarian E. M. Taylor, who had been charged with sedition for having distributed Bibles without a permit, the arrest of a nine-year-old girl for distributing circulars without a licence, and the expulsion of an eleven-year-old girl from school for refusing to make the sign of the cross. After referring to the eight hundred charges "stacked" against Jehovah's Witnesses in greater Montreal, the more than one hundred thousand dollars bail which had had to be raised in their behalf, and the difficulty that they had had in having their cases heard, the leaflet charged that the Catholic Church was responsible for their woes. After stating that "Catholic domination of Quebec courts is so complete that in the courtrooms the imagery of the crucifix takes the place of the British Coat of Arms which appears in the other courts throughout the Dominion", it continued: "All the facts unite to thunderously declare that the force behind Quebec's suicidal hate is priest domination. Thousands of Quebec Catholics are so blinded by the priests that they think they serve God's cause in mobbing Jehovah's witnesses." Finally, it declared:

Quebec, Jehovah's witnesses are telling all Canada of the shame you have brought on the nation by your evil deeds. In English, French and Ukrainian languages this leaflet is broadcasting your delinquency to the nation. You claim to serve God; you claim to be for freedom. Yet if freedom is exercised by those who disagree with you, you crush freedom by mob rule and gestapo tactics. Though your words are, your actions are not in harmony with that for which democracies have just fought a long and bloody global war. And your claims of serving God are just as empty, for your actions find no precedent in the exemplary course laid down for Christians by His Son, Christ Jesus. You should remember that though Christ Jesus and early Christians were often mobbed, they never under any circumstances meted out mob violence. What counts is not whom you claim to serve, but whom you actually do serve by deeds. The Catholic Version Bible says: "Know you not, that to whom you yield yourselves servants to obey, his servants you are whom you obey." (Romans 6:16) Quebec, you have yielded yourself as an obedient servant of religious priests, and you have brought forth bumper crops of evil fruits. Now, why not study God's Word, the Bible, and yield yourself in obedience to its commands, and see how bounteous a crop of good fruits reflecting love of God and Christ and freedom you will bring forth? The eyes of Canada are upon you, Quebec.

As Knorr read from *Quebec's Burning Hate* vigorous applause interrupted him, but what apparently delighted his audience most was the announcement that, beginning on November 15, they and other Witnesses were to distribute one million copies of the leaflet in English, a half-million in French, and seventy-five thousand in Ukrainian throughout the nation. The Watch Tower Society president also brought further joy to his listeners by announcing that 110 additional pioneer evangelists would be sent to the Watch Tower Bible School of Gilead as "specially trained reinforcements" for what gave every indication of being a long and bitter religious struggle in the Province of Quebec. Moreover, Knorr indicated that *Awake!*, which had replaced *Consolation* as a companion magazine to the *Watchtower* in August 1946, "would tell this story of hateful persecution to the world".[20]

The campaign to distribute the searing denunciation of *Quebec's Burning Hate* began as scheduled, and throughout English Canada its distributors were received more sympathetically than ever before; the same could not be said for the reception in Quebec, however. The terrible wrath of the entire province came down on the heads of the small company of Jehovah's Witnesses living within its borders. On November 21, Premier Duplessis called a press conference at which he declared: "My attention has been drawn to certain circulars being distributed by persons describing themselves as Witnesses of Jehovah. I have noticed that there are certain sections which are intolerable and seditious."[21] Two weeks later the Premier remarked further: "The propaganda of the Witnesses of Jehovah cannot be tolerated and there are more than 400 of them before the courts."[22] Duplessis was not alone in his reaction. Mayor Lucien Borne of Quebec City called for an amendment to the city charter "so that we may get rid of Jehovah's Witnesses once and for all".[23] Quebec Sacred Heart Leagues published broadsides calling for Catholics to aid the police "to free the streets of Jehovah's Witnesses".[24] Thus, as the Witnesses walked from door to door to deliver their tracts, they were often met by mobs, particularly of youths, who attacked them and often destroyed their literature.[25]

The police, acting under the direction of Premier and Attorney General Duplessis, took the sternest actions against them. "Arrests ran as high as thirty a day, and by the end of November there were some 1,000 cases pending in the Quebec courts. Some Witnesses had as high as 43 cases stacked against them. Exorbitant bail demands soared as high as $500 cash or $950 property bond."[26] Police also began to raid kingdom halls and homes to seize literature which they proclaimed seditious. On November 25, officers at Sherbrooke entered the local kingdom hall, confiscated thousands of copies of the offending tract, Bibles, and other literature, tore the telephone off the wall, and took money from the contribution box. Nine Witnesses, five men and four women, were arrested on charges of intent to distribute seditious literature.[27] At St. Jerome two homes were entered and thousands of *Burning Hate* leaflets and booklets were seized.[28]

But the most severe blow against the Witnesses was struck on December 4. On that day members of the permit department of the Quebec Liquor Commission arrived at the high-quality Montreal restaurant of Frank Roncarelli to revoke his liquor licence and remove five thousand dollars' worth of liquor from the premises. Roncarelli had, in Duplessis's eyes, committed a cardinal sin. One of Jehovah's Witnesses himself and a victim of the Chateauguay riot, he had willingly supplied between eighty and ninety thousand dollars bail for his arrested brethren. The Premier, therefore, stated openly: "A certain Roncarelli had supplied bail for hundreds of Witnesses of Jehovah and as a result, I have ordered the Liquor Commission to cancel his permit."[29] The courts also eliminated Roncarelli as a bondsman with the apparent hope that arrested Witnesses would be kept in jail.[30] As a result the editors of *Saturday Night* published a piece of doggerel based on the metre of Byron's *The Destruction of Sennacherib* which hailed Duplessis's *Destruction of Roncarelli* with some amusement. It read:

Duplessis came down like a wolf on the fold,
And his edicts were gleaming in purple and gold;
And the sheen of his padlocks was hid by the pall
Of the laws that hang heavy o'er French Montreal.

Like the leaves of the forest when Summer is green,
The Witnesses lying in prison were seen:
Like the leaves of the forest when Winter doth rail,
That host on the morrow was delivered on bail.

For a restaurateur spread his money about
And silenced Duplessis and got them all out.
But the eyes of Duplessis waxed deadly and chill,
Took aim for the liquor, moved in for the kill.

There lay Roncarelli, distorted and pale,
His food all intact, but vanished his Ale;
The Witnesses silent at this sudden act
To discredit the Prophet, suppress every tract.

And the faithful of Rutherford despair at the wreck
For their steps are now dogged through the whole of Quebec;
Their champion is curbed by provincial police,
And his standard is down by the sword of Maurice.[31]

The poetaster was not accurate in his assessment, however; Quebec's modern-day Sennacherib was, in the final analysis, no more successful in his attacks on the servants of Jehovah than his ancient predecessor had been. The Watch Tower Society published a second tract entitled *Quebec, You Have Failed Your People* which, like *Quebec's Burning Hate,* was published in English, French, and Ukrainian and was distributed nation-wide. Even stronger in tone than the *Burning Hate* leaflet, it was described in *Maclean's* magazine as "a detailed tirade against Quebec's police and politicians charging 'hate for free and open study of God's Word and for the principles of Christ' ".[32] In order to get it into the hands of the people of Quebec without again being arrested *en masse,* the Witnesses resorted to the tactic they had used so successfully during the ban—they placed tracts in doorjambs throughout *la belle province* at night and avoided the police as much as possible.[33]

They became—as aptly described by *Maclean's* writer Scott Young —"Jehovah's Secret Agents" and began to see the results of their work. Although they constantly faced arrest and always carried toothbrushes and soap with them in the expectation that they might be jailed at any time, they began to win converts. Young reported in March 1947 that in response to the activities of these "Commando Witnesses", numerous Quebeckers had joined their ranks: "In the last 18 months the Quebec congregation had grown from one to 200. In Montreal, hundreds of Montrealers of all religions have become Witnesses."[34] Even more important was the fact that, by their tenacity and the over-reaction of Quebec authorities, they were able to make the Duplessis government appear to be nothing less than a bigoted despotism.

The outcry against Duplessis and Quebec officialdom in the English-Canadian press was loud. It was quite true that the Witnesses were often described as "obnoxious" and guilty of circulating "scurrilous attacks" on the Roman Catholic Church. B. K. Sandwell, the editor of *Saturday Night*, even published an article entitled "Why French Canada Hates" in which he compared the Witnesses with the communists in making converts among French Canadians.[35] But it was generally recognized that Catholic spokesmen and publishers issued attacks on Jehovah's Witnesses which were equally as severe as anything that the Witnesses had to say about the Catholic Church. The Witnesses were frequently referred to in print as "blasphemers", "heretics", "poor visionaries", "wretches", "scabby sheep", "Witnesses of Lucifer", and "colporteurs of Satan".[36] Premier Duplessis and Catholic writers frequently lumped them in with communists, atheists, and Nazis as enemies of French-Canadian society.[37] Thus, the Witnesses received sympathy from a press which, in the Anglo-Saxon tradition of respect for civil liberties in peacetime, could not approve of the suppression of minority rights or freedom of expression. Above all, the revocation of Roncarelli's liquor licence seemed nothing short of pure vindictiveness and the misuse of the powers of the office of the Attorney General.

Writing in the *Canadian Forum,* Frank Scott chastised Duplessis personally for his actions toward Roncarelli and pointed out that the *Montreal Daily Star,* the *Gazette,* and the *Canadian Register* (the press organ of Ontario English-speaking Roman Catholics) were united in condemning the Premier.[38] The *Toronto Daily Star* reported the arrest and imprisonment for sedition of the Boucher family, including twelve-year-old Lucille, at St. Joseph de Beauce for distributing *Quebec's Burning Hate.* Staff correspondent James Nicol, in a tone of moral outrage, wrote:

Twelve-year-old Lucille Boucher, meek and azure-eyed daughter of a Quebec mountaineer spent two days in the county jail here because her folks belong to Jehovah's Witnesses.

She ate and slept in a notorious cell—the same one in which they kept the woman who eight years ago murdered her husband by a combination of arsenic and witchcraft.

After detailing the story of Lucille's release and that of her sister, twenty-one-year-old Giselle, Nicol told of how her father, Aimé, had to remain in jail until his bondsman could arrive. The *Star* correspondent reported:

"Do not worry for me," he [Boucher] told his wife and five children as the jailer waited. "I sleep well. Better than many others."

As they filed past him the 13 crown witnesses did not turn their heads. Their eyes were steadfastly fixed in the northerly direction toward the capital city of Quebec where Premier Maurice (the noble) Duplessis had blessed religious intolerance for religious purposes.[39]

Reports also appeared in newspapers throughout the land of the convictions of John Maynard How, lawyer Glen How's younger brother, in a Montreal recorder's court and of an alleged comment by Recorder Jean Mercier. According to the press, Mercier had said that a sentence he had imposed on How was "at least 100 times too lenient".[40] It was also reported that the recorder had stated that he would like to sentence How to life imprisonment and that "any measures are justified in ridding our Christian society of these transgressors of all laws, these enemies of all religions, these witnesses of falsehood".[41]

In editorials, the vast majority of English-language newspapers and magazines attacked Duplessis and the government and courts of Quebec. Even *Saturday Night*, a magazine often critical of the Witnesses, reacted negatively to their mass arrest and suggested that the real "crime of the Witnesses is that they are persuading some of the French-Canadians to abandon the faith of their forefathers".[42] The press was not alone in its condemnation either. Some twelve hundred students at McGill University, while indicating a complete lack of sympathy for the tenets of Jehovah's Witnesses, nevertheless argued that "the fundamental right of freedom of speech and worship must be observed in a democratic country".[43] A number of Protestant clergymen denounced the Quebec Premier in the pages of the *Montreal Daily Star*. Ordinary citizens deluged the newspaper with letters of protest, and the Anglican bishop of Montreal wrote an open letter to Duplessis urging that not even a suspicion of "the infringement of the individual's civil and religious liberties" should exist in the enforcement of the law.[44]

Political organizations and individual politicians also censured Quebec's Union Nationale administration. The Co-operative Commonwealth Federation Committee for the Defence of Trade Union Rights reprimanded the Duplessis regime in the strongest terms,[45] while M. J. Coldwell called on Canadians to "awaken to the dangers of this persecution". Further, he coupled his statement with current expressions of anti-Semitic propaganda and remarked: "These persecutions are the beginning of a Fascist movement in this country."[46] Alistair Stewart, CCF Member of Parliament from Winnipeg North, was similarly critical of what was taking place in Quebec and argued that if the Witnesses were guilty of using intemperate language, they were not alone. To prove his assertion he quoted Recorder Mercier's widely published statement and read into the *Debates of the House of Commons* part of an article from *Le Temps* of Quebec which said: "The Witnesses of Jehovah are imposters, scabby sheep, malefactors who must be destroyed before they can corrupt certain of our own people."[47] Perhaps the most severe and important criticism, however, came from the former Air Minister and Quebec federal

Liberal Member of Parliament, C. G. Power. In an address to a civil-liberties meeting held in Montreal to protest Quebec's measures against Jehovah's Witnesses, Power, a Roman Catholic himself, charged the provincial government with "Fascist inclinations" and "bureaucratic tendencies" and went on to remark that "Liberal Ottawa and constitutional Quebec have forgotten the true meaning of Liberalism and constitutionalism".[48]

The Witnesses made great gains as a result of such publicity, and if they were still less than popular with most non-Catholic Canadians, at least they did receive a great deal of sympathy from them. Premier Duplessis and his Union Nationale government were hardly impressed though. After all, the French-Canadian press, French Canadians in general, and the Roman Catholic clergy in particular, heartily approved what Quebec public officials were doing with respect to the Witnesses. In fact, under the heading "Catholic Action Backs Duplessis", a Canadian Press dispatch of December 21, 1946, reported:

Congratulations of the Montreal Diocesan Committee of Catholic Action have been sent to Premier Duplessis for "his energetic action in regard to Witnesses of Jehovah", Msgr. J. A. Valois, general director of the committee, said Friday. In addition, a request has been made to the archdiocese's 62 Catholic groups and 10 other diocesan organizations along the same line.[49]

Watch Tower officials therefore recognized that unless they could, in some way, check police and court actions against the Witnesses in Quebec, the government would eventually be able to curb, or at least minimize, their activities. In consequence, Jehovah's Witnesses throughout Canada were called on to begin a major campaign to legally establish the right of their Quebec brethren to freedom of worship, speech, and publication, even in the face of the almost total opposition of the French-Canadian, Catholic community.

The first step in what was soon to become a crusade for freedom of religion was the launching of a fight for the enactment of a Canadian bill of rights. After all, certainly no religious organization nor any other group (at least until the development of the American civil-rights movement in the 1950s) has experienced such success in appealing to the courts on the basis of a bill of rights as did Jehovah's Witnesses in the United States.[50] In Australia, too, they were able to have a government ban against them declared illegal and unconstitutional, because of the protection afforded by a bill of rights. Protection obtained from courts acting under the provisions of fundamental charters of liberties was thus highly impressive.

Yet how could the Witnesses expect to get the federal Parliament in Ottawa to enact a bill of rights? The Mackenzie King government, and the Minister of Justice in particular, had shown rather dramatically that they had no love for Jehovah's Witnesses and no particular concern about civil liberties. In addition, Quebec remained a major political prop to the federal Liberals, who, at the time, held a narrow grip on power. Undaunted, the Witnesses decided to bring massive pressure to bear on Parliament by circulating a nation-wide petition which read:

The petition of the undersigned people of Canada humbly sheweth the necessity for you to make more secure the fundamental liberties of every person in Canada.

That Canada's participation in the Atlantic Charter and the United Nations Organization are declarations to the world that this country stands for full freedom of speech, press and worship.

That many other nations supporting these world agreements, such as Australia and the United States of America, have, by means of written bills of rights in their constitutions, provided for their people greater protection of fundamental liberties than does Canada.

That recent experiences of Jehovah's Witnesses in the Province of Quebec prove that throughout the whole Dominion basic personal rights are open to attack and loss because of a failure to have them guaranteed by a written constitution.

Wherefore, your petitioners humbly pray that your honourable house take immediate steps to enact or cause to be inserted in the British North America Act a federal bill of rights, similar to those of Australia and the United States, in order to secure freedom of speech, press and worship to all people against municipal, provincial, or national abridgement.

On March 2, 1947, local congregations of Jehovah's Witnesses throughout the nation inaugurated the petition campaign by holding about four hundred public meetings on the subject of the need for stronger provisions for the protection of civil liberties in Canada. Over twelve thousand Witnesses then set out to obtain signatures in support of a bill of rights during what was described as one of the most severe winters on record. Cold, snow, and icy roads were only some of the problems they encountered however; as the journal *Awake!* reported:

It is to be expected that in the circulation of a petition like this not everybody would sign. Some reasons given were silly if not ridiculous. Some demanded that movies and baseball on Sunday be added. Deserted wives wanted a law to bring their husbands back; others would not sign unless a provision was added for reducing taxes.[51]

There was also opposition. According to *Awake!*, at least one Witness was severely beaten and robbed of his petition sheets in New Water-ford, Nova Scotia, while in Verdun, Quebec, "a number of Jehovah's Witnesses were prosecuted for circulating the petition, their sheets were confiscated, and the police visited the persons who had signed, threatening and intimidating them".[52] Yet, in the end, hundreds of thousands of Canadians, including many Roman Catholics, responded favourably to the petition. Over a half-million signatures were affixed to it, and on June 9 it was presented to Parliament.[53] Never before had so many Canadians petitioned their national legislature on a single issue.

The government in Ottawa was forced to respond in some way, and Parliament appointed a joint committee of the House of Commons and the Senate to examine the whole subject of human rights.[54] John Diefenbaker accepted the Witnesses' arguments in favour of a bill of rights and made the crusade for the enactment of such a bill his own—an important fact indeed, as even then he was a rising figure in the Progressive Conservative party. Speaking in the Commons on May 16, 1947, he said: "What would a bill of rights do? It would establish the right of the individual to go into the courts of this country, thereby assuring the preservation of his freedom. These great rights are merely pious ejaculations unless the individual has the right to assert them in the courts of law."[55] The federal cabinet was not anxious to enact the type of bill the Witnesses wanted, even if it would have been constitutionally possible to do so. Even before the human-rights committee had a chance to examine the subjects in detail, the Minister of Veterans Affairs, Ian Mackenzie, suggested publicly that there was no need for a bill of rights, since Canadians already had the needed freedoms and a specific bill might narrow them. Quite accurately he noted that Parliament did not have the power to enact the requested provisions of a charter of fundamental liberties in any case.[56]

The Witnesses were not surprised, nor were they particularly daunted. *Awake!* stated bluntly: "The honorable minister's [Mackenzie's] contentions are as sour as last week's milk and as full of holes as imported Swiss cheese." To the statement that the civil liberties of Canadians were already adequately protected by existing laws, it asked: "If there are such laws, why do Canada's courts permit clean-cut Christian girls to be imprisoned in loathsome cells crawling with vermin[?]" Since Mackenzie had referred to Canadian rights under the Magna Carta and the English Bill of Rights, it reasoned that the Minister had contradicted himself: "How can it be pretended that a written declaration of rights now will be more of a menace than these historic documents?" Finally, *Awake!* suggested that a bill of rights could, and would, be added to the British North America Act by the Imperial Government of Great Britain if Parliament would petition it to do so.[57]

Throughout 1947 and 1948 conditions in Quebec did not improve for Jehovah's Witnesses. In the four months, November 1946 through February 1947, there were 843 arrests of Witnesses throughout the province, and sometimes as many as thirty were thrown into jail on a given day. The majority were charged with peddling without a licence, but sixty-four were charged with sedition, seditious conspiracy, or seditious libel.[58] Then, in the spring session of the legislature, the Duplessis government passed stringent legislation which permitted municipalities to prohibit the distribution of any literature without a licence on pain of a possible maximum penalty of a one-hundred-dollar fine and three months in jail.[59] As a result, Jehovah's

Witnesses were forced to resort to proselytizing with the Bible alone, and even then many of them were arrested. They therefore intensified the struggle for a bill of rights. The January 8, 1948, issue of *Awake!* contained a long article entitled "Magna Carta Myth" which argued quite accurately from a historical standpoint that Magna Carta was essentially a feudal document which in no sense protected civil liberties from the tyrannical acts of legislative bodies. Beyond this, *Awake!* also contended that neither the Petition of Right of 1628 nor the English Bill of Rights guaranteed "the people's liberties of press, worship and speech against the supreme power of Parliament in England, or the colonies, or in the dominions, or in the commonwealth". Thus the vaunted unwritten constitution, like Magna Carta, was described as "a will-o'-the-wisp". Accordingly, what Canada needed was a bill of rights, and *Awake!* called on its readers throughout Canada, the British Commonwealth, the United States, and anywhere else to deluge Prime Minister Mackenzie King and Canadian diplomatic officers with letters supporting it. Undoubtedly, the Prime Minister's mail increased substantially.

Besides carrying on an extensive bill of rights campaign among the general public, the Witnesses decided to bring the matter forcefully to members of the legal profession, public officials, and the press. Hayden Covington published an article entitled "The Dynamic American Bill of Rights" in the April 1948 issue of the *Canadian Bar Review*. A month later Glen How followed with a second article, "The Case for a Canadian Bill of Rights", published in the same journal. To make sure that they were read, the Watch Tower Society reprinted ten thousand copies of each and mailed them "with a personal letter to lawyers, judges, legislators, editors, columnists, members of parliament and professional men throughout the country".[60]

Response from many lawyers and public officials was favourable, but the Witnesses were not satisfied. The Parliamentary Human Rights Committee had suggested that there was much more need for public discussion before Parliament attempted to define the rights and freedoms to be safeguarded. *Awake!* thereupon quoted Robert Gourlay's sarcastic comment—concerning a British parliamentary committee of 1817—to the effect that "they will sit till all their eggs are addled under them, unless they adopt liberal principles".[61] So, taking the committee's statement at "face value", they launched a second petition campaign in September 1948.

After the circulation of the first petition, criticism was levelled at the Witnesses that many people would not have signed it had they been more aware of its authors. The Watch Tower Society carefully determined to blunt such arguments, this time by preparing a small broadside leaflet, *Fight for Freedom!*, which was to be handed to each person before he was invited to sign the petition. In addition, the petition itself was explicitly written so that anyone reading it would be aware that it had been drawn up by Jehovah's Witnesses. It read:

> To the Honourable the House of Commons
> in Parliament assembled:
>
> The Petition of the undersigned people of Canada humbly sheweth:
>
> That in the year 1947 over five hundred thousand Canadian citizens joined in a petition to your Honourable House praying for the enactment of a Bill of Rights to protect the fundamental freedoms of all the people of this nation.
>
> That the persecution of Jehovah's witnesses referred to in that petition has not halted but has continued to further deprive this minority group of the right of freedom of speech, press and worship.
>
> That these rights should properly belong to every Canadian, and we protest against their denial by any authority whether municipal, provincial or national.
>
> That it has been contended our basic liberties are now adequately protected, but the facts of the continuing persecution in Quebec and the decisions of the courts there show that these individual rights are not really guaranteed by Canadian law.
>
> That objection has been taken that the Dominion Government is incompetent from a constitutional standpoint to enact a Bill of Rights that would effectively safeguard freedom of speech, press, worship and due process of law against all official infringements in this country.
>
> Wherefore with the object of preventing deprivation of inherent freedoms such as that experienced by Jehovah's witnesses, your petitioners humbly pray that your Honourable House do submit an address to his Majesty praying that he be pleased to cause a Bill to be

laid before the Parliament of the United Kingdom to enact an amendment to the British North America Act incorporating into that statute constitutional guarantees of freedom of speech, press, worship and due process of law, to make these rights enforceable by the courts.

And your petitioners, as in duty bound, will ever pray.

Remarkably, the Witnesses outstripped themselves in obtaining signatures for another petition to Parliament, this time the largest ever in Canadian history. On February 8, 1949, Alistaire Stewart presented an eleven-foot-high stack of petition sheets containing 625,510 names to the House of Commons.[62] The *Winnipeg Free Press* noted that "only an insignificant fraction of the signatures could have come from members of Jehovah's Witnesses themselves". That paper then remarked: "Such a mobilization of public opinion in protest against discrimination of Jehovah's Witnesses is in itself a victory for the spirit on which genuine civil freedom is based."[63]

In Quebec, itself, the petition obtained about seventy thousand signatures in spite of the fact that its bearers could not distribute *Fight for Freedom!* and were sometimes even arrested for circulating the petition.[64] Jehovah's Witnesses thus raised the concept of a bill of rights throughout Canada and made it a living legal and political issue. Years later, Edward McWhinney, commenting on the Diefenbaker Bill of Rights in 1960, stated:

There is great truth in the statement, made only half in jest, by Glen How, who has been counsel for Jehovah's Witnesses in their main contests before the Supreme Court of Canada, that Jehovah's Witnesses, and not Mr. Diefenbaker, have given Canada her Bill of Rights.

Almost without exception, the great decisions on civil liberties given by the Supreme Court of Canada since the war are the legal by-products of the pangs and sufferings of individual Jehovah's Witnesses at the hands of provincial or municipal authorities.[65]

Eventually the Witnesses' demand for a bill of rights and its entrenchment in the federal constitution was to be taken up not only by opposition parties, but by the Liberal governments of Lester Pearson and Pierre Trudeau. But in 1949, the government, then under the

Witnesses' former opponent Louis St. Laurent, had no intention of providing such a basis for civil liberties. Furthermore, in Quebec, Catholic spokesmen made it abundantly clear that they wanted no bill of rights which would interfere with the provincial government's freedom to suppress Jehovah's Witnesses. *L'Action Catholique* of October 14, 1948, stated: "We must refuse to sign this petition for two main reasons. First of all, because Jehovah's Witnesses want to get liberty to propagate their errors by anti-liberty means; and, secondly, because they are entreating the intervention of the British Government in Canadian affairs."

Consequently, if they were to overcome the effects of Quebec's actions against them, the Witnesses would have to find some other means besides convincing Parliament to pass a bill of rights. Nevertheless, the entire campaign did give them much favourable publicity and did, in the long run, aid them in discrediting the Union Nationale government of Maurice Duplessis.

CHAPTER TEN

victory in the courts

Freedom in thought and speech and disagreement in ideas and beliefs, on every conceivable subject, are of the essence of our life. The clash of critical discussion on political, social and religious subjects has too deeply become the stuff of daily experience to suggest that mere ill-will as a product of controversy can strike down the latter with illegality.

JUSTICE IVAN RAND in *Boucher v. the King*

WATCH TOWER LAWYERS were most anxious to appeal Witnesses' cases from local recorders' courts to higher courts in Quebec and eventually to the Supreme Court of Canada. But during the years immediately following the Second World War this seemed nearly impossible. As the *1948 Yearbook of Jehovah's Witnesses* stated:

We have utilized every known legal remedy to get the cases into higher courts, and many practically unknown methods. Denied protection by one court, we have appealed further. Recourse has even been sought to the Supreme Court of Canada, but we were informed they did not have jurisdiction to hear our cases. Back again into the Recorder's courts our cases have landed. However, the zeal of the Lord's people is undiminished, and the fight starts all over again. Actions, appeals, writs, motions and special remedies have been employed in every case that came to trial. No cases have been abandoned until every avenue of defence was exhausted.[1]

Hayden Covington, Glen How, and the Witnesses' Quebec attorney, Samuel Bard, were firmly convinced that if they could once get their cases into the Supreme Court of Canada, they could legally establish the right of Jehovah's Witnesses to preach openly in Quebec. As How pointed out, however, in an article in the July 1947 issue of the *Canadian Bar Review* entitled "The Jurisdiction of Canada's Supreme Court is Too Limited", and as the *1948 Yearbook* had noted, it was very difficult indeed to have Witnesses' cases adjudicated by Canada's highest national tribunal. One of the major problems was that while Section 36 of the Supreme Court Act stated that "appeal shall lie to the Supreme Court from any judgment of the highest court of final resort now or hereafter established in any province . . . whether such court is a court of appeal or of original jurisdiction", the Supreme Court itself had held that it could hear cases only from the highest court in any province, in every case from an appeal court, if such existed. That fact in itself would not have been too limiting, except that most of the Witnesses' cases heard in recorders' courts could not be appealed to provincial appeal courts. As How stated: "If a case cannot be appealed to the provincial court of appeal then appeal to the Supreme Court is also denied. Under a number of provincial statutes no appeal to the provincial court of appeal is allowed." In Quebec it was true that it was possible to obtain the review of a recorder's decision before a judge of the Superior Court by means of a writ of *certiorari*, but his judgment was final. Therefore, all of the cases against Jehovah's Witnesses in recorders' courts, based on the charge of peddling without a licence, could not be appealed to the higher courts of the land, even though they involved broad constitutional issues.

Appeal to the Supreme Court was also barred in "criminal causes", according to Section 36. Strangely, as lawyer How pointed out, the term did not mean causes which were criminal in substance but, rather, criminal from a procedural standpoint. The Criminal Code did provide for appeal to the Supreme Court in some cases which were criminal in nature. But in all other instances involving criminal causes—any cases, such as traffic violations, in which fines or imprisonment could be imposed—the act stated specifically that there was no appeal to the court. Thus, on this account as well, Jehovah's Witnesses could not hope to take the many licence-tax cases against them before Canada's highest court. The situation was serious; since 1892 there was no longer any possibility of taking criminal appeals to the Privy Council in London.[2] Indeed, the Liberal government in Ottawa was determined to end any and all appeals to that august but non-Canadian body.

Section 36 also prohibited appeal to the Supreme Court by way of the ancient prerogative writs of *habeas corpus*, *certiorari*, or prohibition, when they arose "out of a criminal charge". Section 57 of the Supreme Court Act did provide authority to the court to issue a writ of *habeas corpus* for someone held under a Dominion statute. But this helped the Witnesses very little; in Quebec, most of the "criminal" charges against them were based on provincial legislation. Furthermore, although Section 36 did seem to contemplate non-criminal *habeas corpus* appeals to the Supreme Court, that possibility was evidently ruled out as well by what Glen How called a "collection of ambiguities and repugnancies" in other sections of the act.

Neither were all cases arising out of charges laid under the jurisdiction of the Criminal Code appealable to the Supreme Court of Canada. The Code specifically prohibited it from hearing cases adjudicated by provincial courts of appeal unless there had been a dissenting opinion among the justices of the appeal court in question or the court's opinion conflicted with that of another court of appeal in another province. Jehovah's Witnesses even faced the possibility that they would not be able to appeal sedition cases beyond the Quebec courts.

The Supreme Court did have special rights to hear appeals under Sections 39 and 41 of the Supreme Court Act, but even there its powers were limited. Section 39(a) provided that appeal to the court could be made if the matter in question involved a value of two thousand dollars or more; otherwise, leave had to be sought to have a matter appealed on the basis of Section 41—a difficult procedure. For in order to appeal to the Supreme Court from a provincial appeal court, it was necessary to obtain the latter's approval first. And, even when such authority had been obtained, the Supreme Court always insisted that appeal cases coming before it must have a monetary value. Although Section 41 (c) stated that cases could be heard by the court if they involved "future rights", the Supreme Court held that those rights had to be monetary. The court heard a case involving the right of a Negro to buy beer in Montreal because it had involved damages of $25. It dealt with a trade-union inspector's case concerning damages of $33.80. But in *Greenlees* v. *Attorney General for Canada*, it refused to deal with a major civil-rights issue because no money was involved.[3] Consequently, it seemed that the only way in which Jehovah's Witnesses would be able to win their many legal battles with Premier Duplessis and Quebec officialdom was in the unlikely event that the Quebec courts proved sympathetic.

Nevertheless, time, circumstances, and good planning aided the Witnesses. How's article on the jurisdiction of the Supreme Court, like his and Covington's articles on the bill of rights in the following year, was reprinted and sent to both government and opposition members of Parliament. Fortunately for the Witnesses, the Canadian government was in the process of abolishing the last appeals to the Privy Council in London. Thus, the Supreme Court Act was under review, and the suggestions which the Witness lawyer made in his July 1947 *Canadian Bar Review* article were highly relevant. Specifically, he recommended that:

1. It should be possible to appeal to the Supreme Court from courts other than the provincial court of appeal. Provided appeal has been taken to the final court in the province to which recourse may be had, there is no reason the Supreme Court or a judge thereof should not have power to grant leave to appeal a case raising sufficiently important questions of law.
2. The appeals under the Criminal Code should be broadened to give the Court power to grant leave in cases of general importance irrespective of the decisions of the provincial courts.
3. The exclusion of "criminal causes" (which includes quasi-criminal and "provincial" criminal law) from the jurisdiction of the Supreme Court pursuant to section 36 should be ended and such cases given a right of review with leave granted as suggested for the Criminal Code.

4. Appeals should be permitted on prerogative writs even when they do arise out of what are construed to be "criminal charges".
5. The Supreme Court should be allowed under section 41 unlimited powers to grant leave to appeal the same as the provincial courts already have.

When Parliament did amend the Supreme Court Act in 1949, the substance of those recommendations was included in the new legislation. Though the Supreme Court of Canada continued to be barred from hearing appeals "from a judgment in a criminal cause, in proceedings for or on a writ of *habeas corpus, certiorari* or prohibition arising out of a criminal charge", Parliament saw fit to broaden the powers of the court in most of the ways that How had suggested.[4] Of course the How recommendations fitted nicely into the plans of the federal government. Unless issues arising out of provincial legislation could be tested beyond provincial courts, the provinces could, and no doubt would, extend their powers into areas which the federal government considered its own. It was quite necessary for the Supreme Court to have broad powers of judicial review if Ottawa was going to check the growth of provincial authority. The St. Laurent government therefore chose to facilitate appeal to Canada's highest tribunal, and the door was at last opened to Jehovah's Witnesses—the very thing that How and the Witnesses had specifically wanted.

The first major judicial victory of Jehovah's Witnesses over Quebec authorities also came in 1949, although quite apart from the new federal legislation. It involved the whole issue of seditious libel in the case of *Boucher* v. *the King*.[5] Aimé Boucher, arrested for distributing *Quebec's Burning Hate*, had been tried early in 1947 before Judge Alfred Savard and a French-Canadian, Catholic jury. On the basis of Section 133 of the Criminal Code, Judge Savard charged the jury that if the *Burning Hate* leaflet "might raise up illwill or hostility between different classes of His Majesty's subjects", then they could convict. Boucher was held guilty and sentenced to a month's incarceration. Shortly thereafter, his elder daughter, Giselle, was convicted on the same charge and was given two weeks in jail. Both convictions were appealed, but the Quebec Court of King's Bench upheld the conviction of Boucher. The Witnesses were able to appeal to the Supreme Court of Canada, however, because King's Bench Chief Justice Letourneau and Justice Galipeault dissented on the ground that Judge Savard had misdirected the jury. The Court of King's Bench ordered a new trial for Giselle Boucher which apparently was never held.

Argument before five justices of the Supreme Court—Chief Justice Rinfret and Justices Kerwin, Taschereau, Rand, and Estey—was presented from May 31 to June 4, 1949. On December 5 the court ruled that Boucher deserved a new trial, and two members of that body, Justices Rand and Estey, called for the appellant's conviction to be quashed. Although less than a complete victory, the Witnesses rejoiced, as did most of the English-Canadian press. The comments of Justice Rand were quoted throughout the country. Commenting on the circumstances surrounding the distribution of *Quebec's Burning Hate*, he stated:

The incidents, as described, are of peaceable Canadians who seem not to be lacking in meekness, but who, for distributing, apparently without permits, Bible and tracts on Christian doctrine; for conducting religious services in private homes or on private land in Christian fellowship, for holding public lecture meetings to teach religious truth as they believe it of the Christian religion; who, for this exercise of what has been taken for granted to be the unchallengeable rights of Canadians, have been assaulted and beaten and their Bibles and publications torn up and destroyed, by individuals and by mobs; who have had their homes invaded and their property taken; and in hundreds have been charged with public offences and held to exorbitant bail.

And with respect to Boucher personally, Rand remarked:

The conduct of the accused appears to have been unexceptionable; so far as disclosed, he is an exemplary citizen who is at least sympathetic to doctrines of the Christian religion which are, evidently, different from either the Protestant or the Roman Catholic versions; but the foundation in all is the same, Christ and his relation to God and humanity.

The *Winnipeg Free Press* editorialized: "Mr. Duplessis might well ponder the judgment of Mr. Justice Rand. He might also consider the extent to which his persecution of a minority has brought the operation of law in his province into disrepute."[6] The *Edmonton Journal* hoped that Justice Rand's "blistering criticism" would shame Quebec authorities and put a stop to "organized religious persecution".[7] The *Regina Leader Post* said that Justice Estey had spoken for "all democratic-thinking Canadians" when he said: "The conduct on the part of any group in Canada which denies to, or even interferes with the right of members of any other religious body to worship is a matter of public concern."[8] The Witnesses themselves had their satisfaction expressed when *Awake!* headlined "Canada's Supreme Court Reproves Quebec".[9]

Neither Premier Duplessis nor a great many Quebeckers seemed to take much notice. Only nine days after the Supreme Court handed down its decision on December 5, 1949, two young female pioneer evangelists, Olive Lundell and Winnifred Parsons, were kidnapped and driven out of Joliette, Quebec. The experience was not new to them: along with two other pioneers, Mr. and Mrs. Cecil Jones, they had been expelled from Edmundston, New Brunswick, by a mob aided by the local police only ten months earlier.[10] Yet the situation in Joliette more openly demonstrated the contempt of Quebec public officials, the Catholic clergy, and the general public for the rights of Jehovah's Witnesses and the feelings of English Canadians, including at least two members of the Supreme Court.

According to the two young women, their kidnappers chanted Catholic prayers, threatened to throw them into one of the ice-covered lakes near the city, and frightened them with the possibility of rape. The worst they did was take them to Montreal where they attempted to have the two women jailed as undesirables. But the story did not end there. The police refused to take action against the kidnappers, and when Glen How and another Watch Tower representative, Paul Couture, showed up at a Joliette town meeting the next week, they too were nearly mobbed. Again the two female missionaries were forcibly expelled from the community, and two newspaper photographers were seized and run out of town without their luggage.

The Witnesses once again pointed at the Roman Catholic Church and Catholic organizations as the source of their persecution; this time, they had undeniable proof for their assertion. On December 19 a group of "the best citizens of Joliette", including several physicians and Abbé Felix Gaudry, presented the following petition on behalf of the Knights of Columbus to the city council.

The undersigned respectfully submit that they protest the arrival in Joliette of strangers, Jehovah's Witnesses, who visit their homes falsely posing as missionaries and profiting from the occasion to sow hatred among classes, contempt of authority and encouragement of immorality.

That they are glad to learn that certain citizens have asked these strangers to leave the city and that they congratulate civic authorities, particularly the chief of police for what they have done to rid the town of these sowers of disorder.

That they ask city council to declare publicly and officially that they no longer want in Joliette these pretended missionaries and that the authorities take every means within the law to chase them forever from Joliette.

Later it was admitted that municipal council accepted the resolution in "its form and tenor", and it was published locally in *L'Etoile du Nord* and also in the *Toronto Star*. It was also confessed that the open town meeting had "invited a member of the Catholic clergy to give them a lecture on the doctrines of Jehovah's Witnesses, and in the course of which was confirmed the reaction which the propaganda of the plaintiffs had produced."[11]

Once again the English-Canadian press, supported by civil libertarians, reacted strongly. The *Toronto Evening Telegram* of December 22, 1949, stated: "No mob has any right to tell anyone to get out of town. A reprehensible angle of the events at Joliette has been the manner in which the police had abdicated their responsibility to maintain ordinary rights of Canadian citizens." Although the matter was reported fully to the Attorney General's office, no governmental action was taken.[12] Nevertheless, the Witnesses were beginning to obtain redress of grievances at a higher level—from the Supreme Court of Canada.

A year later, on December 18, 1950, the court handed down a final judgment in the *Boucher* case. By a five-to-four decision the appellant Witness was acquitted on the charge of seditious libel, and "any possibility of further sedition prosecutions in Canada against Jehovah's Witnesses was removed". Upon request from Boucher's lawyers, the court had agreed that instead of returning the case to a lower court for retrial it would hear the matter again itself, this time with all nine justices present. Then, as indicated, it held that *Quebec's Burning Hate for God and Christ and Freedom* in no way constituted seditious libel. Eight of the justices—only Chief Justice Rinfret dissented—agreed that besides causing ill-will, seditious libel must include the intent to produce rebellion or resistance against duly established authority. True, on the question of bringing the system of justice into contempt, the court divided more sharply. Three justices—Cartright, Fauteux, and Taschereau—held that printed attacks on the political and judicial administration of Quebec did constitute seditious libel, even though there was no incitement to violence. Four other justices—Estey, Kellock, Kerwin, and Locke—held that incitement to violence must be present, and when joined by Justice Rand who also moved for Boucher's acquittal, they handed Jehovah's Witnesses a resounding victory over their Quebec adversaries.[13]

The Witnesses had won a judicial battle; yet they still had to win a judicial war. Until, and unless, they could have the restriction against the circulation of their literature lifted, their preaching activities would continue to be limited. Consequently, to test the validity of Quebec City Bylaw 184, which allowed the chief of police to license or prohibit the distribution of printed matter, a pioneer evangelist, Damase Daviau, sought an injunction against the city to restrain it from interfering with the activities of Jehovah's Witnesses. The case was first heard in Superior Court in November 1948 before Judge Léon Casgrain. Samuel Bard, counsel for Daviau, argued that the matter of control over the distribution of all publications was within the exclusive authority of the Dominion government, that Bylaw 184 was a violation of the unwritten constitution of the British Commonwealth, and that it was a violation of the pre-Confederation Freedom of Worship Act to which Hayden Covington had referred in 1945. Lawyers for the City of Quebec and the Attorney General argued that Article 92 of the British North America Act placed civil rights (hence the right to control the circulation of printed literature) within the authority of the provinces; they also tried to make a strong case that Jehovah's Witnesses did not constitute a religion.

In the Superior Court trial, the deep animosity existing between the Witnesses and their religious adversaries was expressed. Hayden Covington took the stand and openly branded the Roman Catholic hierarchy as a part of the whore of Revelation.[14] On the other hand the defendants' attorneys brought forward four expert witnesses—Hervé Gagné, a Laval University priest; Rabbi Solomon Frank; an Anglican theologian, Dr. Kenneth Evans; and Roman Catholic advocate Dr. Damien Jasmin—to support their case against Jehovah's Witnesses. Although Frank and Evans admitted that Jehovah's Witnesses were, from a theological point of view, "religious", the two Roman Catholic experts stoutly denied this assertion. Jasmin called for the "strict enforcement of the law" against "the underhanded dealings and deadly propaganda of Jehovah's Witnesses", which he openly labelled seditious, while Gagné stated, "what they teach is philosophically and theologically false, and morally evil." Furthermore he asserted: "That is why they cannot even be tolerated in a society which is Christian and which intends to remain Christian."[15]

In a way, the Witnesses were seemingly hoist with their own petard. Their publications had long used the term "religion" pejoratively to mean false worship, and Judge Rutherford had thundered that "religion is a snare and a racket". Yet, they had also reasoned that, in a legal sense at least, they were a religion, and Judge Casgrain did not concern himself particularly with that issue. He simply ruled that the Quebec City municipal government was exercising a legitimate police power under the authority of provincial law.

On appeal, the Court of King's Bench sustained Judge Casgrain's decision, but the Witnesses determined to have the matter settled before the Supreme Court of Canada. Surprisingly, Damase Daviau became disheartened and refused to proceed with the case. For that reason it was taken forward in the name of Laurier Saumur, who, with over one hundred charges against him,[16] was perhaps the most frequently arrested man in Canadian history. Since Saumur was involved in litigation identical to that involving Daviau, he was accepted by agreement as substitute plaintiff. Thus his name became attached to the constitutionally important case of *Saumur* v. *Quebec*.

The Supreme Court of Canada handed down its decision, a very complicated one indeed, on October 6, 1953. Seven judgments were forthcoming from the nine justices, but the final outcome, at least as far as Jehovah's Witnesses were concerned, was that they had won what was to prove a decisive victory over Roman Catholic Quebec. Four members of the court—Justices Rand, Estey, Locke, and Kellock, all of whom were English-Canadian Protestants—ruled on the precedent of the *Alberta Press Act* decision that provinces and municipalities acting under provincial jurisdiction had no right to restrict the freedoms of press, speech, or religion by prohibiting the distribution of printed matter on the streets of a city. Two justices, Chief Justice Rinfret and Justice Taschereau, took just the opposite position and found that the whole matter was *intra vires* of the province. Justices Cartright and Fauteux simply reasoned that control over the streets was a legitimate police power subject to exclusive provincial authority. It was Mr. Justice Kerwin, the only English-speaking Roman Catholic on the court, who decided the case in favour of Saumur by taking a middle position. In the main, he agreed with those justices who ruled that Bylaw 184 was an entirely legitimate outgrowth of provincial powers. However, on the basis of the Freedom of Worship Act alone, he held that Jehovah's Witnesses could not be denied the right to circulate printed matter of a religious nature throughout the Province of Quebec.[17]

The act on which Justice Kerwin based his opinion was the 1852 Freedom of Worship Statute of the Province of Canada, which was included in the *Revised Statutes of Quebec*, 1941. Interestingly, this act had never been used as a basis for judgment by the Supreme Court before, and had seldom been used at all until the Witnesses appealed to it.[18] But now Justice Kerwin demonstrated the significance of it by declaring that hundreds of the prosecutions of Jehovah's Witnesses in Quebec were quite illegal. The *Montreal Daily Star* of January 13, 1954, noted that the *Saumur* judgment disposed of more than seven hundred cases against Jehovah's Witnesses throughout the province. They were, of course, quite jubilant and immediately set about the distribution of their literature, which had been clearly defined as religious by the Supreme Court of Canada. Still, Maurice Duplessis did not agree with Hayden Covington's assertion that the

Freedom of Worship Act was as strong in its guarantees of freedom as was the United States Constitution; he determined to change the law.

On January 12 the first minister rose in the provincial legislature and proposed amendments to the Freedom of Worship Act designed to nullify the effects of *Saumur* v. *Quebec*. The Canadian Press reported: "Quebec: Drastic steps to deal with distribution of religious tracts by Witnesses of Jehovah were announced Tuesday by Premier Duplessis in the Legislature." The "drastic steps" were Bill 38, which provided stiff penalties in the form of fines from one hundred to one thousand dollars, and sentences from thirty days to six months in prison, for distributing printed matter of any kind, making speeches, lectures, or remarks, in any fashion which "insulted members or adherents of a religious profession within the province". Furthermore, the bill contained a provision for the seizure of all books containing such insults throughout the province by the police, enabling them to search without warrants. And to the shock of civil libertarians throughout Canada, charges could be laid for the offence of simply contemplating the act of insulting the members or adherents of a religious profession "upon petition supported by the oath of a credible person". Any of the insults or contemplated insults were, of course, no longer to constitute the free exercise or enjoyment of religious profession and worship.[19]

Newspapers expressed great alarm. Although it was assumed that Jehovah's Witnesses would be practically outlawed for criticism of the Catholic and Protestant clergy, no one expected anyone to be prosecuted for insulting Jehovah's Witnesses. But if the freedom of the Witnesses was in jeopardy, so was that of every Canadian. As a result, the *Winnipeg Free Press* issued an editorial pamphlet entitled *Constitutional Freedom in Peril*, in which it criticized the Supreme Court for taking a less definite stand on civil liberties than in the *Alberta Press* case, censured the St. Laurent government in Ottawa for ignoring the implications of the *Saumur* decision, and forthrightly took up the Witnesses' campaign for a bill of rights.[20] Yet it was the swift action of Watch Tower lawyers, rather than a charter of fundamental liberties, which once again saved the small band of Witnesses in Quebec from the wrath of their adversaries.

Bill 38 became law on January 22, 1954; the next day, lawyers for Jehovah's Witnesses appeared before Judge Choquette of the Superior Court of Quebec in order to obtain "protection of their constitutional rights" and a declaration to the effect that the new legislation was *ultra vires* of the province. Their argument, already presented to the Supreme Court of Canada during the *Saumur* proceedings, was an ingenious one. According to How and Bard, religious freedom was a basic right belonging to all Canadians, not reducible in any one province. In the first place, Justices Rand and Estey were of the opinion that freedom of worship had been granted in Canada by the Articles of Capitulation of Montreal in 1760, the Treaty of Paris in 1763, and the Quebec Act in 1774. In addition, the Witnesses' advocates claimed, the Freedom of Worship Act was not subject to amendments by a provincial legislature. It had been enacted by the unitary legislature of the Province of Canada prior to Confederation and, although it could be amended, they contended that according to Article 129 of the British North America Act only Parliament in Ottawa had the power to do so.[21]

Though taken before the Supreme Court, again in Saumur's name, the matter was never adjudicated. That body ultimately held that since no one was ever charged under the terms of Bill 38, there was no legal issue.[22] Nevertheless, by opening another long legal battle the Witnesses were able to forestall the enforcement of Duplessis's statutory thunderbolt. Writing in the late summer of 1954, Percy Chapman reported:

There was probably a feeling of satisfaction in the camp of our enemies, but it was short-lived, for by a swift move in the courts a case for an injunction against Duplessis and his bill was launched, and that is still pending. The desired effect has been obtained, for the bill at the present lies inactive and the Kingdom-publishing work goes on apace throughout the province.[23]

Therefore, if the Supreme Court's ruling in the first *Saumur* v. *Quebec* case did not have a completely sobering effect on Quebec officialdom, it did curb the mass arrests of Witnesses in that province and disposed of a great many pending cases against them. What really put a stop to the harassment of the servants of Jehovah in Quebec was another judgment, this time in the case of *Chaput* v. *Romain et al.*[24]

On September 4, 1949, a small congregation of Jehovah's Witnesses had been holding its Sunday meeting in the home of Esymier Chaput, their local overseer, at Chapeau, Quebec. Suddenly, to the surprise of the assembled group, three officers of the Quebec Provincial Police arrived, were admitted to the house, and proceeded to break up the services. Without warrant, the officers in question—Edmond Romain, Roger Chartrand, and Linden Young—seized a copy of the Roman Catholic Douay Version of the Bible from the hands of a visiting Watch Tower representative and circuit minister; as well as the Bible, several hymn books, a number of pamphlets, and the congregational contribution box were confiscated. Then, after dispersing the congregation of about forty persons, they forcibly took the visiting minister, Albin Gotthold, to the police car, in which they transported him to the Pembroke ferry, which carried him across the Ottawa River to Ontario.

The Attorney General's office ignored the whole matter, but Chaput filed civil suit for damages. The Quebec courts upheld the three policemen, ruling that they had acted in good faith under the terms of Section 7 of the Magistrate's Privilege Act, although Glen How raised the constitutional question of the right to freedom of worship and pointed out that Romain, Chartrand, and Young could have been charged under the Criminal Code on four counts—interfering with a religious service, interfering with a minister, theft, and kidnapping. When the case reached the Supreme Court of Canada, however, it held for the plaintiff Chaput and awarded him two thousand dollars damages.

The Chaput case was a serious blow to Quebec police. During the trial of his fellow constables, Chartrand admitted that the local parish priest, Abbé Harrington, had requested that the police stop the Witness meeting. Chartrand thereupon called his superior, Sergeant Perreau, who ordered him and his colleagues to break up the gathering. The justices of the Supreme Court were shocked. Justice Rand called the event an "offensive outrage", while Justice Taschereau referred to the conduct of the three respondents as "highly reprehensible", and went on to make a rather famous pronouncement on freedom of worship in Canada. He declared:

In our country there is no state religion. All religions are on an equal footing, and Catholics as well as Protestants, Jews, and other adherents of various religious denominations, enjoy the most complete liberty of thought. The conscience of each is a personal matter and the concern of nobody else. It would be distressing to think that a majority might impose its religious views upon a minority, and it would also be a shocking error to believe that one serves his country or his religion by denying in one province, to a minority, the same rights which one rightly claims for oneself in another province.

In addition, neither Justice Taschereau nor the other members of the court were willing to excuse the police on the grounds that they were simply carrying out orders. "Obedience to the order of a superior is not always an excuse," he said.

By 1956, Jehovah's Witnesses in Quebec began to experience an unfamiliar tranquillity. Percy Chapman indicated that during the period from September 1, 1955, to August 31, 1956, "not one arrest or serious interference by the police was reported", and referring to the Supreme Court's judgment in the *Chaput* case, he wrote: "This decision has helped police officers to realize they are acting illegally when interfering with our sacred service and pure worship to Jehovah."[25] But the Witnesses were not prepared to stop appealing to the courts; they still faced serious problems.

For one thing it was difficult to send their children to school. Quebec law had long provided for the existence of two school systems, a Roman Catholic and a Protestant; the Catholic system was divided into a French section and an English section, but the Protestant school system provided education only in English. No general provision had been adopted to provide schools for children who were neither Catholic nor Protestant, although Article 588 of the Education Act placed Jewish children on the same footing as Protestants; and it was generally assumed that if a child were not Catholic, for educational purposes he would be treated as a Protestant. Thus, in most places, such as Montreal, Jehovah's Witnesses regularly sent their children to Protestant schools, particularly since many of them were English-speaking, of Protestant or Eastern Orthodox backgrounds. But when French-Canadian families became Witnesses, problems often arose. In the first place, they were usually required to remove their children from Catholic schools, where French was used, and place them in Protestant schools, even though the children might not understand more than a few words of English, as they often lived in overwhelmingly French-speaking communities. This factor did not upset their parents as a rule, since they were often anxious to have their children become bilingual; what was most disturbing, however, was that even Protestant schools sometimes refused to accept these children.

During the early 1950s, the situation was especially serious in the Rouyn area where fourteen children were, for a time, refused admission to the Protestant school, although ten or twelve other children were in much the same circumstances in other parts of Quebec. As a result of this problem, one Witness father, Paul Emile Perron, filed suit against the Rouyn Protestant school trustees to force them to accept his three children—Ronald, age nine; Réal, age seven; and Giselle, age six—as students in the local Protestant school. As usual in cases involving Witnesses, he lost at Superior Court level. In August 1954, Justice Eugene Marquis held that Jehovah's Witnesses were not Protestants, and, in fact, were not a religion. Therefore, the Protestant school system did not have to admit their children. He stated that, in any case, they would be better off in the Catholic system where they could receive instruction in French.[26]

Glen How remarked bitterly that the children, who could not attend Catholic schools without receiving Catholic instruction, had the option of giving up school or giving up their religion. He branded Judge Marquis's assumption that they could attend Catholic schools "a lie", and declared hotly: "I believe that Witnesses might be considered the only true Protestants left, because the other churches are too dead to protest anything."[27] And How was not alone in his protestation. The *London Free Press* snorted:

If the Jehovah [*sic*] Witnesses are not a religious group, then what are they? A political party, a service club, a limited company, or what? The Free Press does not support the views of the Jehovah [*sic*] Witnesses, but it does seem shocking that their children are to be denied an education in a Canadian school because a judge rules that they are not a religion. The Witnesses are manifestly as Christian as the Protestant and Roman Catholic authorities who have frustrated them in securing an education for their children.[28]

Most Canadians seemed to agree, and so did the Quebec Court of Queen's Bench. In a decision of the following year, Justice Brissonet held for the court that "to be considered a Protestant it is sufficient to be a Christian and to repudiate the authority of the Pope".[29] The Witnesses were delighted; for once they had won a major issue without having to appeal to the Supreme Court of Canada. At the same time, they could hardly look upon the fact that their children had been denied education in the first place as anything short of persecution, when the children of Jews, Moslems, and atheists had been attending Protestant schools throughout the province without question.

The *Perron* case did not solve all of the school problems, however. There were Witness families in predominantly Catholic areas where no Protestant schools existed: Witness children must, perforce, attend Catholic schools or receive no education. Another Witness father, Cajetan Chabot, took action on behalf of his two sons, eight-year-old Jean-Pierre and seven-year-old Marcel. The Chabot boys had originally been expelled from the Catholic school in the parish of Lamorandière. Their crime had been the refusal to make the sign of the cross, kneel, or recite Catholic prayers. Chabot thereupon sought a writ of *mandamus* from the Superior Court at Amos, Quebec, to have his children readmitted to class without taking part in Catholic religious exercises. Glen How, arguing on Chabot's behalf, claimed that since there was no Protestant school in the area, and the plaintiff paid taxes to the Catholic system, he had a right to send his children to a Catholic school which must recognize his right to raise his children in the faith of his choice.

The difficulty was that the regulations of the Catholic Committee of the Council of Education, created under the authority of the Quebec Education Act, expressly provided that children in Catholic schools must participate in Catholic religious exercises. Glen How asked the Superior Court to declare that both the regulations and the section of the act under which they had been formulated were in violation of the Freedom of Worship Act and, hence, were *ultra vires* of provincial authorities. He also requested that the school in question, located in an area where there was no alternative one, should be regarded as "common in the sight of the law". This challenge to provincial authority brought the Attorney General's office into the case on the side of the school commissioners, and Superior Court Judge Fernand Choquette refused to issue the writ.

On appeal to the Court of Queen's Bench, Choquette's decision was reversed. Although the Queen's Bench judges declared both the sections of the Education Act in question and the regulations of the Catholic Committee to be valid, they held that they applied to Catholic children only, and therefore granted Cajetan Chabot a writ of *mandamus*. Justice Pratt noted that under the terms of the law Chabot was required to send his children to school, and was forced to pay taxes to the Catholic system, because no Protestant school existed in the area. He therefore had a right to demand that the Lamorandière school be regarded as "common to all", and that it accept Jean-Pierre and Marcel as pupils.

It was important, too, that several members of the court indicated that Chabot had a transcendent *natural right* to teach his children the tenets of his faith without outside interference. Justice Pratt quoted the dictum of the Irish jurist Lord O'Hagan, to the effect that the right of a father over his children was a God-given thing, "to be sustained to the utmost by human law". In addition, he restated Thomas Aquinas's principle that "the father is the primary ancestor, with respect to education and discipline and all that which is required for the protection of human life". And in summation of this line of thought, he reasoned: "Thus if one considers natural law, first of all our laws, it is necessary to conclude that children who attend school are not obliged to follow a religious teaching to which their father is opposed."[30]

To all intents and purposes, the *Chabot* case brought an end to what both Jehovah's Witnesses and the higher courts considered to be official persecution. But at the time no one was aware of the fact. The Witnesses' request for a declaration to the effect that the Bill 38 amendments to the Freedom of Worship Act were unconstitutional dragged on through the courts. In June 1957 Glen How was able to force Premier Duplessis to take the witness stand in Quebec Superior Court and to pillory him for three hours. The Toronto *Globe and Mail* reported:

Mr. Duplessis, who is 67, was in the witness box for almost three hours. He stood most of the time. The courtroom was hot as the morning hearings opened and in a few minutes the Premier's face was flushed.

He relaxed later, but as the hearing dragged and counsels argued, seemed annoyed and mentioned he had much urgent work to attend to.[31]

How tried to force Duplessis to admit that Bill 38 was directed against Jehovah's Witnesses on the basis of statements the Premier had made in the Legislative Assembly. Duplessis took refuge in the rules of that body and denied that they were within the scope of the court. When Judge Lizotte supported him, How complained that he was not getting a fair hearing and questioned the Premier's credibility. Duplessis angrily called How a "nervy and impudent person", and Judge Lizotte asked the Witness attorney to be polite. How, nevertheless, went on to suggest that the Premier wanted to evade the Supreme Court. When Duplessis said the remark was "absolutely out of place and indecent", How replied: "Maybe the Supreme Court will decide whether this is so."[32] Of course Canada's highest tribunal did not decide on the issue under examination, but the Witnesses were to obtain great satisfaction in any case. On January 27, 1959, the Supreme Court of Canada handed down two decisions which climaxed the Witnesses' long struggle for religious freedom in Quebec.

The first of the two was the now famous action of *Roncarelli* v. *Duplessis*.[33] For over eleven years it had been moving through the courts. Originally, Justice MacKinnon of the Superior Court of Quebec had heard the case and had awarded Roncarelli $8,123 damages as a result of the cancellation of his liquor permit by Duplessis. The Court of Queen's Bench reversed MacKinnon's judgment by a four-to-one vote, holding that Premier and Attorney General Duplessis had acted within his discretionary powers. McGill law professor Frank Scott, acting on Roncarelli's behalf, then took the matter to the Supreme Court of Canada and won. That body held that, since Duplessis had openly admitted that he had cancelled the

Montreal restaurateur's liquor licence because he had put up bail for Jehovah's Witnesses, the Premier had acted arbitrarily and capriciously. The court therefore awarded Roncarelli $33,123 and assessed Duplessis interest and court costs—in all, an amount of over $50,000. In addition, the court spanked Duplessis verbally. Justice Rand said:

To deny or revoke a permit because a citizen exercises an unchallengeable right totally irrelevant to the sale of liquor in a restaurant is equally beyond the scope of the discretion conferred. There was here not only revocation of the existing permit but a declaration of a future, definitive disqualification of the appellant to obtain one: it was to be "forever".

He remarked also:

The act of the respondent[Duplessis] through the instrumentality of the [Liquor] Commission brought about a breach of an implied public statutory duty toward the appellant; it was a gross abuse of legal power expressly intended to punish him for an act wholly irrelevant to the statute, a punishment which inflicted on him, as it was intended to do, the destruction of his economic life as a restaurant keeper within the Province.

The other case decided on the same day was that of *Lamb* v. *Benoit*.[34] Louise Lamb had been charged on December 7, 1946, at Verdun, Quebec, along with several other Witnesses for distributing *Quebec's Burning Hate*, although she had had no copies of the leaflet in her possession at the time. She had been held in the Verdun jail, from the Saturday on which she was arrested until the following Monday morning, in a cell with "a sick and terribly diseased prostitute" who used the same conveniences. The officer who had arrested her, Paul Benoit, offered to let her go on Monday if she would agree to sign a statement that she would not take action against him; otherwise, he threatened to lay a criminal charge against her. When she refused, he did release her and did lay the charge. When it was speedily dismissed by the court, Miss Lamb took civil action against Benoit for false arrest and malicious prosecution. Benoit was able to win at both Superior Court and Queen's Bench levels on legal technicalities, but the Supreme Court gave a ruling favourable to

Jehovah's Witnesses. Benoit was required to pay Miss Lamb twenty-five hundred dollars damages plus costs. Then, he too received a tongue-lashing from Justice Rand:

The arrest and prosecution, as the Court of Queen's Bench found, were quite without justification or excuse and the detention of the appellant over the weekend was carried out in a manner and in conditions little short of disgraceful. . . .

To Benoit it was patent that the appellant was not distributing the issue of the paper containing the alleged libel, nor was there a scrap of evidence on which he could have acted to connect her with the acts of the other three distributors. All this is concluded by what took place at the police station when, in what is said to be a routine practice, Miss Lamb was offered her liberty in exchange for a release of claims, a proposal which she spurned.

The English-Canadian press hailed the Roncarelli and Lamb decisions for what they were—final proof that the Supreme Court of Canada would not permit the victimization of even an unpopular minority such as Jehovah's Witnesses. The *Ottawa Citizen* editorialized:

Mr. Duplessis' laws for discouraging opinion of which he disapproves have taken quite a battering. In 1950 in the Boucher case the Supreme Court of Canada rejected Quebec's claim that a Jehovah's Witness pamphlet was "seditious libel". In 1953 in the Saumur case it ruled that a Quebec City bylaw used to stop distribution of Jehovah's Witnesses' publications contravened the Quebec Freedom of Worship Act.[35]

The *Telegram* of Toronto hailed the judgment in the Roncarelli case as "a declaration championing the rights of individuals", and went on to say: "No man, however high and mighty, may inflict injustice upon an individual however low his station."[36] The *Toronto Daily Star* probably summed up the matter for Jehovah's Witnesses and most Canadians when it stated: "Premier Duplessis of Quebec said in effect: 'I am the law.' The Supreme Court of Canada ruled otherwise."[37]

In a real sense the *Roncarelli* and *Lamb* decisions were anti-climactic. The Witnesses had already won their war with Quebec officialdom. They were also being welcomed more favourably by the people of Quebec, and to create a better public image they began to print books and articles which flattered the natural beauties of the province and its culture. The July 8, 1956, issue of *Awake!* had carried an article entitled "Quebec—Land of Interest and Charm", and in 1958 the Watch Tower Society at Toronto issued a small booklet entitled *Saviez-vous?*, especially designed for French-Canadian Catholics. After all, the Witnesses, with a desire "to preach to men of all nations", were far less prejudiced toward *les Canadiens* than were many other non-Catholic groups. Many, in fact, were themselves French Canadians, and they were very pleased, when, after the first *Perron* decision, the Quebec City Protestant school system established classes in French for French-Canadian Witness children.[38] Although this action was largely designed to avoid problems, it showed that the Witnesses were at last being accepted as a permanent part of Quebec society.

Other factors also were beginning to make life easier for what Justice Rand had called that "militant religious sect". The Union Nationale government of Quebec was losing its grip on the society it had ruled since the Second World War. Labour was restless, and even elements within the Roman Catholic Church questioned the extreme parochialism of provincial life. A new generation of intellectuals was also coming to the fore, many of whom admired Jehovah's Witnesses for having shown, more than anyone else, that with persistence the Duplessis regime's semi-dictatorial methods could be stopped. Pierre Trudeau noted with approval their fight for civil liberties,[39] and René Lévesque, then a radio and television commentator, favourably interviewed two of their representatives on station CBFT-TV, Montreal.[40] When the Witnesses' old parliamentary advocate, John Diefenbaker, became Prime Minister of Canada and introduced the Canadian Bill of Rights, they obtained a major psychological victory, although they considered the bill to be less than satisfactory.[41] It was the death of their long-time adversary, Maurice Duplessis, in September 1959, however, which indicated to the Witnesses of Jehovah that their fight for freedom in Quebec was over. Duplessis's successor was willing to let them live and worship in peace. They had overcome Quebec's burning hate.

CHAPTER ELEVEN

ABSTAIN FROM BLOOD

I consider it preferable that certain individuals should die before their time than that we should undermine their ultimate right and duty of being the custodian of their own health.

DR. ARTHUR D. KELLY *Canadian Medical Association Journal*
February 18, 1967

THE STUNNING VICTORIES of Jehovah's Witnesses over the Duplessis regime gave them a prominence and acceptability in Canadian society where nothing else had. Many old judicial decisions which had denied them the right to be classed as a "religious denomination" and their young men and women as "ministers" were overturned by the Supreme Court of Canada itself.[1] Ordinary Canadians generally accepted them, too; their door-to-door evangelism no longer evoked so much opposition, even in Quebec. They had come to form "part of the picture". By 1962 Laurier Saumur was able to muse that he could hardly remember the last time a door had been slammed in his face, and he remarked: "Catholics don't slam the door oftener than Protestants."[2] In 1968 *Awake!* published an article entitled "Jehovah's Witnesses in Quebec, Yesterday and Today", which gave a brief résumé of the struggles of the past and the changes which had taken place in that province. It stated that the number of French-speaking Witnesses had increased from ten in Montreal, and a few others spread throughout Quebec in 1935, to several thousands by 1968.[3] More important, however, were the changed attitudes of the populace: the clergy had lost much of its influence; neither clergy nor laity was particularly hostile to the Witnesses; both Roman Catholic and Protestant school auditoriums were being used for Watch Tower conventions; and at least one Catholic bishop advised his parishioners to read *The Watchtower* and *Awake!*[4] During the decade of the 1960s large congregations began to appear in formerly hostile places such as Joliette. The number of French-Canadian Witnesses continued to grow, perhaps faster than that of their English-Canadian brethren.[5] In Montreal, as in Toronto and other large cities, many immigrants—particularly Italians, Greeks, Portuguese, and Spanish—became converts.[6] In most ways the average Jehovah's Witness found his civil liberties as well protected as those of other Canadians—throughout the nation.

True, old prejudices died hard and occasional instances of anti-Witness feeling flared up. At least five times during the 1950s, 1960s, and 1970s, public-school officials raised the old issue of enforced patriotic exercises.[7] But, in every instance, the matter was settled out of court, or at least before trial. In 1968 the most serious case arose at Brooks, Alberta, when a number of children were dismissed from the local grade school for refusing to stand for the national anthem. After repeated attempts to return them to class, one of the parents, Robert Preston, filed suit against the teachers, the principal, and Brooks School Board. Meanwhile, much emotion was generated. The Witnesses charged that their children had been manhandled. Local and national newspapers picked up the story, and CBC television made it a national news item. The Witnesses agreed not to proceed with legal action when lawyers for the respondents accepted a binding agreement: the children were to return to school and would be excused from the exercises.[8] In the following year the Alberta legislature made the Witnesses' victory complete when it passed a new school act. The wording of the new legislation on patriotic exercises was made much clearer than the terms of the previous act were: henceforth parents would have the unquestioned legal right to have their children excused from all religious and patriotic exercises or ceremonies.[9]

In other ways the Witnesses were made to realize they were still less than universally popular. Occasional assaults on door-to-door preachers by furious householders or clergymen still occurred.[10] Congregations still had to fight at times to obtain building permits to construct kingdom halls,[11] and in 1969 officials at Chicoutimi, Quebec, stated flatly that they would not allow the Witnesses to purchase a meeting site there, since a majority of the people in that community were Roman Catholics.[12] In 1969 a Saskatchewan judge fined a Jehovah's Witness, Ernest Zepik of Saskatoon, for refusing jury duty. Zepik had argued that his Christian-trained conscience would not allow him to judge his fellow man in a secular court, and the law exempted ministers of religion from jury duty. But the judge simply regarded Zepik's refusal as a failure to accept civic responsibility and denied his status as a minister.[13] Glen How also experienced some criticism for his strong public stand against the Trudeau government's "Hate Bill", which he labelled a threat to freedom of speech.[14] The press sometimes made attacks on the Witnesses, too. The *Calgary Herald*, an old adversary, subjected them to harsh criticisms over the Brooks patriotic-exercises case[15] and a small Alberta weekly attacked them on the same issue in terms little short of scurrilous.[16] Still, if Jehovah's Witnesses continued to face opposition in the 1960s and early 1970s, they probably received as much praise as censure. Many Canadians thought that school boards were bigoted for trying to force Witness children to stand for anthems or salute flags when large numbers of teenagers wore the Union Jack or the Canadian flag stitched to the seats of well-worn blue-jeans. Old-style patriotism seemed more like chauvinism. Libertarians felt Witnesses should be left off juries if they chose, and many, both inside and outside Parliament, agreed with Glen How on the "Hate Bill". If Chicoutimi engaged in old-fashioned discrimination more in keeping with the Duplessis era, other communities generally proved more liberal.

The Witnesses rarely experienced direct persecution. They seemed, also, to be both more tactful and more sophisticated.[17] Yet prosperity appeared to affect them as adversely in Canada as it did in other prosperous nations of the Western world. During much of the decade of the 1960s their increase seemed far smaller than in the dramatic years of the Depression, the war, and the battle with Quebec.[18] Young men and women still moved to Quebec from English Canada. But they were faced more with the everyday responsibilities of evangelism and pastoral care for the now sizable Quebec Witness community than with a bitter-sweet struggle against Quebec authorities and the Church of Rome. The decline of the churches caused many Canadians to become either luke-warm or openly hostile toward religion. Thus, instead of being met at the doors with either anger or warmth, Witnesses often encountered indifference. As one pioneer evangelist stated: "We used to tell the people religion is a snare and a racket; now they tell us that."

In spite of everything, Jehovah's Witnesses seemed extremely adept at swimming against the tide of religious indifferentism that swept Europe and the Americas in the 1960s. The *Watchtower* took a strong stand against materialism, the sexual revolution, and increased social permissiveness.[19] Yet, according to at least one outside observer, the Witnesses continued to have an amazing appeal to youth.[20] In fact, their long-standing opposition to militarism and involvement in politics appealed to many young men and women who had become disillusioned with the larger society. The Watch Tower Society took steps both to strengthen the internal élan of the Witnesses and to broaden their appeal to outsiders. Greater emphasis was placed on family life and the education of children in the home, and in 1967, at the yearly district conventions, the Society introduced the use of dramas to stress adherence to strict moral values. The dramas, types of morality plays, are highly developed, well-staged, and colourful events which have had great appeal and, undoubtedly, great impact on Witness life. Several new publications—*Did Man Get Here by Evolution or Creation?* and *Is the Bible Really the Word of God?*— have tended to strengthen their faith in revealed religion and have also been useful tools in making converts. More important, however, has been the book *The Truth That Leads to Eternal Life*. Released in the summer of 1968 and placed at doors for twenty-five cents, well over seventy million copies of it have now been published in approximately ninety languages.[21] It is basically a fairly simple synopsis of Witness doctrines used in studying with newly interested persons, and it has been a most effective tool. Since its publication, the world-wide growth of Jehovah's Witnesses has been truly phenomenal.[22] Their numbers in Canada have also increased more rapidly than during the years just before it began to roll from the presses. In the spring of 1974, well over 100,000 persons gathered to celebrate the memorial of the Lord's Supper,[23] and in November, just over 60,000 Witnesses reported preaching to non-Witnesses throughout the country.[24] But the most dramatic statistics which demonstrate the increase in numbers of Jehovah's Witnesses during a period of general religious decline are found in the 1971 census of Canada. During the decade 1961–71 the number of persons listed as Jehovah's Witnesses throughout the Dominion of Canada increased from 68,018 to 174,810! By the same token, the Witnesses had grown far faster in percentage terms than any other Canadian religious organization. While the Roman Catholic Church increased slightly, largely as the result of a traditionally high (though declining) birth rate and high immigration, and while membership in all the major, and many of the minor, Protestant churches failed to climb at the same rate as the total population, Jehovah's Witnesses grew an amazing 157.01 per cent. Even the Pentecostals, the group with the next highest increase in number of adherents, experienced an increase of only 53.18 per cent.[25]

TABLE 2

Growth in the Number of Active Jehovah's Witnesses Under the Canadian Branch of the Watch Tower Society*

Year	Total Active Publishers	Pioneers
1942	9,000	?
1949	14,305	1,212
1953	22,350	994
1958	35,324	1,135
1963	40,625	1,431
1968	41,661	1,795
1973	52,773	2,882
1974	58,452	3,904

*These figures do not include Jehovah's Witness publishers in Newfoundland, who have their own branch, or those in the Yukon, who are under the Alaska branch. According to the latest reports, there are just over 1,000 in Canada's most easterly province and about 200 in the Yukon. Thus, as of 1974, there were approximately 60,000 Witness preachers in the entire Dominion.

TABLE 3

The Number of Jehovah's Witnesses in Each Canadian Province and
Territory According to the National Censuses from 1901–71
(The totals of all Jehovah's Witnesses in the provinces and territories may be
different from the totals for Canada because of census revisions.)

Year	Canada	Nfld.	P.E.I.	N.S.	N.B.	Que.	Ont.
1901	101			17	4		63
1911	938		1	112	25	1	507
1921	6,689		16	460	98	53	2,655
1931	13,582		16	477	117	90	4,486
1941*	7,007		8	142	44	62	828
1951	34,596	556	111	1,401	522	1,422	11,485
1961	68,018	1,145	250	2,749	1,333	4,287	23,921
1971	174,810	1,860	415	4,960	2,850	17,130	67,710

Year	Man.	Sask.	Alta.	B.C.	Yukon	N.W.T.
1901	7	1		7		
1911	72	25	86	96		
1921	756	800	627	1,213		
1931	2,316	3,152	1,252	1,596		
1941*	485	1,074	504	415		1†
1951	3,173	5,077	3,493	7,339	2	15
1961	4,580	7,564	7,523	14,583	54	29
1971	8,635	9,880	17,930	42,315	585	530

*Report highly inaccurate because of ban.
†In 1941 all members of each religious denomination in the Yukon and
Northwest Territories were counted together.

Jehovah's Canadian Witnesses remained apart from society, too.
Basically they had not changed; they continued to consider them-
selves at war with Satan's world. Frequent reports of the persecution
of their brethren in Spain, Portugal, Greece, Communist lands, and
the newly independent nations of Africa—particularly Malawi—
made them feel that even in Canada they were not entirely safe.[26]
When Prime Minister Trudeau invoked the War Measures Act in
October 1970 against the Front de Libération du Québec, many
Witnesses felt uncomfortable at the revocation of civil liberties; the
Watch Tower Society cautioned them to remain strictly neutral in
the matter, however.[27] But in another dramatic way they continued

to make known what many Canadians considered to be a fanatic devotion to their faith along with a willingness to clash with authority over religious principle: for religious reasons they totally rejected the medical use of blood transfusions.

During the time between the organization of the first Bible Student congregation in Pittsburgh and the Second World War, Jehovah's Witnesses had seldom taken any position with regard to medical treatment. The *Golden Age* and *Consolation* magazines had criticized the use of smallpox vaccination and aluminum cookware as dangerous to health, but no attempt was made to claim that they were in violation of any scriptural principle. Individual Witnesses, therefore, usually went to physicians without any serious conflict. By the Second World War this situation began to change.

The Witnesses had long accepted the strict Biblical injunctions against the eating of blood and refused blood sausages or blood puddings. The question of their use of transfusions did not arise, however, until after the establishment of the first large-scale blood bank at Cook County Hospital in Chicago in 1937. Even when transfusions were used on the battlefields of the Second World War, most Witnesses objected to their ministration to soldiers as a means of aiding war and warriors as spillers of blood rather than as a violation of the apostolic requirement to abstain from blood. But before the war ended the *Watchtower* took a stand against transfusions *per se*. In its issue of July 1, 1945, it discussed Psalm 16, and in the exegesis of verse 4 dealt with the drinking of human blood and the unsuccessful attempt to transfuse Pope Innocent VIII in 1492. Shortly after the war, a series of articles appeared in *Awake!* and the *Watchtower* which called on Witnesses to avoid transfusions, in that they were both morally wrong and medically dangerous.[28]

Since then the Watch Tower Society has taken strong exception to other medical practices and popular customs which affect the human body. To Jehovah's Witnesses abortion is simply murder of the unborn;[29] organ transplants are regarded as little more than a macabre form of cannibalism;[30] vasectomies or the sterilization of women simply for the purpose of birth control are seen as unnecessary violations of the sanctity of the body,[31] as is tattooing of the skin.[32] The Witnesses have run into few problems with these stands, however. On the issue of abortion they have as an ally the old enemy, the Roman Catholic Church. Transplants are neither so common nor so successful as to have really affected the Witnesses as yet. And their position on sexual sterilization and tattooing has never approached the proportions of a serious issue.

Many non-Witnesses have cared about their rejection of blood transfusions, however. In fact, during the last two decades it has become a *cause célèbre* throughout Canada, the United States, and much of the civilized world. The Witnesses have never budged an inch on their stand, and many have refused transfusions for themselves and their children, often in the face of demands from physicians that they accept them as a means of saving life itself. Many members of the medical profession have been extremely irritated; the press has often pictured the Witnesses' belief in the matter as a struggle between fanaticism and modern science; much concern has been aroused about the plight of children who may die for "want of life-saving blood"; the courts have frequently removed children from parents' custody upon requests from physicians; legislatures have debated the matter; and the public has sometimes been aroused to the point of violence against the Witnesses. A few cases illustrate well just what has happened, and the publicity and emotion generated.

Witnesses in the United States first received serious adverse publicity for their position on blood in the spring of 1951, when a young Chicago couple, Darrell and Rhoda Labrenz, refused to allow physicians to give their new-born baby daughter, Cheryl, an exchange transfusion.[33] In Canada the issue became a matter of grave public concern when, in January 1954, Mr. and Mrs. Fred Prudum of London, Ontario, would not grant permission for a transfusion for their eight-year-old daughter, Margaret.[34] Shortly after, Neron Gaudreau, a French-Canadian Witness and fifty-nine-year-old father of twelve, also made headlines by spurning blood after a serious haemorrhage with the words: "Jehovah will look after his faithful witness."[35] But it was not until the late winter and early spring of 1956 that a rash of hysterically publicized Canadian transfusion cases occurred.

The Witnesses were subjected to merciless publicity in the press, and over radio and television. On February 8 the *Winnipeg Tribune* reported that the funeral of an Englehart, Ontario, woman, Mrs. James Grant, was held up two hours before the service was to take place. Coroner Dr. J. S. Ellis ordered an autopsy, since Mrs. Grant had died after refusing a transfusion. The *Tribune* also reported that local citizens were in an "ugly mood", that rumours indicated that the Witnesses might be denied entrance to the Orange Hall where they usually held their meetings, and that an Ontario Provincial Police constable had been assigned to protect mourners at the Grant funeral. On February 10 the public was made aware that Hamilton Judge Hugh Aurrell had removed custody of a new-born child from Mr. and Mrs. David Byron of that city, when they refused to allow the baby to be given an exchange transfusion for Rh blood factor incompatibility.[36] On February 19 another Hamilton child, baby Robert Cole, was severely burned. Doctors recommended a transfusion, but again the parents refused. Much publicity was given to the case, and Robert's mother charged that the family was being subjected to religious discrimination. By March 5 the press announced that Robert had pulled through without blood.[37] A third baby case was announced on February 20. The *Toronto Daily Star* reported on Witness child Bradley Carlton whose parents also rejected their doctor's request that he be given a transfusion when he had been burned six months earlier. The *Star* showed pictures of a healthy Bradley and a Witness woman, Mrs. Annie Wilson. She had been given a transfusion when her physicians did not realize that she was a Jehovah's Witness—and had died. Bradley Carlton's survival was declared a "vindication" by his parents.[38] Meanwhile, Toronto newspapers also focused attention on the case of seventeen-year-old Donna Jones. In its February 17 issue, the *Daily Star* headlined in two-and-one-half-inch type, "NEED GIRL, 17, DIE?" and went on to indicate that Donna refused blood at least a dozen times in spite of the danger of death. The *Star* quoted her as having said, "I'd rather die than violate the laws of Jehovah." A week later she was released from hospital, well.[39] Finally, on May 1, 1956, the *Calgary Albertan* dealt with the case of Judy Madison, a fourteen-year-old girl with a defective heart from Turner Valley, Alberta. Alberta surgeons agreed to operate on her but only with permission to give blood. Her parents refused. Though neighbours in the nearby community of Black

Diamond collected money for Judy's operation, many people in Turner Valley, angered at her parents, refused to contribute. The Madisons then took Judy to the Mayo Clinic at Rochester, Minnesota, where physicians indicated that they could operate without transfusions. They did so—successfully.[40]

In March 1957 the Toronto *Telegram* headlined, " 'Witness' Mother Spurns Blood, Dies". The account that followed dealt with the case of Mrs. A. W. Routliffe of Aylmer, Quebec, a thirty-six-year-old housewife who had died in still-birth.[41] But a number of better publicized and more emotional cases took place in the following year. These involved fourteen-year-old Donald Holland of Neepawa, Manitoba, and Lori Lynn Campbell, born at Newmarket, Ontario, on December 8, 1958.

On November 4, 1958, while on his parents' farm near Neepawa, Donald Holland was accidentally shot in the thigh with a .22 calibre bullet. The femoral artery was severed, but his physician tied it off, and the boy seemed to do reasonably well. On November 14 he died, however. The events received much publicity and while he lived, tremendous pressure was brought to bear on both the boy and his parents to permit a transfusion.[42] However, Manitoba Attorney General Sterling Lyon had indicated that the doctors were legally bound not to give him blood without parental consent.[43] After his death, a coroner's jury recommended to the Manitoba legislature that the law be amended to simplify legal machinery so that, in future, physicians would be able to give transfusions to minors when they considered them medically necessary.[44] As a result, the Manitoba Child Welfare Act[45] was changed. Under new legislation, Section 2 of the act was made to read:

Where a child is apprehended pursuant to an information alleging him to be a neglected child within the meaning of clause 'o' of ss (1) of section 19, the judge, on investigation may require and hear the evidence of at least three duly qualified medical practitioners who have been appointed by the minister to examine and have examined the child to determine whether any particular surgical operation or medical or remedial care or treatment is necessary for health or well-being of the child.

Section 6 was also amended as follows:

a) if he deems that the exigencies of the case require it, after giving to the persons entitled to receiving notice under s.s. 6, only such notice as the judge deems reasonable and practicable in the circumstances; or
b) without notice to those persons, if he is satisfied that the child may die or suffer serious injury if the operation, care, or treatment is not performed or given without further delay.

In the minds of the coroner's jury, the legislature, and much of the general public, there was no doubt that Donald Holland had died for want of a blood transfusion. However, at least one Canadian medical man, Dr. H. Angus Boright of Montreal, voiced dissent. In a letter to the Montreal *Gazette*, he wrote:

I would take objection to the article printed in the *Gazette* under the headline "Denied blood by faith, boy dies of wounds". This statement would seem to imply that had the boy received blood, his life would have been saved. Perhaps such an implication is unfair to both the parents and the Jehovah's Witness sect in general. . . . By implication the story suggests that the loss of blood was largely responsible for the boy's death, yet, although the accident occurred on Nov. 4, he did not die until Nov. 14. Such an interval is strong evidence against the likelihood that blood loss alone was responsible, for if such were the case death would have occurred shortly after the accident . . . blood transfusions per se would not necessarily have altered the ultimate course. . . . The loss of a son is one thing but to be accused publicly (by inference) of partial responsibility for that death is the inhumane act of an irresponsible press.[46]

The Lori Lynn Campbell case, occurring shortly after Donald Holland's death, created a storm. As Glen How was later to note: "A real wave of hysteria was whipped up by the press." One Toronto newspaper carried five large articles on blood transfusion in one day.[47] According to the Witness lawyer, what also happened was that a sudden hearing was held on a Sunday afternoon before a family-court judge, a former clergyman untrained in law, to which Lori Lynn's father was given an hour and fifteen minutes' notice to get thirty-five miles from his home to the trial. The infant, an Rh baby, was made a ward of the Toronto Children's Aid Society, was given a transfusion, and was later returned to her parents.[48]

Most of the publicity resulting from these cases was seriously damaging to the Witnesses. The old animosities against them had begun to die, or at least subside. Now the public was often stimulated to renewed anti-Jehovah's Witness feeling. What made it worse for them, too, was that by taking a stand against blood therapy, they seemed to set religion against science—a highly unpopular stand in the mid twentieth century. Furthermore, the press often played on public emotions when Witness children or mothers were involved in transfusion cases. But beginning in the early 1960s the Witnesses began an all-out counter-attack over the issue of blood, and once again they were able to find many public supporters for one of their beliefs.

Characteristically, the Witnesses met the issue on a number of fronts. In the first place, numerous articles on the question appeared from time to time in *Awake!* and the *Watchtower*.[49] Individual Witnesses were, therefore, constantly fortified to refuse blood in any form. The Watch Tower Society pointed out that the prohibition to eat blood had originally been given to Noah, was included in the Mosaic Law, and was restated in the Acts of the Apostles 15:20, 29. Jehovah's Witnesses were therefore abiding by Christian principles, not just those given to the Jews. To the objection from most clerics that blood transfusions were unknown in the ancient past and that the Bible prohibited eating blood, not intravenous transfusions, the Witnesses replied that the ancient Egyptians had used blood therapy, that Roman mobs had drunk the blood of fallen gladiators to gain strength, and that in any case transfusions were no more than a form of intravenous feeding. They also stressed Acts 15:20 which, as rendered in the *New World Translation*, states that Christians should "abstain from things polluted by idols and from fornication and from what is strangled and from blood", and Acts 15:29 which reads: "Keep yourselves free from things sacrificed to idols and from blood and from things strangled and from fornication. If you carefully keep yourselves from these things, you will prosper. Good health to you."

Accordingly, the Witnesses argued that the words "abstain" and "keep free" prohibit any form of ingestion of blood.[50]

In an appeal directed more at the public—particularly the medical and legal professions—they argued that transfusions took more lives than they saved. The Witnesses had long believed that revealed religion is in harmony with natural law; if blood therapy is morally wrong, it is therefore dangerous to health. And in their attempt to deal with the matter from that standpoint, they were able to collect an amazing amount of medical data to support their contention. Writing in the *Canadian Bar Journal* of October 1960, Glen How asserted bluntly that "blood transfusions can kill" and went on to quote a veritable plethora of reputable medical sources to prove his contention. Among others he was able to cite Dr. Alexander Wiener's statement, made at a Boston Society of Hematology convention in 1956, that three thousand Americans each year perished from faulty transfusions[51] and a declaration made by Dr. Arthur Kelly, secretary of the Canadian Medical Association:

Patients and parents have a perfect right to accept or reject treatment offered. No doctor can be positive that a person will die if he doesn't get a transfusion or live if he does. . . . The principle is an important one relating to the liberty of citizens. The same thing applies to any other medical treatment, and right or wrong people have a right to decide.[52]

In the following year the Watch Tower Society released a sixty-four-page booklet entitled *Blood, Medicine and the Law of God*. Although it stated clearly the Witnesses' religious objections to blood transfusions and gave a brief historical account of the medical usage of blood, most of its contents dealt strictly with medical arguments against blood therapy. Employing copious references and directed specifically to doctors, it discussed the problems of matching blood types, reactions to transfusions, Rh blood factor incompatibility, the danger of transmitting numerous diseases (for example, syphilis, malaria, hepatitis), the health of blood donors, the nature of blood banks, and means whereby Jehovah's Witnesses could be treated medically without blood. Attention was given to surgery without blood and the use of artificial blood expanders. Brief mention was also made of the rights of parents to choose, or not to choose, a certain form of treatment for their children.

The Witnesses were now armed with something more than a religious argument in dealing with physicians. Every effort was made to place copies of *Blood, Medicine and the Law of God* with medical doctors wherever Witnesses resided. Of course the Watch Tower Society was under no illusions. Witnesses believed that many of their problems were the direct result of emotional prejudice against them which would be stopped only after a long and bitter struggle. After all, wrote Glen How: *"The beliefs of the Roman Catholic Church, Christian Scientists and others cause their adherents to refuse at least some forms of medical treatment but such religious conflict with medical practice is considered quite acceptable though the result in lives lost may be much more serious than among Jehovah's witnesses."*[53] If Pope Pius XII could state that it is "illicit—even in order to save the mother—to cause directly the death of the small being that is called [the unborn child]",[54] and if Christian Scientists could refuse all types of medical treatment, why such a terrible outcry about Jehovah's Witnesses' refusal to accept blood?[55] The Witness lawyer also sharply criticized members of the medical profession for their dual standard with respect to religion:

So far as Jehovah's Witnesses are concerned, the only thing that is of importance is unfettered medical power; "saving lives" as they like to describe it. They are more than prepared to sacrifice the religious liberty of Jehovah's Witnesses on the altar of science. In Saskatchewan, however, in the medical battle against state medicine, the College of Physicians and Surgeons has used as an important plank in its propaganda the following argument: "A government-controlled plan offers latent but potential threat to certain dogmas and views of the Catholic Church relating to maternity, birth control and the state."[56]

Numerous outsiders were already coming to the Witnesses' defence, and by their statements began to bring a gradual shift in public opinion over the transfusion issue. Even before his *Bar Journal* article, Glen How had raised an important legal question: if the courts could force blood on the children of Jehovah's Witnesses almost without notice, what was to stop them from doing what they liked to the children of anyone who objected to a particular type of treatment for religious or other reasons? The *Toronto Daily Star* had agreed:

The Witnesses are not the only religious group which collides with 20th century scientific practice. Christian Science doctrine has nothing in common with modern medicine. Roman Catholic doctrine conflicts with some medical practice, when it forbids birth control by mechanical means or abortion even when the life of a woman might be at stake. Yet there is no mass outcry because of these beliefs, and properly so. . . . [The] Witness lawyer poses a danger: "If one of the Witnesses can lose custody of his child because he disagrees with a certain form of medical treatment, then any parent who happens to disagree with any form of medical treatment can immediately have his child removed from his home and declared a neglected child." If precedent widened out to snatching children for other medical treatment, let us consider first how much medical treatment of just 50 years ago is now regarded useless or even harmful.[57]

More important than editorial agreement that the seizure of Witness children to give them transfusions was a danger to civil liberties were several statements from medical men. The chief coroner of Manitoba had said that Jehovah's Witnesses should have the right to reject transfusions if they so desired.[58] Dr. T. L. Fisher, secretary-treasurer of the Canadian Medical Protective Association, had emphasized: "To the best of our knowledge, a doctor has no right to do anything to any person without his permission, or in the case of a child, parental or guardian's permission."[59] Dr. Arthur Kelly had remarked:

It is perhaps better that the odd person die rather than the fundamental human right of refusing medical treatment become impaired. Right. wrong or maybe, the final decision in these matters should rest with the patient or guardian. Patients have the right to accept or reject a doctor's advice according to their own desires. A doctor has no right to insist you accept his advice. I deplore methods of trying to force a transfusion or any kind of treatment. You are putting yourself in the position of God.[60]

Two Manitoba anaesthetists, Dr. Max Minuck and Dr. Ronald S. Lambie, were to go much further. Writing in the *Canadian Medical Association Journal* of May 27, 1961, they agreed that the Witnesses were victims of religious intolerance: "So often in the case of the Jehovah's Witnesses the surgical team becomes emotional, confused and irrational, because the patient's liability is religious rather than physical." In their summary, they stated: "Our experience has revealed that a great deal of intolerance exists towards the Jehovah's Witness order. An irrational, intolerant, and confused aura surrounds the participants, especially when children are involved." They criticized colleagues for secretly administering transfusions to unconscious patients and noted several points. Witnesses would accept auto-transfusions if their blood was not stored. That is, blood shed during surgery could be reinfused. Also, like the Witnesses themselves, the two Manitoba physicians stressed the possible use of synthetic blood volume expanders, more careful surgery, and special anaesthetic procedures. Then, too, they stated: "Other groups such as Roman Catholics must also refuse some forms of medical treatment, and we accept their point of view. Similarly the Jehovah's Witnesses beliefs should be respected and tolerated."

Three months after the Minuck and Lambie article appeared in a journal read largely by medical doctors, Dr. F. B. Bowman and Sidney Katz jointly published an article in *Maclean's* which was entitled "A Doctor of 45 Years' Standing Brings A Grave Charge Against the Majority of Hospitals and Physicians: THREE BLOOD TRANSFUSIONS OUT OF FOUR ARE MORE LIKELY TO HARM THAN HEAL".[61] Bowman and Katz quoted many of the same sources used earlier by Glen How, such as American blood specialist Dr. W. H. Crosby's remark that careless use of transfusions was "playing Russian Roulette with a bottle of blood instead of a revolver". Although the authors of the article did feel that there were times when transfusions should be used, they stated: "Unfortunately, too many doctors don't limit transfusions to these extreme medical emergencies. It can be said with honesty, that they are 'blood happy'."[62]

The appearance of the Bowman-Katz article did much to dampen public hostility to the Witnesses' stand on blood transfusions. There could be no doubt, either, that Glen How's statements in the *Cana-*

dian Bar Journal, the Minuck-Lambie article in the *Canadian Medical Association Journal*, and *Blood, Medicine and the Law of God*, all had much the same effect. On June 8, 1961, *Toronto Daily Star* writer Glenn Julian reported: "Mr. How has written a lengthy report on religion, medicine and law which has created quite a stir in medical and legal circles." Not long before, no less a publication than the *Canadian Register*, official organ of the Roman Catholic Archdiocese of Toronto and other Ontario dioceses, had come forward with a strong editorial statement arguing that no one had a right to force transfusions on anyone. Though the *Register* reasoned that "the blood transfusion had proved its worth as medical treatment in certain situations", and Catholics should consider themselves morally bound to make use of it when needed, the matter must be left with the conscience of the individual:

However, because this obligation rests on the conscience of the patient, no medical or civil authority has the right to force him to accept such treatment against his conscience. And since the responsibility for the life of a child rests on the parents, as long as the parents are physically and mentally capable of assuming it, the state cannot force them to subject the child to treatment which they consider morally wrong.

The state has no right to over-ride the rights of the individual patient, or of the parents in the case of a child, unless such intervention is necessary for the common good, as for example, to quarantine a case of a contagious disease.[63]

This statement was significant and served as a milestone. The *Canadian Register* did not miss the point stressed by Glen How that Catholics as well as Jehovah's Witnesses opposed certain forms of medical treatment regarded as life-saving. It was well aware that the state could, and sometimes would, invade the privileged areas of individual and family life contrary to the dictates of faith. Thus the *Register* took a strong stand in defence of the rights of Jehovah's Witnesses. Times had changed.

Articles questioning the value of blood transfusions and sympathy for the Witnesses' conscientious beliefs written by some members of the medical profession and by others did not, of course, solve the problem. The idea, still adhered to by most physicians, that blood therapy saves lives caused many to insist that Jehovah's Witnesses accept transfusions. Furthermore, constant appeals by the Red Cross for blood donors continued to popularize the concept that transfusions are life-saving, largely without risk to recipients. As a result, when new transfusion cases arose in the 1960s and 1970s, certain doctors and children's aid societies determined to force blood on Witness children even when there seemed little or no reason to do so. *Vancouver Sun* staff writer Simma Holt, in an article on battered babies written in 1967, contrasted the lack of public concern shown for children who were actually tortured and beaten by their parents, sometimes to death, with that manifested toward the children of Jehovah's Witnesses. Although there were forty-seven reported cases of battered babies in British Columbia in 1966, all of which required hospitalization and seven of which died, "the supervisor of the Richmond welfare office explained that 'it is very difficult to apprehend a child'. Yet it only takes a social worker a few minutes to apprehend a Jehovah's Witness child to give a blood transfusion, even where it may not be a matter of life or death as it is with these battered children."[64]

Thus, at about the same time as Jehovah's Witnesses began a campaign to counteract unfavourable publicity over their refusal to accept blood therapy, they decided to fight the issue in the courts. In the spring of 1960, Mrs. Ronald Wolfe of London, Ontario, gave birth to a child with haemolytic disease of the newborn (Rh incompatibility). Doctors demanded that the child be given a transfusion, but the Wolfes refused to consent. The child was then made a ward of the local Children's Aid Society and given the transfusion. Shortly thereafter, the child died. A coroner's jury received evidence from attending physicians and, on their word, ruled that the child's death had occurred because the transfusion had not been administered earlier.[65] Mr. and Mrs. Wolfe then tried to have the matter brought before a higher court. Glen How argued that the jury's verdict was entirely unwarranted as, under the law, there was no way whereby witnesses testifying before a coroner's jury could be cross-examined. "It is well known as a feature of cases involving medical testimony that they (doctors) are loath to testify against each other and often the sole means of introducing medical evidence is by cross examination,"[66] said How. None the less, the Wolfes' attempt to have the jury's decision reversed, or the case even heard by an appeal court, failed. The Ontario Supreme Court[67] and, ultimately, the Supreme Court of Canada refused leave to have the matter reopened.[68] In effect, Canadian courts proved unwilling to examine the blood-transfusion issue.

The best that the Witnesses could achieve by litigation in a Canadian court occurred in the fall of 1962. On Sunday, August 26, Mrs. Alexander Livingston of Galt, Ontario, gave birth to a daughter, Teresa Ella, with Rh blood factor incompatibility. On the same day, wardship over her was granted to the Waterloo Children's Aid Society so that she could be given a blood transfusion without her father's consent. Livingston later asked that the society's guardianship be revoked and Ontario Supreme Court Justice Samuel Hughes agreed. His decision was made simply on the narrow ground that the original order making the Livingston child a ward of the Waterloo Children's Aid Society had been issued on a Sunday.

Another case brought before Justice Hughes on the same day did give the Witnesses a more substantive minor victory, however. It involved Gregory Russell Forsyth, the infant son of Mr. and Mrs. Robert Forsyth of Kingston, Ontario, born on September 29, 1962, and also an Rh baby. Though there was no great danger to the child and there was no strong indication to show that he might need a transfusion, Dr. D. J. Delahaye, the attending physician, had called the boy's father to a "discussion" at the hospital. The discussion turned out to be an impromptu court hearing before Judge James Garvin. At the hearing Dr. Delahaye stated: "This child may need transfusions within the next three days. We cannot, at the moment, be absolutely certain but the need for it may arise within the next few days." The parents were never asked for their permission to give a transfusion. But, since they were Jehovah's Witnesses, the physician and Judge Garvin removed Gregory from their custody and placed him under the guardianship of the Kingston Children's Aid Society; in fact, he had already been taken into the society's custody before the hearing.

Justice Hughes questioned the legality of the action, but the legal counsel for the society claimed the Witness infant was a neglected child and someone had to act in his defence. Lawyer How, representing the parents, charged that the medical profession and the children's aid societies were going "too far" and indicated that Jehovah's Witnesses henceforth might avoid hospitals. Although Justice Hughes felt that the Kingston Hospital, Dr. Delahaye, and Judge Garvin had acted in the child's best interest, he returned him to his parents' custody. He remarked that he was unable to say that "the haphazard affair [the hearing before Judge Garvin] which emerges from the transcripts meets the test [of a fair judicial proceeding]".[69] At best, all the Witnesses gained was an admission from Justice Hughes that the medical profession, children's aid societies, and family and juvenile courts were not acting with due respect for parents' legal rights. Still, that in itself was important, for Witnesses hoped that it would stop rapid seizures of their children for treatment without a chance to have the issue argued in court.

In the United States, Jehovah's Witnesses also sought recourse to the courts. Doctors not only obtained legal authorization to give transfusions to children who were legally minors, but also insisted on giving them to Witness adults, with or without court permission. Consequently, the Witnesses' case against the medical profession in that country seemed stronger than it did in Canada. While many members of the general public undoubtedly disagreed with the Witnesses when they refused blood for their children, far fewer felt that adults should be forced to accept a specific form of medical treatment —good or bad—if they did not want it. The United States Constitution also seemed to guarantee the Witnesses or anyone else the right to decide the matter privately. The Fourth Amendment specifically stated: "The right of the people to be secure in their persons, houses, papers and effects against unreasonable searches and seizures shall not be violated." American lawyers for Jehovah's Witnesses therefore took the position stated by the Watch Tower Society's Canadian counsel—that giving transfusions to unwilling patients was nothing less than "unreasonable seizure". If doctors could force blood on Jehovah's Witnesses in the name of science, could not anyone be treated against his will in any way that members of the medical profession saw fit? Lawyers for the Witnesses also stressed the rights of Americans under the First and Fourteenth Amendments to the Constitution, as well as the Fourth; and with the support of certain medical authorities, they emphasized again and again the dangers of blood transfusions. Yet they were little more successful than were Jehovah's Witnesses in Canada. The Supreme Court of Illinois did rule that adults could not be made to accept transfusions unwillingly.[70] But the Witnesses lost a hard-fought case in the State of Washington in the late 1960s,[71] and their request to appeal was denied by the United States Supreme Court.[72] As late as 1971 the Supreme Court of New Jersey granted a hospital in that state permission to give a twenty-two-year-old woman blood on the ground that she did not have the legal right to commit suicide. A transfusion was administered over her cries for help.[73] Thus there seemed little use in pursuing the matter legally; most American courts were no more willing to hear Jehovah's Witnesses' arguments against blood therapy than their Canadian counterparts. With some bitterness Glen How remarked privately that many American jurists were more concerned about the well-being of murderers and rapists than the constitutional rights of God-fearing Christians.[74] So by the late 1960s Jehovah's Witnesses no longer took the initiative in pressing transfusion cases in North American courts.

If they could not win by appealing to Caesar, as they had so many times in the past, the Witnesses refused to give ground. And many events began to make the transfusion issue easier for them to deal with. In the first place, they began to take great care in seeking out both doctors and hospitals that would agree not to give them blood, even in extreme emergencies.[75] As a result, there were far fewer cases of bad publicity. Then, as Jehovah's Witnesses began to find physicians—some Witnesses themselves—who would respect their wishes, they began to make medical history. In 1962 Dr. Denton Cooley of the Texas Heart Institute—a pioneer in heart transplants and the first physician to implant an artificial heart in a human being—agreed to perform heart surgery on a Witness, without blood. That operation and others like it were so successful that Cooley and his surgical team decided to dispense with transfusions during operations on non-Witness patients as well. Numerous newspapers and medical journals gave favourable reports. The *San Diego Union* headlined

"Patients' Beliefs Aid Surgery",[76] and the *Journal of the American Medical Association* commented that not only did the Cooley team's techniques "have a significant bearing on medical practice, particularly, the use of blood transfusions and emergency treatment of traumatic and hemorrhagic shock", but stated "the practical advantages of employing crystalized solutions [blood expanders] rather than plasma or whole blood are obvious".[77]

Numerous articles appearing in medical texts, journals, and the public press also began to strengthen the Witnesses' contention about the extreme dangers of blood transfusions. The medical profession throughout North America was made more aware of the "frightening revelation of transfusion morbidity", since approximately 16,500 persons each year were dying from transfusion.[78] According to one authority, "the computed annual death rate from blood transfusions exceeds that reported for many common surgical illnesses such as rectal cancer, appendicitis, diverticulitis, duodenal ulcer, cholecystitis or intestinal obstruction."[79] The *Chicago Tribune* reported in 1969 that one out of every twenty of some forty-eight thousand patients who had received transfusions at Cook County Hospital had had negative reactions, many of which were serious.[80] A director at a St. Petersburg, Florida, blood bank stated that blood is like "a loaded gun".[81] Toronto's flamboyant ex-coroner, Dr. Morton Shulman, made headlines in 1967 when he charged that a Hamilton woman had died of an overload transfusion, and that authorities were trying to keep the matter quiet. According to the medical report, she had died of lung congestion, perhaps drowning in blood from a too rapidly administered transfusion.[82] The *Toronto Star* of April 5, 1968, announced that the American National Research Council had called for the banning of pooled, stored blood plasma because of the possibility of hepatitis being transmitted. The article stated that a three-year study at the University of California had indicated that ten per cent of all patients who had received plasma had become ill with acute hepatitis.

Medical opinion began to change on the advisability of exchange transfusions for Rh babies suffering from hyperbilirubinemia (haemolytic disease of the newborn). Several physicians writing in medical journals suggested that the danger to infants' lives and mental health

246 / JEHOVAH'S WITNESSES IN CANADA

from hyperbilirubinemia was not as great as had been thought in the past.[83] An Alberta physician also admitted that many babies had died from exchange transfusions.[84] Furthermore, a far safer and more simple treatment had been discovered for Rh babies: phototherapy, the use of blue light or direct sunlight.[85]

As a result of much of this information and Jehovah's Witnesses' struggles over the transfusion issue, many began to seek a re-examination of the whole situation. Dr. Arthur Kelly again warned his fellow physicians not to coerce Witnesses, even if they believed that "Big Brother knows best".[86] R. C. Cornish, editor of the Trent, Ontario, *Trentonian*, suggested that Canadians ought to give the Witness belief on blood "a more sympathetic hearing than it has so far been given".[87] But if some manifested a greater willingness to listen to the Witnesses' request "to abstain from blood", others were not convinced. Thus, between 1967 and 1971, four rather dramatic transfusion cases occurred in Canada, which were advertised widely by the news media. In the long run, the publicity proved largely favourable to the Witnesses, as did that which resulted from Glen How's appearance before the Manitoba legislature in July 1970.

The first case involved fifteen-year-old Miriam Myllyniemi, a girl from the Okanagan Valley, British Columbia, who was suffering from a serious malfunction of the kidneys. Doctors claimed that in order to keep her alive she must be given regular transfusions. Since her mother was a Witness, she refused consent, and Miriam was made a ward of the Children's Aid Society. Over a period of time, numerous transfusions were administered to the girl over her strong protests. Then early in May 1967, Miriam fled the hospital with her mother and went into hiding. A Canada-wide alert was sent out for the missing child, and police began raiding Witness homes in the Okanagan Valley in an attempt to find her. Newspapers loudly proclaimed that she would die unless found and given life-saving blood. Months later the Watch Tower Society released a statement: Miriam Myllyniemi—still in hiding—was receiving treatment and doing well without blood.[88]

The second case occurred at Kingston, Ontario, in the spring of 1970. Early in the morning of April 1, Mrs. Lynn DeWaal, attended by Dr. T. O. Ashwell, gave birth to a baby girl at St. Francis General

Hospital, Smiths Falls, Ontario. Later in the day the baby, Eunice Devina, was found to be suffering from a mild case of blood incompatibility. At six in the evening, Mrs. DeWaal was obliged to leave the hospital to attend court in order to obtain a divorce from her husband, who had deserted her. Two hours later, after being granted the divorce and full custody of her child, she returned to St. Francis Hospital. Although the hospital staff had assured her that her baby would be there when she returned, in fact the Children's Aid Society had removed the infant to Kingston, some sixty miles away, during the mother's absence in court. Accompanied by her parents and brothers, Mrs. DeWaal drove to Kingston and, upon arrival there, discovered that her baby had been placed in the care of Dr. D. J. Delahaye. When Mrs. DeWaal discussed the child's condition with the doctor, he informed her that Eunice Devina's bilirubin count had risen to eighteen milligrams per one hundred millilitres of blood. The mother, as one of Jehovah's Witnesses, requested that her baby be given phototherapy treatment. But Dr. Delahaye insisted on an exchange transfusion. He was quoted as saying: "I am going to give that child a transfusion if I have to go to jail for it." Thereupon one of Mrs. DeWaal's brothers suggested that she take the baby, which she was holding in her arms, and leave. A scuffle followed. Dr. Delahaye tried to restrain the man forcibly, and two nurses who tried to grab the baby badly bruised Mrs. DeWaal's arm in the process. As Dr. Delahaye struggled all the way from the hospital's seventh floor to the street with Mrs. DeWaal's father and brothers, she went down the elevator with the baby, reached her car, and drove away. *Awake!* described what followed:

Newspapers spoke of the baby as being abducted; the police were instructed to hunt for her. Questions were raised in the provincial legislature. John Yaremko, Minister of Social and Family Services, announced that a charge had been laid against the mother. An official in Mr. Yaremko's department immediately denied that a charge had been laid. A warrant was issued to search the mother's home; then the Crown Attorney ordered it canceled.

The Children's Aid Society applied for wardship and complained when the judge would not make the order. Judge Garvin, being a man who believes in law, wanted to give the parents a fair hearing and refused to be stampeded. He recalled that the Supreme Court of Ontario had said in an earlier case of Jehovah's Witnesses that they were entitled to notice and a trial. Showing his due respect for the Supreme Court, he refused to act till proper procedures were put before him.

The Crown Attorney, C. J. Newton, commended the actions of Dr. Ashwell at Smiths Falls but also admitted: "The mother had an equal right to remove the child from hospital."

Faced with these crosscurrents of opinion, the *Globe and Mail* (Toronto) remarked: "Confusion clouded legal issues yesterday in the disappearance of a three-day-old baby."

On top of this, Dr. Ashwell stated that "the chances of this little girl living or not suffering irreparable brain damage are about the same as me winning the Irish Sweepstakes today", although he admitted, "quite honestly, I can't simply describe the disease to you because I have only a slight grasp of it myself". Dr. Delahaye, angered at events, criticized the Children's Aid Society for "laxity" and the Supreme Court of Ontario for "ducking the issue". In remarks to the *Toronto Telegram*, he related the case of another Witness child who had suffered from leukemia. "Before the doctor gave a transfusion its parents came to Kingston Hospital and took the child. Toronto doctors decided to abide by the wishes of the parents and ironically the child survived." *Awake!* remarked with bitterness:

Ironically so did the DeWaal baby. Ironically, so has every other infant of Jehovah's witnesses that has been removed from a hospital to avoid exchange transfusion. Not so ironically, six children of Jehovah's witnesses in Canada have been taken from their parents, given forced blood transfusions and brought back dead.

In the meantime, Mrs. DeWaal had taken her baby to another municipality where she was given phototherapy by a nurse widely experienced in the field. Though Dr. Delahaye had made the direst predictions and had suggested that there was a good chance the baby was dead, she made a complete recovery. On June 3 Mrs. DeWaal appeared on television in Ottawa with Eunice Devina and legal counsel "to explain what happened and why". The program was later shown across Canada. With satisfaction *Awake!* stated: "In view of the events in this case, one is reminded of law professor Howard Oleck's commentary in *Medical World News* (Dec. 5, 1969) advising that medical relationships would improve 'if physicians generally would stop acting as though they are somehow the anointed ones of God'."[89]

Only a few months later, Arlene Hansler, a fifteen-year-old Toronto girl, was admitted to Sunnybrook Hospital for what the hospital described as severe uterine bleeding. According to the girl, the hospital physician advised her that he might force her to accept a transfusion even before he examined her. She also claimed that she had been in hospital only a few hours when she was told that court proceedings were under way to make her a ward of the Toronto Children's Aid Society. Before any such action could be taken, however, Arlene's mother removed her from the hospital. When Judge Margaret Chambers signed an order giving custody of Arlene to the Children's Aid Society, she went into hiding in a friend's home somewhere in North Toronto. Thereupon the police began an all-out search for her. Some twenty days later, members of the press were invited to meet with Arlene, who had recovered completely under the treatment of a general practitioner. She had been given iron pills and other medication, but not blood.

The Witnesses claimed that the police had not only talked to Arlene Hansler's friends but had searched homes, tapped telephones, and posted policemen outside kingdom halls and the Hansler home. Thus, even though she was well and could return to high school, she did not dare do so. Hospital authorities and the police denied the statements made by the Witnesses. The Sunnybrook Hospital public relations officer claimed that if the Witness girl was no longer ill, the hospital had no more interest in her. Yet a spokesman for the Children's Aid Society verified Witness charges by stating that the police would continue to look for her as she was "lawfully in the care of the society" under the terms of a thirty-day court order.[90]

The fourth and final case involved the Raymond Randall family of Wawota, Saskatchewan. In February 1971 Mr. and Mrs. Randall had their three-month-old daughter, Esther, admitted to the Regina

General Hospital. Their physician indicated that abdominal surgery was necessary but refused to operate on the infant unless the Randalls gave permission for a blood transfusion. The Randalls then attempted to make contact with doctors in Houston, Texas, and in Toronto to determine if surgery could be performed in one place or the other without blood. Their local doctor angrily refused to allow them to remove their child, however, and stated that she was in critical condition. Randall then called a surgeon in Winnipeg and made arrangements to have Esther operated on at that city's Victoria General Hospital. The Randalls then went to the Regina General, removed the child, and started at once for Winnipeg. But as they neared the Manitoba capital they were stopped by the RCMP; Randall was handcuffed and he, Mrs. Randall, and the baby were driven in a police car to another hospital. Upon request from Saskatchewan authorities, Esther was made a ward of the Winnipeg Children's Aid Society and, after a thirty-six-hour delay, was operated on without blood.

The events caused a public storm in the press and over radio. Local radio stations used the occasion to interview representatives of both Jehovah's Witnesses and the Winnipeg Children's Aid Society. The Randalls gave their own account over the air, and both the local Witness circuit overseer and Glen How were interviewed on several programs. Glen How pointed out that the Randalls were completely within their rights in removing their child from Regina. They were in no sense "abducting" her, since parents have a perfect right to take their child anywhere they like and certainly to any physician they like, unless the child has been made a ward of the state, or someone representing it. Furthermore, the police had no right and no reason to seize Randall and handcuff him. When asked about the matter over radio, a spokesman for the Winnipeg Children's Aid Society admitted that doctors had recognized that there was no need to administer blood to the infant except in the case of a surgical accident. He also stated that after examining her, doctors had agreed that there was no need for an immediate operation, and they had decided to wait until she was made a ward of the Children's Aid Society.[91]

Jehovah's Witnesses received much public sympathy. One physician, Dr. G. J. Froese of East Kildonan, wrote to the *Winnipeg Free Press* in some bitterness over the way society seemed willing to destroy hundreds of unborn children through abortion and yet, at the same time, castigate Jehovah's Witness parents for not allowing blood to be given to an occasional new-born child such as Esther Randall. Wrote Froese: "If this one baby had died everybody would have shouted 'shame, murder' but if 600 are ruthlessly done away with by doctors who are more interested in money than Judean Christian principles this is 'liberation'."[92] Another writer to the *Free Press* who stated that he was not a member of Jehovah's Witnesses said that the police owed Randall a public apology and suggested that he be compensated for the humiliation he had suffered.[93] At the same time, many persons who identified themselves as non-Witnesses called local phone-in programs to protest the fact that Randall had been treated like a common criminal.

The Witnesses used the Randall case, like the Myllyniemi, DeWaal, and Hansler cases before it, to charge that the medical profession and children's aid societies were carrying on a vendetta against them. Glen How, who argued that the law was being turned into a sham, asked bitterly over a Winnipeg radio station, "Is this Canada or Russia?" and went on to compare Manitoba and Saskatchewan officials to Nazis "who had also known what was best for the children of Jehovah's Witnesses". Such officials, he said, were "meddlesome little public officials" who wanted to get their names in the newspapers.

By this time, Manitobans, especially members of the province's New Democratic Party government, should have been somewhat accustomed to such strong language. In the previous summer, Minister of Health René Toupin had proposed an amendment to the Manitoba Child Welfare Act, which was quite evidently directed at the Witnesses. It read:

Where any person who is actually or apparently under eighteen years of age is in a hospital and who is likely to die or suffer serious injury if a surgical operation or other remedial care or treatment is not performed, either immediately or within a period of seven days, the surgical operation or remedial care or treatment may be performed without notice to or the consent of the parent or guardian and without an order of the court, if the superintendent or medical director of the hospital so certifies in the prescribed form, and upon such certification and the forwarding of a copy thereof to the director within a period of three days, the person in need of such treatment shall be deemed to be a temporary ward of the government at the expense of the government until such time as he is discharged from the hospital.

When Jehovah's Witnesses became aware of the proposed amendment, they acted immediately. They attacked it publicly, as a possible violation of the rights of the family, and as an attack on minority rights. Glen How discussed the issue over radio with René Toupin, and the Witnesses made direct contact with Manitoba's Premier Schreyer. Early in July, How appeared before the provincial legislature, meeting as a committee of the whole, and delivered a strongly worded statement. After detailing the common-law position on parental rights, he stated:

Every time this statute has been mentioned, the Minister of Health has spoken only about seizing, without trial, the children of Jehovah's Witnesses. It seems to be thought that, as long as you are only tramping on the rights of a minority, this is a palatable assault on civil rights.

The dictator, Hitler, pretended he was only attacking Jews and Jehovah's Witnesses! Remember the damage he did to everyone else!

The present law is an attack on Jehovah's Witnesses, a manifest effort to make them second-class citizens, not entitled to even the semblance of a fair trial.

The history of discriminatory legislation is a history of injustice and oppression that sprays damage like a scattergun instead of a rifle. Many will be damaged who did not expect it.

He followed these remarks with a long and detailed analysis of the demerits of blood transfusions, buttressed with copious quotations and whole articles from medical journals. He also claimed there was much medical experimentation on patients—"not ordinarily a subject that is advertised". Accordingly, he stated: "The legislation will make your children, every child in the province, a subject for experimentation. Those members of the legislature who are convinced that doctors are absolutely right, absolutely infallible, should have no trouble agreeing to make them absolutely liable for damage caused."[94]

These strong words evidently caused an uproar in the legislature and confounded both the Minister of Health and his colleague, the Minister of Mines, Sidney Green. A few days later Health Minister Toupin withdrew the proposal. He stated that, after investigation, his staff had been able to find only two cases in eight years in which children had been denied blood by their parents in serious circumstances. In each of those cases the responsible provincial government minister and the courts dealt with the situation in time to save the child's life. The Witnesses replied that the children's lives would have have been saved without blood, but they gave a sigh of relief that the Minister of Health had backed down, and they commended the government. The NDP caucus voted unanimously to withdraw the amendment.[95] Apparently the Witnesses had convinced them it was bad legislation.

Meeting a few days later in Winnipeg's Hotel Fort Garry, the Canadian Pediatrics Society expressed "disappointment and discouragement". "It's time we stop letting minority groups intimidate us and push things down our throats," said Dr. K. O. Wylie, president of the society. "I don't think it's right that any person or group of people should make medical decisions other than the M.D."[96] Jehovah's Witnesses indicated that they weren't trying to push anything down anyone's throat; they simply did not want blood pushed into their veins. Also, they asked, should not parents, as well as physicians, have some rights over medical issues related to their children?

All these events demonstrated several things. The blood-transfusion issue remained, and remains, a live one. In spite of taking what was so long an unpopular stand against a large proportion of the medical profession, the courts, the legislatures, and the news media, Jehovah's Witnesses have won some important victories—legally, medically, and in the court of public opinion. No matter what has happened, or will happen, respecting the issue they remain totally determined to abstain from blood. The *Edmonton Journal* commented in 1967 with regard to Miriam Myllyniemi: "Witnesses take their religion seriously."[97]

To many, this position still seems based on fanaticism. But by their stand on blood, Jehovah's Witnesses continue to challenge many of the popular concepts, ideas, and values of the larger society. If John Stuart Mill's statement about the value of dissent in his famous work *On Liberty* is to be believed, they serve a useful purpose. By acting as medical guinea-pigs they have certainly proved this. Yet it is not primarily for the good of society that they stand so firm; they are determined "to render unto God the things that are God's".

RUSSELL V. ROSS

THE ALLEGATION that Pastor Charles T. Russell perjured himself in a Hamilton, Ontario, courtroom in March 1913 by stating that he "knew Greek" has proved to be one of the most damaging charges made against him. Over the years, it has been repeated by Martin and Klann,[1] Anthony Hoekema,[2] William Whalen,[3] Gérard Hébert,[4] and Alan Rogerson[5]—to name but a few—in works which are both openly polemical and supposedly objective. Russell made a personal defence of himself in the *Watch Tower*,[6] and J. F. Rutherford dealt briefly with the issue in *A Great Battle in the Ecclesiastical Heavens*.[7] In 1955 Marley Cole also discussed it and quoted a brief section from the transcript of record which seems to exonerate Russell.[8] But both Russell's and Rutherford's statements have generally been ignored, and Cole has been accused of leaving out the relevant section of the transcript which, it is asserted, proves Russell guilty of perjury.[9] What, then, are the facts?

The charge originally made by the Reverend J. J. Ross is found on page 18 of *Some Facts and More Facts about the Self-Styled "Pastor" Charles T. Russell*.[10] Ross gives the following version of what occurred:

"Do you know the Greek?" asked the Attorney. "Oh, yes," was Russell's reply. Here he was handed a copy of the New Testament in Greek, by

Westcott & Hort, and asked to read the letters of the alphabet as they appear on the top of page 447. He did not know the alphabet. "Now," asked Mr. Staunton, "Are you familiar with the Greek language?" "No," said Mr. Russell, without a blush.

However, an examination of the transcript of record indicates, in fact, that Ross, who accused Russell of "devising falsely" and of being "a fabricator",[11] was himself guilty of serious dishonesty.

In the first place, Russell had already specifically stated in court that he had not been trained in Greek. When questioned by Ross's lawyer, George Lynch-Staunton, he had given the following testimony:

Question: "You don't profess, then, to be schooled in the Latin language?"

Answer: "No, Sir."

Question: "Or in Greek?"

Answer: "No, Sir."

At that point Lynch-Staunton asked Russell if he knew the Greek alphabet. The testimony quoted from the transcript of record reads:

Question: "Do you know the Greek alphabet?"

Answer: "Oh yes."

Question: "Can you tell me the correct letters if you see them?"

Answer: "Some of them, I might make a mistake of some of them."

Question: "Would you tell me the names of the letters of those on top of the page, page 447 I have got here [from Westcott and Hort]?"

Answer: "Well, I don't know that I would be able to."

Question: "You can't tell what those letters are, look at them and see if you know?"

Answer: "My way . . ." [At this point he was interrupted by the court and not allowed to explain.]

Immediately after this, Lynch-Staunton asked Russell the question: "Are you familiar with the Greek language?" Russell's reply was an emphatic "No."

Russell explained later in the *Watch Tower* what he had undoubtedly intended to say when he was cut off. All he meant when he indicated he "knew" the Greek alphabet was that he had developed a schoolboy's ability to recognize Greek words in Strong's and Young's concordances of the Bible. William Whalen, an advocate of the perjury theory, says as much.[12] No doubt, too, Russell could repeat from memory the names of the Greek letters from alpha to omega. Besides, before Lynch-Staunton showed him the Greek text of Westcott and Hort, he had already stated that he might not be able to recognize all of the letters of the Greek alphabet in print. Thus, when he asserted that Russell had claimed to "know the Greek" in court, it was Ross, not Russell, who was guilty of twisting the truth. The most that Russell claimed was that he "knew" the Greek alphabet, and he admitted that he could not recognize all the letters in print.

Those present at the trial did not seem to feel that Pastor Russell had perjured himself in any way. Magistrate George H. Jelfs did not;[13] neither did the correspondent for the *Hamilton Spectator*, who simply mentioned questions relating to the Watch Tower president's education in passing.[14] George Lynch-Staunton wrote that he personally felt that Russell was a "first-water fakir" and stated that he had been led to believe that Russell had "accumulated a great amount of wealth from his victims". He admitted that "this was never verified", however, and said nothing about Russell's having committed perjury.[15] Hence, the perjury story grew entirely out of Ross's account of the matter and has been perpetuated by bitter adversaries of Jehovah's Witnesses, most notably Martin and Klann.

In their 1953 edition of the book *Jehovah of the Watchtower*, Walter Martin and Norman Klann quoted directly from Ross's *Some Facts and More Facts About the Self-Styled "Pastor" Charles T. Russell*. Their account of the trial reads as follows:

The cross examination continued for five hours. Here is a sample of how the "Pastor" perjured himself.

Question: (Attorney Staunton)—"Do you know the Greek?"

Answer: (Russell)—"Oh yes."

At this point Russell was handed a copy of Westcott and Hort's Greek New Testament and asked to read the letters of the alphabet as they appeared on the top of page 447. Russell did not even know the alphabet. Counsellor Staunton continued—

Question: (Counsellor Staunton)—"Now, are you familiar with the Greek?"

Answer: (Russell)—"No."

Here is conclusive evidence, the "Pastor" under oath perjured himself beyond question.[16]

As made evident by these quotations, Martin and Klann were so convinced by the account of their fellow Baptist clergyman that they did not bother to examine the transcript of record to determine its accuracy. In a later version of *Jehovah of the Watchtower*, they did publish an accurate version of the transcript of record as quoted above.[17] Yet, strangely, they still assert that Russell "perjured himself" and take no note of the fact that both they and Ross earlier distorted the facts of the case and maligned Russell unfairly.

ᴄɦє ꝼiꝛꞅᴄ woꝛlꝺ waꝛ

As INDICATED in Chapters 2 and 3, much hostility was directed against Bible Students during the First World War because of their opposition to involvement in combatant military service. Conscription of many of them and their subsequent travails in the army and prisons both in Canada and in England arose out of Justice Lyman Duff's decision in *Re Cooke* (January 14, 1918) quoted in full.

Re COOKE (Serial No. 548250 JC.)

January 4, 1918.

This was an appeal by the subject of the application by leave against the decision of a Tribunal refusing exemption to David Cooke, a member of an organization known as the "International Bible Students Association".

The Central Appeal Judge: The applicant claims exemption as a member of the "International Bible Students Association" on the ground that in the language of Section 11 (1) (f) "he conscientiously objects to the undertaking of combatant service and is prohibited from so doing by the tenets and articles of faith, in effect on the sixth day of July, 1917, of any organized religious denomination existing and well recognized in Canada at such date, and to which he in good faith belongs."

There is an unlimited company known as the "International Bible Students Association" incorporated under the Companies Acts of 1908 and 1913 (United Kingdom). By the memorandum of association the objects of the company are stated as follows: —

a) To promote Christian knowledge by the dissemination of Bible truths, orally and by the printed page, and by means of the distribution of Bibles and the printing and publication of Bible study helps, tracts, pamphlets, papers and other religious documents, and by the use of all other lawful means which may seem to the *Council of the Association* directly or indirectly conducive to the furtherance of the above objects of the Association.

b) To purchase or otherwise acquire sketches, photographs, drawings, publications, manuscripts, notes, data and memoranda bearing upon the above objects of the Association and to print, publish, display and distribute the same.

c) To enter into any arrangement with any Government or authority, supreme, municipal, local or otherwise, and to obtain from any such Government or authority all rights, concessions or privileges that may seem conducive to the above objects or any of them.

d) To promote any association or associations, whether limited or not, for the purpose of its or their acquiring all or any of the property, rights and liabilities of the Association, or for any other purpose which may seem, directly or indirectly, calculated to further the objects of the Association.

e) To purchase, take on lease or in exchange, hire or otherwise acquire, and to sell, exchange, surrender, lease, mortgage, charge, convert, turn to account, dispose of and deal with any estate or interest in any lands, buildings, easements, rights, privileges, mortgages, debentures, options, contracts, licenses or other rights, and any real or personal property of any kind necessary or convenient for the attainment of the objects of the Association mentioned in paragraph 3 (a) hereof, and to erect, construct, enlarge, alter, furnish, maintain and improve buildings of all kinds.

f) To make donations to such persons and in such cases, and in either of cash or other assets, as may be thought directly or indirectly conducive to any of the objects of the Association, or otherwise expedient, and to subscribe or guarantee money for charitable or benevolent objects, or for any exhibition, or for any public, general or other objects, and to grant pensions and allowances and to make payments towards insurance.

g) To borrow or raise, or secure the payment of money in such manner as the Association shall think fit.

h) To pay out of the funds of the Association all expenses of or incident to the formation and registration of the Association.

i) To do all such other things as are incidental or conducive to the attainment of the above objects.

The Company as appears from the evidence, issues publications, in which certain views are advocated touching the interpretation of the Bible, and certain religious beliefs advanced and supported; and of the subscribers to these publications, who accept the doctrine so expounded, there are in various countries, including Canada, groups who meet for the study of the Bible and the discussion of questions of theology and ethics.

These groups are not associated by any bond other than their adherence to, and advocacy of, these views and beliefs, but are among themselves collectively known by the same designation as that given to the Company.

These writings, as far as I have examined them, leave some doubt whether according to the beliefs advocated by the writers of them, a member of the Association might conscientiously under the compulsion of legal necessity, engage in combatant military service. I do not, I must admit, find them entirely self-consistent.

It is not necessary, however, to form any opinion upon the exact nature of the doctrine, as touching the subject of non-resistance and kindred subjects advocated in these writings.

The evidence before me does not justify the conclusion that these groups or associations so-called, either individually or collectively come within the description—"organized religious denomination existing and well recognized in Canada" within the contemplation of the Military Service Act.

First:—There is much room for doubt whether these associations so called have for the primary object a common worship, which is, I think, an essential characteristic of a "religious denomination" within the meaning of Section 11. The evidence is certainly consistent with the view that the primary objects of them in so far as they can be said to have a common object, are those expressed in the passage quoted above from the memorandum of association, which in themselves are certainly not sufficient to constitute even an organized body clearly proved to be pursuing them in common, a "religious denomination".

Second: The Statute plainly implies as a characteristic of religious denominations, falling within its scope, that there should be conditions of membership, compliance or non-compliance with which can be ascertained by reference to some practical criterion, and of such conditions there is, although I pressed for it on hearing, no evidence, and there are no indicia to serve as reliable guides for the Tribunals.

Though the Bible Students' conscientious objection was certainly a factor which made them unpopular in 1917 and 1918, their anti-clericalism was undoubtedly of even greater importance. As well as the letter from the Reverend E. A. Cooke on behalf of the Vancouver Ministerial Association as quoted in Chapter 2 and the various Catholic complaints quoted and cited in Chapter 3 over the *Morning Messenger* affair, there were other clerical requests for governmental actions against the Bible Students. The *Golden Age* of September 29, 1920, claimed that in January 1918 about six hundred clergymen had signed a petition asking for the suppression of Watch Tower literature. The public press was full of clerical, anti-Bible Student statements, and numerous men of the cloth wrote to government officials to report on Bible Student activities or to support stringent actions against them. Some of this correspondence from the files of the chief public censor appears below. Among these is the letter from the Reverend George Bousfield to Colonel Sir Percy Sherwood which instigated the chief press censor's all-out campaign against the Bible Students:

> 656 Rideau St.
> Ottawa
> 23–9–17

Dear Col. Sherwood:

The enclosed was put into my letter box Sunday a.m. I do not think,

from the sentiments expressed in the passage marked, that it should
be allowed to enter Canada, and those distributing it should be punished.

Yours sincerely,

Geo. Bousfield

A press clipping from the *Vancouver World* of January 22, 1918,
concerning a sermon by the Reverend Charles G. Patterson of Winnipeg played a major part in having the ban imposed on *The Finished
Mystery* and the *Bible Students Monthly*. It was sent to the chief
press censor shortly after its publication by Malcolm Reid, Dominion
Immigration Inspector for British Columbia; Chambers forwarded
it to the Secretary of State on January 28. The ban on the two
publications followed immediately thereafter. It read as follows:

WINNIPEG, Jan. 22—Unpatriotic literature is being circulated in
Western Canada relating to the war and the attorney-general of
Manitoba is investigating the charge. Pamphlets issued in the International Bible Students monthly, published in Brooklyn, N.Y., were
referred to in a sermon by Rev. Wm. Paterson [*sic*] in St. Stephen's
church on Sunday. Some passages denounce all ministers for preaching
thousands into dreadful death in the trenches. Dr. Paterson declared:
"They assert that preachers have made thousands of men cannon-
fodder for blood-lusty kings and Kaisers."

The Bible Students organization attracted much attention here
recently by a number claiming exemptions as conscientious objectors,
but they were refused.

Yet some time after, the chief press censor denied that the clergy
had any part in bringing any influence to bear on the Canadian
government in having a ban placed on Bible Student publications.
In a letter dated March 25, 1918, to C. E. Heard of Vancouver, he
wrote:

The objectionable character of these statements [in *The Finished
Mystery* and *Bible Students Monthly*] and the pernicious results flowing
from their circulation were reported to the Chief Press Censor for
Canada, by Military, Police and other public officials from one end of

Canada to the other, and there was no clerical influence whatever exercised in securing the banning of these objectionable publications.

On the following day, he wrote to Leslie V. B. Mais of Medicine Hat, Alberta:

While writing you I would draw your attention to the circulation in various centres of Canada of a certain false and misleading circular relating to the action taken to prevent the possession within Canada of copies of The Bible Students Monthly and The Finished Mystery. These circulars represent the action of the Censorship Authorities as having been due to clerical influence which is absolutely untrue, action having been taken on the representations of the injurious effect produced throughout the Country by the circulation of these publications. The representations in question did not come from clergymen but from military, police and other public officials from one end of Canada to the other.

Yet, throughout the spring of 1918, the Canadian government, and Chambers personally, continued to receive letters from clergymen calling for the extension of bans to cover all Bible Student publications. Among them were the following:

i *A letter from the Regina, Saskatchewan, Ministerial Association*

St. Peter's Rectory
Regina, Sask. Canada
March 7th, 1918.

Hon Martin Burrell,
Secretary of State,
Ottawa
Dear Sir:
At a meeting of the Regina Ministerial Association held on Monday last, March 4th, the following resolution was unanimously passed and I was instructed to forward it to you.

"That the Ministerial Association of Regina, Saskatchewan, desire to express to the Government at Ottawa their appreciation of the abolition of the book 'The Finished Mystery'. And to say that from reports placed before the association it would seem that the movement for distributing this literature is being actively supported from German districts in Saskatchewan."

Yours very sincerely,
Frederic Stanford
Hon Secretary
Regina Ministerial Association.

ii   *A letter from the editor of the* Presbyterian Witness *at Halifax, Nova Scotia.*

Halifax, N.S.,
April 1/18.

Ernest J. Chambers, Esq.,
Chief Censor's Office
Ottawa.

Dear Sir:

I am enclosing a note which I have just received from Truro with regard to Russellite literature. The correspondent has forgotten to sign her name, but I enclose the letter to show you the methods being used by Russellite agents to secure signatures to their petition for the removal of the ban on the circulation of their books. I have received other letters of a similar nature. The Russellites are very German in their methods and I hope your department will not be influenced by the petition which they are circulating. They really represent but a very insignificant fraction of the people of Canada.

With kind regards.
Yours truly,
G. S. Carson

Che SECOND WORLD WAR

Jehovah's Witnesses' outspoken criticisms of their adversaries in Canada during the early days of the Second World War are clearly indicated by the tract *"It Must Be Stopped!"*. The Roman Catholic response to this broadside and the general activities of Jehovah's Witnesses was a campaign to have them banned by the Canadian government. This is made clear by an editorial from *L'Action Catholique*, dated June 20, 1940, and correspondence between Cardinal Villeneuve's office and that of Minister of Justice Ernest Lapointe. The success of the Catholic program is also evident from this correspondence and a second editorial from *L'Action Catholique*, dated July 5, 1940.

"IT MUST BE STOPPED!"

"The author of the pamphlet concerned might have sung a different tune had he met a good Anglican or a good Catholic who had a horsewhip handy!" Such was the distinctly biased statement recently made by a certain judge, presiding over the Court of King's Bench in the Province of Quebec, in his address to the jury just prior to their deliberation before bringing in a verdict. The occasion was the trial of seven of Jehovah's witnesses, charged with the crime of sedition for having in their homes a Bible text-book entitled *Enemies*.

"It Must Be Stopped!" said the same judge. This remark was levelled at the work of Jehovah's witnesses of preaching the Gospel of God's Kingdom, the particular method under fire being the distribution of *Enemies*, which book carries the message of the Kingdom, honors the name of the Most High God, exposes the enemies of truth and points out the way of complete protection for those who love righteousness.

The seven Christians involved in this case, after being haled into court with their "seditious" equipment of Bibles and Bible text-books, were found guilty and sentenced to prison terms at hard labor, being compelled to associate with criminals of every description. Twenty-one others still await trial on the same charge.

On a previous occasion two of Jehovah's witnesses had been convicted on a charge of sedition and sentenced to six months' imprisonment for distributing a pamphlet entitled *The Peoples' Greatest Need*, which, like the book *Enemies*, points the people to the Kingdom of God. Fourteen thousand letters were thereupon dispatched to business and professional men of the Province of Quebec, acquainting them with this gross injustice and enclosing a copy of the so-called "seditious" pamphlet. On learning the facts many people of good will expressed their righteous indignation at this treatment of Christians, while others showed a bitter spirit of hatred, openly identifying themselves as being against the Kingdom, one prominent politician stating: *"Within a short time we will have our own Canadian Hitler, and he will quickly settle your case!"*

Many will ask, What is the cause of this bitter spirit of opposition to Jehovah's witnesses, and who are they?

Who Are Jehovah's Witnesses?

The name "Jehovah's witnesses" is taken from God's Word, the Bible, which name the Almighty God gives to those persons who have devoted themselves wholly to His service. Such persons must witness to the name of the Almighty. "Ye are my witnesses that I am God." (Isaiah 43:10–12) They carefully study and consider the Word of God that they may ascertain His will and, doing His will, have God's approval. They follow Christ Jesus, and therefore do not follow any earthly leader. Their work is done at the command of the Almighty God and because they rejoice to obey His commandments.

To carry out God's commandments, they must preach the Gospel of the Kingdom. (Matthew 24:14) This good news is that Jehovah's Theocratic Government, under Christ the King, has come and will soon eliminate Satan and his organization, and then bring lasting blessings to all who desire peace, prosperity and happiness. They are commanded to warn the people of Christendom of the impending disaster of Armageddon and to inform them that the only means of safety is to escape from religious organizations and flee to God's Kingdom.

Jehovah's witnesses do not constitute a sect. They are not reds or Communists, as the religionists and the press have unfairly tried to make it appear. They have no political ambitions, and hence, do not support any worldly organization, but follow the admonition of the Scriptures to keep themselves "unspotted from the world." Their work is not for any selfish reason nor worldly honor that might come to them. They seek only the honor that comes from the Almighty. They are truly Christians.

Why Opposed and Persecuted?

Jehovah's witnesses are opposed because they publish the name of Jehovah and His Theocratic Government of peace and righteousness, and are therefore the special targets of Satan and his agents. The Devil makes war with all who are God's people. (Revelation 12:17) During the three and a half years that Jesus went about preaching and teaching the people concerning the Kingdom of God, the Devil constantly reproached Him and tried to kill Him, and finally had Him convicted on a charge of sedition and put to death. (Luke 23:5) Jesus suffered this persecution at the hands of the Devil and his agents because of His love and zeal for doing His Father's will.

Jesus warned His disciples that they would have to suffer like reproach. He said: "If the world hate you, ye know that it hated me before it hated you. If ye were of the world, the world would love his own: but because ye are not of the world, but I have chosen you out of the world, therefore the world hateth you. Remember the word that I said unto you, The servant is not greater than his lord. If they have persecuted me, they will also persecute you." (John 15:18–20) Among these faithful ones was Stephen, the first Christian martyr, whom the religionists charged with the crime of sedition. They had him arrested, brought into court, and bribed witnesses to testify falsely against him; and when Stephen stood before the court and testified to the name of Jehovah God and Christ Jesus and denounced the religionists, these wicked ones rushed upon him and put him to death.—Acts 7:51–60.

Saul of Tarsus, then a religionist, stood by and saw Stephen die. When Saul became Paul the Christian, he also suffered for righteousness. He then delighted to be in the class in which Stephen was found as a follower of Jesus Christ. The same is true today of those who are disciples of Christ, and attempts are continually made to prevent their work being done, either through the courts or through other forms of persecution. This hatred and persecution of Jehovah's witnesses is not because they are evil-doers or that they do anything to interfere with the property or personal rights of others, but because they boldly and fearlessly proclaim the name of Jehovah God and His King, Christ Jesus.

Persecution in Germany

A book, entitled *Crusade Against Christianity,* published in German, French and Polish, has been widely distributed throughout Europe and America. Commenting on this book, *The Montreal Daily Star* of January 6, 1940, stated: "It is a completely documented story of the persecutions suffered by the German members of the witnesses of Jehovah organization under the Nazi regime." These Christians were there shown to be the targets of brutal and bestial persecution, imprisonment and even death itself. They were thrown into filthy jails, herded into concentration camps, families separated, homes where Bible studies were in progress broken into and Bibles, Bible helps and books which contained songs of praise to the Almighty God seized and burned. These Nazis broke up meetings where the Lord's Supper was being celebrated and removed hundreds of Christians to unknown destinations. It is known that upwards of 6,000 of the Earnest Bible Students (Jehovah's witnesses) have been confined to prison and concentration camps in Germany—some of them for more than five years—where they have been tortured and even put to death. Through all this, the faith of Jehovah's witnesses in the Almighty God and the righteousness of their cause could not be shaken, and their determination to serve God, no matter what the cost, has even won the respect of some of their sadistic guards. The *White Paper,* recently published by the

British Government, on the treatment of German nationals in concentration camps during the period 1938–39, further exposes the maltreatment of Jehovah's witnesses in Germany.

It is important to note that this wicked and devilish persecution of these Christians began in the year 1933, the same year which was proclaimed by the head of one religious organization a "Holy Year" and which, according to him, would "usher in a golden flood of peace and prosperity."

Persecution in Quebec

Freedom to proclaim the Gospel of the Kingdom and to serve the Lord according to the dictates of one's own conscience is still allowed to some extent under the democratic governments. The Province of Quebec is an exception. For some years in that province Jehovah's witnesses have been bitterly opposed by the religionists, who have sought every means to stop their work and have caused these witnesses to be brought into the courts on various trumped-up charges of "disturbing the peace", "unlawful assembly", "peddling without a license", "distributing circulars without a permit", "defamatory libel", "blasphemous libel", "uttering seditious libel", "seditious conspiracy", etc. However, they have not been successful in having Jehovah's witnesses convicted in every case, as evidenced by a recent trial in which two of Jehovah's witnesses were charged with blasphemy. The judge, in addressing the jury, said: "These people believe these statements to be true; they have faith in these teachings, hence they have a right to promulgate them, and even if it does hurt some of us, that does not constitute blasphemy." The jury brought in a verdict of "Not guilty".

During the year 1939 about 115 of Jehovah's witnesses were brought before the courts of Quebec, charged with crimes of which they were entirely innocent, and some have yet to be tried. Many of their homes have been raided and literature, phonographs, records and even private papers have been seized. They have been accosted by police officers on the streets and their preaching equipment taken away from them. For three months Jehovah's witnesses operated a mission boat along the Quebec river, equipped with an amplifying machine for preaching the Gospel to the people at the various villages and camps. At every point they encountered hostility and religious intolerance. Word was passed from town to village along the whole river front. At the City of Quebec, where they landed to move some phonographs and recorded Bible speeches, the police seized everything that had been placed on the dock. At other places they were stoned, mooring ropes were cut, and at one village they were even fired upon from the shore with rifles.

Religionists Deny the Bible

Jehovah's witnesses have repeatedly pointed out that there is a clear distinction between religion and Christianity; that religion is the open and violent adversary of all Christians—which fact is apparently recognized by the judge whose remarks appear at the beginning of this article. Religion and the practices thereof are the result of demon power and influence. Christianity stands for the truth and full obedience to the law of Almighty God. Religion is demon-worship. Christianity is the worship of Jehovah God in spirit and in truth. Religionists follow the traditions and teachings of men. Christians obey the commandments of Jesus Christ.

At the trial of the seven witnesses of Jehovah aforementioned, two clergymen appeared as witnesses for the Crown. In testifying, one of these clergymen made the statement that the name "Jehovah" appearing repeatedly in the book *Enemies*, was merely that of the "*tribal God*" of the nation of Israel. It is evident that such a profane and impious declaration concerning the name of the Most High God puts this man in the class spoken of in the Scriptures as blasphemers. To state that the Most High, whose name alone is JEHOVAH, is merely a "tribal God" tends to lessen reverence for the name of Jehovah and is a grave indignity to the Creator of the universe. Such person, who does not ascribe honor and glory to the name of the Almighty has no right to lay claim to be the representative of God and is certainly an unsafe guide for the people to follow. This clergyman apparently overlooked, or else deliberately ignored, the following scriptures:

"That men may know that thou, whose name alone is JEHOVAH, are the Most High over all the earth."—Psalm 83:18, *King James* Version.
"Before me there was no God formed, neither shall there be after me. I, even I, am JEHOVAH; and besides me there is no saviour: . . . therefore ye are my witnesses, saith JEHOVAH, that I am God."—Isaiah 43:10-12, *American Revised* Version.
"I am JEHOVAH, that is my name; and my glory will I not give to another." —Isaiah 42:8, *American Revised* Version.

"I appeared unto Abraham, unto Isaac, and unto Jacob, by the name of God Almighty; but by my name JEHOVAH was I not known to them."— Exodus 6:3, *King James* Version.

These "reverends" and other theologians should know that this so-called "tribal God", JEHOVAH, is the name of the God of Israel, whom Jesus worshipped. A clergyman should be familiar with the following scriptures:

"And there came to him [Jesus] great multitudes, . . . and he healed them: . . . and they glorified the *God of Israel*"—Matthew 15:30, 31, *Douay* Version.

"And Jesus answering, said to them: . . . Have ye not read that which was spoken by God, saying to you: I am the God of Abraham, the God of Isaac, and the God of Jacob?"—Matthew 22:32, *Douay.*

"The God of Abraham, and the God of Isaac, and the God of Jacob, *the God of our fathers*, hath glorified his Son Jesus, whom ye indeed delivered up and denied before the face of Pilate, when he judged he should be released."—Acts 3:13, *Douay.*

The fact is, these religionists deny the Bible. They have accepted and taught the traditions of men and have kept the people in ignorance of the truth. THEY DO NOT WANT YOU TO KNOW:

THAT the scriptures declare that the dead are unconscious, out of existence, and are not alive, suffering conscious punishment in some place called purgatory.—See Ecclesiastes 9:5, 10, *Douay*; Psalm 146:4, *King James* and *American Revised*; Psalm 6:5; 115:17.

THAT no one has an "immortal soul". The doctrine of the "inherent immortality of man" is absolutely false, God alone having immortality, as stated by the Scriptures.—1 Timothy 6:16; Ezekiel 18:4.

THAT hell is not the abode of evil spirits, where the wicked are tormented. The Scriptures teach that hell is the grave, where all go at death. Even Jesus went to hell.—Acts 2:27, 30, 31.

THAT the doctrine of "purgatory" is pure imagination and is not even mentioned in the Scriptures. In fact, the Bible flatly contradicts the "purgatory" doctrine.

THAT prayers for the dead are of no avail whatever, but are a religious practice, based upon tradition and unsupported by the Word of God.

THAT the bowing before, or even the making of, images is expressly forbidden by God's Word.—See Exodus 20:4, 5.

THAT no priest or company of priests has any power whatsoever to remit sins. No organization on earth has such power.—1 John 1:7; 1 John 2:1, 2; Acts 10:42, 43, *Douay.*

THAT the doctrine of the trinity is false, wholly unreasonable, and in direct conflict with the Scriptures.—1 Corinthians 8:6.

THAT the baptism of infants is not taught in the Bible.

THAT all theological titles are contrary to the Word of God.—Matthew 23:8, 9; Psalm 111:9.

Are you willing to risk your eternal existence by accepting and following the false doctrines taught by these religious clergymen? Or will you be guided by the Word of the Almighty God? You can properly decide that matter by gaining a knowledge of God and Christ Jesus, as set forth in the Word of God.—John 17:3.

The Reason

What is the reason for thus keeping the people in darkness or ignorance concerning God's Word of truth? We quote from the book *Enemies*:

> "The reason now clearly appears as to why religionists try to keep the people in ignorance of the Bible and books that explain the Bible, and that reason is, because the Bible condemns all religion and all traditions of men, and the Bible alone makes clear the pathway of righteousness. The Devil and his agents attempt to withhold the Bible from the people, lest the people should learn the truth and then flee from the Devil religious organizations and find refuge in the Lord."—Pages 349, 350.

"Enemies" Points the Way to Life

The author of *Enemies* (whom the learned judge in the sedition case above referred to considered worthy of a horsewhipping) shows who are man's true friends and who are his enemies. He points the only way to salvation. He shows from God's infallible Word how all the meek can gain that much-needed knowledge. We quote:

> "The Bible was not written for fools, nor is this book published for the benefit of fools. The Bible was written and given to man for his aid and guidance, that such man of good will and purpose might be fully advised as to the right way to go and that he might stay on the side of God and refuse to serve the Devil. (2 Timothy 3:16) This publication attempts to put the Bible in a simple way before the people who want to know the truth. It is not expected it will be appreciated or used by others. The Scriptures contain the Word of God, and the same is true and is the proper guide for the man who wants to know and to do what is right. 'Thy word is a lamp unto my feet, and a light unto my path. Thy word is true from the beginning.' (Psalm 119:105, 160) 'Thy word is truth.'—John 17:17.
> "Let no man conclude, however, that the mere possession of the Bible or an occasional reading over texts thereof is sufficient to enable him to be wise. Many persons say: 'I have the Bible and know what it teaches'; and yet they

are entirely ignorant of what it contains, and of the meaning thereof. The Bible is the greatest storehouse of knowledge and wisdom. A man who desires to know the truth must study the Bible and thus study to show himself approved of God and not be ashamed to acknowledge to all that all good things proceed from the Almighty God. (2 Timothy 2:15)" Pages 81, 82.

"Many are the marvelous blessings to flow to those of humankind who love and obey God and his Kingdom, and amongst those great blessings, and that which is the chief one to man is life in happiness. . . . To have life everlasting in health, strength, peace and happiness, and to know God and Christ Jesus and serve them, is the greatest blessing any creature could enjoy. All of those blessings will result to those who know, love and obey God and his King; as Jesus stated: 'This is life eternal that they might know thee, the only true God, and Jesus Christ whom thou hast sent.' (John 17:3) God and Christ Jesus will be the everlasting Friends of obedient men and will minister blessings to such obedient ones without end.

"All these blessings come as a gracious gift and are therefore prompted entirely by love. Only the Devil, the great enemy, and his agents, the religious organizations, could attempt to deprive men of such marvelous blessings or to keep them in ignorance of what God has provided for those who know and serve him. Therefore when all of these enemies are for ever removed, the obedient ones will dwell with the Lord, their great Prince and Helper, and nothing will interfere with their boundless blessings and eternal happiness."—Pages 354, 355.

'Fighting Against God'

The judge who gave expression to the words appearing at the beginning of this article that the work of Jehovah's witnesses "must be stopped" and that "the author of this pamphlet might have sung a different tune had he met a good Anglican or a good Catholic who had a horsewhip handy", would do well to bear in mind the words of an eminent lawyer of Bible fame who preceded him: "Then stood there up one in the council, a Pharisee, named Gamaliel, a doctor of the law, had in reputation among all the people, and commanded to put the apostles forth a little space; and said unto them, Ye men of Israel, take heed to yourselves what ye intend to do as touching these men. . . . And now I say unto you, Refrain from these men, and let them alone: for if this counsel or this work be of men, it will come to nought: but if it be of God, ye cannot overthrow it; lest haply ye be found even to fight against God."—Acts 5:34, 35, 38, 39.

LES PIRES SABOTEURS

On parle beaucoup de sabotage.

On surveille avec raison les gens qui pourraient faire sauter les navires en construction, les manufactures d'obus, etc., etc. Il y a saboteurs plus dangereux encore; ce sont les gens qui préparent les esprits et les coeurs aux actes subversifs en semant des idées révolutionnaires et en attisant des sentiments de révolte.

Parmi ces ennemis publics, il n'en est pas de plus hypocrites ni de plus néfastes que les témoins de Jéhovah et leurs agents.

A tous les instants du jour, en une paroisse ou en l'autre, à la campagne ou à la ville, cette secte dangereuse distribue des plaquettes qui sont des poisons.

Nos tribunaux ont jugé les témoins de Jéhovah et leurs agents. Plusieurs ont été condamnés. On devrait donc déployer un certain zèle pour les empêcher de distribuer leur littérature venimeuse.

Pourquoi les officiers de vitesse et les limiers de la police des liqueurs ne recevraient-ils pas l'instruction de surveiller ces agents qui parcourent les campagnes? Les citoyens pourraient même les prévenir de l'arrivée des "témoins" dans une localité.

Quoi qu'il en soit, nous n'hésitons pas à dire que les autorités devraient faire davantage pour la protection publique dans ce domaine. Ces tracts qui viennent la plupart du temps des Etats-Unis ne devraient pas pouvoir traverser les frontières, encore moins être distribué par le service postal de Sa Majesté.

Ces brochures ignobles s'attaquent à toutes les religions et à toutes les autorités. Elles sont d'autant plus pernicieuses que ces attaques sont distillées lentement à la faveur de considérations édifiantes sur la Bible.

Or, aux heures critiques que nous vivons, il est essentiel de protéger l'autorité quelle qu'elle soit et de préserver les bases de la morale. Sans morale et sans autorité, la société sombrerait à une allure vertigineuse.

N'achetons jamais de ces livres car nous contribuerons à en imprimer d'autres. Si on nous donne ces plaquettes ou volumes, acceptons-les et insistons pour en avoir davantage . . . afin de les faire brûler. Si le cadeau vient par voie postale, jetons-le au feu immédiatement. On ne doit pas goûter au poison intellectuel plus qu'on ne goûte au poison du corps.

En garde donc contre l'oeuvre de démoralisation qu'exerce cette littérature où toute autorité est vilipendée, où tout ordre établi est sapé.

La secte des Témoins de Jéhovah constitue une cinquième colonne plus dangereuse que toute autre.

Louis-Philippe Roy

Québec, le 27 juin 1940.

A Monsieur
le Secrétaire particulier
du T. H. M. Ernest Lapointe,
Ministre de la Justice,
Ottawa, Ont.
Cher Monsieur,
Son Eminence le Cardinal serait heureux que vous attiriez l'attention du Très Honorable Monsieur Ernest Lapointe, Ministre de la Justice, sur le *premier-Québec* que voici, concernant les publications de la *Tour de garde* ou *Témoins de Jéhovah*.

Certains livres et certains fascicules adressés récemment encore par la poste, et en particulier le périodique *Consolations*, sont tout ce qu'il y a de plus démoralisant et de plus destructeur des forces spirituelles de la nation.

Je vous remercie par avance, cher Monsieur, de l'attention que vous voudrez bien donner à cette communication, et vous prie de me croire,

Votre très dévoué,

PAUL BERNIER [signed]
Chancelier

PERSONNELLE   le 4 juillet 1940
Monseigneur Paul Bernier,
Chancelier de l'Archidiocese,
Palais Cardinalice,
Québec

Monsieur le Chancelier,
Je me suis fait un devoir, sur réception de votre lettre du 27 juin, de me rendre en désir de Son Eminence le Cardinal et d'attirer l'attention du Ministre sur vos représentations ainsi que sur l'article éditorial publié

par l'Action Catholique, au sujet de la Tour de garde, Témoins de Jéhovah et Consolation.

Monsieur Lapointe m'a autorisé à vous communiquer, par téléphone, le renseignement confidentiel que l'organisation dite des Témoins de Jéhovah serait déclarée illégale, aujourd'hui même, avec prière d'en faire part à Son Eminence le Cardinal.

La présente est pour confirmer ce que je viens de vous dire au téléphone.

Je comprends que Son Eminence le Cardinal sera dûment informé de l'arrêté ministériel relatif aux Témoins de Jéhovah.

Agréez, Monsieur le Chancelier, avec mes remerciements, mes civilités empressées.

Secrétaire particulier.
Maurice Bernier

LE TÉMOINS DE JÉHOVAH HORS LA LOI

L'action Catholique a trop souvent réclamé la mise au ban de la secte faussement nommée "Témoins de Jéhovah" pour ne pas se réjouir de la décision prise par les autorités fédérales.

Hier en effet, l'hon. Ministre de la Justice a présenté un projet de loi dans le but de rendre illégale cette organisation de saboteurs intellectuels et moraux.

Les Témoins de Jéhovah et leurs agents poursuivaient une propagande intensive dans nos villes et nos campagnes. Ils vendaient ou distribuaient gratuitement des tracts qui constituaient de véritables poisons. Ces brochures ignobles s'attaquaient sournoisement à toutes les religions et à toutes les autorités.

A plusieurs reprises, nos tribunaux avaient condamné ces distributeurs de poisons; mais c'était toujours à recommencer, les prévenus prétendant que leurs produits ne contenaient rien de nocif et qu'ils usaient tout simplement de la liberté religieuse.

Maintenant que la secte est mise hors la loi, la répression sera plus facile, plus expéditive, plus efficace.

N'allons pas croire pour autant que les Témoins vont cesser immédiatement toute propagande. Restons vigilants et brûlons, sans pitié pour leur belle apparence, ces publications dangereuses que l'on déposera encore à nos portes. Si nous voyons un agent de la secte à l'oeuvre, rendons à la société le service de signaler sa présence à qui de droit.

Les autorités ont donc fait preuve de sagesse. C'est le temps moins que jamais de laisser la liberté à ceux qui voudraient saboter les principes moraux sans lesquels aucun ordre public véritable n'est possible.

Louis-Philippe Roy

PERSONNELLE   Québec, le 8 juillet 1940.
A Monsieur Maurice Bernier,
Secrétaire particulier
du T. H. M. Ernest Lapointe,
Ministre de la Justice,
Ottawa.

Monsieur le Secrétaire,
Votre empressement à bien vouloir attirer l'attention du Très Honorable Monsieur Lapointe sur l'objet de ma lettre du 27 juin dernier m'oblige infiniment.

Je n'ai pas besoin d'ajouter,—puisque déjà Son Eminence aura Elle-même écrit à Monsieur Lapointe pour lui dire sa satisfaction de l'arrêté ministériel en question,—combien une aussi prompte et aussi heureuse solution mérite nos félicitations et nos remerciements.

Je me permets seulement, au cas où il aurait pu échapper à votre attention, de glisser ici copie du premier-Québec, par lequel, dès samedi dernier, 6 juillet, *L'Action Catholique* accueillait la mise au ban de ces soi-disant "Témoins de Jéhovah", fléau de la chrétienté en Amérique.

Veuillez recevoir, Monsieur le Secrétaire, l'expression réitérée de ma gratitude et de ma haute considération.

(Mgr) Paul Bernier,
Chancelier.

The ban on Jehovah's Witnesses was fully supported by the Royal Canadian Mounted Police. When H. R. Fleming, MP for Humboldt,

Saskatchewan, asked why they had been declared illegal, Maurice Bernier, Lapointe's private secretary, wrote Commissioner S. T. Wood to request that he supply a "suitable" answer for Fleming. Wood's reply to Bernier appears below. The letter, as prepared by the RCMP commissioner, was copied verbatim and sent to Fleming by Bernier.

SECRET   October 10th, 1941.

J. M. Bernier, Esq.,
Private Secretary to the
Rt. Honourable the Minister of Justice
Ottawa, Ontario

Dear Mr. Bernier:

With reference to the communication written to the Honourable the Minister of Justice by H. R. Fleming, Esq., M.P. of Humboldt, Sask., on September 29th, it is desired to advise you that the two anonymous letters forwarded therewith have been retained for investigation.

2. In connection with a suitable reply which might be made to Mr. Fleming it is suggested that he be communicated with, somewhat along the following lines:

It is observed that similar letters to the two forwarded by you have been turned over to the R. C. M. Police and similar action has been taken with respect to the two letters and the envelope forwarded by you.

For your information "Jehovah's Witnesses", "Watch Tower Bible and Tract Society", "International Bible Students Association" and the "Watch Tower Bible and Tract Society Incorporated" were declared illegal organizations pursuant to the provisions of Regulation 39c of the Defence of Canada Regulations. This action was taken owing to the activities of their followers in stirring up animosity between all religions and what they term "man-made governments". All religions are regarded as "rackets" and "Jehovah's Witnesses", to use the name by which they are more commonly known, are definitely opposed to the Red Cross, describing it as the "devil's work" and "belonging to the devil". In its teaching of fanatical pacifism,

Jehovah's Witnesses urge their followers, particularly children, to refuse to salute the flag or stand when "God Save the King" is sung. Jehovah's Witnesses maintain that their object is the dissemination of Bible truths and their activities are guided by a peculiar interpretation of the Bible, thus giving the organization a religious complexion.

If the teachings of Jehovah's Witnesses were confined to religious matters alone there would not be any particular grounds for concern, but they claim to recognize only a heavenly sovereign, maintaining that "how could one who is wholly devoted to Almighty God and to His Kingdom under Christ Jesus, take sides in a war between nations, both of which are against God and His Kingdom".

Their literature has been the cause of much concern and it is of interest to mention that in an appeal case dealt with by the Court of the King's Bench in the Province of Quebec some time ago, the judgment mentioned in part that "if the pamphlets meant anything they constituted an appeal to all to condemn and have a supreme contempt for every form of organized authority, whether civil or ecclesiastical". It is of interest to also mention that certain enemy aliens commenced to take an active part in the work of Jehovah's Witnesses, obviously for the purpose of using the cloak of religion to justify their activities. Following consideration of the situation, it was decided that their activities could not be regarded as other than subversive and their organizations were therefore declared illegal.

It is suggested that the referring of any communications you may receive concerning Jehovah's Witnesses, to the R. C. M. Police is the proper course to take should you continue to receive such material.

3. The letter written by Mr. H. R. Fleming, M.P., is returned herewith.

Yours sincerely,

S. T. Wood

ᴛhε ʙᴀᴛᴛʟε οϝ ϙᴜεʙεϲ

THE TRACTS *Quebec's Burning Hate* and *Quebec You Have Failed Your People* were major propaganda weapons used by Jehovah's Witnesses against the Duplessis Union Nationale government and also against the Roman Catholic Church in the late 1940s. After the Witnesses' victory in the Supreme Court of Canada Saumur decision, the Quebec legislature passed Bill 38, which became Chapter 15 of the *Statutes of Quebec* (1953). Only the English version of this statute appears below. To the present time, it has not been repealed in spite of its extremely anti-libertarian nature.

QUEBEC'S BURNING HATE

FOR GOD AND CHRIST AND FREEDOM IS THE SHAME OF ALL CANADA

Before the hot denials and protests and false countercharges boom out from the priestly keepers of Quebec province and whip up an unreasonable frenzy, calmly and soberly and with clear mental faculties reason on the evidence presented in support of the above-headlined indictment. Words in lip service to God and Christ and freedom can be as cheap as the free wind it takes to utter them, but actions speak louder to reasoning minds. As God's Word says, "Let us not love in word, nor in tongue, but in deed." (1 John 3:18, *Catholic Douay Version Bible*) Is your mind reasonable enough to let you listen to loud-speaking deeds that count for more than easy words? Are you willing and unafraid to allow the evidence to be weighed in the just balances of God's true Word, and see whether Quebec is found wanting in love for God and Christ and freedom? The few minutes so spent in reasoning will not make it too late for you to thereafter believe the hot denials and protests and false countercharges booming out of religious Quebec, if you still wish to. But now, pause and consider:

Is it love for God that moves Quebec mobs to tear copies of God's Word, the Bible, to shreds and burn them in the flames? Is it an evidence of love for Christ for these same religious mobs to club and stone Christ's followers, hound them throughout the province, damage their property, and otherwise go on deliriously wild rampages of vandalism against Christ's brethren? Did not Christ say: "As long as you did it to one of these my least brethren, you did it to me"? (Matthew 25:40, *Douay*) Did the parish priests that have stood by and approvingly witnessed such outrages show regard or disregard for Christian principles? And what about Quebec's law-making bodies that frame mischief by law to "get" those not favored by the ruling elements? and her police forces that allow mobsters to riot unchecked while they arrest the Christian victims, sometimes for no more than distributing Bibles or leaflets with Bible quotations, or even as these followers of Christ walk along the streets or wait for a streetcar? and what of her judges that impose heavy fines and prison sentences against them and heap abusive language upon them, and deliberately follow a malicious policy of again and again postponing cases to tie up tens of thousands of dollars in exorbitant bails and keep hundreds of cases pending? Do such legislators and police and judges of Quebec thereby show their love for freedom? Honestly, do you think such fruits are borne by love, or by hate? "By their fruits you shall know them."—Matthew 7:20, *Douay Version Bible.*

In a torrential downpour all the foregoing violences and injustices rain down daily upon Jehovah's witnesses in Quebec province. Now do we hear you say to yourself, "Ah, Jehovah's witnesses! I thought so. They are always in trouble"? Because they are often persecuted, or because they are an unpopular minority, or because they may have been misrepresented to you by incorrect reports, that is not just cause for a hasty dismissal of the matter. On the contrary, it is all the stronger reason for fair-minded persons to hear out all the evidence.

Were not Christ and early Christians persecuted often? an unpopular minority? and grossly misrepresented by religious liars? If you can identify enemies by their fruits, by the fruits of Jehovah's witnesses you may also know them as true followers of Christ. Both the message they preach and the methods by which they preach it have full backing and foundation in the Bible, as you will soon see if you allow one of Jehovah's witnesses to explain them to you instead of listening to the lying and prejudicial reports of the witnesses' persecutors. But neither space nor subject permit full discussion of these matters here, and such discussion is not at all necessary. It does not alter the issue here at stake. Whether you agree or disagree with the witnesses, you do know for a certainty that it does not show love for God, Christ, Bible principles and freedom to burn Bibles and to mob and stone and falsely arrest and imprison those endeavoring to serve God. Such deeds are the outgrowth of burning hate, and cause the finger of shame to point to Canada.

Hateful Persecution of Christians

A brief sketch of only a few of the instances of persecution of and violence against Jehovah's witnesses in Quebec province is now submitted as concrete evidence. These facts are well known to many of the inhabitants of Quebec, and can be proved. Listen:

In Lachine, September 15, 1945, mob action blazed fiercely against Jehovah's witnesses as they advertised the holding of a Bible lecture. Street assaults reached their height when the large Catholic mob laid siege to the shop and home of Joseph Letellier, who, with three other witnesses, was inside. The plate glass display window was shattered and rocks and tomatoes poured through the windows in a steady stream. Witness Joyce was struck full in the chest, and as Witness Letellier tried to phone police one vandal dashed in and smashed the elderly man in the face, inflicting a long gash on his face and knocking his glasses to the floor. The witnesses barricaded themselves in and endured the rain of rocks for more than five hours. Until midnight, two hours after other witnesses had helped the besieged ones escape under cover of darkness through a narrow 25-foot rear passage, irate mobsters bombarded the building. The entire front was wrecked, and the valuable clocks inside the shop destroyed.

In the mobocratic city of Chateauguay, September 9, 1945, witnesses were advertising a Bible lecture to be held that afternoon in City Hall Park. City officials instigated the unlawful arrest of fifteen witnesses and decreed they could not use City Hall Park for the Bible talk. The lecture location was moved to the yard of R. W. Weaner's private home. Some 125 attended the lecture to hear, but by starting time a mob of 1,200 were there to break up. They had brought along a truck loaded with tomatoes and potatoes, and to these missiles added a generous sprinkling of stones as the barrage got under way. Two big fire sirens had been brought, and these were used to drown out the speaker's voice. In vain did the witnesses appeal to Provincial Police who had arrived following the emergency call to Montreal. The meeting broke up amid violence, and damage to the Weaner home was heavy.

Previously laid plans called for another Bible lecture in Chateauguay the Sunday following. This time the city's mob-ruled officials arrested 17 witnesses (Quebec police never molest the mobsters), and a mob of 1,500 was on hand at the Weaner home to break up the second meeting. Not satisfied with throwing tomatoes and potatoes and rocks, this time the Catholic hoodlums added to the bombardment cucumbers, rotten eggs and *human excrement!* The police ordered the witnesses' loudspeakers silenced or Mrs. Weaner would be arrested for disturbing the peace. Some of the buses that had brought the witnesses were returned to Montreal empty, stranding scores of witnesses. After several beatings at the hands of the mob, the Christian assemblers were evacuated. The last group, about 40, were fleeing cross country when they were overtaken by mobsters in cars. Though under the protective escort of five Provincial and three Chateauguay policemen, many witnesses were injured in the attack that followed and their literature, including Bibles (and the witnesses often carry Catholic Bibles, too), was forcibly seized and torn to bits and burned. And note this: it is reliably reported that during the mobbing the Catholic priest in his long black robes stood just across the street calmly looking on! This is no insignificant fact, in a province where the priest rules the parish and one word from him would dispel any mob!

One year later, September 8, 1946, a riot at Caughnawaga, a village on the outskirts of Montreal, was reported. Resident Indian witnesses had invited fellow witnesses from Lachine to assist in their Bible service, and extended invitations to other residents of the reserve to attend.

Strenuous effort was made to incite the Indians to violently break up the meeting. Upon being asked to furnish protection, the Royal Canadian Mounted Police flatly refused; but they did arrest the chairman of the Bible meeting and drove off with him amid the yells of the mob. The undispersed mobsters continued for half an hour to pelt with missiles the house into which the assembly had retired for shelter.

Here are some instances revealing Quebec's hatred for God's Word as well as for freedom: In Hull, E. M. Taylor, septuagenarian, of Namur, Quebec, was sentenced to seven days in prison for having distributed Bibles without a permit. In Recorder's Court his attempted explanation was curtly ended by the recorder's ordering him off to prison. Two of Jehovah's witnesses were arrested for distributing free a Bible pamphlet, charged with sedition, and sentenced to 60 days imprisonment or $300 fine. All the French Canadian courts were so under priestly thumbs that they affirmed the infamous sentence, and it was not until the case reached the Supreme Court of Canada that judgment was reversed. One Quebec witness of Jehovah was distributing a leaflet bearing only the words "The Holy Bible Is the Word of God. Read It", and some familiar verses of the *Crampon Version Bible*. So incensed were the Mounted Police that they arrested her, searched her home, and jailed her.

The following affidavit of one of Jehovah's witnesses reports what is regularly happening on the streets of Quebec City:

"Two men came to me while I was displaying the magazines *The Watchtower* and *Consolation* and asked if I had a license to do it. One was very filthy-mouthed and caused quite a commotion. He suddenly tore my case and magazines and then used me for a punching bag for a few seconds until my teeth were rattling. They crossed the road, evidently with the intention of molesting my companion, an elderly minister. I crossed also, thinking he would get the same dose as I. They tore his magazines, and there was much confusion and ripping of magazine bag. Then they turned on me again, but two taxi drivers interfered and things cooled off. As I went back to get my magazine bag and gather up the torn magazines one of these men shouted, 'Don't let him do that; get him!' So again they gave me a good pounding. Eventually breaking away, I escaped and took refuge in a store by locking the door. The manager of the store refused to phone the police on my request. When the crowd cleared I gathered up my torn magazines and continued preaching at another intersection."

Still Quebec City, but with scene shifted to a private home, another recent affidavit of a witness paints this picture of vandalism and hate:

"A mob of 25 young men gathered around one of the homes where a Bible study was in progress and a chunk of ice was hurled through a double window into the kitchen of the house. The owner had been a commando in the army, but has now taken a definite stand for God's kingdom. When he ran into the street the mob disappeared into the community building next to the church. The next night, about 11:00 p.m., following the closing down of the recreation hall, a small gang began to gather. Finally a carload came, but two local policemen chased them away. The following morning the owner and his friend reported the matter at the police station, to have the man who was caught questioned. They soon found out that the priest had phoned the officers and told them to lay off. Similar mobs were active every night during the week and windows were smashed. The police caught 6 of the gang and obtained 45 other names, but nothing was done. The mob, seeing that no action was taken, got more daring each night. Last night the mob began collecting at 8:00 p.m., and was the worst yet. More windows were broken. The gang got onto the roof and some made their way up onto the roof of the two-story house opposite and were throwing missiles down at the doors if anyone went in or out. The police were called twice and finally came."

Christ Jesus taught at the homes of the people, and also the apostles and other early Christians went "from house to house, to teach and preach". (Acts 5:42; 20:20; *Douay Version Bible*) Judge how they would now be received in the proud capital city of Quebec province, as indicated by what was meted out to one of Christ's followers as he trudged from house to house there:

"I had placed a Bible textbook with a woman and was standing at the next door when a man climbed over the verandah rail with the book in his hand, telling me to come with him, that he was going to phone the police. He was not the householder of the premises where I had left the textbook, but just a neighbor of this woman. He opened the door, bidding me go in. There was another man standing in the hall, and of course I refused. With this he seized me and told the young man to phone the police, and due to his violence he ripped my coat. I warned him not to carry his actions too far. He then told me he was a policeman and that I had to go in. The lady with whom I had placed the book then came to the door of the house and was very displeased with this man's action. Ignoring her, he put on his uniform and laid the charge himself when we arrived at the police station."

Religionists know no bounds in their zeal to persecute. A 9-year-old girl, daughter of one of Jehovah's witnesses, was distributing circulars when she was picked up and detained at police court, charged with soliciting without possessing a $25 city permit. She had to appear at juvenile court for a hearing. Again, an 11-year-old child of one of Jehovah's witnesses in the district of Ste. Germaine had been expelled from school for refusing to make the "sign of the cross" and to say the catechism. The parents explained the child's beliefs, and the teacher excused it from participating in the ceremony. But two weeks later a priest visited the school, and soon after the child was expelled. Capping religious zeal, however, was the time when Royal Canadian Mounted Police charged into a hall in Montreal where Jehovah's witnesses were celebrating the Lord's Supper. The police broke up the meeting, refusing the presiding minister's request that the service might be completed. Can the most fantastic imagination picture the police disrupting mass at a Roman Catholic Church?

Jehovah's witnesses have waged battles for freedom in seeking to dislodge its haters from their entrenched position in Quebec. Due to the large number of arrests that have taken place in Montreal and district, the witnesses challenged the constitutionality of Montreal and Verdun by-laws, under which the charges are made. Jehovah's witnesses won in Superior Court, and Justice C. Gordon Mackinnon ordered writs of prohibition issued against the Recorders' Courts of Montreal and Verdun to restrain further proceedings against the witnesses. He ruled the by-laws were suppressive of free worship, press and speech.

But regardless of this decision, the lawless arrests of Jehovah's witnesses continue almost daily in Montreal and district, and in the Recorders' Courts they are subjected to abusive tirades. For example, in June of 1946 Recorder Leonce Plante denounced the witnesses as a "bunch of crazy nuts", set cash bail as high as $200, and threatened that if some witnesses came before him again bail would be $1,000. At present, 1946, there are about 800 charges stacked up against Jehovah's witnesses in Greater Montreal, with property bail now involved being $100,000 and cash bails more than $2,000. Court cases are adjourned time after time, to inconvenience and increase expense for Jehovah's witnesses. To have their cases heard, during one short period the witnesses had to appear on 38 different occasions!

The Force Behind Quebec's Burning Hate

Why this hate for God and His Word? for Christ and his followers? Why this hate for righteous principles and freedom? *Why? WHY?* Jehovah's witnesses preach in all the other Canadian provinces, without any smouldering hate bursting into flaming mobocracy. Why should it be so in Quebec province? Wherein is Quebec different? The following will enlighten you to see clearly the moving force behind Quebec's hate:

An officer arresting one of Jehovah's witnesses in Quebec City told the witness he was ordered to do it by Mr. Lavergne, the parish curate. A French Catholic lawyer defending one of Jehovah's witnesses was told by the city attorney, the court clerk and the deputy chief of police that the arrests were illegal, but that they were so hard pressed by the clergy that they had to make it as difficult as possible for the witnesses. Four witnesses arrested in Quebec City were told by representatives of the police department that delegations from the bishop's palace called daily and insisted that the witnesses were a menace to the Catholic Church and that it was the duty of police to get rid of them, law or no law. A deputy chief of police once admitted that he was never so annoyed by priests as when cases against Jehovah's witnesses were pending. And it is so often noticed that the officer emerges from the back door of the church or convent before making the arrest! Why, Catholic domination of Quebec courts is so complete that in the courtrooms the imagery of the crucifix takes the place of the British Coat of Arms, which appears in other courts throughout the Dominion!

All well informed persons in Canada grant that Quebec province with its 86-percent-Catholic population is under church-and-state rule. In the Quebec legislature the crucifix is placed above the Speaker's Chair, and in the Quebec Parliament buildings alongside the throne of the lieutenant-governor of Quebec is installed a throne for the cardinal. It was reportedly the cardinal who instigated the notorious Padlock Act, supposedly against a mere handful of Communists, but which Act left "Communist" undefined so that anyone not suiting the priests and their puppet politicians could be prosecuted. The Act was used against Jehovah's witnesses. The Quebec cardinal also headed a campaign for a corporate state to regiment the people behind the clergy, a program based on Pius XI's encyclical *Quadragesimo Anno*. Catholic secret societies, backed by French Canadian hierarchy, have been charged before the Canadian Senate as conspiring to turn Quebec province into a French Catholic Corporate state; and these charges were made by Senator Bouchard, a Frenchman, a Catholic, and from Quebec! Quebec has an unsavory reputation for isolationism, fascism and anti-Semitism. She lives up to it hatefully well, and now seeks to root herself deeper in religious totalitarianism by her legislature's demand that the

Canadian prime minister "bring before the Parliament of Canada the measures required to institute an embassy at the Holy See".

All the facts unite to thunderously declare that the force behind Quebec's suicidal hate is priest domination. Thousands of Quebec Catholics are so blinded by the priests that they think they serve God's cause in mobbing Jehovah's witnesses. Jesus foretold this, saying to his followers: "The hour cometh, that whosoever killeth you, will think that he doth a service to God." (John 16:2, *Douay Version Bible*) Such blind course will lead to the ditch of destruction. To avoid it turn from following men and traditions, and study and follow the Bible's teaching; that was Jesus' advice. (Matthew 15:1–14) So doing, honest Quebec Catholics will show love for God and Christ and freedom not only by words but also by righteous deeds. They will join with the many thousands of other Quebec people, Catholic and Protestant and non-religious, that have vigorously protested the wicked treatment meted out to Jehovah's witnesses in that benighted, priest-ridden province.

Quebec, Jehovah's witnesses are telling all Canada of the shame you have brought on the nation by your evil deeds. In English, French and Ukrainian languages this leaflet is broadcasting your delinquency to the nation. You claim to serve God; you claim to be for freedom. Yet if freedom is exercised by those who disagree with you, you crush freedom by mob rule and gestapo tactics. Though your words are, your actions are not in harmony with that for which democracies have just fought a long and bloody global war. And your claims of serving God are just as empty, for your actions find no precedent in the exemplary course laid down for Christians by His Son, Christ Jesus. You should remember that though Christ Jesus and early Christians were often mobbed, they never under any circumstances meted out mob violence. What counts is not whom you claim to serve, but whom you actually do serve by deeds. The Catholic Version Bible says: "Know you not, that to whom you yield yourselves servants to obey, his servants you are whom you obey." (Romans 6:16) Quebec, you have yielded yourself as an obedient servant of religious priests, and you have brought forth bumper crops of evil fruits. Now, why not study God's Word the Bible and yield yourself in obedience to its commands, and see how bounteous a crop of good fruits reflecting love for God and Christ and freedom you will bring forth? The eyes of Canada are upon you, Quebec.

QUEBEC YOU HAVE FAILED YOUR PEOPLE!

Quebec's burning hate for God and Christ and freedom is still the shame of all Canada. In recent weeks the eyes of Canada have been turned towards Quebec province, and what they have seen has deepened the national shame. Quebec rulers, your actions since November 15, 1946, have screamed out to the nation and to the whole world your hate for free speech, your hate for free press, your hate for free worship. Your deeds have even shouted out your hate for free and open study of God's Word and for the principles of Christ.

When Jehovah's witnesses distributed nation-wide a folder exposing this burning hate as demonstrated in recent years and months, the only rebuttal Quebec's infuriated officials could muster was a colossal smear campaign, misrepresentation and name-calling in mass production, and a sweeping wave of false charges and false arrests. By their actions Quebec rulers themselves piled mountain-high additional proof for the heavy charges Jehovah's witnesses levelled against them in the folder entitled "Quebec's Burning Hate for God and Christ and Freedom". The undemocratic and anti-freedom tactics are a stench in the nostrils of Quebec's many freedom-lovers. Now a second folder circulates through-out the nation to focus Canada's eyes on the continued hate rampant in the province of Quebec. You look for yourself, and see how miserably Quebec has failed her people!

On November 15, 1946, Jehovah's witnesses began distributing the first folder exposing Quebec's hate for God and Christ and freedom. The heavy charges were supported by a detailing of unlawful police interference, unjust recorder discrimination, vandalism and mob violence launched against Jehovah's witnesses, their Bible literature, and even their Bibles. Moreover, the pamphlet pointed out evidence that convicted Roman Catholic priests as being the moving force behind the burning hate. (That pamphlet was distributed free throughout Canada. If you did not get your copy, it will be sent free to you upon request. Address the publishers, listed at the close of this folder you are now reading.)

Apparently, Quebec's rulers did not feel equal to any sensible refutation of the charges. Instead, they turned to the weapons of the professional rabble-rouser, to the hurling of misrepresentations, false charges and inflammatory name-callings calculated to whip up a hysterical frenzy of hate against Jehovah's witnesses. Though highly charged with emotional content, the reckless denunciations were empty of logic or reason. The arm of the law was drafted to parallel the smear campaign. The statements in the folder could not be refuted; so their distribution must be suppressed. No less personage than the premier of the province, Mr. Duplessis, who is also attorney general, spearheaded the drive on the legal front. But at the same time he did not overlook the strategy of the two-pronged offensive against the Witnesses; he did not forget the smear front.

At a press conference on November 21 Duplessis declared: "My attention has been drawn to certain circulars being distributed by persons describing themselves as witnesses of Jehovah. I have noticed that there are certain sections which undoubtedly are intolerable and seditious. These people, among other things, apparently complain about crucifixes being hung in the legislative assembly and the legislative council." To say that Jehovah's witnesses complained about the presence of the crucifixes is to distort the facts. To bandy such distortion about the province is stooping to rabble-rousing, and betrays that vulnerable religious susceptibilities are the concern more than sedition. As was expected, many newspapers took the premier's cue, caught up the distortion, and carried it a little farther. They reported: "One extract of the sect's writings that has aroused ire in Quebec is that demanding removal of a crucifix from the throne in the legislative council."

Now, you fair-minded persons, read what the folder actually said. Here is the setting: the force behind Quebec's burning hate for Jehovah's witnesses was being discussed; the facts indicating Roman Catholic power and influence in the courts and in the government were being recounted. Imbedded in this series of facts was the following sentence: "In the Quebec legislature the crucifix is placed above the Speaker's Chair, and in the Quebec Parliament buildings alongside the throne of the lieutenant-governor of Quebec is installed a throne for the cardinal." No complaint voiced, no demands for removal; only a statement of fact to prove Hierarchy influence. This one example of many misrepresentations only proves that when politicians and newspapers speak of Jehovah's witnesses you should not believe them hastily.

Religious Persecution Through Prosecution

But settle attention, now, on the all-out blitz against the Witnesses on the legal battle-front. Prior to the distribution of the folder the Witnesses had been repeatedly arrested on charges of distributing literature without a license. Jehovah's witnesses do not ask men for permission to do God's work; in this they are backed up by the legal guarantees of free worship. Early arrests made during the distribution of the folder were on the no-permit grounds, but newspapers stated that the report was current that Duplessis was going to have all Witnesses that were arrested during the last two weeks of November re-arrested on the new charges of "conspiracy and distributing libelous and seditious literature". Two weeks after he launched the drive against the Witnesses, the admittedly intolerant Duplessis stated to the press: "The propaganda of the Witnesses of Jehovah cannot be tolerated and there are more than 400 of them now before the courts in Montreal, Quebec, Three Rivers and other centers." Arrests ran as high as thirty a day, and by the end of November there were some 1,000 cases pending in the Quebec courts. Some Witnesses had as many as 43 cases stacked up against them. Exorbitant bail demands soared as high as $500 cash or $950 property bond.

Through all trials Jehovah's witnesses prove their unquenchable love for God by obedience to His commandments to preach, and in standing fast for freedom they make more secure the civil liberties of all men. Misrepresented, maligned, discriminated against, mobbed, hounded throughout the province, systematically hunted down and falsely arrested, and then held in vermin-infested, disease-ridden jails on exorbitant bail demands—still they maintain integrity toward God and are back in His service upon release. And it is a question as to which is the severest test, the filthy jails or the field work. Sometimes Catholic youths precede the Witnesses from door to door warning and prejudicing the people, or they follow after and gather up the folders and destroy them. Persons who would like to read are often fearful because of their neighbors. In less educated sections where people are mere puppets of the priests, by the time three or four homes are worked the first house-holder is out screaming threats and rousing the neighborhood. Soon many are on their porches or in the street filling the air with abusive filth and cursings, while others are phoning the police. Often it is necessary for the Witnesses to work a half dozen homes, go to another section and work a few minutes, and then return to finish the original section. It would be a harrowing and unbearable ordeal if it were not for the sustaining strength and spirit of Jehovah God.

Rabid Catholic leaders co-operate closely with the police in rounding up these Christian ministers. In the notorious Quebec City the Sacred Heart Leagues printed a 9" x 12" sheet in French crying out for all Catholics to work with the police in running down all of Jehovah's witnesses. Made up in big, splashy advertising style, the bold black type had a message from the chief of police. It blustered that the "chase against every last one of Jehovah's witnesses is being pursued with more intensity than ever", and placed the Radio-Police at everyone's disposal "to free the streets of Jehovah's witnesses". Prominently set off by itself is the phone number of Radio Police. It is one of the Hierarchy's modern versions of hunting down "heretics" for another inquisition.

Generous Quebec City shares with others her experience at suppressing freedom. For instance, Sherbrooke newspapers of November 20 reported how Mayor Lucien Borne, of Quebec, counseled the city of Sherbrooke on getting rid of Jehovah's witnesses. The City Charter is to be amended so as to prohibit even free distribution of religious material without first securing permission of the chief of police. The chief can then censor what might be unpleasant to his priest. The resolution passed unanimously, and began with these words: "So that we may get rid of Jehovah's witnesses once and for all. . . ." Such openly frank discrimination is unusual, except in Quebec.

A few days pass, and the Sherbrooke municipal police make league with the provincial police and raid the Kingdom Hall of Jehovah's witnesses in that city. Twelve officers storm through the front door on the evening of November 25 without so much as a push on the bell. Books, booklets, 7,000 of the folders, records, mail, office equipment, and even Bibles, including the Catholic Douay version, all this material valued at several hundred dollars was seized and thrown into an open truck. En route to provincial police headquarters rain damaged many of the books. In the hall the money was taken from the contribution box mounted on the wall, and then in a typical display of spitefulness the emptied box was torn from the wall and the plaster damaged. Nine Witnesses, five men and four women, were arrested by the raiders and their bail was set at $500 cash or $900 property bond each. The charge was intent to circulate seditious literature.

Three evenings later the raiders swooped down once again on the hall, only to find it as bare as they had left it. Frustrated and desperate, they went so far as to raid the flat above the hall, which was occupied by people not even interested in the work of Jehovah's witnesses. Other raids were aimed at private homes scattered throughout the province. At St. Jerome the invasion of two homes netted 4,000 of the Quebec exposure folders and 3,000 booklets containing Bible treatises. Oddly enough, it seems that the appearance of the folder has in the eyes of Quebec rulers somehow transformed all the Bible literature into sedition. How they will sweat trying vainly to prove it so!

Not all of the police of Quebec, however, are in such heart sympathy with Duplessis' *putsch*. Some of the Witnesses taken into the station but not arrested reported that the chief and his men listened attentively to the testimony, then told them of the pressure being brought to bear upon the police. In another case officers had been sent out to arrest the Witnesses, but did not want to do so. They suggested that the ministers might change territory for a while, and they would tell their police captain that they could not locate the Witnesses. Again, one police captain told publishers: "The first ten phone calls we get don't bother us at all, but when we get twenty-five or thirty, then, of course, we have to do something." The priests may be able to stir many of the people into goading the police, but there are many thousands of freedom-loving persons in Quebec that not only turn a deaf ear on priestly agitations but also raise a loud voice in opposition to such suppression. Their voice is being added to that of Jehovah's witnesses in telling Quebec's rulers they have failed the people.

And how that chorus of voices did swell in number and volume from and after December 4! On that day officers of the Permit Department of the Quebec Liquor Commission swooped down on Roncarelli's restaurant, demanding its liquor license. No reason was given this restaurateur (who had held liquor licenses since 1911) for the action, and Liquor Commission trucks hauled off liquor valued at $5,000. Frank Roncarelli has operated a cafe in Montreal for many years; he is also one of Jehovah's witnesses and has supplied bail bond for the Witnesses to the extent of some $80,000 or $90,000. This greatly irked rulers and frustrated the persecution-through-prosecution drive; so on November 22 the Montreal courts said that hereafter the policy would be "a different bondsman for each accused". This would eliminate Roncarelli as a future bondsman; it would keep the Witnesses locked up while the trials were indefinitely postponed. But that was not enough. Bitter hate wanted revenge in the form of ruin for Roncarelli! Hence it was that on December 4 the liquor license was revoked, and the reason was given on the same day by Duplessis himself: "A certain Roncarelli has supplied bail for hundreds of witnesses of Jehovah. Today, Roncarelli is identifying himself with the odious propaganda of the witnesses of Jehovah and as a result, I have ordered the Liquor Commission to cancel his permit."

Frank Roncarelli termed this arbitrary and capricious cancellation "another example of the odious discrimination in Quebec and which the Witnesses claim is a shame upon Canada". If it is wrong to supply bail, then arrangements providing for bail are wrong, and courts are wrong in accepting any bail. If it is not wrong for courts to accept bail, and for laws to provide for it, and for persons to supply it, then Roncarelli has committed no wrong. He has not, and the people of Quebec say he has not; but they do say Duplessis has committed a wrong and a rank discrimination against a man because of his Scripture beliefs. As the storm of protest swelled ominously Duplessis realized many Quebecers were not yet willing to stomach such tyranny; so he thought up a new reason. Vague, tenuous, far-fetched, it failed to quiet fears. His new theory was that Roncarelli made money from the license, the money was used to bail out Witnesses, and since the state granted the license, the state was an accomplice to the bails. But bails are lawful; so even if the premier's specious, tricky, sleight-of-hand reasoning were true the state would not be an accomplice to any crime. Furthermore, days before Duplessis made his hateful stab at Roncarelli's livelihood the Montreal courts had eliminated the restaurateur as a bondsman! This fact alone strips Duplessis of excuses and exposes him as a rank discriminator. Premier Duplessis, you in particular have failed your people. And, what is more, they are telling you so!

Stormy Protest Against Duplessis' Discrimination

By telephone, by letter, by public platform, by radio and by newspaper persons not Witnesses but who favor freedom for all have raised a flood of protest. Dozens of editorials and scores of letters have appeared in Quebec papers. They protest that "Duplessis is only corroborating certain charges which appeared in the pamphlet *Quebec's Burning Hate*"; that "the methods employed bring reproach on us all"; that "they constitute a brazen and shocking denial of a citizen's civil rights"; that the Witnesses are "not getting a square deal in this province"; that they should not be "subjected to a twentieth-century inquisition"; that Duplessis' act was "intolerant if not tyrannical, and certainly contrary to the spirit of Christ" and his "categorizing of this sect with the Nazis, in fact his whole attitude, only makes one's blood boil"; that the drive against the Witnesses "deeply involves the whole principles of freedom of religion"; that advocates of religious liberty are aroused over "the vindictiveness of Mr. Duplessis' persecution by court prosecution"; that in this issue "Mr. Duplessis constitutes himself accuser, lawyer, witness and judge in a case to which, as he says, the attorney general has become a party", and hence sits as judge in his own case; that the government seems to have "proceeded outside the law"; that "to make a bludgeon of the law and to wield it arbitrarily is beyond the function of the state"; that if Duplessis continues denying liberty citizens will be "compelled to ask our federal government to intervene"; and that "an uprising of public opinion should force him back to the ways of civilized, democratic government or throw him out of office". In the heat of indignation one citizen queried: "Has anyone got the guts to stand up and demand freedom, now? Or shall we wait until it is our turn—until it is too late? Is it a crime to criticize a political party, or a religious group who are in power? Only in a dictatorship!"

The foregoing are only samples of many editorials and letters published; hundreds of phone calls and additional letters were received by Quebec papers. Many letters protesting Quebec's failure to protect freedoms were from orthodox ministers. The Church of England bishop of the Montreal diocese penned an open letter of protest to the premier. On December 9 the Montreal *Daily Star* published a joint protest signed by nine "Reverends". That issue of the *Star* carried an editorial and ten letters on the hot controversy, and the editor advised: "Owing to the great number of letters on the Jehovah's witnesses matter, on hand and arriving, the *Star* regrets that space will not permit the publication of any more." And it is with similar regret that we heed the demands of limited space and move along.

Organizations took group action to tell Quebec's rulers that they have failed their people on issues of religion and freedom. On December 6 thirty McGill University students met to organize student-body protest against Duplessis' use of police power "to further religious intolerance". In the group were represented campus religious and political organizations, and petitions of protest were signed by 1,200 students. The Cooperative Commonwealth Federation Committee for the Defence of Trade Union Rights scored Duplessis' actions as "high-handed and unconstitutional", charging Roncarelli's business was to be ruined because his providing of bail "temporarily interferes with Mr. Duplessis' mass persecution of a religious minority", and claiming that "such contempt for liberty and justice it would be difficult to match outside a fascist state". Prominent citizens endorsed the protest.

Also, the Montreal Civil Liberties Association urged citizens to flood Duplessis with protests by wire and letter; and went further in calling a mass meeting of protest. It was held December 12 in Montreal at Monument Nationale, which was packed out. Principal speaker was Hon. C. G. Power, K.C., M.P., who was Canada's wartime air minister. Round after round of applause roared out the audience's approval of his and other prominent speakers' condemnation of Duplessis' denial of freedom. Chairman of the Civil Liberties group had previously deplored Duplessis' methods as "repugnant to anyone who supports the democratic process" and claimed that he "destroys the process we have elected him to maintain". Over the radio this liberty-lover stated: "Incipient tyrants have usually begun the exercise of arbitrary authority on the most outrageous grounds. . . . Now is the time for believers in freedom to speak and act. Today it is Mr. Roncarelli. Tomorrow it may be you. Today it is the Jehovah's witnesses. Tomorrow it may be your particular minority group." Leslie Roberts, writer and chairman of a Democratic Action Committee, asked at the mass meeting: "Do we turn the press into the jackals of a one-party dictatorship, change the courts from halls of impartial justice into the tools of a fuehrer?" Previously he had evaluated the premier as follows: "This situation is nothing new for Mr. Duplessis. People would do well to think back to the Padlock

Law, to the premier's anti-war position in 1939 which swept him from office, to his attempts to disunite the country with his constant autonomy cries. What has happened is profoundly shocking, but it is certainly no new approach on the part of a man who is fundamentally a minor league Franco."

Jehovah's Witnesses Refute the False Charges

The freedom-loving people of Quebec have in an amazing way come forward to champion civil liberties, and to prove that certainly not all Quebecers hold hate for freedom. Now it seems appropriate that Jehovah's witnesses offer some answers to the charges Quebec rulers have so recklessly tossed about through the columns of the public press. Some are so absurd that they only prove the effort to create prejudice against the Witnesses, such as the one that appeared in the French paper *Le Petit Journal* on November 24: "In the Quebec capital indignation is very great against the Witnesses, since it was revealed Friday evening that these sectaries had even offered $10 in cash to a little lad if he would tramp on a crucifix."

That paper's policy to print lies was exposed in the same article, when it claimed that the Witnesses sold copies of *Quebec's Burning Hate* folder "at fantastic prices, varying from 5c to 50c according to the interest manifested". Practically every household in Quebec and all Canada knows the distribution of this folder was free; and anyone who wants one now may have it free for the asking. Recorder Mercier slandered the Witnesses as commercial agents who profiteered by selling 5c pamphlets for 25c. But Recorder Plante, who repeatedly denounces the Witnesses and alludes to them as "a bunch of crazy nuts", was very loquacious on the morning of November 16 in court when 14 Witnesses were to appear. He had not seen the folder that had started circulating the day before, and talked to defendants' counsel for 20 minutes about the Witnesses, about the nuns soliciting, and then: "I have seen with my own eyes where they say the Roman Catholic Church is a racket. Maybe it is a racket—you pay when you are born, you pay when you die, you pay after you die, you pay, pay, pay all the time—maybe it is a racket. But they shouldn't say so!" As for Jehovah's witnesses, if their work were commercial they would choose a pleasing, ear-tickling message that would sell. They only deliver God's message.

But in the little space remaining, let us concentrate on the main charges of serious import. Premier Duplessis, at his press conference on November 21 when he revealed his orders for a drive against the Witnesses, showily emoted: "The province of Quebec, jealous of its traditions, reputation and religious beliefs, would not and will not tolerate atheism, the twin brother of communism, nor will it permit such illegal publicity [referring to the *Quebec's Burning Hate* folder] to be made here in its favor." In a statement to the press on December 4, when he announced his dictator-like action against Roncarelli, Duplessis summed up: "The Communists, the Nazis as well as those who are the propagandists for the Witnesses of Jehovah, have been treated and will continue to be treated by the Union Nationale government as they deserve for trying to infiltrate themselves and their seditious ideas in the province of Quebec." In these releases to the public news channels the premier accuses the Witnesses of being atheists, charges them with sedition, and by linking in Communism and Nazism purposely plants and cultivates the charge that they are also supporters of these alien isms. So we settle attention on these four charges.

COMMUNISTS. The premier reasons that Jehovah's witnesses are Communists because he believes them to be atheists, the 'twin brothers of Communists'. Does he believe the many educators and scientists who are atheists are also Communists? Is it not true that during the past decade or so the Hierarchy's established policy is to label as Communist anyone who opposes her? And certainly Canada knows that the Catholic legislators of Quebec left the term Communism undefined in the Padlock Law so that it might embrace this broad meaning. But since the premier's smear that the Witnesses are Communists is based on his charge that they are atheists, we will let the two false charges fall together.

ATHEISTS. If the premier knows a Bible citation when he sees it, and if he has ever examined any of the literature of Jehovah's witnesses, he knows that he can hardly turn to a page that does not have Bible citations or quotations. As you note the following comparison, observe that the quotations are all taken from the Catholic Douay version Bible (not a Protestant Bible or Catholic catechism or prayer-book):

Jehovah's witnesses believe the Bible where it says: "He spared not their souls from death" (Psalm 77:50); "the living know that they shall die, but the dead know nothing more" (Ecclesiastes 9:5). But the Catholic Church teaches that the human soul is immortal and lives on, conscious. She teaches the Serpent's lie to Eve, "No, you shall not die."—Genesis 3:4.

Jehovah's witnesses believe the Bible where it says: "The soul that sinneth, the same shall die" (Ezechiel 18:4, 20); "the wages of sin is death" (Romans 6:23). But the Catholic Church teaches that punishment for sin is either eternal torment in fiery hell or a long period of purging in purgatorial fires, out of which the victim can be ultimately delivered by the prayers of priest, for money consideration.

Jehovah's witnesses believe the Bible where it says: "Thou shalt not make to thyself a graven thing" (Exodus 20:4); "fly from the service of idols" (1 Corinthians 10:14); "what agreement hath the temple of God with idols?" (2 Corinthians 6:16). But the Catholic Church revels in graven images, among which are graven crucifixes, which items the Bible never mentions as instruments of worship.

Jehovah's witnesses believe this Bible testimony about Jesus: "The Father is greater than I" (John 14:28); "there is one God, and one mediator of God and men, the man Christ Jesus" (1 Timothy 2:5). But the Catholic Church teaches the mysterious pagan trinity doctrine that claims God and Christ are the same; and the priest is set up in Christ's stead as man's mediator with God.

Jehovah's witnesses believe and obey Jesus' command, "Call none your father upon earth; for one is your father, who is in heaven" (Matthew 23:9). But the Catholic Church teaches that men must call her priests "Father".

Jehovah's witnesses believe and teach Bible truths, but the Catholic Church preaches contrary doctrine. Unsuspecting, sincere Catholics are pumped full of pagan doctrine and ritual that are contrary to their own Catholic Bibles. Actually, this makes them and their church the atheists; not Jehovah's witnesses. And to go along a bit with Duplessis in his folly of reasoning that atheists are Communists, then it is the Catholics and their church that are the Communists, because they certainly do not base their teachings on the Catholic Bible. How the tables are turned!

NAZIS. In Germany Jehovah's witnesses were known for years as "Earnest Bible Students". A Catholic priest of Berlin, writing in *The German Way* of May 29, 1938, quoted Hitler as saying: "These so-called

'Earnest Bible Students' are trouble-makers; they disturb the harmonious life amongst the Germans; I consider them quacks; I do not tolerate that the German Catholics be besmirched in such a manner by this American 'Judge' Rutherford; I dissolve the 'Earnest Bible Students' in Germany; their property I dedicate to the people's welfare; I will have all their literature confiscated." The priest added, "Bravo!" More than 6,000 Witnesses were held in Nazi concentration camps; many died there; and many were released only when the Allies whipped Germany in World War II. To call them Nazis is to lie.

But the Vatican made a concordat with Hitler in 1933, and despite repeated pleas by Catholics the pope would never excommunicate Catholic Hitler. The pope blessed Mussolini's rape of Ethiopia as a glorious crusade; he whitewashed Butcher Franco by calling him a "fine Christian gentleman"; Hitler's invasion of Austria was welcomed by a swastika flown from Cardinal Innitzer's cathedral; "Father" Tiso was made Hitler's puppet ruler in Czechoslovakia (the Allies are now trying him as a war criminal); priests followed Hitler's legions into Poland and on into Russia in a modern crusade; the pope lauded Traitor Petain as a "Good Marshal"; and the Vatican recognized the Japanese-sponsored government of the Philippines when that land was overrun. There is ample documentary evidence to support these facts, as informed persons know. What gall for a Catholic politician to even hint someone else might be a Nazi!

SEDITIONISTS. To date this charge remains in the category of name-calling. Neither the premier nor any one of his henchman has backed the charge with a seditious statement from *Quebec's Burning Hate.* They have babbled about references to Catholic images in legislative buildings and criticisms of mobsters and delinquent police and court officials. But no intelligent person considers that sedition. Since Quebec rulers do not cite backing for the charge, suffice it to say here that the accusation is an ancient one against God's servants. When the Jews were God's chosen and faithful nation, enemies hurled that charge against them. (See Ezra 4:12, 15, 19, Catholic Bible.) The evil scribes and Pharisee priests had a religious ax to grind against Jesus, and to grind it they trumped up a charge of sedition against Him and pressured it through on perjured testimony. At the insistent uproar of a religious mob goaded on by the priests Jesus was murdered as one guilty of "perverting our nation". (See Matthew 26:59, 60; Luke 23:1–24, Catholic Bible.) Years later religious rabble-rousers were still busy stirring up the populace against the apostles and early Christians, saying that because the Christians advocated Christ's kingdom they were against the state. (Acts 17:4–8, Catholic Bible) Then there were orating slick-tongues, like Tertullus, who went before the rulers accusing the apostle Paul to be "a pestilent man, and raising seditions", to be the "author of the seditions"; and he was said to "profane the temple". (See Acts 24:1–6, Catholic Bible.) So Premier Duplessis is no pioneer when he accuses the Christian Jehovah's witnesses of being pests and authoring and circulating seditions.

A conclusion for the preceding body of material is hardly required. Indeed, public reaction indicates that the people have already reached right conclusions on the failure of Quebec officialdom. How true for the religious kingdom of Quebec is the divine decree!—"Thou are weighed in the balance, and art found wanting." (Daniel 5:27, Catholic Bible) Wanting in love for God because Quebec rulers do not respect or follow the righteous principles of His Word, the Bible. Wanting in love for Christ because Quebec rulers hound and persecute His followers. Wanting in love for freedom because Quebec rulers trample underfoot a minority that disagrees with them. Where the spirit of the Lord is, there is liberty"; but that is not in Quebec officialdom despite the presence of crucifixes. (2 Corinthians 3:17, Catholic Bible) Quebec rulers, the eyes of Canada were upon you, but by now they have turned away in disgust. You have failed your people.

Readers, what do you think? Why not write to the Prime Minister of Canada, at Ottawa, Ontario, and ask him to investigate the action of Mr. Duplessis in denying Canadian citizens their liberty? Shall not Canada also have the Four Freedoms?

(Reprint from January 8 issue of *Awake!*)

STATUTES OF QUEBEC 1953–1954
2–3 Elizabeth II

CHAPTER 15

An Act respecting freedom of worship and the maintenance of good order

HER MAJESTY, with the advice and consent of the Legislative Council and of the Legislative Assembly of Quebec, enacts as follows:

1. The Freedom of Worship Act (Revised Statutes, 1941, chapter 307) is amended by adding, after section 2, the following sections:

"2a. It does not constitute the free exercise or enjoyment of religious profession and worship

a. to distribute, in public places or from door to door, books, magazines, tracts, pamphlets, papers, documents, photographs or other publications containing abusive or insulting attacks against the practice of a religious profession or the religious beliefs of any portion of the population of the Province, or remarks of an abusive or insulting nature respecting the members or adherents of a religious profession; or

b. to make, in speeches or lectures delivered in public places, or transmitted to the public by means of loud-speakers or other apparatus, abusive or insulting attacks against the practice of a religious profession or the religious beliefs of any portion of the population of the Province, or remarks of an abusive or insulting nature respecting the members or adherents of a religious profession; or

c. to broadcast or reproduce such attacks or remarks by means of radio, television or the press.

"2b. Every act mentioned in paragraph a, paragraph b or paragraph c of section 2a is an act endangering the public peace and good order in this Province.

"2c. Every act contemplated in paragraph a, paragraph b or paragraph c of section 2a is prohibited in this Province."

2. The said act is amended by adding, after section 10, the following sections:

"10a. Whosoever commits an act mentioned in paragraph a, paragraph b or paragraph c of section 2a is guilty of an infringement of section 2c and is liable, on proceeding under Part 1 of the Quebec Summary Convictions Act, to a fine or not less than one hundred dollars nor more than two hundred dollars for the first offence, of not less than two hundred dollars nor more than four hundred dollars for a second offence and of not less than four hundred dollars nor more than one thousand dollars for each subsequent offence, with costs in each case; and, on failure to pay the fine and costs, to imprisonment for not less than fifteen nor more than thirty days for the first offence, for not less than thirty days nor more than sixty days for the second and for not less than one hundred and twenty days nor more than one hundred and eighty days for each subsequent offence.

When the offence consists in distributing a book or writing mentioned in paragraph a of section 2a, such book or writing may be seized without warrant and all their copies in the Province may be seized with warrant. In case of a conviction, the judge pronouncing it must order the destruction thereof.

"10b. Upon petition supported by the oath of a credible person and alleging an infringement or the impending infringement of the provisions of section 2c, presented by the Attorney-General or with his authorization or by the municipal corporation in whose territory the infringement has been or is about to be committed, the Superior Court or a judge thereof may issue an interlocutory order of injunction to prevent the commission, continuance or repetition of such infringement.

An interlocutory injunction may be applied for and pronounced against any person and against any organization, association or body of persons, whether a juridical entity or not, who or which infringes or is about to infringe the provisions of section 2c.

In the cast of an organization, association or body of persons not a juridical entity, it shall be sufficient, for the purposes of the petition, the order of injunction and the proceedings relating thereto, to designate it by the collective name by which it designates itself or by which it is commonly known and designated, and the service of the petition, the order of injunction or any other proceeding may validly be made upon it at any of its offices or at any place where it is organized or meets or at any of its places of business in the Province.

The order of injunction made against such organization, association or body shall bind all persons who are members thereof and shall be executory against each of them.

The application for an injunction may be made and the injunction granted without the issuance of a writ of summons. Such application shall then itself constitute a suit.

The recourse contemplated in this section shall also, saving inconsistency with the foregoing provisions, be subject to the application of articles 959 to 972 of the Code of Civil Procedure, except that in no case shall any security be required.

"10c. The exercise of one of the recourses contemplated in sections 10a and 10b shall not prevent the exercise of the other."

3. This act shall come into force on the day of its sanction.

NOTES

NUMEROUS ABBREVIATIONS which refer to files in the Public Archives of Canada are used in the notes in the following pages. In order to make these comprehensible to the reader, an explanation of their full meaning appears below:

CPC 206-B-6   A file of the Department of the Secretary of State, office of the chief press censor, relating to *The Bible Students Monthly*, Pastor Russell's Organization, etc. (Public Archives of Canada reference R.G. 6 F-I, Vols. 49, 53, 54, and 55)

CPC 206-W-I   A file of the Department of the Secretary of State, office of the chief press censor, relating to the *Watch Tower* (Public Archives of Canada reference R.G. 6 E-I, Vol. 67)

EL-TJ   A file in the Ernest Lapointe Papers entitled "Témoins de Jéhovah" (Jehovah's Witnesses) (Public Archives of Canada reference M.G. 27 III BIO, Vol. 34)

MD H.Q. 54-21-10-21   A headquarters file of the Department of Militia and Defence which contains information relating to the position taken by the International Bible

Students with respect to war in 1915 and 1916 (Public Archives of Canada reference R.G. 24 A, Vol. 2199)

MD H.Q. 1064-30-67 A headquarters file of the Department of Militia and Defence relating to the treatment of conscientious objectors drafted into the Canadian Army in 1918 (Public Archives of Canada reference R.G. 24 A, Vols. 2028 and 2029)

M & F-IBSA A file of the Department of Marine and Fisheries with materials relating to International Bible Students Association radio station CHUC Saskatoon (Public Archives of Canada reference R.G. 42, Vol. 493)

NANRP Department of Northern Affairs and National Resources Papers (Public Archives of Canada reference R.G. 22 B, Vols. 217 and 218)

RLB 2309 A file in the Robert L. Borden Papers relating to the treatment of conscientious objectors drafted into the Canadian Army in 1918 (Public Archives of Canada reference M.G. 26 H 1(c), Vol. 238)

INTRODUCTION

1. D. A. Schmeiser, *Civil Liberties in Canada* (London: Oxford University Press, 1964), pp. 54, 55.

2. *Ibid.*

3. At first the Church of England claimed that "Protestant clergy" applied to Anglicans alone. However, as early as November 1819, the law officers of the Crown gave an opinion to the British colonial secretary, Lord Bathurst, that the term "may be extended also to Clergy of the Church of Scotland if there are any such settled in Canada". Yet they held that other Protestant clergymen or "dissenting Ministers" could not receive support from the reserves, since, as they said, "we think, the terms protestant Clergy can apply only to Protestant clergy recognized and established by law". "Opinion of the Law Officers of the Crown, to Earl Bathurst", reprinted in John S. Moir, ed., *Church and State in Canada 1627–1867* (Toronto: McClelland and Stewart Limited, 1967), pp. 161, 162.

4. For the relevant legislation, comments theron, and a discussion of the marriage-laws problems in Upper Canada between 1792 and 1859, see Moir, pp. 140–49.

5. *Statutes of Canada,* 14–15 Victoria, Chapter 175. Much of the Act is reprinted in Moir, pp. 246–48. It was not given royal assent until June 9, 1852.

6. The portion of the statute quoted above was reprinted in the *Revised Statutes of Canada* (1859), Chapter 74. It also appeared in the *Revised Statutes of Quebec* (1888), Article 3439, without any preamble and in the *Revised Statutes of Quebec* (1941), Chapter 307, which is entitled "An Act Respecting Freedom of Worship and Maintenance of Good Order in and Near Places of Public Worship".

7. *Statutes of Canada,* 18 Victoria, Chapter 2. Reprinted in Moir, pp. 243–45.

8. The BNA Act, Section 93.

9. See Chapter 10, pp. 231–35.

10. *Bintner v. Regina Public School Board No. 4,* (1965) 55 D.L.R. (2d) 646 (Sask. C.A.).

11. The BNA Act, Section 92 (12).

12. In the pre-Confederation period exemption from military service was granted to Quakers and Tunkers. The same privilege was extended by orders in council to Mennonites, Doukhobors, and Hutterites in 1873, 1898, and 1899 respectively.

13. The Military Service Act of 1917 provided no exemption for anyone not a member of a religion which regarded combatant service as specifically wrong. Thus, no member of the major churches of Canada could escape conscription as a conscientious objector; neither, of course, could any person claim conscientious objection on purely philosophical grounds. At the same time, under the provisions of the War-time Elections Act, Mennonites, Doukhobors, and other persons who claimed exemption from military service under the Military Service Act were disfranchised.

14. These denominations included the Church of Christ (Christians), the Disciples of Christ, the International Bible Students, the Pentecostal Assemblies, and the Plymouth Brethren. Strangely, two other groups, the Seventh-Day Adventists and Christadelphians, were recognized. Letter from J. Lorne McDougall, clerk to the Central

Appeal Judge, to Captain O. S. Tyndale, secretary to the military service sub-committee, Department of Militia and Defence, Ottawa, May 20, 1918. This letter may be found in MD H.Q. 1064-30-67.

15. "Alternative Service Work Camps", *The Mennonite Encyclopedia*, 1955, Vol. I, pp. 76–78.

16. See Chapter 8, pp. 177, 178.

17. *Statutes of British Columbia* (1920), Chapter 27, Section 6 (2) (b) (c). In fact, the legislation denied the franchise to Mennonites, Doukhobors, Hutterites, and all who had been exempted under the terms of the Military Service Act of 1917. However, the only body of people in the province to be affected in a major way were the Doukhobors. There were almost no Mennonites or Hutterites in British Columbia, and few other conscientious objectors in the province had been recognized as such.

18. The Dominion Franchise Act of 1934 specifically disfranchised "in the province of British Columbia, every Doukhobor person and every descendant of any such person, whether born in that province or elsewhere, who is by law of that province disqualified from voting at an election of a member of the Legislative Assembly of that Province". *Statutes of Canada* (1934), Chapter 51, Section 4 (c) (12).

19. *Perepolkin* v. *Superintendent of Child Welfare* (No. 2), (1957) 23 W.W.R. 592, pp. 599–600.

20. S. M. Katz, "The Lost Children of British Columbia", *Maclean's*, May 11, 1957.

21. Under Section 92 of the BNA Act all matters involving property and civil rights fall within provincial jurisdiction. Thus, though the Communal Property Act was directed against Doukhobors and Hutterites alone by prohibiting them from establishing new colonies less than forty miles from any other colony and limiting such new colonies to a maximum size of 6,400 acres, the court denied that their religious freedom was affected. In addition it ruled that the Freedom of Worship Statute of 1852 had no validity outside Ontario and Quebec. *Walter et al.* v. *Attorney-General for Alberta, Fletcher* v. *Attorney-General for Alberta*, [1969] S.C.R. 383; 66 W.W.R. 513.

22. *Time*, July 23, 1956.

23. *Statutes of Alberta* (1972), Chapter 103.

24. Actually, Jehovah's Witnesses are the only religion to have been placed under ban in Canada since the British Conquest, but reference is made here to the "victory of voluntarism" because from 1852 onward Canadian legislation supposedly guaranteed "the free exercise and enjoyment of religious profession and worship", at least in Ontario and Quebec.

CHAPTER I

1. Though there are numerous accounts of Russell's life, there is no good biography of him. Most of the following information concerning him is taken from *The Laodicean Messenger* (Chicago: The Bible Educational Institute, 1923); a "Biography of Pastor Russell", which appears in a late edition of his book, *The Divine Plan of the Ages* (Brooklyn, N.Y.: Watch Tower Bible and Tract Society, 1924); J. F. Rutherford, *A Great Battle in the Ecclesiastical Heavens* (New York: printed privately, 1915); and *Jehovah's Witnesses in the Divine Purpose* (Brooklyn, N.Y.: Watch Tower Bible and Tract Society, 1959). Some details of his life and work are also taken from Timothy White, *A People for His Name* (New York: Vantage Press, Inc., 1968).

2. *Jehovah's Witnesses in the Divine Purpose*, p. 15.

3. On January 1, 1909, the magazine's name was changed to the *Watch Tower and Herald of Christ's Presence*; on October 15, 1931, it became the *Watchtower and Herald of Christ's Presence*; from January 1 to March 1, 1939, it was the *Watchtower Announcing Christ's Kingdom*; and since then it has been known as the *Watchtower Announcing Jehovah's Kingdom*.

4. *Jehovah's Witnesses in the Divine Purpose*, pp. 25, 26.

5. *Ibid.*, p. 26.

6. *The Laodicean Messenger*, p. 99.

7. *Ibid.*, pp. 105, 106. *Jehovah's Witnesses in the Divine Purpose*, p. 62.

8. The present name is the Watchtower Bible and Tract Society of New York, Inc.

9. Incomplete statistics indicate that 15,430 Bible Students gathered to celebrate the memorial of the Lord's Supper throughout the world in the spring of 1915. It is therefore probably quite safe to estimate

that there were more than 20,000 world wide. The quantity 55,000 for copies of the *Watch Tower* in circulation is a firm figure. *Jehovah's Witnesses in the Divine Purpose*, p. 50. For a detailed statement of Russell and the Bible Students' later public work, see White, pp. 41–63.

10. Most of the information respecting Rutherford's life and career are taken from *Jehovah's Witnesses in the Divine Purpose*; Marley Cole, *Jehovah's Witnesses* (New York: Vantage Press, 1955) ; and A. H. Macmillan, *Faith On The March* (Englewood Cliffs, N.J.: Prentice-Hall, Inc., 1957).

11. There is no warrant for the practice of placing quotation marks around the title judge before Rutherford's name. The argument expressed by most of his critics is that, since he held the position of special or substitute judge on only a few occasions, he was not entitled to be called "judge". Since he was in fact a judge, even if only for short periods of time, such reasoning is mere casuistry. In any case Rutherford never used the title personally.

12. Macmillan, p. 68.

13. *Jehovah's Witnesses in the Divine Purpose*, pp. 64, 65.

14. Macmillan, pp. 46–63.

15. See Chapter 3, pp. 81, 82.

16. William J. Whalen, *Armageddon Around the Corner* (New York: John Day Company, 1962), p. 66.

17. *Jehovah's Witnesses in the Divine Purpose*, p. 312.

18. *Ibid.*, p. 195.

19. Most of the information presented here on Knorr is taken from Cole and from *Jehovah's Witnesses in the Divine Purpose*.

20. *Watchtower*, 1971, pp. 748–62. A list of the original eleven members of the governing body of Jehovah's Witnesses may be found in the *1973 Yearbook of Jehovah's Witnesses*. Since the creation of the body at least two of its members have died, and eight new members have been added to it. (References to *International Bible Student Association Yearbooks* or the *Yearbooks of Jehovah's Witnesses* appear without bibliographical data, since all are Watch Tower Society publications, printed in Brooklyn, New York.)

21. Acts 6:1–7; 15:1–29; 16:4.

22. Alan Rogerson disputes this assertion, but his argument that the

Witnesses are not growing as fast as the Mormons and Seventh-Day Adventists does not bear careful analysis. In the first place he takes total membership statistics from the former two groups and places them against the number of *active* Jehovah's Witnesses. If the Witnesses were to count members as do the Mormons and Adventists their numbers would be greatly inflated indeed. Furthermore, Rogerson's statement that the term "fastest-growing religion" is simply a journalistic device is inaccurate. It was not originated by the Witnesses themselves but by outside observers. See Alan Rogerson, *Millions Now Living Will Never Die* (London: Constable & Co. Ltd., 1969), pp. 75, 76.

23. *1975 Yearbook of Jehovah's Witnesses*, pp. 32, 257.
24. *Ibid.*, pp. 30, 31.
25. Rogerson, pp. 169–72.
26. *Ibid.*
27. *Vancouver Sun*, July 21, 1969.
28. For the Witnesses' position on "progressive revelation" see the *Watchtower*, 1964, pp. 360–72, and 1965, pp. 424–29. To the Witnesses, "progressive revelation" means the progressive understanding of truths delivered to the patriarchs, prophets, and men of faith in the early Christian church. It no longer means new direct revelations, as is understood in Mormonism for example.
29. Though evidence of their interest in history, archeology, and linguistics is frequently demonstrated in the pages of many of their publications, an outstanding example of their scholarship in these areas is the huge Bible dictionary *Aid to Bible Understanding* (Brooklyn, N.Y.: Watch Tower Bible and Tract Society, 1971).
30. See, for example, the *Watchtower*, 1962, p. 762.
31. *Jehovah's Witnesses in the Divine Purpose*, pp. 12–15. Cole, pp. 26–49.
32. Brian R. Wilson, "A Typology of Sects", in Roland Robertson, ed., *Sociology of Religion* (Harmondsworth, England: Penguin Books, 1969), p. 366.
33. Discussions of all of these topics may be found in *The Divine Plan of the Ages*, the other five original volumes of *Studies in the Scriptures*, the *Watch Tower*, and in many of Russell's sermons as they appeared in newspapers.

34. This point is stressed continually in Witness literature today. For example, see *The Truth That Leads to Eternal Life* (Brooklyn, N.Y.: Watch Tower Bible and Tract Society, 1968), Chapters 10 and 11.

35. This is the case with even a severe critic like Salem Kirban who acknowledges Jehovah's Witnesses' untiring zeal. Salem Kirban, *Jehovah's Witnesses: Doctrines of Devils No. 3* (Chicago: Moody Press, 1972), p. 44.

36. In his *Cur Deus Homo*, Anselm (1033?–1109), Archbishop of Canterbury, held that in order to redeem mankind at Calvary, Jesus had to be both God and man.

37. Rutherford, p. 10.

38. *Ibid.*, pp. 9–11.

39. *Ibid.*, pp. 17–20. The separation is often referred to as a "divorce" and Alan Rogerson says that "the Witnesses are excessively coy in refusing to speak of Russell's divorce". Rogerson, p. 195, n. 46. In fact, the problem is a semantic one. At the time, Maria Russell was granted a "divorce" from bed and board, an expression which means a legal separation. However, she was not given an absolute divorce with the right to remarry. So, in the generally accepted sense of the term, Russell was not a divorced man. The best detailed and documented account of Russell's relations with his wife is his own defence published in *Zion's Watch Tower*, 1906, pp. 212–27 (reprints pp. 3808–19). Mrs. Russell obtained her "divorce", or separation, on grounds of mental cruelty.

40. A partial reproduction of the transcript of record of Mrs. Russell's testimony in the case in which she related the "jellyfish story" may be found in Appendix iv of Gérard Hébert, s.j., *Les Témoins de Jéhovah* (Montréal: Les Éditions Bellarmin, 1960), pp. 292–303.

41. Rutherford, p. 17.

42. *Zion's Watch Tower*, 1906, pp. 220–22 (reprint p. 3815).

43. When Mrs. Russell's own lawyer questioned her: "You don't mean by that that your husband was guilty of adultery?" she replied "No." This portion of the transcript is reprinted in Hébert, p. 292.

44. The *Post*'s article of May 4, 1906, is reproduced in Hébert's Appendix v, pp. 302–4, and appears also in Whalen, p. 40.

45. Rutherford, pp. 19, 20. Cole, pp. 64–65.

46. Rutherford, p. 20.

47. As Timothy White and Alan Rogerson point out, many clergymen and others distorted the facts surrounding Russell's troubles with his wife. White, p. 34, Rogerson, p. 195, n. 46. This tradition has continued up until lately. Professor William Whalen completely ignores the facts relating to Russell's suit against the *Washington Post* and leaves the distinct impression that he was guilty of adultery.

Only very recently have religious critics of Jehovah's Witnesses begun to admit that there was no fairness in Mrs. Russell's charges regarding his "improprieties" and that she may simply have been seeking more alimony. See Kirban, p. 9.

It is also significant that Russell's critics have almost completely ignored his published defence in which he gives documentary proof that it was after the date when Mrs. Russell claimed that he had made the "jellyfish" statement to Ros Ball that she, Maria Russell, presented the theory that her husband was the faithful and wise servant of Matthew 24:45–51. *Zion's Watch Tower*, 1906, pp. 213–16 (reprints pp. 3810–11).

48. There is no evidence that Russell was in any way guilty of fraud. He, like many non-Bible Students, simply believed that Miracle Wheat had amazingly productive qualities. Neither was he originally responsible for the idea that it should be sold through the *Watch Tower*. Rutherford, pp. 20–30; Cole, pp. 65–69. The one thing that he can be charged with in the Miracle Wheat episode is naïveté. He should have realized that the very name "Miracle Wheat" would give his critics an opportunity to attack him and the Watch Tower Society. Since this time the Society has been most careful in not allowing the advertisement of anything in its publications except other Watch Tower publications.

A full copy of the transcript of record of Russell's suit against the *Brooklyn Eagle* is in the Watch Tower Society's Bethel Library at 124 Columbia Heights, Brooklyn.

49. See n. 47 and Appendix A.

50. Whalen, p. 18.

51. *Jehovah's Witnesses in the Divine Purpose*, p. 142.

52. White, pp. 324–34.

53. For the details see Chapter 7.
54. *Jehovah's Witnesses in the Divine Purpose*, pp. 153, 154.
55. *Newsweek*, March 25, 1963.
56. *Awake!* April 22, 1957. *Washington Post*, March 21, 1959. White, pp. 349–51.
57. Jehovah's Witnesses are either banned or under severe restrictions in about fifteen African countries and all of the Arab nations of the Middle East. They have been most cruelly treated in Malawi, however, when as late as 1973 nearly 36,000 of them were forced to flee to Portuguese Mozambique to escape beatings, torture, and murder. *ABC* (Madrid), October 12, 1972. *The Nation*, July 16, 1973. *1974 Yearbook of Jehovah's Witnesses*, pp. 14–17.
58. *Time*, September 9, 1966.
59. Jesús Jiménez, *La objeción de conciencia en España* (Madrid: Editorial Cuadernos para el Diálogo, 1973). Since the spring of 1974, the Spanish government has changed its policy toward conscientious objectors. Witness objectors are now being sentenced to terms of from five to eight years in prison for failing to do two years' military service.
60. *1972 Yearbook of Jehovah's Witnesses*, pp. 109–11.
61. For many years the *Watchtower* was available to French Witnesses only in a plain-covered edition which could not be distributed to the public. However, the partial ban on the magazine and its distribution has just recently been lifted.
62. *Walsh* v. *The Lord Advocate*, [1956] 3 All E.R. 129; I W.L.R. 1002; 100 Sol. Jo. 585; S.C. (H.L.) 126; Sol. T. 283, H.L.
63. White, pp. 341–43.
64. Charles A. Beard, *The Republic* (New York: The Viking Press, 1943), p. 73.
65. Charles S. Braden, *These Also Believe* (New York: The Macmillan Company, 1950), p. 380.
66. Dissenting in *Prince* v. *Massachusetts*, 321 U.S. 158, 175, 176, 64 s. ct. 438, 447, 448, 88 L. Ed. 645 (1944).
67. William E. Mann, *Sect, Cult and Church in Alberta* (Toronto: University of Toronto Press, 1955), p. 36.
68. *Ibid.*, p. 35.

69. Douglas J. Wilson, *The Church Grows in Canada* (Toronto: Committee on Missionary Education, Canadian Council of Churches, 1966), p. 189.

70. Brian R. Wilson discusses a particularly "gross" oversimplification of sect-type religions by D. A. Martin. According to Martin, sects worship "in a wild communal rant, or, like the Seekers [in] utter silence". As Wilson says: "The different Darbyist groups, Jehovah's Witnesses, Church of God in British Isles and Overseas, the holiness movements do not worship in a wild rant nor in total silence." Brian R. Wilson, "A Typology of Sects", pp. 362, 363.

71. Said Cumberland: "Some students of the movement have placed the Witnesses in the lowest social category. My own observations lead me to believe that they are moving into the middle class, and while there are as yet few college graduates in the movement, most Witnesses under forty have had at least a High School education." In his conclusion Cumberland remarked: "In manner of dress, speech and education the Witnesses do not appear distinct from the majority of Americans. If anything they are neater and more courteous since Jehovah would not be pleased to be represented by a slovenly, rude people." William H. Cumberland, *A History of Jehovah's Witnesses* (unpublished doctoral dissertation, University of Iowa, Iowa City, 1958), pp. 5, 295.

72. Rogerson, pp. 174, 175.

73. A careful examination of the files of the alternative-service camps in the Public Archives of Canada indicates that the largest number of Witnesses in the camps were farm owners of British or Northern European stock. Other conscientious objectors were mainly farm labourers.

74. See Table 3, p. 229.

75. This assertion is based upon the fact that, in 1961, while 34 per cent of all Canadians were under fifteen years of age, 34.5 per cent of Jehovah's Witnesses were within the same age group. In 1971 only 29.6 per cent of the population and 30 per cent of Canadian Witnesses were under fifteen.

76. According to the 1961 census 32.9 per cent of all persons within the United Church were under fifteen; in 1971 the percentage had dropped to 28. While in both instances birthrates among United

Churchmen were slightly lower than among Jehovah's Witnesses, perhaps because many Witnesses are converts from groups with high birthrates such as Roman Catholics, it is important to note that Witness families are much closer to those of United Churchmen in size than to those of religions such as the Mennonites, Mormons, Pentecostals, and Roman Catholics, all of whom still tend to have many more children.

77. Douglas J. Wilson, *The Church Grows*, p. 189.
78. Although the British and Germans have assimilated completely with English-speaking or, more rarely, French-speaking congregations, there are Italian, Greek, Portuguese, Spanish, and Ukrainian Witness congregations throughout the country.
79. According to the offices of the Watch Tower Society in Toronto there are twenty-five Italian congregations in Canada, some of which are quite large.
80. See Chapter 11, pp. 227.
81. *Watchtower*, 1956, pp. 306, 307. *Awake!* December 8, 1965, pp. 12–15.
82. William Cumberland has noted accurately: "Witnesses are not opposed to education, but they are critical of American colleges because they fear the liberal ideas of college professors, especially the concept of evolution, may result in a weakening of their faith." Cumberland, p. 296.
83. The Mormons, concentrated in Southern Alberta, maintain close ties with the United States. Many are noted for their "Mormon drawl".
84. Cole, pp. 124, 125.
85. Thomas F. O'Dea, *The Sociology of Religion* (Englewood Cliffs, N.J.: Prentice-Hall, Inc., 1966), pp. 66–69.
86. Whalen, p. 224. Cumberland, p. 296.
87. Brian R. Wilson, *Sects and Society* (Berkeley: University of California Press, 1961). See also O'Dea, p. 69.
88. For their positions on other medical practices see Chapter 11, pp. 230, 231.
89. In the past, the Watch Tower Society explained the term fornication, taken from the Greek word πορνεία, to mean vaginal intercourse between two persons, male and female, who are not married

to one another. However, since 1972, the *Watchtower* has stated that on the basis of further research the Society has been forced to broaden its understanding of the meaning of the biblical term. Accordingly πορνεία is now held to mean any illicit sexual intercourse including sodomy, lesbianism, and bestiality. The *Watchtower*, 1972, pp. 766–68, and 1974, pp. 703, 704.

90. An up-to-date view of the Witnesses' positions on all these matters is stated in *True Peace and Security—From What Source* (Brooklyn, N.Y.: Watch Tower Bible and Tract Society, 1973), pp. 145–54.

91. *Make Sure of All Things* (Brooklyn, N.Y.: Watch Tower Bible and Tract Society, 1965), pp. 54, 162–65. *Organization for Kingdom-Preaching and Disciple-Making* (Brooklyn, N.Y.: Watch Tower Bible and Tract Society, 1972), pp. 154–82.

92. Rogerson quotes Watch Tower Vice-President F. W. Franz's remark that in the United States roughly 500 Witnesses were disfellowshipped each year between 1952 and 1957. However, in 1958 there was a sharp increase in disfellowshipments. Since the 1950s the average number of disfellowshipments per year has generally tended to increase as Jehovah's Witnesses are determined "to keep the organization clean". It is also true, though, that many disfellowshipped persons are later readmitted to Witness society upon repentance.

93. *The Truth That Leads to Eternal Life* (Brooklyn, N.Y.: Watch Tower Bible and Tract Society, 1968), pp. 170–80.

94. *Ibid.*

95. As pointed out earlier the democratic, congregational system of government was gradually abandoned among Jehovah's Witnesses, and elected "elders" and "deacons" were replaced by congregational officers appointed by the Watch Tower Society. The office of service director, established in the 1920s, became that of "company servant" in the 1930s, then "congregation servant", or "overseer", in the 1950s. Assistants to the company or congregation servant were called "servants". In 1971, however, the Watch Tower Society announced that the Witnesses should return to a system of congregational government under elders supported by ministerial servants or deacons. Although the bodies of elders are more autonomous than formerly,

and authority is shared by all elders equally under rotating chairmen, they are still appointed by the Watch Tower Society rather than elected congregationally. "Appointed Elders to Shepherd the Flock of God", *Watchtower*, 1972, pp. 9–27. *Organization for Kingdom-Preaching and Disciple-Making*, pp. 53–93.

96. Cole, pp. 3–19; Whalen, pp. 126–39; Rogerson, pp. 167–73.

97. In 1974 only 10,723 partook of the bread and wine. The *Watchtower*, 1975, p. 27.

98. Jehovah's Witnesses believe that most of the "elect" were chosen by 1935 and that after that date most persons have been called to hope for everlasting life on a paradise earth. For further details of this belief see Chapter 6, p. 116.

99. In the spring of 1974 a total of 4,550,457 gathered to celebrate the Memorial Supper. During the same "service year" (September 1973 through August 1974), the peak of active Witness preachers for any one month was 2,021,432. *1975 Yearbook*, p. 31.

100. Braden, p. 380.

101. The call to serve where "the need is greater" first went forth at a series of district conventions held in the summer of 1957.

102. Matthew 19:11, 12. 1 Corinthians 7:28, 32–35.

103. According to the *1975 Yearbook*, pp. 24–31, during the 1974 service year there were 127,135 pioneers throughout the world of whom 3,904 were active under the Canadian branch. On this basis roughly one in fifteen active Canadian Jehovah's Witnesses is a pioneer evangelist.

104. Many of the Watch Tower Society's branch overseers in foreign lands have been Canadians, as have many Witness missionaries in Africa, Asia, Latin America, and the islands of the seas.

CHAPTER 2

1. W. G. How, L. W. Greenlees, and P. Chapman, *History of Jehovah's Witnesses in Canada* (an unpublished manuscript submitted as a report to the Watch Tower Society at Brooklyn, 1958).

2. *Ibid.*

3. *Zion's Watch Tower* (reprints) 1886, p. 851.

4. There were among them men whose professions were that of newspaper editor, printer, magistrate, realtor, accountant, etc. The names

and pictures of some of those early Ontario Bible Students are found in J. F. Rutherford, *A Great Battle in the Ecclesiastical Heavens* (New York: printed privately, 1915), pp. 32, 33, 54.

5. How, Greenlees, and Chapman.

6. *Ibid.*

7. *Zion's Watch Tower*, 1901, pp. 192, 208, 223, 288, 304, 320.

8. George Naish, *The Early Times* (an unpublished manuscript, 1971).

9. Based on information submitted to the Toronto offices of the Watch Tower Society by Clifford Roberts of Victoria, British Columbia, April 1, 1958.

10. Based on information given to the author by Aitchison's daughter, Mrs. Mary Eckmire of Winnipeg, Manitoba, in August 1973.

11. Based on information submitted to the Toronto offices of the Watch Tower Society by George Naish of Saskatoon, Saskatchewan, March 1958.

12. Based on information given the author by Arnold Melin of Calgary, Alberta, October 1973.

13. Based on information submitted to the Toronto offices of the Watch Tower Society by George Naish, March 1958.

14. How, Greenlees, and Chapman. *Zion's Watch Tower*, pp. 192, 208.

15. *Watch Tower*, 1909, p. 304.

16. Based on information submitted to the Toronto offices of the Watch Tower Society by Mr. and Mrs. James Orr of Montreal, Quebec, during 1958.

17. How, Greenlees, and Chapman.

18. *Ibid.*

19. *Zion's Watch Tower*, 1904, p. 196.

20. *Ibid.*, 1906, pp. 272, 336.

21. *Ibid.*, 1908, p. 32.

22. *Watch Tower*, 1909, p. 240.

23. *Zion's Watch Tower*, 1907, p. 80; *Watch Tower*, 1909, p. 38.

24. *Watch Tower*, 1909, pp. 304, 307.

25. *Ibid.*, 1910, p. 2.

26. How, Greenlees, and Chapman.

27. *The People's Pulpit* was later known as *Everybody's Paper* and was superseded by the *Bible Students Monthly* during the First World War.

28. *Jehovah's Witnesses in the Divine Purpose* (Brooklyn, N.Y.: Watch Tower Bible and Tract Society, 1959), p. 49.

29. *The Laodicean Messenger* (Chicago: The Bible Educational Institute, 1923), p. 99. *Jehovah's Witnesses in the Divine Purpose*, p. 50, puts the estimated number at a more conservative ten million.

30. *Jehovah's Witnesses in the Divine Purpose*, pp. 50, 51.

31. I have in my possession notes from one such debate held between a fundamentalist clergyman and a woman Bible Student, the wife of a pioneer country doctor. The issue in contention was the nature of hell.

32. J. F. Rutherford, p. 31.

33. J. J. Ross, *Some Facts and More Facts About the Self-Styled "Pastor" Charles T. Russell* (Philadelphia: Philadelphia School of the Bible, 1913), p. 18.

34. Marley Cole, *Jehovah's Witnesses* (New York: Vantage Press, 1955), pp. 70, 71.

35. For full details of the issue see Appendix A.

36. C. T. Russell, *The New Creation* (Pittsburgh: Watch Tower Bible and Tract Society, 1904), pp. 594, 595.

37. A copy of this affidavit may be found in MD H.Q. 54-21-10-21.

38. Dated March 7, 1916, MD H.Q. 54-21-10-21.

39. See, for example, a letter from Lieutenant-General Mewburn to Lieutenant-Colonel C. S. MacInnis, March 24, 1916, MD H.Q. 54-21-10-21.

40. Dated April 3, 1916, MD H.Q. 54-21-10-21.

41. *Winnipeg Free Press*, July 8, 1916.

42. A. H. Macmillan, *Faith on the March* (Englewood Cliffs, N.J.: Prentice-Hall Inc., 1957), pp. 67, 68, 71–73.

43. *Jehovah's Witnesses in the Divine Purpose*, p. 66.

44. *Watch Tower*, 1918, p. 2.

45. C. T. Russell, *The Battle of Armageddon* (Pittsburgh: Watch Tower Bible and Tract Society, 1897), pp. 613, 614; *The Finished Mystery* (Brooklyn, N.Y.: Watch Tower Bible and Tract Society, 1917), pp. 53, 125, 416–23; Macmillan, pp. 126, 127.

46. Macmillan, pp. 71–73; *Jehovah's Witnesses in the Divine Purpose*, p. 69.

47. *Jehovah's Witnesses in the Divine Purpose*, pp. 69–72; Macmillan,

pp. 75–81; Cole, p. 89. *1973 Yearbook of Jehovah's Witnesses*, pp. 100–16. Alan Rogerson presents a very different view based upon Johnson's account of what happened. As he states, Johnson had full powers to act on behalf of the Society in Britain. Alan Rogerson, *Millions Now Living Will Never Die* (London: Constable & Co. Ltd., 1969), pp. 32–39. However, it is certain that neither Rutherford nor the Society had given him the right to claim to be Russell's successor. On that basis alone, it is no wonder that Rutherford regarded him as mad and recalled him.

48. During the last years of his life Russell was becoming increasingly militant in his attitude towards "the world"; many of the harshest quotations in *The Finished Mystery* were from articles he had written personally in the *Watch Tower*.

49. *Jehovah's Witnesses in the Divine Purpose*, pp. 70, 71.

50. *Ibid.* Macmillan, pp. 75–81. Cole, pp. 86–89.

51. *Jehovah's Witnesses in the Divine Purpose*, p. 73.

52. Johnson and the directors did not maintain unity among themselves but almost immediately split into separate factions. Thus, although numerous Bible Student organizations exist to this day, none of them has become an influential religious force of any size.

53. Cole, pp. 89, 90.

54. *Ibid.*

55. *The Finished Mystery*, pp. 248–53.

56. March 7, 1916.

57. Canadian Press Service bulletin, April 9, 1917. *Ottawa Evening Journal*, April 10, 1917.

58. Kenneth McNaught, *A Prophet in Politics* (Toronto: University of Toronto Press, 1959), pp. 70, 71.

59. CPC 206-B-6.

60. Letter from Sherwood to Chambers, August 14, 1916. Chambers to Scott, August 14, 1916. Scott to Chambers, August 21, 1916. All in CPC 206-W-1.

61. Dated August 25, 1917, in CPC 206-B-6.

62. Letter from Chambers to Evans, August 29, 1917, CPC 206-B-6.

63. Found in CPC 206-B-6.

64. Letter from Sherwood to Chambers, August 25, 1917. Chambers to Bousfield, August 25, 1917. Both in CPC 206-B-6.

65. Letter from Chambers to Burrell, August 27, 1917, in CPC 206-B-6.
66. Letter from D. A. Campbell to Chambers, October 23, 1917, in CPC 206-B-6.
67. Letter from Chambers to Burrell, October 23, 1917, in CPC 206-B-6. In this letter Chambers indicated that he considered Bible Student literature to be "objectionable and dangerous, doubly so on account of the insidious attacks on the military system".
68. Dated November 12, 1918, in CPC 206-B-6.
69. *Vancouver World*, January 22, 1918.
70. Letter from Campbell to Chambers, January 22, 1918, in CPC 206-B-6.
71. Letter from District Intelligence Officer No. 2 (Toronto) to Chambers, January 24, 1918, in CPC 206-B-6.
72. Telegram from Johnson to Chambers, January 24, 1918, in CPC 206-B-6.
73. Letter from Chambers to Burrell, January 14, 1918, in CPC 206-B-6.
74. Most major newspapers announced the ban. The *Ottawa Journal Press* of February 13, 1918, headlined: "TEUTONIC PLOT NIPPED IN BUD BY THE CENSOR—BIBLE STUDENTS' MONTHLY WAS THE CHIEF MEDIUM".

CHAPTER 3

1. *Statutes of Canada* (1917) Chapter 19, Section 11 (1) (f). See also Section 11 (2) (a), and Schedule Exemption 6.
2. *Re Cooke*. See Appendix B.
3. George Naish, *The Early Years* (an unpublished manuscript, 1971). At least one Bible Student, Ernest Edward Spalding, was court-martialled and sentenced to fifteen years in prison, though the sentence was reduced to ten years by the Governor General in Council. The report of this case may be found in CPC 206-B-6.
4. The commander of the depot battalion stated that while Clegg, Naish, and Matheson were subjected to "school boy pranks" or "ragging", he asserted that "brutality was never practiced for a moment" and "the matter has been very much exaggerated". *Winnipeg Free Press*, January 25, 1918.
5. *Winnipeg Tribune*, January 24, 1918.
6. This telegram may be found in MD H.Q. 1064-30-67.

7. "Following up the telegram I have just dispatched to you re the torture of conscientious objectors there is no doubt about the facts of the case. On Monday last, the 21st, in Minto Street Barracks, two conscientious objectors, Robert Clegg and Frank Naish, were first placed in a hot room until they perspired profusely and then placed under a cold water shower and left there until they became unconscious. As a result Clegg is now lying in St. Boniface hospital." Quoted in a letter from Crerar to Mewburn, January 28, 1918, in MD H.Q. 1064-30-67.

8. *Ibid.*

9. *Winnipeg Free Press*, January 25, 1918.

10. *Winnipeg Tribune*, January 24, 1918.

11. *Winnipeg Free Press*, January 25, 1918.

12. RLB 2309, documents 132767 and 132771.

13. *Winnipeg Tribune*, January 24, 1918.

14. The full transcript of the proceedings may be found in MD H.Q. 1064-30-67.

15. Lieutenant R. Carr, one of the three-member court, was identified as one of the officers who had tried "to reason" with Matheson when he refused to obey military commands.

16. A glaring example of such was when one witness, Sergeant H. Mackinnon, described Clegg's condition after the cold-shower treatment. He indicated that Clegg had trembled a good deal, had rolled, pitched, and would not speak at all. Lieutenant Carr then asked: "So he was perhaps trembling with rage?" Mackinnon replied: "He might have been, Sir."

17. Transcript of the inquiry.

18. "96 Your wire 5254 twenty fifth instant [.] Reports greatly exaggerated [.] Full investigations already under way which will be completed today [.] Clegg being returned to barracks to-day [.] He never has been unconscious [.]" Telegram from Ruttan to Mewburn, January 26, 1918. MD H.Q. 1064-30-67.

19. Telegram from Ruttan to the Adjutant-General, January 28, 1918. MD H.Q. 1064-30-67. See also the *Winnipeg Telegram*, January 24 and 26, 1918; February 6, 7, and 13, 1918.

20. *Winnipeg Telegram*, February 13, 1918.

21. Memorandum from Mewburn to the Adjutant-General, January 24, 1918. MD H.Q. 1064-30-67.
22. Letter from Mewburn to Crerar, January 29, 1918. MD H.Q. 1064-30-67.
23. Letter from Mewburn to Borden, February 9, 1918. RLB 2309, document 132777.
24. Decision No. 116 of the Militia Council made at a meeting held February 6, 1918. MD H.Q. 1064-30-67.
25. *Winnipeg Telegram*, February 27, 1918.
26. Ivens was one of the few clergymen who showed any sympathy for "unrecognized" groups such as the Bible Students. Letter from Ivens to Crerar, February 25, 1918. RLB 2309, document 132789.
27. Letter from Crerar to Borden, March 4, 1918. RLB 2309, document 132780.
28. RLB 2309, document 132799.
29. Telegram from Mrs. W. Elliott to Prime Minister Borden, April 6, 1918, plus an attached hand-written memorandum to the Prime Minister. There is much additional correspondence on this matter in MD H.Q. 1064-30-67. Ultimately the Judge Advocate General decided that the men should never have been sent overseas.
30. Various telegrams, cablegrams, and letters in MD H.Q. 1064-30-67. *Golden Age* (special edition for Canada and Great Britain), September 29, 1920. C. F. Wainwright, *Appreciating Years of Joyful Service* (an unpublished manuscript, 1971). Interview with C. F. Wainwright, April 1972.
31. *Golden Age*, September 29, 1920.
32. *Ibid.*
33. *Ibid.*
34. *Ibid.*
35. *Ibid.*
36. Wainwright, *Years of Joyful Service*.
37. *Ibid.*
38. Many of these may be found in CPC 206-B-6.
39. *Winnipeg Tribune*, February 14, 1918.
40. In CPC 206-B-6.
41. *Golden Age*, September 29, 1920.

42. See, for example, the book *Babylon the Great Has Fallen!* (Brooklyn, N.Y.: Watch Tower Bible and Tract Society, 1963), pp. 498–505.

43. *Winnipeg Tribune*, February 14, 1918; Elizabeth Kelly Wainwright, *Account of My Life* (an unpublished manuscript, 1971). The Bible Students were not sure what they should do from an ethical standpoint. Russell's earlier teaching as expressed in *The New Creation* indicated that they should obey the "higher powers" of Romans 13. That caused many to co-operate with the police by surrendering banned publications or by destroying them. Others took the stand that they "ought to obey God rather than men" and kept their literature. Many who co-operated with the authorities suffered persecution. According to first-hand accounts, Menyhert Revesz, a Hungarian immigrant at Lethbridge, Alberta—at the time not a Bible Student—was fined ten dollars for surrendering *The Finished Mystery*; and at Roseland, Saskatchewan, several Bible Students were heavily fined when they voluntarily gave banned books and tracts to the police.

44. *Winnipeg Tribune*, February 14, 1918. Letter from A. J. Cawdron, chief commissioner of the Royal North West Mounted Police for Saskatchewan, to Ernest Chambers, April 25, 1918. CPC 206-B-6.

45. *Jehovah's Witnesses in the Divine Purpose*, p. 76; Montreal *Gazette*, February 28, 1918. Letter from the British ambassador to the United States to the Duke of Devonshire, Governor General of Canada, March 4, 1918. Letter from Chambers to Senator George Lynch-Staunton, June 15, 1918. Both in CPC 206-B-6.

46. Memorandum for Office File, February 19, 1918, and notes on a conference between Chambers and Toronto attorney Denton with his client, W. Ernest Whelpton. CPC 206-B-6.

47. Found in CPC 206-B-6.

48. A copy of the broadside containing Rutherford's letter and the other documents may be found in CPC 206-B-6.

49. "The Chief Press Censor specially asks that editors will bear in mind, in connection with the activities of the International Bible Students in Canada, that their campaign will be more benefited than deterred by the wide publicity which is being given to it. The publication in Canadian newspapers of lengthy interviews with these 'conscien-

tious objectors' is most undesirable, being the sort of pacifist campaign the enemy would be glad to see prosper at this time.

"The Canadian Press Limited will decline to carry any more publicity of this kind. Announcements of action by the authorities to suppress this pacifist propaganda are the only items we require in connection with the International Bible Students.

"Your co-operation will be greatly appreciated." Confidential Memorandum for Editors from J. F. B. Livesay, March 20, 1918. CPC 206-B-6.

50. Letter from F. G. Aldham (Office of the Censor for the West) to Chambers, March 24, 1918. CPC 206-B-6.

51. Letter from J. H. Woods to Chambers, April 15, 1918. CPC 206-B-6.

52. In CPC 206-B-6.

53. Dated April 1, 1918. CPC 206-B-6.

54. In CPC 206-B-6.

55. Dated February 8, 1918. CPC 206-B-6. For further examples of anti-Bible Student clerical pressure on public officials see Appendix B.

56. Dated April 5, 1918. CPC 206-B-6.

57. *Ibid.*

58. Letter from Whelpton to Chambers, March 25, 1918. CPC 206-B-6.

59. In a letter to Bible Student Ernest E. Spalding, dated April 4, 1918, Chambers wrote "Considering that so much matter published in the recent publications of the International Bible Students Association is of a type pre-eminently advantageous to the insidious propaganda being conducted by enemy agents and sympathizers . . . it is only to be expected that suspicion should be aroused.

"It is unquestionably the fact that if this recent literature is not pro-German propaganda, it is certainly anti-War, anti-Ally, anti-British, anti-Canadian and altogether objectionable from a national standpoint."

To the editor of the *Victoria Daily Times* he wrote as of June 24, 1918: "I firmly believe that these International Bible Students, either as willing accomplices or misled dupes, are engaged in a very active and pernicious enemy propaganda, and if I had my way, I would like to see everyone concerned in the campaign of these people put behind bars." Both letters are in CPC 206-B-6.

60. These included the *Berean Studies of the Finished Mystery, The*

Battle of Armageddon (one of Pastor Russell's *Studies in the Scriptures*), and *Berean Studies in the Battle of Armageddon*. Notices of the bans were published in the *Canada Gazette*, April 13, 1918, p. 3569; April 27, 1918, p. 3824, May 25, 1918, p. 4133.

61. *United States, Congressional Record* (Vol. 56 Part 6), Senate, April 24, 1918, p. 5542; May 4, 1918, pp. 6051, 6052. See also A. H. Macmillan, *Faith on the March* (Englewood Cliffs, N.J.: Prentice-Hall, Inc., 1957), Chapter 6.

62. Macmillan, Chapter 6.

63. *Jehovah's Witnesses in the Divine Purpose*, p. 79; Macmillan, Chapter 7.

64. *Rutherford v. the United States*, (May 14, 1919) 258 F. 855, Transcript of Record, Vol. I, p. 12. Quoted in *Jehovah's Witnesses in the Divine Purpose*, p. 79.

65. In sentencing them Judge Howe stated: "The religious propaganda in which these men engaged is more harmful than a division of German soldiers. They have not only called in question the law officers of the Government and the army intelligence bureau but have denounced all the ministers of all the churches. Their punishment should be severe." Macmillan, p. 99.

66. *The Case of the International Bible Students* quoted in *Jehovah's Witnesses in the Divine Purpose*, pp. 81, 82. *Golden Age*, September 29, 1920.

67. *Jehovah's Witnesses in the Divine Purpose*, p. 83. On September 1, 1918, the *Watch Tower* gave notice of the suspension of *The Finished Mystery*, the *Watch Tower* of March 1, 1918 (ZG), all issues of the *Bible Students Monthly* and *Kingdom News*.

68. Letter from Livesay to G. Pringle, May 10, 1918. CPC 206-B-6.

69. Livesay stated: "I have been over the enclosed manuscript of the 'Watch Tower' people, and cannot see that it is objectionable from the point of view of Press Censorship." *Ibid.*

70. In CPC 206-B-6.

71. Dated June 14, 1918. CPC 206-B-6.

72. Dated June 18, 1918. CPC 206-B-6.

73. An undated letter and one dated June 17, 1918, from Lynch-Staunton to Chambers. CPC 206-B-6. Lynch-Staunton had been the Reverend J. J. Ross's lawyer at the time Pastor Russell had pressed

charges against him in 1912 and 1913.

74. Dated June 10, 1918. CPC 206-B-6.

75. Dated June 11, 1918. CPC 206-B-6.

76. In CPC 206-B-6.

77. In CPC 206-B-6.

78. In CPC 206-B-6.

79. Dated June 15, 1918. CPC 206-B-6.

80. Dated June 18, 1918. CPC 206-B-6.

81. Letter from Livesay to Chambers, June 18, 1918. CPC 206-B-6. At the same time, Livesay argued that he did not feel that the *Morning Messenger* was objectionable. He said: "I read the thing very carefully—as I thought—and as it had no bearing to all seeming on the prosecution of the war, I could not see that it could be prohibited on the ground that it was an attack on religion that not being, to my idea, the business of Press Censorship."

Though Chambers disputed this point in a letter to F. G. Aldham in Winnipeg by stating that the *Morning Messenger* was "unquestionably a contravention" of censorship regulations, he admitted that "I am in great trouble about the 'Morning Messenger'", and "I am in a decidedly uncomfortable position". Chambers's reaction to the Bible Student publication was therefore undoubtedly more a response to Catholic anger over its distribution than because of its nature. Chambers's letter to Aldham, dated June 13, 1918, may be found in CPC 206-B-6.

82. Letter from Chambers to Livesay, June 19, 1918. CPC 206-B-6.

83. Letter from Chambers to Cutforth, July 2, 1918. CPC 206-B-6. Said Chambers: "In the best interests of many simple minded dupes of slim designing scoundrels, who for the furtherance of their own treasonable schemes have represented national duty and national service as Babylonian sin, and who have been convicted of the foul crime of treason, it certainly appears desirable that the law should take its course and that a firm and notable example should be made for the purpose of demonstrating that the laws of Canada specially designed for the safety and protection of this country during the continuance of its great effort on behalf of righteousness and human freedom are not to be lightly flaunted and set at naught."

84. Letter from T. R. Slaught, Crown Attorney of Norfolk County,

Simcoe, Ontario, to Chambers, July 10, 1918. CPC 206-B-6.

86. *Ibid.*

85. *Victoria Daily Colonist,* June 11, 1918.

87. Letter from Aldham to Chambers, June 18, 1918. CPC 206-B-6.

88. George Naish, *The Early Years.*

89. Letter from Chambers to R. Macdonald, editor of the *Patriot* (Charlottetown, P.E.I.), July 11, 1918. CPC 206-B-6.

90. Letter from Chambers to Aldham, July 1, 1918. CPC 206-B-6. A general notice had been sent to all newspapers on June 22 ordering them not to accept Bible Student advertisements.

91. Letter from Chambers to Burrell, July 13, 1918. CPC 206-B-6. Chambers wrote: "Convinced that the only way to deal with this most disturbing and dangerous propaganda is to forbid the circulation of all books, periodicals, pamphlets and other publications of this organization, I consequently have the honour to recommend that a warrant be issued forbidding the possession in Canada of any and all publications printed by or under the auspices of the International Bible Students' Association, the Watch Tower Bible and Tract Society, and the Associated Bible Students."

92. *Canada Gazette,* July 20, 1918, p. 259.

93. Letter from I. C. Edwards to Chambers, July 8, 1918. CPC 206-B-6.

94. Letter from Malcolm Reid, chief inspector of immigration for British Columbia, to Chambers, July 11, 1918. CPC 206-B-6.

95. Letter from Police Chief Langley of Victoria, British Columbia, to Chambers, August 23, 1918. CPC 206-B-6.

96. *Vancouver World,* August 21, 1918.

97. Under-Secretary of State Thomas Mulvey asked to have secret-service agents visit Bible Student meetings in the West. Memorandum for Colonel Chambers from Ben Deacon, September 1, 1918. CPC 206-B-6.

98. Letter from Langley to Chambers, August 21, 1918. CPC 206-B-6.

99. Letter from Chambers to Langley, August 27, 1918. Letter from Chambers to Mulvey, August 27, 1918. Both in CPC 206-B-6.

100. Letter from Mulvey to Chambers, August 28, 1918. CPC 206-B-6.

101. *Ibid.* Letter from Chambers to Sir Percy Sherwood, August 29, 1918. CPC 206-B-6.

102. Sherwood to Chambers, August 31, 1918, CPC 206-B-6. Sherwood

did indicate, however, that the police had already asked for amendments to federal legislation which would make the wearing of IBSA buttons illegal. Without such amendments the police could do nothing and, evidently, the government did not think highly of banning buttons.

103. Letter from Campbell to Chambers, September 10, 1918. Telegram from Campbell to Chambers, September 13, 1918. Both in CPC 206-B-6.

104. Telegram from Campbell to Chambers, September 17, 1918. CPC 206-B-6.

105. Letter from Chambers to the Minister of Justice, September 13, 1918. CPC 206-B-6.

106. Letter from E. L. Newcombe, Deputy Minister of Justice, to Chambers, September 28, 1918. CPC 206-B-6.

107. *Ibid.*

108. Letter from Chambers to Newcombe, October 1, 1918. CPC 206-B-6.

109. Examples can be found in a North West Mounted Police report dated December 23, 1918, as found in CPC 206-B-6, and the *Victoria Daily Colonist*, February 23, 1919.

110. Jehovah's Witnesses from southern Saskatchewan still recall the activities of C. R. Day, a customs and immigration officer at East Poplar River, who broke up a Bible Student meeting and deported a pilgrim speaker to the United States.

111. Except in one or two cases, Bible Students were most respectful in their letters to Chambers and other public officials.

112. *Victoria Daily Colonist*, September 1, 1918.

113. Letters from Sutherland to Chambers, January 17, February 17, and March 24, 1919. Chambers's assistant to Sutherland, January 24, 1919. Chambers to acting Under-Secretary of State Colson, February 28, 1919. Colson to Chambers, March 1, 1919. All in CPC 206-B-6. Chambers finally closed the matter by assuming that the police must have been right all along in seizing the Bible in question.

114. Postal officials, Chambers, Aldham, and Chambers's U.S. contact were involved in this matter for nearly a month. The correspondence may be found in CPC 206-B-6.

115. Dated April 2, 1919. CPC 206-B-6.

116. Dated April 7, 1919.

117. Dated July 25, 1919. CPC 206-B-6.

118. In CPC 206-B-6.

119. Letter from Chambers to T. D'Arcy Finn, news editor of the *Ottawa Citizen*, November 23, 1918. CPC 206-B-6.

120. Letter from Chambers to G. C. Wilson, MP, March 26, 1919. CPC 206-B-6.

121. Letter from the Department of the Postmaster General to Chambers, April 24, 1919. CPC 206-B-6.

122. The Watch Tower's letter, Harding's reply, and RNWMP Assistant Controller Col. C. F. Hamilton's letter to Chambers, November 27, 1919, plus Chambers's reply to Hamilton may be found in CPC 206-B-6.

123. Royal North West Mounted Police report, November 29, 1919, which may be found in CPC 206-B-6.

124. *Golden Age*, September 29, 1920. Letter from Hamilton to Chambers, December 17, 1919. CPC 206-B-6.

125. The censorship orders based on the War Measures Act were repealed. Notice of this action appeared in the *Regina Leader Post*, December 22, 1919.

126. Dated January 12, 1920. CPC 206-B-6.

127. In CPC 206-B-6.

CHAPTER 4

1. *New York Tribune*, June 22, 1918.

2. *Jehovah's Witnesses in the Divine Purpose* (Brooklyn, N.Y.: Watch Tower Bible and Tract Society, 1959), p. 85.

3. *Ibid.*, pp. 85, 86.

4. *Ibid. St. Paul Enterprise*, March 18, 1919.

5. *Rutherford* v. *the United States*, 258 F. 855, 863 as quoted in *Jehovah's Witnesses in the Divine Purpose*, pp. 86, 87. A. H. Macmillan, *Faith on the March* (Englewood Cliffs, N.J.: Prentice-Hall, Inc., 1957), pp. 107, 109.

6. *Watch Tower*, 1920, p. 162.

7. *Jehovah's Witnesses in the Divine Purpose*, p. 88; Macmillan, p. 112.

8. Alan Rogerson, *Millions Now Living Will Never Die* (London: Constable and Company, Ltd., 1969), p. 45; *Jehovah's Witnesses in the Divine Purpose*, pp. 88–90.

9. *Jehovah's Witnesses in the Divine Purpose*, pp. 91–93.
10. Macmillan, pp. 117, 118; *Jehovah's Witnesses in the Divine Purpose*, p. 95, 96.
11. *Watch Tower*, 1926, pp. 3–8.
12. *Watch Tower*, 1927, pp. 55, 56.
13. Rogerson, pp. 39, 40.
14. *Ibid.*
15. George Naish, *The Early Years* (an unpublished manuscript, 1971).
16. *Watch Tower*, 1922, pp. 200, 201; 1925, p. 263.
17. During the period in question practically every *Yearbook* published by the Watch Tower Society showed increases in the numbers of publications printed and the numbers of new persons associating with the Society. By 1928 some 21,776 Bible Student "class workers" were engaged in public preaching in the United States while, at the same time, 9,705 were involved in that work in Germany. *1929 Yearbook of the International Bible Students Association*, pp 55, 119.
18. *The International Bible Student Year-book for 1922*, pp. 19–21.
19. *Ibid.*, pp. 35–37.
20. *International Bible Students Association Yearbook for 1925*, pp. 16–22.
21. *Ibid.*
22. *Ibid.*
23. Joseph Hupalo, *A History of the Wakaw Congregation* (an unpublished manuscript, 1968). Roy Hook, *Memoirs of the Hook Family* (an unpublished manuscript, 1971).
24. Hook.
25. *IBSA Yearbooks* for 1927, pp. 65, 66; 1928, pp. 72–74; 1929, p. 101.
26. *IBSA Yearbooks* for 1927, pp. 64, 65; 1928, p. 72; 1929, p. 98.
27. *IBSA Yearbook* for 1929, pp. 96–98.
28. *IBSA Yearbooks* for 1931, pp. 113, 114; 1932, pp. 102, 103.
29. *Watch Tower*, 1920, p. 374.
30. J. F. Rutherford, *Deliverance* (Brooklyn, N.Y.: Watch Tower Bible and Tract Society, 1926), p. 269.
31. J. F. Rutherford, *Creation* (Brooklyn, N.Y.: Watch Tower Bible and Tract Society, 1927), p. 300.
32. J. F. Rutherford, *Life* (Brooklyn, N.Y.: Watch Tower Bible and

Tract Society, 1929), p. 211.

33. During Pastor Russell's day, early Bible Students were concerned over the question of whether wine or unfermented grape juice should be used in the celebration of the Memorial of the Lord's Supper. It was quickly decided that since the Bible indicated that the word "wine" meant an alcoholic beverage, fermented wine would have to be used. Since that time Jehovah's Witnesses have had no restriction against the moderate use of alcoholic beverages.

34. *Jehovah's Witnesses in the Divine Purpose*, pp. 101–19.

35. Letter from J. F. Rutherford to the Department of Labour, Ottawa, September 13, 1920, entitled, "A Protest—Malicious Libel of Bible Students Induced by Maddened Clergy".

36. J. F. Rutherford, *Liberty to Preach: Points and Authorities in Re Sunday and License Laws as Applied to the International Bible Students Association* (Toronto: International Bible Students Association of Canada, undated), p. 12.

37. *Ibid.*

38. *Ibid.*, p. 18.

39. *Ibid.*, pp. 17, 18.

40. *Ibid.*

41. *Golden Age*, June 12, 1929.

42. *Ibid.*; *Le Soleil*, August 29, 1924.

43. *Golden Age*, June 12, 1929.

44. *Montreal Standard*, April 18, 1925.

45. *Golden Age*, June 12, 1929.

46. *Ibid.*

47. *Rex* v. *Kinler*, (1925) 63 Que. s.c. 483. The two women charged were Myra Kinler and Janet McCoy.

48. *Golden Age*, June 12, 1929.

49. Rutherford, *Liberty to Preach*, p. 16.

50. *Ibid.*, pp. 16, 17.

CHAPTER 5

1. *Jehovah's Witnesses in the Divine Purpose* (Brooklyn, N.Y.: Watch Tower Bible and Tract Society, 1959), pp. 121–23; *Debates of the House of Commons of Canada*, 1928, Vol. III, pp. 3618–25, 3644–51, 3654–72; *Golden Age*, June 13, 1928. *1929 Yearbook of the Inter-*

national Bible Students Association, pp. 93–96.

2. *Golden Age,* June 13, 1928. *Debates,* 1928, Vol. III, pp. 3664–65.

3. Letter from J. Macham, radio inspector at Saskatoon, to C. P. Edwards, director of radio at Ottawa, August 17, 1925. M&F-IBSA.

4. *1929 Yearbook,* p. 93.

5. J. J. Maloney, *Darkness, Dawn and Daybreak* (Vancouver, printed privately, undated).

6. Maloney.

7. Correspondence in M&F-IBSA; George Naish, *The Early Years* (an unpublished manuscript, 1971).

8. Correspondence in M&F-IBSA; Naish.

9. Dated January 7, 1928; M&F-IBSA.

10. Published in the *Star* of February 10, 1927.

11. In M&F-IBSA.

12. In M&F-IBSA.

13. *Ibid.*

14. Edward's memorandum and Johnston's statement are the first serious expression of governmental displeasure with CHUC to be found in M&F-IBSA. See also *Debates,* 1928, Vol. III, pp. 3621–24.

15. *Debates,* 1928, Vol. II, p. 1951; Vol. III, p. 3666. Walter Salter made a careful analysis of the filed correspondence and submitted an affidavit giving evidence for the Bible Students' position in the matter to Members of Parliament. According to Salter some of the statements in the letters submitted by Radio Inspector S. J. Ellis of Toronto to the Department of Marine and Fisheries were false, based on "hearsay and gossip . . . without foundation in fact". T. T. Lardner used some of Salter's statement in the House of Commons and the Minister of Marine and Fisheries made no attempt to deny Salter's allegations. More seriously, A. A. Heaps accused Cardin himself of unfairly trying to collect additional anti-Bible Student correspondence after J. S. Woodsworth had asked to have tabled the materials on which the Minister had based his decision not to renew the IBSA stations' licences. Said Heaps: "In the first place there is a letter sent from the Department of Marine and Fisheries, dated on the 12th of April, when the motion, I believe, was already on the order paper, practically asking for information against the International Bible Students. A letter came back on the 17th day

of April. I find also several other letters on this file dated about the same period. In other words, the department cancelled the licenses, and after they had done so, they looked around for evidence to justify them in taking their action."

16. *Debates*, 1928, Vol. III, p. 3644.

17. *Globe and Mail* (Toronto) March 17, 1928. *1928 Yearbook*, pp. 93–95. Frank W. Peers, *The Politics of Canadian Broadcasting— 1920–1951* (Toronto: University of Toronto Press, 1969), pp. 29– 34.

18. *Debates*, 1928, Vol. III, p. 3348.

19. *Ibid.*, pp. 3248, 3294, 3295, 3348.

20. *1929 Yearbook*, p. 94. *Golden Age*, June 13, 1928; *Debates*, 1928, Vol. III, pp. 3649–50.

21. *Golden Age*, June 13, 1928; *Debates*, 1928, Vol. III, pp. 3649, 3650.

22. Dated March 15, 1928. M&F-IBSA.

23. Dated April 2, 1928, M&F-IBSA.

24. In M&F-IBSA.

25. *Ibid.*

26. The main issues which upset Saskatchewan Protestants were the school and immigration questions which were used by Orangemen and Klansmen against the Liberals. However, the refusal to renew IBSA radio licences undoubtedly seemed one of the most outstanding and obvious of Catholic pressure tactics, especially since such refusal had come, in part at least, over the fact that CHUC had rented time to J. J. Maloney. The importance of religion in the election of the Anderson government is a commonly acknowledged fact. J. F. C. Wright, *Saskatchewan* (Toronto: McClelland and Stewart, 1955), pp. 212–14. J. P. Kyba, *The Saskatchewan General Election of 1929* (unpublished master's thesis, University of Saskatchewan, Saskatoon, 1964); William Calderwood, *The Rise and Fall of the Ku Klux Klan in Saskatchewan* (unpublished master's thesis, University of Saskatchewan, Saskatoon, 1968), Chapter 9.

27. *Debates*, 1928, Vol. III, pp. 3618–25, 3644–47, 3667–72.

28. *Debates*, 1928, Vol II, p. 2049.

29. *Debates*, 1928, Vol. III, pp. 3618, 3619, 3644, 3645; *Golden Age*, June 13, 1928.

30. *Debates*, 1928, Vol. III, pp. 3654–59, 3672.

31. *Golden Age*, June 13, 1928.
32. The article in question, dated May 8, 1928, appeared in the *Golden Age* of June 13, 1928.
33. *Debates*, 1928, Vol. III, pp. 3663, 3664.
34. *Ibid.*, pp. 3659–63, 3368–72. Baptists, Catholics, the Christian and Missionary Alliance, and the United Church of Canada, all continued to hold radio licences.
35. *Ibid.*, p. 3669.
36. *Ibid.*, p. 3670.
37. *Ibid.*, p. 3665.
38. *Ibid.*, p. 3672.
39. Peers, pp. 29–34.
40. *1933 Yearbook*, pp. 106, 107.
41. *Debates*, 1932–33, Vol. III, p. 2619; *Golden Age*, March 1, 1933.
42. *Watch Tower*, 1927, pp. 307, 308.
43. Peers, p. 120; *Debates*, 1932–33, Vol. IV, p. 4150.
44. Quoted in the *Golden Age*, March 1, 1933. See also the *Winnipeg Free Press*, January 28, 1933.
45. Reprinted in the *Golden Age*, March 1, 1933.
46. *Debates*, 1932–33, Vol. V, p. 4672.
47. *1934 Yearbook*, pp. 84–86.
48. *Ibid.*
49. *Winnipeg Free Press*, January 28, 1933.
50. February 4, 1933.
51. February 18, 1933.
52. January 20, 1933.
53. February 4, 1933.
54. February 23, 1933.
55. *Ibid.*
56. *Debates*, 1932–33, Vol. IV, p. 4151.
57. *Ibid.*
58. *Debates*, 1932–33, Vol. III, p. 2619.
59. *Ibid.*, Vol. IV, p. 3581.
60. *Ibid.*, pp. 3631, 3632.
61. *Ibid.*, p. 4149.
62. *Ibid.*, p. 4150.
63. *Ibid.*

64. *Ibid.*

65. *Golden Age,* May 24, 1933.

66. Edward Noseworthy and other Witnesses at the Toronto offices of the Watch Tower Society indicate that Woodworth made this clear at a Witness convention held shortly after the battle with Charlesworth and the radio commission.

67. *Debates,* 1932–1933, Vol. v, p. 5156.

CHAPTER 6

1. *Jehovah's Witnesses in the Divine Purpose* (Brooklyn, N.Y.: Watch Tower Bible and Tract Society, Inc., 1959), pp. 129, 134–38; David R. Manwaring, *Render Unto Caesar* (Chicago: The University of Chicago Press, 1962), pp. 23, 24; A. H. Macmillan, *Faith on the March* (Englewood Cliffs, N.J.: Prentice-Hall, Inc., 1957), pp. 163, 164.

2. *Jehovah's Witnesses in the Divine Purpose,* pp. 129–33; Manwaring, pp. 26–28; Macmillan, p. 164–71.

3. *Jehovah's Witnesses in the Divine Purpose,* p. 141. J. S. Conway, *The Nazi Persecution of the Churches 1933–1945* (New York: Basic Books, Inc., 1968), p. 195.

4. Guenter Lewy, *The Catholic Church and Nazi Germany* (New York: McGraw-Hill Book Company, 1965), p. 43.

5. The following declaration was made by Karl R. A. Wittig and signed before a notary at Frankfurt am Main, November 13, 1947: "DECLARATION—On October 7, 1934, having been previously summoned, I visited Dr. Wilhelm Frick, at that time Minister of the Interior of the Reich and Prussia, in his home office of the Reich, located in Berlin, 6 am Köenigsplatz, since I was a plenipotentiary of General Ludendorff. I was to accept communications, contents of which were an attempt to persuade General Ludendorff to discontinuance of his objection to the Nazi regime. During my discussion with Dr. Frick, Hitler suddenly appeared and began taking part in the conversation. When our discussion obligatorily dealt with the action against the International Bible Students Association [Jehovah's Witnesses] in Germany up until now, Dr. Frick showed Hitler a number of telegrams protesting against the Third Reich's persecution of the Bible Students, saying: 'If the Bible Students do

not immediately get in line we will act against them using the strongest means.' After which Hitler jumped to his feet and with clenched fists hysterically screamed: 'This brood will be exterminated in Germany!' Four years after this discussion I was able, by my own observations, to convince myself, during my seven years in protective custody in the hell of the Nazis' concentration-camps at Sachsenhausen, Flossenburg and Mauthausen—I was in prison until released by the Allies—that Hitler's outburst of anger was not just an idle·threat. No other group of prisoners of the named concentration-camps was exposed to the sadism of the SS-soldiery in such a fashion as the Bible Students were. It was a sadism marked by an unending chain of physical and mental tortures, the like of which no language in the world can express." *Jehovah's Witnesses in the Divine Purpose*, pp. 141–43, 162–74.

Conway claims: "Foremost amongst the opponents of Nazism were the Jehovah's Witnesses, of whom a higher proportion (97 percent) suffered some form of persecution than any of the other churches." Conway, p. 196.

6. *Jehovah's Witnesses in the Divine Purpose*, p. 129.

7. *Ibid.*, p. 132; *Intolerance* (Brooklyn, N.Y.: Watch Tower Bible and Tract Society, Inc., 1933).

8. *1934 Yearbook of Jehovah's Witnesses*, pp. 46, 47; *Jehovah's Witnesses in the Divine Purpose*, p. 133; Manwaring, p. 28.

9. *Jehovah's Witnesses in the Divine Purpose*, p. 135.

10. *1934 Yearbook*, pp. 127–46.

11. *1935 Yearbook*, pp. 118, 119.

12. *Ibid.*, p. 119.

13. *1934 Yearbook*, pp. 81, 82.

14. *1935 Yearbook*, pp. 83, 84. *Quebec Chronicle-Telegram*, October 3 and 4, 1933. Kenneth Johnstone, "Who Exactly Are These Jehovah's Witnesses?" *Montreal Standard*, January 4, 1947.

15. *Quebec Chronicle-Telegram*, October 17, 1933.

16. Johnstone. *1935 Yearbook*, pp. 83, 84.

17. *Quebec Chronicle-Telegram*, October 3, 1933.

18. *Ibid.*, October 4, 1933.

19. *Ibid.* See also the *Chronicle-Telegram* of October 5, 1933.

20. Johnstone. *Quebec Chronicle-Telegram*, October 17, 1933.

21. *Ibid.*, October 18, 1933.

22. *Ibid.*

23. *Ibid.* October 6, 1933.

24. Quoted in the *Quebec Chronicle-Telegram*, October 18, 1933.

25. *1935 Yearbook*, pp. 83, 84. Johnstone.

26. *1935 Yearbook*, p. 83.

27. *Ibid.*, p. 86.

28. *Quebec Chronicle-Telegram*, October 21 and 25, 1933.

29. *1934 Yearbook*, pp. 81, 82.

30. *Ibid.*

31. *Jehovah's Witnesses in the Divine Purpose*, pp. 139, 140.

32. Conway, p. 197; Manwaring, pp. 30–33; *Jehovah's Witnesses in the Divine Purpose*, pp. 143, 144.

33. As David Manwaring shows, though the flag salute had begun in the United States as early as 1898, and various religious groups had opposed it in several states during the 1920s, it did not become a common practice in most of the country until the early 1930s. It was the Witnesses' resistance to nationalism as a form of idolatory that caused them in both the United States and Canada, as in Germany, to refuse to participate in the ceremony. Manwaring, pp. 1–16, 30–33.

34. *Ibid.*; J. F. Rutherford, *Loyalty* (Brooklyn, N.Y.: Watch Tower Bible and Tract Society, 1935); *Jehovah's Witnesses in the Divine Purpose*, pp. 143, 144.

35. See Chapter 7, pp. 130, 131, 137–43.

36. The Witnesses also objected to other patriotic exercises at this time. On March 16, 1937, "twelve youthful Witnesses in Quarryville, N.B., refused to sing the National Anthem". Johnstone.

37. *Jehovah's Witnesses in the Divine Purpose*, pp. 143, 144. Marley Cole, *Jehovah's Witnesses* (New York: Vantage Press, 1955), pp. 102–8.

38. *Jehovah's Witnesses in the Divine Purpose*, pp. 189, 190. The zone conventions, later to be known as circuit assemblies, were placed on a semi-annual basis following the Second World War.

39. *1936 Yearbook*, p. 111.

40. *1940 Yearbook*, p. 125.

41. *Ibid.*

42. Kenneth Johnstone says that many referred to the time during which Jehovah's Witnesses used the portable phonographs as the "Pest Period". Although not very effective as a teaching device, the phonograph probably caught householders' attention in a way that oral preaching could not have done.

43. *1938 Yearbook*, p. 113.

44. *1937 Yearbook*, pp. 126–28. *1938 Yearbook*, pp. 108, 109.

45. Interview with Mr. and Mrs. Frank Wainwright, April 1972, and interview with Roberta Davies, August 1973.

46. *1938 Yearbook*, pp. 108, 109.

47. *1937 Yearbook*, pp. 127, 128.

48. *1936 Yearbook*, pp. 110, 111.

49. *Ibid.*, pp. 109, 110.

50. *Brodie and Barrett* v. *the King*, [1936] S.C.R. 118; 65, C.C.C. 289; 3 D.L.R. 81.

51. *Duval et al.* v. *the King*, (1938) 64 Quebec K.B. 270.

52. *Ottawa Journal*, February 1, 1937.

53. *1938 Yearbook*, p. 17.

54. *Statutes of Quebec* (1937), Chapter 11.

55. *Maclean's*, August 1, 1937.

56. *1939 Yearbook*, p. 126.

57. *1940 Yearbook*, p. 130.

58. *1939 Yearbook*, p. 126; David K. Kernaghan, *Freedom of Religion in the Province of Quebec with Particular Reference to the Jews, Jehovah's Witnesses and Church-State Relations* (unpublished dissertation, Duke University, Durham, N.C., 1966), pp. 201, 218.

59. *1940 Yearbook*, p. 130.

60. *Ibid.*, pp. 129, 130. See also an open letter from Gerald Barry to the Attorney General of the Province of Quebec, March 27, 1939. In EL-TJ.

61. *1940 Yearbook*, p. 130.

62. *Golden Age*, July 15 and 26, 1936. *Jehovah's Witnesses in the Divine Purpose*, pp. 136–38. Manwaring, p. 24.

63. *1940 Yearbook*, p. 74.

64. *Ibid.*

65. J. F. Rutherford, *Fascism or Freedom* (Brooklyn, N.Y.: Watch Tower Bible and Tract Society, 1939), pp. 18–22.

66. The riot was heard around the world. Not only did many Jehovah's Witnesses tied into the New York convention by long-distance telephone to twenty-eight conventions in Australia, Britain, and Hawaii hear the shouting, but the whole event was recorded on the phonograph record "Government and Peace" and later replayed at homes throughout the English-speaking world.

67. Conway, pp. 196–99. Franz Zuercher, *Kreuzzug gegen das Christentum* (Zurich: Europa-Verlag, 1938). Eugen Kogon, *The Theory and Practice of Hell* (New York: Berkley Medallion Books, 1958), pp. 42, 43. *1939 Yearbook*, pp. 128–37, 148–51. The *1974 Yearbook of Jehovah's Witnesses* also carries a complete history of the Nazi persecution of German Witnesses. Upon receipt of a copy of *Kreuzzug gegen das Christentum*, Dr. Thomas Mann wrote the following letter: "I still owe you my thanks not merely as an act of politeness, but also a debt of the heart for the present of your book, *Crusade Against Christianity*. I have read your book and its terrible documentation with the deepest emotion. I cannot describe the mixed feeling of abhorrence and loathing which filled my heart while perusing these records of human degredation and abominable cruelty. Human speech fails in the presence of such unspeakable perversity which is revealed in the pages on which the awful sufferings of these innocent men and women, who firmly hold fast to their faith, are recorded."

68. *1939 Yearbook*, pp. 151–53.

69. *1940 Yearbook*, pp. 81, 82. *Jehovah's Witnesses in the Divine Purpose*, pp. 152, 153. The *1973 Yearbook of Jehovah's Witnesses*, pp. 117–19, gives a historical account of mob action against British Witnesses just before the outbreak of the Second World War.

70. *Face the Facts* (Brooklyn, N.Y.: Watch Tower Bible and Tract Society, 1938), pp. 60, 61.

71. Rutherford, *Fascism or Freedom*, p. 12.

72. *Jehovah's Witnesses in the Divine Purpose*, p. 145, indicates that placard marches began in 1936 in New Jersey. They, like the use of the portable phonograph, gave the Witnesses a prominence far out of proportion to their numbers.

73. Letter from Cabana to Minister of Justice Lapointe, March 8, 1939. According to his own statement, Cabana was able to get the help

of the RCMP in seizing the Witnesses' literature, probably quite illegally.

74. Letter from Cabana to Lapointe, January 13, 1939. EL-TJ.

75. *Ibid.* Letters from Cabana to Lapointe, February 15 and March 8,
1939. EL-TJ.

76. Dated March 6, 1939. EL-TJ.

77. Letter from Maurice Bernier, secretary to the Minister of Justice,
to Florent Hébert, secretary for L'Union des Jeunesses Catholiques
Canadiennes de Sherbrooke, March 29, 1939. EL-TJ.

78. Dated March 14, 1939. EL-TJ.

79. A letter from Maurice Bernier to N. H. MacDonald, private secretary to the Postmaster General, March 29, 1939, states that Pigeon's
letter was being forwarded under the same cover for "whatever
action . . . deemed advisable". EL-TJ.

80. In fact, so many references to the Witnesses' use of the mails appear
that it is obvious that there was a general campaign to force the
government to deny postal services to the Watch Tower Society. It
is also evident that Roman Catholics in general equated criticism of
their church with "sedition", a term used time and again in the
protests cited above.

81. Copies of such correspondence may be found in EL-TJ.

82. October 1939.

83. *1939 Yearbook*, p. 126.

84. *1940 Yearbook*, p. 126.

85. *Ibid.*

86. *Ibid.*, p. 129.

CHAPTER 7

1. Interview with Ralph Brodie, August 1973.

2. *"It Must Be Stopped!"* (Toronto: Watch Tower Bible and Tract
Society, 1940). *1941 Yearbook of Jehovah's Witnesses*, pp. 158, 159.

3. *"It Must Be Stopped!"* One non-Witness wrote to Minister of Justice Lapointe concerning Justice Greenshields' remarks: "If this
does not show complete pre-judgment and partisanship—you would
find it hard to find a parallel unless it be that of a judge trying the
case of a nonconformist preacher in the middle of the seventeenth
century.

"Such imbecility should certainly be removed from the bench."
Letter from Alfred Myerson to Ernest Lapointe, February 15, 1940.
EL-TJ.

4. *1941 Yearbook*, p. 159.

5. 310 U.S. 586, 60 S. ct. 1010, 87 L. Ed. 1375.

6. David R. Manwaring, *Render Unto Caesar* (Chicago: The University of Chicago Press, 1962), pp. 163–86.

7. *Debates of the House of Commons of Canada*, 1940, Vol. I, p. 729. Dr. Bruce claimed a list of "subversive" organizations, read in the House of Commons on June 12, 1940, had been given to him by the police.

8. A copy of the resolution may be found in EL-TJ.

9. A copy of McMurray's letter may be found in EL-TJ.

10. Letter from Lapointe to Crerar, July 4, 1940. EL-TJ.

11. "Attendu que sous l'empire du règlement numéro 39c des Règlements concernant la défense du Canada, certains organismes ont été déclarés illégaux y compris toute association ou société, tout groupe ou organisme que le Gouverneur en conseil a déclaré illégal par un avis publié dans la *Gazette du Canada*; et

"Attendu que le ministre de la Justice signale qu'il existe un organisme connu sous le nom de 'Témoins de Jéhovah' [Jehovah's Witnesses] qui est jugé être d'une nature subversive et qu'il est opportun de déclarer ledit organisme illégal;

"Par conséquent, à la recommandation du ministre de la Justice et sous l'empire des dispositions de l'alinéa (6) du paragraphe (1) du règlement numéro 39c des Règlements concernant la défense du Canada, il plaît à Son Excellence le Gouverneur général en conseil de déclarer illégal l'organisme connu sous le nom de 'Témoins de Jéhovah.'

"Il plaît en outre à Son Excellence en conseil de décréter qu'un avis à cet effet soit publié dans la *Gazette du Canada*." *Canada Gazette*, Vol. 74 (July–September, 1940), p. 87, under "Arrêtes en Conseil", dated Thursday, July 4, 1940.

12. In EL-TJ.

13. In EL-TJ.

14. Letter from Lapointe to Gallagher, June 18, 1940. Letter from Maurice Bernier, private secretary to the Minister of Justice, to

Commissioner S. T. Wood, RCMP, June 18, 1940. Letter from Maurice Bernier to Charpentier, June 20, 1940. Copies of all three letters may be found in EL-TJ.

15. In EL-TJ.
16. Letter from Charpentier and Eggleston to Lapointe, June 28, 1940. EL-TJ.
17. *Calgary Herald*, June 10, 1940. Letter from Grote Stirling, MP, to Lapointe, June 22, 1940. EL-TJ.
18. Stirling to Lapointe, June 22, 1940.
19. See Appendix C.
20. EL-TJ. See Appendix C.
21. EL-TJ. See Appendix C.
22. Letter from Paul Bernier to Maurice Bernier, July 8, 1940. EL-TJ. See Appendix C.
23. *Debates*, 1940, Vol. II, p. 1646.
24. *Defence of Canada Regulations* (Consolidation, 1941), Section 39C, pp. 54, 55.
25. *1941 Yearbook*, pp. 165, 166.
26. "I draw your attention to the fact that the group of organizations—Jehovah's witnesses, Watch Tower Bible and Tract Society, International Bible Students Ass'n, etc., had considerable property seized. The premises known as 38-40 Irwin Avenue are worth between twenty-five and fifty thousand dollars. Their premises in Saskatoon known as the Regent Hall would be of equal value and there was property in Winnipeg and elsewhere of lesser values.

    "These organizations, engaged in the Christian work of preaching the Gospel, will likely have lost property aggregating $100,000." Letter from Charles Morrell to Sir Ellsworth Flavelle, March 29, 1943, a copy of which may be found at the Toronto offices of the Watch Tower Society.
27. *Debates*, 1941, Vol. II, p. 1190.
28. *1942 Yearbook*, p. 157. *Edmonton Bulletin*, December 10, 1940. There is much correspondence regarding this "blitz" in EL-TJ and many press reports concerning it appeared throughout the nation.
29. Interviews with Jack Nathan, Ralph Brodie, and George Naish, August 1973.
30. *Edmonton Bulletin*, July 9, 1940.

31. Kenneth Johnstone, "Who Exactly Are These Jehovah's Witnesses?" *Montreal Standard*, January 4, 1947.

32. *Ibid.*

33. A typewritten memorandum from Charles Morrell to Percy Chapman, some time in 1942.

34. Typewritten report of "Conditions Involving the Children of Jehovah's Witnesses in Hamilton, Ontario, 1940–41" from the Toronto offices of the Watch Tower Society. See also the *Globe and Mail* (Toronto) for September 12 and 13, 1940.

35. *Globe and Mail*, September 19, 1940.

36. *Ibid.* The investigators under Police Inspector E. D. L. Hammond pointed out: "The anthem issue is not so clear, inasmuch as the singing of the National Anthem is a recognized part of the school opening exercises. At the same time it is recognized as a principle that students whose religious beliefs are not in harmony with the Protestant form of opening exercises may be excused from taking part in those exercises."

37. *Consolation*, November 7, 1945.

38. In December 1943, one Witness mother, Mrs. Violet Archer of New Westminster, British Columbia, wrote: "Our children Wilfred, 14, Kathleen, 12, and Gwendolyn, 9, have been out of school three years this coming March. Gwendolyn had only six months schooling."

    Consolation stated in November 1945 that over forty Witness children were suspended throughout Canada, twenty-six in Hamilton alone. In fact, probably twice that many were expelled from classes and many more were voluntarily placed in private schools to avoid difficulties. However, in many places such as Toronto, school officials simply ignored the flag-salute issue and Witness children continued to attend school without any problem. Letter from Violet Archer to Jehovah's Witnesses of Canada, December 30, 1943. *Consolation*, November 7, 1945; *Globe and Mail*, September 19, 1940.

39. Letter from William Aberhart to Mrs. C. McGregor, September 26, 1940.

40. Transcript of record in *Rex* v. *Clarence and Agnes Leeson* as held in the County Police Court for the County of Middlesex, November 6, 1940.

41. *Ibid.*
42. *Ibid.* Letter from Clarence Leeson to the author, September 21, 1973.
43. Leeson to author. *London Daily Free Press*, October 12 and November 6, 1940. *Rex* v. *Clarence and Agnes Leeson*, unreported.
44. *Rex* v. *Clarence and Agnes Leeson. London Daily Free Press*, November 29, 1940. Leeson to author.
45. *London Daily Free Press*, December 5, 1940, and January 30, 1941; Leeson to author.
46. *Edmonton Journal*, November 28, 1940.
47. *Rex* v. *Clark*, [1941] 3 w.w.r. 229, 234 (Man. Police Ct.); [1941] 4 d.l.r. 299. (Man. c.a.).
48. Judgment of H. A. Burbidge, January 6, 1941. "Conditions involving the Children of Jehovah's Witnesses in Hamilton, Ontario." Many references to these events appeared in the press throughout Canada. See for example the *Edmonton Journal* of October 9, 10, 22, and 30, 1940.
49. *Edmonton Journal*, December 7, 1940.
50. Letter from Harold Cox of Langbank, Saskatchewan, to Colonel Ralston, May 17, 1941, in el-tj. Cox, a school trustee, complained bitterly to the federal authorities about the Saskatchewan education minister's policy. Many statements concerning this policy may be found in the files of the Department of Education in the Archives of Saskatchewan.
51. For example see the *Edmonton Journal*, December 7, 1940.
52. *Ibid.*
53. Much pressure on Jehovah's Witnesses over the flag salute and other issues came from provincially organized veterans' organizations such as the Saskatchewan Veterans' Civil Security Corps. British settlers such as Harold Cox (cited in note 50 above) were frequently the most vocal adversaries of the Witnesses in many communities, a point often emphasized by individual Jehovah's Witnesses in many areas of western Canada even today. Many of these Britons were, of course, former soldiers or officers in the Imperial Army.
54. *Canada Gazette*, Vol. 74 (January–March 1941), pp. 2681, 2682.
55. *Ibid.*, pp. 2846, 2847.
56. In a number of documented instances the Royal Canadian Mounted

Police brought pressure on employers to dismiss Jehovah's Witnesses and even their non-Witness relatives. Frequently this was done in the name of national security, but not always.

57. *1942 Yearbook,* p. 158.

58. *Ibid.*

59. *Edmonton Bulletin,* September 9 and 13, 1941. *Edmonton Journal,* September 10, 11, and 13, 1941. Further details on this case may be found in File 1231 (Box 117) of the Files of the Province of Alberta at the Provincial Archives, Edmonton.

60. A copy of this letter may be found in EL-TJ.

61. *Debates,* 1940, Vol. I, pp. 752, 753; 1941, Vol. II, p. 1206.

62. *Ibid.,* 1940, Vol. II, p. 1068.

63. *Ibid.,* pp. 1070, 1071, 1078, 1079, 1206, 1207, 1215. According to the *Edmonton Bulletin* of July 5, 1940, some 117 United States periodicals had been denied entry into Canada during the war and eight or ten more were about to be prohibited.

64. *Debates,* 1941, Vol. II, pp. 1069, 1070, 1188–201, 1203–17. The pamphlet contained remarks made by Mrs. Nielsen speaking in the House of Commons.

65. *Ibid.,* pp. 1067, 1069, 1070, 1188–201, 1203–17, 1251, 1252.

66. *Ibid.,* pp. 1089, 1189, 1190.

67. *Ibid.* p. 1189.

68. *Ibid.,* p. 1199.

69. *Ibid.,* p. 1190.

70. *Ibid.,* p. 1199.

71. *Toronto Telegram,* May 12, 1942.

72. *1943 Yearbook,* p. 148.

73. *Debates,* 1943, Vol. I, p. 615.

74. Charles Morrell, *Report on the Hearing Before the Select Committee of the House of Commons* (an unpublished report to Percy Chapman, June 27, 1942). This report is on file at the Toronto offices of the Watch Tower Society.

75. The committee recommended "That sub-paragraph 'a' of paragraph 1 of Regulation 39c be amended by striking therefrom: Technocracy Inc.; Jehovah's Witnesses; Watch Tower Bible and Tract Society; International Bible Students Association; Watch Tower Bible and Tract Society Incorporated." It then stated: "Your

Committee believes that it is not now necessary to continue the organizations named in this recommendation as illegal organizations among those listed in Regulation 39c." *Votes and Proceedings of the House of Commons of Canada*, Ottawa, Thursday, July 23, 1942, p. 59.

76. *Debates*, 1943, Vol. i, p. 615.

77. *Ibid.*, p. 606.

78. *Ibid.*

79. Speaking in the Commons, Angus MacInnis stated: "The committee was unanimously in favour of raising the ban on this particular sect, and no evidence was put before the committee by the Department of Justice which indicated that at any time Jehovah's Witnesses should have been declared an illegal organization, nor did the representatives of the department raise any objection to the recommendation made by the committee."

Yet in July 1943, Minister of Justice St. Laurent stated: "I should not like anyone to feel that I would attempt to set up my own views against those of the majority of the house. But from what knowledge I had of what took place last year I did not feel that it was the view of the majority of the house that this recommendation should be implimented, and I felt I was at perfect liberty to wait until the house had expressed its views." *Ibid.*, Vol. i, p. 606; Vol. v, p. 4861.

80. *Ibid.*, Vol. i, p. 615.

81. *Ibid.*, p. 616.

82. Order in council P.C. 1266 as quoted in *Debates*, 1943, Vol. v, p. 5202.

83. *Debates*, 1943, Vol. v, p. 5201.

84. *Ibid.*, p. 5199.

85. *Ibid.*, pp. 4853, 5197–210.

86. *Ibid.*, p. 5199.

87. *Ibid.*

88. *Ibid.*, p. 4853. Speaking in the following year St. Laurent remarked: "This matter was raised at the last session and I stated frankly that I had seen these tracts and they were extracts from the French edition of the Bible published over the name of l'abbé Crampon, which is a well recognized edition that is used by Roman Catholics of the

French language, and there did not seem to be anything but that. It certainly was a mistake to prosecute anyone for distributing copies of pages of the Bible if there was nothing more. There have been overzealous officials in all administrations, and that was certainly something that should not have been done. I may say that it was one of the reasons which made it appear necessary to me to go farther than had first been done in respect of Jehovah's Witnesses." *Ibid.*, 1944, Vol. v, pp. 4861, 4862.

89. *Ibid.*, 1943, Vol. v, p. 4862.

90. *Ibid.*, p. 5202.

91. *Ibid.*

92. *Ibid.*, p. 5200.

93. *Ibid.*, pp. 5204–6.

94. *Ibid.*, pp. 5207, 5208.

95. *Ibid.*

96. *Ibid.*, p. 5209.

97. *Ibid.*, p. 5215.

98. *Ibid.*

99. *Ibid.*

100. *Ibid.*

101. *Ibid.*, pp. 4861, 5205, 5214, 5215. In addition, St. Laurent would not agree to promise that Jehovah's Witnesses would not be prosecuted for writing signed letters to Members of Parliament.

102. *Ibid.*, Vol. i, p. 615.

103. By the spring of 1943 the government even permitted communists to operate through "front" organizations such as the Workers' Election Committee and the Communist Labour Total War Committee. Members of Parliament noted the sharp contrast between governmental policy toward the communists on one hand and Jehovah's Witnesses on the other. *Ibid.*, pp. 606–32.

104. *Jehovah's Witnesses in the Divine Purpose* (Brooklyn, N.Y.: Watch Tower Bible and Tract Society, 1959), pp. 208–11.

105. (1943) 319 U.S. 105.

106. (1942) 316 U.S. 584.

107. (1943) 319 U.S. 583.

108. (1943) 319 U.S. 624.

109. [1943] 67 C.L.R. 116, 124.

110. *Globe and Mail,* February 24, 1943.

111. The *Herald* had editorialized: "The Communist Party has been declared an illegal organization in Canada. Technocracy, Inc., has now won the same treatment. Now Jehovah's Witnesses are under the ban.

"Many Canadians feel this action should have been taken long ago and that these organizations, come what may, must not return.

"In its firm removal of them, democracy loses nothing. The constant infusion of strife and dissension is not an essential quality of democratic life. It is possible—it is imperative even—to have an efficient democracy freed from endless bickering and boring-from-within. There is an obvious distinction between honest criticism and calculated agitation.

"The press and the people of Canada are free to exercise a large measure of criticism. But they are not free to encourage sabotage, and talk dissension.

"The Communists have had their day. They have accomplished nothing useful; they have done a great amount of harm. They stand for nothing but destruction and brutality. They ape the barbarism of their masters in the Kremlin. The same might well be said of the other organizations which Ottawa has declared illegal, and there are still some groups in Canada the government has not yet reached. They were and are parts of our Fifth Column. When we are at peace, they cause uncertainty and instability, a millstone around our necks; when we are at war, they stab us in the back.

"Bury them. Keep them buried for all time." *Calgary Herald,* July 6, 1940.

112. "Order in Council amending the Defence of Canada Regulations (Consolidation) 1942", P.C. 8022, October 14, 1943, as published in *Canadian War Orders and Regulations,* 1943, Vol. IV, No. 3, October 25, 1943, p. 127.

CHAPTER 8

1. J. W. Noseworthy, CCF Member of Parliament for York South, stated: "Will the Minister of Justice explain to the house just what is or wherein lies the difference between the treatment we are meting out to those people and the treatment that is being meted out under

similar circumstances in Germany today? There is this difference. Under the present administration fewer than one thousand Jehovah's Witnesses have been prosecuted. In Germany more than six thousand members have been prosecuted. They are being prosecuted in Germany much the same as they are here, and for much the same reason."

John Diefenbaker remarked: "I believe there have been some five hundred prosecutions of Jehovah's Witnesses, none of which had to do with subversive activities, the entire offence being that of belonging to an organization banned under the defence of Canada regulations." *Debates of the House of Commons of Canada,* 1943, Vol. I, pp. 611, 612; Vol. III, p. 2912.

2. *1945 Yearbook,* p. 116.

3. *Ibid.,* 1944, Vol. III, p. 2918; Kenneth Johnstone, "Who Exactly Are These Jehovah's Witnesses?" *Montreal Standard,* January 4, 1947; *Calgary Herald,* August 30, 1943.

4. That a great many raids on Witnesses' homes were made at the request of unfriendly neighbours is shown by the files of the Saskatchewan Veterans' Civil Security Corps in the Archives of Saskatchewan, at Saskatoon.

5. Based on information given the author by Ernest Rosvold of Lethbridge, Alberta. Rosvold relates that he was personally ordered not to talk to a fellow Witness on the streets of the village of Bengough, Saskatchewan, by an RCMP constable. Other Witnesses throughout Canada relate similar experiences.

6. Based on a statement by William Cook, RCMP officer, deceased, to the author in June 1967.

7. *1945 Yearbook,* p. 116.

8. *Ibid.,* p. 118.

9. *Ibid.,* p. 117.

10. *Ibid.*

11. *Ibid.,* pp. 117, 118.

12. *Debates,* 1943, Vol I, pp. 611, 616; 1944, Vol. III, p. 2910.

13. *Ibid.*

14. *1945 Yearbook,* pp. 118, 119.

15. *Ibid.*

16. "Order-in-Council Amending Defence of Canada Regulations re

International Bible Students Association", P.C. 4476, June 13, 1944, in *Canadian War Orders and Regulations*, June 26, 1944, pp. 615, 616. *1945 Yearbook*, p. 119.

17. [1943] 3 W.W.R. 340.

18. *Statutes of Alberta* (1944), Chapter 46, Section 9.

19. [1945] O.R. 518; 3 D.L.R. 424; O.W.N. 526; reversing [1944] O.R. 475; 4 D.L.R. 227; O.W.N. 559.

20. Alone, the *Donald* decision did not serve as a strong judicial precedent, but taken along with later decisions of the Supreme Court of Canada (see Chapter 10) it probably makes compulsory flag salutes legally unenforceable under Canadian law.

21. *1946 Yearbook*, pp. 101, 102.

22. *Ibid.*

23. *Ibid.*

24. *Ibid.*

25. *Canadian War Orders and Regulations 1945*, June 4, 1945, p. 461.

26. "Order in Council Amending the Defence of Canada Regulations (Consolidation) 1942", P.C. 3635, in *ibid.*, May 28, 1945, p. 402.

27. *Consolation*, January 3, 1945.

28. *1946 Yearbook*, p. 98.

29. *Ibid.*, pp. 98, 99.

30. *Ibid.*, pp. 97, 99.

31. *Ibid.*

32. For a discussion of this matter in Parliament, see *Debates of the House of Commons*, 1941–42, Vol. IV, pp. 4311–15.

33. Frank H. Epp, *Mennonite Exodus* (Altona, Man.: D. W. Friesen & Sons, Ltd., 1962), pp. 328–31.

34. *Ibid.*, pp. 74, 103, 104, 125, 156, 206, 245, 252, 271, 392–94.

35. J. D. B. MacFarlane, "Operation of Alternative Service Work Camps in National Parks for the Years 1941–1945". NANRP.

36. G. Tunstall, "Alternative Service Work Camps—Summer Operations, 1941". NANRP.

37. Most of the camps were under the Parks Bureau, but those at Kananaskis, Petawawa, and Montreal River were under the supervision of the Dominion forester. MacFarlane, "Operation of Alternative Service Work Camps in National Parks for the Years 1941–1945". Department of War Services memorandum on "Num-

ber of Alternative Service Workers in Each of the Camps at February 28th, 1943". NANRP.

38. "Disposal of Men Called Up for Alternative Service". NANRP.

39. *Ibid.*

40. The files of the Watch Tower Society in Toronto contain records and newspaper clippings of more than thirty Witnesses sentenced to prison for refusing military or alternative service prior to 1943. The sentences given pioneers were particularly severe.

41. *Debates,* 1943, Vol. I, p. 606.

42. "Disposal of Men Called Up for Alternative Service".

43. Memorandum from J. G. Rattray to Major Benoit "re: Circular Memorandum No. 576", June 4, 1942. NANRP.

44. *Debates,* 1944, Vol. III, p. 2917.

45. *1945 Yearbook,* p. 118.

46. *Debates,* 1944, Vol. III, pp. 2905–9.

47. *Ibid.*

48. *Ibid.*

49. *Ibid.*

50. *Ibid.*

51. *Ibid.*

52. The details of this case may be found in the records of the Department of National Defence—Army, file H.Q. 54-27-67-9, Vol. I, in the Public Archives of Canada (R.G. 24A, Vol. 2199).

53. For information on these cases see the records of the Department of National Defence—Army, file H.Q. 1161-3-4, Vol. 4 in the Public Archives of Canada (R.G. 24A, Vol. 6573).

54. *Debates,* 1944, Vol II, p. 1862.

55. A memorandum from Major-General Letson to the Minister of National Defence, April 20, 1944. H.Q. 1161-3-4, Vol. 3.

56. *Ibid.,* Vol. 4.

57. Found in NANRP.

58. *Ibid.*

59. "Order in Council Amending the National Selective Service Mobilization Regulations and National Selective Service Civilian Regulations—Service of Doukhobors, Mennonites and conscientious objectors", P.C. 2821, *Canadian War Orders and Regulations,* April 19, 1943, Section 252 (5) (6) (7), pp. 5, 6.

60. Though there was no definite proviso which required farm owners who were conscientious objectors to pay money to the Red Cross, Selective Service officers demanded that they make such payments, and most of them did. Yet speaking in the District Court of Humboldt, Saskatchewan, in the case of *Leonard Ratz* v. *Gill* (unreported) Judge J. M. Hanbidge held: "I also find that there is no evidence that the minister had fixed the amount that this man [Ratz, a farm owner] should pay to the Red Cross if he was liable to pay anything."

61. Judge Hanbidge agreed with Jehovah's Witnesses. He said: "I do not think a man may be confined in an alternative service camp merely because he is a conscientious objector; such an interpretation of the Regulations would mean that in place of having been passed to assist the war effort, the Regulations were merely a subterfuge for the imprisonment of men on account of their conscientious belief or religious view." *Leonard Ratz* v. *Gill.*

62. *Debates,* 1944, Vol. III, p. 2561.

63. *Frank Ratz* v. *Gill,* unreported.

64. As a consequence, many farmers, supposedly not liable to military service, were jailed and later sent to alternative-service work camps. That this was so can be seen from a simple examination of the occupational lists in NANRP files. See also "Alternative Service Work Camps", *The Mennonite Encyclopedia,* 1955, Vol. I, pp. 76–78.

65. *Debates,* 1944, Vol. V, pp. 5260, 5261, 5509.

66. Letter from J. Smart, controller, to the acting superintendent, Kootenay Park, January 11, 1945. NANRP. Copies of this letter were sent to the superintendents at Banff, Jasper, and Riding Mountain.

67. Personal account by Ross Bletsoe in the files of the Watch Tower Society, 150 Bridgeland Avenue, Toronto.

68. *Calgary Albertan,* March 13, 1942.

69. Interview with Walter Bachous, June 5, 1971.

70. *Debates,* 1944, Vol. III, p. 2615.

71. *Ibid.*

72. *Ibid.*

73. *Ibid.* pp. 2615, 2616.

74. *Ibid.,* pp. 2616, 2617.

75. This letter may be found in NANRP.

76. *Debates,* 1944, Vol. I, pp. 296, 325, 326.

77. Letter from L. E. Westman, Chief Alternative Service Officer, to R. A. Gibson, Director of Lands, Parks and Forest Branch, Department of Mines and Resources, January 25, 1945. NANRP.

78. *Ibid.*

79. *National War Services Regulations, 1940—Recruits,* Section 6 (c), p. 4.

80. *United States, Service in Wartime, Second Report of Director of Selective Service 241* (1943); Marley Cole, *Jehovah's Witnesses* (New York: Vantage Press, 1955), pp. 201–6.

81. *Hull* v. *Stalter,* [1945] 151 F. 2d 633.

82. *Grundy* v. *the King,* unreported.

83. *Offord* v. *Hiscock,* [1917] 86 L.J.K. B. 941.

84. *Re Bein and Cooke,* [1944] 1 W.W.R. 237; 81 C.C.C. 316; [1944] 2 D.L.R. 187.

85. *White* v. *Coverly,* [1946] unreported. *White* v. *Regem,* [1946] 2 W.W.R. 337.

86. *Rex* v. *Stewart,* [1944] 2 W.W.R. 86; 81 C.C.C. 349; [1944] 3 D.L.R. 331 at 338 affirming; 1 W.W.R. 469.

87. [1945] O.R. 411; [1945] 2 D.L.R. 641 808.

88. [1946] O.R. 90; [1946] 1 D.L.R. 550 affirming.

89. *Rex* v. *Stewart.*

90. *Ibid. Greenlees* v. *Attorney-General for Canada.*

91. See *Bein and Cooke.* Also *Rex.* v. *Jazewsky* (No. 1), [1945] 1 W.W.R. 95; 85 C.C.C. 175, and (No. 2), [1945] 1 W.W.R. 107; 85 C.C.C 186.

92. [1946] S.C.R. 462.

93. R. S. Kale and F. Rasky, "Jehovah's Witnesses: Are They Draftable?" *Saturday Night,* January 20, 1945.

94. See *Rex* v. *Jazewsky* (No. 2).

95. Dated October 26, 1944. NANRP.

96. Letter from Westman to Gibson, September 14, 1944. NANRP.

97. Eugen Kogon, *The Theory and Practice of Hell* (New York: Berkley Medallion Books, 1958), p. 43.

98. J. D. B. MacFarlane, "Operation of Alternative Service Work Camps in National Parks for the Period April 1st, 1944, to March 31st, 1945". NANRP.

99. J. D. B. MacFarlane, "Operation of Alternative Service Work

Camps in National Parks for the Period April 1st, 1945, to March 31, 1946". NANRP.

100. This problem was not solved until the Witnesses won a major victory in the *Evans* case discussed below.

101. Letter from MacNamara to J. H. Blackmore, MP, June 6, 1946; *Debates,* 1946, Vol. I, pp. 213, 214.

102. MacNamara to Blackmore.

103. *Rex* v. *Evans,* 2 C.R. 91; [1946] O.W.N. 594 (C.A.)

104. *Saturday Night,* June 8, 1946.

105. W. Glen How, "Representations with Respect to Alternative Service", 1946.

106. *Ibid.*

107. A copy of this letter is on file at the offices of the Watch Tower Society in Toronto.

108. *Debates,* 1944, Vol I, p. 296; 1945, Vol. I, pp. 592, 710, 1077, Vol. II, p. 1911; 1946, Vol. I, pp. 960, 993, Vol. II, pp. 1544, 2102, Vol. III, pp. 3210, 3211.

109. *Ibid.,* 1946, Vol. III, p. 3308.

CHAPTER 9

1. [1949] 2 W.W.R. 195.

2. [1950] 1 W.W.R. 987.

3. *Rex ex rel. Atkinson* v. *Montague,* [1950] C.C.C. 29.

4. Quebec has not yet granted Jehovah's Witnesses the right to solemnize marriages.

5. See Appendix D.

6. *Montreal Star,* September 17, 1945.

7. Montreal *Gazette,* September 17, 1945.

8. *Ibid.,* September 10, 1945.

9. *Ibid.,* September 17, 1945.

10. *Montreal Star,* September 17, 1945.

11. Montreal *Gazette,* September 17, 1945.

12. Only a year after the Lachine and Chateauguay riots, Villeneuve wrote in a letter dated September 17, 1946: "C'est un service urgent à rendre à la société et à la religion que de découvrir le vrai caractère des Témoins de Jéhovah qui ne se réclament de la Bible que pour mieux servir leur fanatisme antireligieux et leur esprit de sé-

dition." Damien Jasmin, *Les Témoins de Jéhovah* (Montreal: Les Éditions Lumen, 1947), p. 7.

13. Kenneth Johnstone, "Who Exactly Are These Jehovah's Witnesses?" *Montreal Standard*, January 4, 1947; *L'Action Catholique* (Quebec), November 8, 1946; *Le Droit* (Montreal), April 11, 1947.

14. Jasmin, pp. 114, 115.

15. *1945 Yearbook of Jehovah's Witnesses*, pp. 92, 93.

16. *Ibid.*

17. *Ibid.* Of the 300 only about half were French speaking.

18. *Awake!* December 8, 1946.

19. *Ibid.*

20. *Ibid.*

21. Johnstone. *Awake!* January 8, 1947.

22. *Awake!* January 8, 1947.

23. *Ibid.* David Kenneth Kernaghan, *Freedom of Religion in the Province of Quebec with Particular Reference to the Jews, Jehovah's Witnesses and Church and State Relations* (unpublished dissertation, Duke University, Durham, N.C., 1966), p. 184.

24. Kernaghan. Even before the distribution of *Quebec's Burning Hate*, a small article on the front page of *L'Action Catholique* of Quebec (November 8, 1946) had read in translation: "The chase against every last one of Jehovah's Witnesses is being pursued with more intensity than ever in the City of Quebec. As these ministers try now to inconvenience the people, by offering their books free, the chief of police informs the public that Radio-Police is at everyone's disposition to free the streets of Jehovah's Witnesses. People who are approached by these accused have only to appeal to Radio-Police which will make it its duty to respond immediately to their call."

25. *Awake!* January 8, 1947.

26. *Ibid.* Johnstone; Scott Young, "Jehovah's Secret Agents", *Maclean's*, March 1, 1947.

27. *La Tribune* (Sherbrooke), November 26, 1946. *Awake!* January 8, 1947.

28. *Awake!* January 8, 1947.

29. *Roncarelli* v. *Duplessis*, [1959] S.C.R. 121; 16 D.L.R. (2d) 689. Johnstone. *Awake!* January 8, 1947.

30. *Awake!* January 8, 1947. *Roncarelli* v. *Duplessis*.

31. *Saturday Night*, February 8, 1947.

32. Young.

33. *Ibid.*

34. *Ibid.*

35. *Saturday Night*, December 28, 1946.

36. Examples of such can be found in the *Social Bulletin* of December 1945 of the École Sociale Populaire, 1961 Rue Rachel Est, Montreal; *L'Action Catholique*, November 8, 1946; *Le Droit* (Ottawa), April 11, 1947; and in an article from *Les Temps*, as quoted in *Saturday Night*, January 4, 1947.

37. *Awake!* January 8, 1947; *Saturday Night*, January 18, 1947; Jasmin, pp. 109–18; *Le Droit* (Ottawa), April 11, 1947. Several years later, at a Knights of Columbus banquet in Quebec City attended by Prime Minister St. Laurent, Chief Justice Thibault Rinfret of the Supreme Court of Canada, and Quebec Lieutenant-Governor Gaspard Fauteux, the then Attorney General of Quebec, Antoine Rivard, attacked Jehovah's Witnesses and said there should be no tolerance for them. Judge Fabio Monet also referred to the Witnesses negatively. *Le Soleil* (Quebec), May 7, 1951.

38. *Canadian Forum*, January 1947.

39. *Toronto Star*, January 11, 1947.

40. *Saskatoon Star-Phoenix*, December 19, 1946; *Globe and Mail* (Toronto), December 19, 1946.

41. *Saskatoon Star-Phoenix*, December 18, 1947.

42. *Saturday Night*, January 4, 1947.

43. Young, *Globe and Mail*, December 12, 1946; *Awake!* January 8, 1947.

44. *Montreal Star*, December 9, 1946; *British Columbian* (New Westminster), December 10, 1946; *Toronto Telegram*, December 11, 1946; *Awake!* January 8, 1947.

45. *Awake!* January 8, 1947.

46. *Toronto Star*, December 19, 1946.

47. *Debates of the House of Commons of Canada*, 1947, Vol. III, pp. 3162, 3163.

48. *Vancouver Daily Province*, December 13, 1946.

49. See also the article "R.C.'s Applaud Duplessis For Drive On Witnesses", in the *Toronto Telegram*, December 20, 1946.

50. For a discussion of the forty-six cases which Jehovah's Witnesses took to the U.S. Supreme Court between 1937 and 1945 see Marley Cole, *Jehovah's Witnesses* (New York: Vantage Press, 1955), pp. 179–84.

51. *Awake!* July 22, 1947.

52. *Ibid.*

53. *Debates*, 1947, Vol. IV, p. 3912.

54. *Ibid.*, pp. 3139–49.

55. Diefenbaker was not alone in his support of a Bill of Rights; spokesmen for the CCF and Social Credit parties indicated that they favoured the enactment of one as well. In fact the CCF had included a proposal for one in their 1945 election manifesto. However, speakers in the House of Commons recognized clearly that it was Jehovah's Witnesses who had popularized the idea. *Ibid.*, pp. 3139–83.

56. *Ibid.*, pp. 3145, 3146.

57. *Awake!* July 22, 1947.

58. *1948 Yearbook*, pp. 101, 102.

59. *Statutes of Quebec* (1947), Chapter 77, Section 13, Article 371, paragraph 2, and Section 18, Article 413, paragraph 11.

60. Letter from W. Glen How, B.A., to "Members of the Bar and those responsible for making laws", August 10, 1947.

61. *Awake!* May 8, 1949.

62. *Ibid. Debates*, 1949, Vol. I, p. 371.

63. *Winnipeg Free Press*, February 12, 1949.

64. *Awake!* May 8, 1949.

65. Edward McWhinney, "The Bill of Rights, The Supreme Court, and Civil Liberties in Canada", *The Canadian Annual Review for 1960* (Toronto: The University of Toronto Press, 1961), p. 271.

CHAPTER 10

1. *1948 Yearbook of Jehovah's Witnesses*, pp. 102, 103.

2. *Statutes of Canada* (1892), Chapter 29, Section 751.

3. *Greenlees* v. *Attorney General for Canada*, [1946] S.C.R. 462.

4. *Statutes of Canada* (1949, 2nd Session), Chapter 37, Sections 36 to 44, inclusive.

5. *Boucher* v. *the King*, 9 C.R. 127; 96 C.C.C. 48; [1950] 1 D.L.R. 657;

reversing 8 c.r. 97; 95 c.c.c. 119.

6. December 7, 1949.

7. December 16, 1949.

8. December 7, 1949.

9. April 8, 1950.

10. *Awake!* May 8, 1949.

11. *Lundell* v. *Joliette,* [1954] Que. s.c. 10. *Lundell* v. *Masse,* [1954] Que. s.c. 59. *Toronto Star,* December 20, 1949. *Awake!* April 8, 1950.

12. *Awake!* April 8, 1950.

13. *Boucher* v. *the King,* 11 c.r. 85; [1951] s.c.r. 265; 99 c.c.c. 1; [1951] 2 d.l.r. 369; reversing 8 c.r. 97; 95 c.c.c. 119. D. A. Schmeiser, *Civil Liberties in Canada* (Glasgow: Oxford University Press, 1965), pp. 209–14.

14. This portion of the transcript of record is quoted in *Saumur* v. *the City of Quebec,* [1953] 2 s.c.r. 299; 106 c.c.c. 289; [1953] 4 d.l.r. 641. See also *Awake!* January 22 and April 8, 1949.

15. Taken from memoranda submitted by Gagné, Frank, Evans, and Jasmin to Ernest Godbout, Attorney for the City of Quebec, and presented on behalf of the city in *Daviau* v. *the City of Quebec.* This evidence was used later in *Saumur* v. *the City of Quebec* as cited above. See *Daviau* v. *the City of Quebec,* [1951] Que. p.r. 140.

16. David Kenneth Kernaghan, *Freedom of Religion in the Province of Quebec with Particular Reference to the Jews, Jehovah's Witnesses, and Church and State Relations* (unpublished dissertation, Duke University, Durham, N.C., 1966), p. 177.

17. *Saumur* v. *the City of Quebec.*

18. The act had been used successfully before in Quebec by the Salvation Army in *Regina* v. *Bice,* (1889) 15 Que. l.r. 147.

19. *Statutes of Quebec* (1953–54), Chapter 15.

20. *Constitutional Freedom in Peril: The Jehovah Witness Case, Winnipeg Free Press* Pamphlet No. 40 (January 1954), pp. 16, 17.

21. *Quebec Chronicle-Telegram,* January 30, 1954; *Vancouver News Herald,* January 30, 1954; Appellants' Supplementary Factum presented in the Supreme Court of Canada in *Saumur* v. *the City of Quebec,* pp. 24–27.

22. *Saumur* v. *Attorney-General of Quebec,* [1964] s.c.r. 262; 45 d.l.r.

(2d) 627; affirming [1963] Que. Q.B. 116; 37 D.L.R. 703; 1963 Can. Abr. 249.

23. *1955 Yearbook*, p. 114.

24. [1955] S.C.R. 834; 114 C.C.C. 170; 1 D.L.R. (2d) 241; Schmeiser, p. 115; *Awake!* January 22, 1956.

25. *1957 Yearbook*, p. 107.

26. *Toronto Telegram*, August 25, 1954.

27. *Ibid.*

28. *London Free Press*, August 27, 1954.

29. *Perron* v. *Syndics d'Écoles de Rouyn*, [1955] Que. Q.B. 841, [1956] 1 D.L.R. (2d) 414.

30. *Chabot* v. *Les Commissaires d'Écoles de Lamorandière*, [1957] Que. Q.B. 707; 12 D.L.R. (2d) 796.

31. June 15, 1957.

32. *Ibid.*

33. [1959] S.C.R. 121; 16 D.L.R. (2d) 689. *Awake!* April 8, 1959.

34. [1959] S.C.R. 321; 123 C.C.C. 193; 17 D.L.R. (2d) 369. *Awake!* April 8, 1959.

35. January 28, 1959.

36. January 28, 1959.

37. January 28, 1959.

38. This class was established at St. George Protestant School in 1954.

39. Pierre Elliott Trudeau, *Federalism and the French Canadians* (Toronto: Macmillan of Canada, 1968), pp. 112, 171, 210.

40. Over station CBFT Montreal with Étienne Ouellette and Paul Couture, November 16, 1955.

41. *Awake!* February 8, 1961.

CHAPTER 11

1. J. T. Eyton, "The Jehovah's Witnesses and the Law in Canada", *The Faculty of Law Review* (Toronto), April 1959.

2. *Maclean's*, August 25, 1962.

3. *Awake!* December 22, 1962.

4. *Ibid.*

5. According to the 1961 and 1971 censuses of Canada, the increase in the numbers of Jehovah's Witnesses in Quebec was proportionately greater than in any other province; and while some of this

growth occurred among Anglophones, more took place among French-speaking *Québécois*.

6. According to the Toronto offices of the Watch Tower Society, at last count there were six Italian Witness congregations in Montreal and a newly formed Spanish congregation.

7. These instances of friction over patriotic exercises have occurred in Nova Scotia, Ontario, Manitoba, Alberta, and British Columbia. In no case, however, has a provincial government been willing to press the matter very far against the Witnesses in support of local school authorities.

8. *Calgary Albertan*, October 28, 1968. *Lethbridge Herald*, November 6, 1968.

9. The new legislation read: "Upon receipt by a teacher of a written statement signed by a parent requesting that a pupil be excluded from religious or patriotic exercises, or both, the pupil shall be permitted to leave the classroom or may be permitted to remain without taking part." *Revised Statutes of Alberta* (1970), Chapter 329, Section 154 (1).

10. *Ottawa Journal*, October 27, 1962, and February 20, 1964; *Kingston Whig-Standard*, April 21, 1964; *Lethbridge Herald*, February 16, 1974.

11. *Globe and Mail* (Toronto), November 11, 1971.

12. *Toronto Star*, August 19, 1970.

13. *Calgary Herald*, January 10, 1969.

14. *Maclean's*, January 2, 1965; *Montreal Star*, April 25, 1969; *Globe and Mail*, April 25, 1965.

15. October 29, 1968.

16. In an editorial printed in the *Brooks Bulletin*, the editor of the *Innisfail Province* referred to "the Brooks Den of Jehovah Witness" and stated: "The entire problem of the Jehovah Witness at Brooks is plain stupidity on the part of leaders of a sect that apparently is making every effort to avoid being good Canadian citizens." *Brooks Bulletin*, November 14, 1968.

17. *Maclean's*, August 25, 1962.

18. See Table 2, p. 228.

19. See, for example, the *Watchtower*, 1964, pp. 694, 695; 1965, pp. 409–11, 766–67. *Awake!* May 8, 1965.

20. R. W. Armstrong, "I Went to Jehovah's Witness Rallies", *United Church Observer*, February 15, 1960.

21. *Watchtower*, 1975, p. 48.

22. See Table 1, p. 13.

23. *Kingdom Ministry* for Canada, June 1974.

24. *Kingdom Ministry* for Canada, March 1975.

25. *1971 Census of Canada*.

26. The *Watchtower* and other Watch Tower literature frequently carry articles written to fortify Jehovah's Witnesses against persecution which, they feel, might come upon them at any time. See, for example, the *Watchtower*, 1972, pp. 133–46.

27. Letters were sent to all Witness congregations throughout the country from the Society's offices in Toronto warning individual Jehovah's Witnesses not to take a stand either for or against the proclamation of the War Measures Act.

28. *Awake!* September 22, 1949; August 8, 1950; May 22, 1951; *Watchtower*, 1950, pp. 79, 80; 1951, p. 414.

29. *Watchtower*, 1969, pp. 765–68.

30. *Ibid.*

31. *Ibid.*

32. See "Tattoo" in *Aid to Bible Understanding* (Brooklyn, N.Y.: Watch Tower Bible and Tract Society, 1971), p. 1577.

33. *Toronto Star*, April 20, 1951.

34. *London Free Press*, January 23, 1954.

35. *Montreal Herald*, February 10, 1954.

36. *Toronto Star*, February 10, 1956.

37. *Toronto Telegram*, March 1 and 5, 1956; *Toronto Star*, March 1, 1956.

38. *Toronto Star*, February 20, 1956; *Truro Daily News*, March 5, 1956.

39. *Toronto Telegram*, March 1, 1956.

40. See also the *Victoria Colonist*, May 25, 1956.

41. *Toronto Star*, April 1, 1957.

42. *Winnipeg Free Press*, November 11, 1958; *Awake!* March 22, 1959.

43. *Winnipeg Free Press*, November 11, 1958.

44. W. Glen How, "Religion, Medicine and the Law", *Canadian Bar Journal*, October, 1960.

45. *Statutes of Manitoba* (1959), Chapter 9.

46. Montreal *Gazette*, November 20, 1958. Reprinted in *Awake!* March 22, 1959.

47. How.

48. *Ibid. Toronto Star*, December 16, 1958.

49. For example, see the *Watchtower*, 1961, pp. 63, 64, 284, 285; 1964, pp. 680–82. *Awake!* September 8, 1964.

50. A full, official statement of the Witnesses' position on blood transfusions may be found quoted in How's article, "Blood, Medicine and Religion".

51. Published originally in the *Post Standard* of Syracuse, New York, September 3, 1956.

52. Published originally in the *Toronto Star*, November 26, 1958.

53. How.

54. Based on a statement made to the International College of Surgeons at a convention held in Rome in May 1948, and published originally in *Time*, May 31, 1948.

55. How.

56. *Ibid.*

57. December 11, 1958; reprinted in How, "Religion, Medicine and Law".

58. *Winnipeg Free Press*, November 11, 1958.

59. *Toronto Star*, November 26, 1958.

60. *Globe and Mail*, April 15, 1960; reprinted in How, "Religion, Medicine and Law"

61. August 26, 1961.

62. Crosby's statement appeared originally in "Misuse of Blood Transfusions", in *Blood*, December 1958.

63. January 14, 1961.

64. *Vancouver Sun*, June 13, 1967.

65. *Wolfe* v. *Robinson*, [1962] O.R. 132; 132 C.C.C. 78; 31 D.L.R. (2d) 233; affirming [1961] O.R. 250, 27 D.L.R. (2d) 98; 129 C.C.C. 361; 1961 Can. Abr. 298.

66. *Toronto Star*, January 25, 1962; *Ottawa Citizen*, January 25, 1962.

67. *Wolfe* v. *Robinson* as cited above.

68. *Ottawa Citizen*, January 25, 1962; *Ottawa Journal*, January 25, 1962; *Toronto Star*, January 25, 1962; *Winnipeg Tribune*, January 26, 1962.

69. *Kingston Whig-Standard,* October 23, 1962; *Ottawa Journal,* October 23, 1962; *Globe and Mail,* October 26, 1962; *Toronto Star,* October 24, 1962; *Forsyth* v. *Children's Aid Society of Kingston,* [1963] 1 O.R. 49; 35 D.L.R. (2d) 690. For further details see How, "Religion, Medicine and the Law".

70. The case in question, *In re Brooks Estate,* (1965) 32 III. 2d 361, 205 N.E. 2d 435, was discussed fully in *Awake!* May 22, 1967 under the name *Brooks* v. *Aste.*

71. *Vancouver Sun,* June 19, 20, 22, 1967; *Seattle Times,* November 21, 1967; *Awake!* March 8, 1968.

72. *Awake!* July 8, 1968.

73. *Ibid.,* November 22, 1971.

74. Made to the author, August 1973.

75. *Globe and Mail,* May 25 and 26, 1967. *Awake!* August 22, 1970.

76. December 27, 1970.

77. Seymour Gollub, PH.D., M.D., and Charles P. Bailey, M.D., D.SC., "Management of Major Surgical Blood Loss Without Transfusion", *Journal of the American Medical Association,* December 12, 1966. See also C. Wilton Simmons, Jr. M.D., Bruno J. Messmer, M.D., Grady L. Hallman, M.D., and Denton A. Cooley, M.D., "Vascular Surgery in Jehovah's Witnesses", *Journal of the American Medical Association,* August 10, 1970.

78. Ben J. Wilson, M.D., "Complications of Blood Transfusions", Curtis P. Arty, M.D., F.A.C.S., and James D. Hardy, M.D., F.A.C.S., eds., *Complications in Surgery and Their Management* (Philadelphia: W. B. Saunders Company, 1960), p. 80. In fact, according to Wilson the 16,500 computed deaths occurred "from only 3 complications of blood transfusion (Hemolytic reactions, overload and serum hepatitis)".

79. *Ibid.*

80. October 10, 1969.

81. *St. Petersburg Times,* December 13, 1970.

82. *Ottawa Citizen,* July 29, 1967.

83. Hans G. Keitel, M.D., "Our Care of Newborn Infants Is Often Not Good Enough", *Consultant,* March 1965. In "Pitfalls in Neonatology", published in *The Pediatric Clinics of North America,* May 1965, Dr. Hans Keitel and Dr. Keith Hammond wrote: "The

routine performance of an exchange [transfusion] if the bilirubin level rises to or approaches 20 mg. per 100 ml. in the first week of life is unfortunate. We must have the fortitude to tell parents the whole truth and to inform them of the uncertainties and the risks. Many believe it far better to have a live child who has only a small chance of brain damage (if the bilirubin level does not rise over 25 mg. per 100 ml. for less than a day in the first week of life) than to risk the chances of a fatality." In "Uncomplicated Hyperbilirubinemia of Prematurity", Jack G. Shiller, M.D., and William A. Silverman, M.D., wrote: "The present study [involving 110 infants] fails to demonstrate a significant correlation between uncomplicated hyperbilirubinemia in premature infants and neurologic deficit at three years of age." *American Journal of Diseases of Children*, May 1961.

84. W. C. Taylor, "Mortality and Morbidity of Exchange Transfusions", *Canadian Medical Association Journal*, December 15, 1962.

85. Richard P. Wennberg, M.D., "Phototherapy and the Jaundiced Child", *Northwest Medicine*, April 1970; J. Donald Ostrow, M.D., and Roger V. Branham, M.D., "Photodecomposition of Bilirubin and Biliverdin in Vitro", *Gastroenterology*, January 1970; "Hyperbilirubinemia Prevented with Phototherapy", *Medical Tribune*, May 10, 1967; Frank Giunta, M.D., and Jogeswar Rath, M.D., "Effect of Environmental Illumination in Prevention of Hyperbilirubinemia of Prematurity", *Pediatrics*, August 1969; *Hamilton Spectator*, November 5, 1968; "Blue Light for Babies in Bilirubin Peril", *Medical World News*, June 13, 1969.

86. *Canadian Medical Association Journal*, February 18, 1967.

87. *Trentonian*, June 9, 1967.

88. *Vancouver Sun*, March 29 and May 10, 1967; *Lethbridge Herald*, May 9 and 12, 1967; *Evening Reporter* (Galt, Ontario), May 13, 1967; *Edmonton Journal*, May 20, 1967. The Watch Tower Society's statement was broadcast over nation-wide CBC-TV.

89. *Awake!* November 22, 1970; *Smith Falls Record-News*, April 9 and 30, 1970; *Saskatoon Star-Phoenix*, April 2, 4, and 7, 1970; *Toronto Telegram*, May 6 and August 4, 1970; *Kingston Whig-Standard*, May 14, 1970.

90. *Toronto Star*, September 25, 1970; *Toronto Telegram*, September 25, 1970; *Vancouver Sun*, September 26, 1970.

91. Based on tape recordings of the radio interviews discussed above, February 1971.

92. *Winnipeg Free Press* of February 27, 1971.

93. Also published in the *Free Press* of February 27, 1971.

94. W. Glen How's brief on proposed Amendment III to the Manitoba Child Welfare Act as presented to the Manitoba legislature, July 9, 1970.

95. *Winnipeg Tribune*, June 10, 1970; *Winnipeg Free Press*, July 10 and 17, 1970; *Victoria Daily Colonist*, August 8, 1970. How's brief as presented to the Manitoba legislature and various public statements made subsequently by How.

96. *Winnipeg Free Press*, July 21, 1970.

97. *Edmonton Journal*, May 20, 1967.

APPENDIX A

1. Walter J. Martin and Norman H. Klann, *Jehovah of the Watchtower* (New York: Biblical Truth Publishing House, 1953; rev. and enl. ed., Grand Rapids, Mich.: Zondervan Publishing House, 1956).

2. Anthony Hoekema, *The Four Major Cults* (Grand Rapids, Mich.: Wm. B. Eerdman's Publishing Company, 1963).

3. William J. Whalen, *Armageddon Around the Corner* (New York: John Day Company, 1962).

4. Gérard Hébert, s.j., *Les Témoins de Jéhovah* (Montreal: Les Éditions Bellarmin, 1960).

5. Allan Rogerson, *Millions Now Living Will Never Die* (London: Constable & Co. Ltd., 1969).

6. *Watch Tower*, 1914, pp. 286–91.

7. J. F. Rutherford, *A Great Battle in the Ecclesiastical Heavens* (New York: printed privately, 1915).

8. Marley Cole, *Jehovah's Witnesses* (New York: Vantage Press, 1955), pp. 70, 71.

9. Rogerson, p. 209, n. 47.

10. J. J. Ross, *Some Facts and More Facts About the Self-Styled "Pastor" Charles T. Russell* (Philadelphia: Philadelphia School of the Bible, 1913).

11. *Ibid.*, p. 20.
12. Whalen, pp. 42, 43.
13. He committed Ross to appear before a grand jury of the High Court of Ontario. At that level the judge instructed the jury: "Unless the jury finds that this alleged libel would cause a breach of the public peace in Canada then no indictment should be returned, but the parties should resort to civil suit for damages." Rutherford, p. 31. Ross's account of these events is a strangely garbled one. If one follows what occurred in the pages of the *Hamilton Spectator*, the dates given for the hearings in *Some Facts and More Facts* are out by several weeks.
14. *Hamilton Spectator*, March 17, 1913.
15. Letter to Ernest Chambers, June 17, 1918. CPC 206-B-6.
16. Martin and Klann, pp. 19, 20.
17. Martin and Klann (1956 edition), pp. 21, 22.

biBLioGRApby

Works of Russell and Rutherford as Published by the Watch Tower
Society or Associated Corporations

RUSSELL, CHARLES T. *Pastor Russell's Sermons.* 1917.

————. *Studies in the Scriptures.* 7 Vols., 1886–1917. Numerous editions published.

    Vol. I: *The Divine Plan of the Ages.* 1886

    Vol. II: *The Time is at Hand.* 1889

    Vol. III: *Thy Kingdom Come.* 1891

    Vol. IV: *The Battle of Armageddon.* 1897

    Vol. V: *The Atonement Between God and Man.* 1899

    Vol. VI: *The New Creation.* 1904

    Vol. VII: *The Finished Mystery.* 1917. *The Finished Mystery* was styled as the posthumous work of Russell since it was based largely on his notes and writings. It was prepared by George Fisher and Clayton Woodworth immediately after Russell's death.

RUTHERFORD, JOSEPH F. *Children.* 1941.

————. *Creation.* 1927.

————. *Deliverance.* 1926.

————. *End of Nazism.* 1940.

————. *Face the Facts.* 1938.

————. *Fascism or Freedom.* 1939.

———. *Intolerance.* 1933.

———. *Liberty to Preach: Points and Authorities in Re Sunday and License Laws as Applied to the International Bible Students Associated.* Undated.

———. *Life.* 1929.

———. *Loyalty.* 1935.

———. *Prohibition; League of Nations: Of God or the Devil, Which?* 1930.

Periodicals of the Watch Tower Society, Listed Chronologically

Zion's Watch Tower and Herald of Christ's Presence (1879–1907).
Watch Tower and Herald of Christ's Presence (1908–31).
Watchtower and Herald of Christ's Presence (1931–38).
Watchtower and Herald of Christ's Kingdom (1939).
Watchtower Announcing Jehovah's Kingdom (1939 to date).
Golden Age (1919–37).
Consolation (1937–46).
Awake! (1946 to date).

Bulletins of the Watch Tower Society, Listed Chronologically

Kingdom News. Various broadside leaflets published during the First World War.
Morning Messenger. 1918.
Kingdom Ministry for Canada. Monthly bulletins distributed by the Canadian offices of the Watch Tower Society to all Jehovah's Witnesses under the Canadian branch at Toronto. Known formerly as the *Informant.*

Other Publications of the Watch Tower Society Since 1942

Aid to Bible Understanding. 1971.
Blood, Medicine and the Law of God. 1961.
Did Man Get Here by Evolution or by Creation? 1967.
Is the Bible Really the Word of God? 1969.
Jehovah's Witnesses in the Divine Purpose. 1959.
Let God Be True. 1946.

Organization for Kingdom-Preaching and Disciple-Making. 1972.

True Peace and Security—From What Source? 1973.

The Truth that Leads to Eternal Life. 1968.

Yearbooks of Jehovah's Witnesses (known until 1934 as *International Bible Students Association Yearbooks*).

Other Works Concerning the General History of Jehovah's Witnesses

"Alternative Service Work Camps". *The Mennonite Encyclopedia.* 1955. Vol. I.

BACH, MARCUS. *They Have Found a Faith.* Indianapolis: The Bobbs-Merrill Company, 1946.

BRADEN, CHARLES SAMUEL. *These Also Believe.* New York: The Macmillan Company, 1949.

COLE, MARLEY. *Jehovah's Witnesses.* New York: Vantage Press, 1955.

———. *Triumphant Kingdom.* New York: Criterion Books, 1957.

CONWAY, J. S. *The Nazi Persecution of the Churches 1933-1945.* New York: Basic Books, Inc., 1968.

CUMBERLAND, WILLIAM H. *A History of Jehovah's Witnesses.* Unpublished doctoral dissertation, University of Iowa, Iowa City, 1958.

CZATT, MILTON STACEY. *The International Bible Students. Jehovah's Witnesses.* New Haven: Yale University Press, 1933.

HÉBERT, GÉRARD. *Les Témoins de Jéhovah.* Montreal: Les Éditions Bellarmin, 1960.

HOW, W. G., GREENLEES, L. W., and CHAPMAN, P. *History of Jehovah's Witnesses in Canada.* An unpublished typescript submitted as a report to the Watch Tower Society at Brooklyn, 1958.

JASMIN, DAMIEN. *Les Témoins de Jéhovah.* Montreal: Les Éditions Lumen, 1946.

JIMÉNEZ, JESÚS. *La objeción de conciencia en España.* Madrid: Editorial Cuadernos para el Diálago, 1973.

KERNAGHAN, DAVID K. *Freedom of Religion in the Province of Quebec with Particular Reference to the Jews, Jehovah's Witnesses and Church-State Relations.* Unpublished doctoral dissertation, Duke University, Durham, N.C., 1966.

KIRBAN, SALEM. *Jehovah's Witnesses—Doctrines of Devils* No. 3. Chicago: Moody Press, 1972.

KOGON, EUGEN. *The Theory and Practice of Hell*. New York: Berkley Medallion Books, 1958.

The Laodicean Messenger. Chicago: The Bible Educational Institute, 1923.

MACMILLAN, A. H. *Faith on the March*. Englewood Cliffs, N.J.: Prentice-Hall, Inc., 1957.

MANWARING, DAVID R. *Render Unto Caesar*. Chicago: The University of Chicago Press, 1962.

MARTIN, WALTER R., and KLANN, NORMAN H. *Jehovah of the Watchtower*. New York: Biblical Truth Publishing Society, Inc., 1953. Revised and enlarged edition. Grand Rapids: Zondernan Publishing House, 1956.

ROGERSON, ALAN. *Millions Now Living Will Never Die*. London: Constable, 1969.

ROSS, J. J. *Some Facts and More Facts About the Self-Styled "Pastor" Charles T. Russell*. Philadelphia: Philadelphia School of the Bible, 1913.

RUTHERFORD, J. F. *A Great Battle in the Ecclesiastical Heavens*. New York: printed privately, 1915.

STROUP, HERBERT H. *The Jehovah's Witnesses*. New York: Russell and Russell, 1945.

WHALEN, WILLIAM J. *Armageddon Around the Corner*. New York: The John Day Company, 1962.

WHITE, TIMOTHY. *A People for His Name*. New York: Vantage Press, Inc., 1968.

ZUERCHER, FRANZ. *Kreuzzug gegen das Christentum*. Zurich: Europa Verlag, 1938.

INDEX